T   9-8
W   9-9.
Th 9-8
F   9-5
S

INTRODUCTION TO COMPUTER SYSTEMS
Using the PDP-11 and Pascal

McGraw-Hill Computer Science Series

Allen: *Anatomy of LISP*
Bell and Newell: *Computer Structures: Readings and Examples*
Donovan: *Systems Programming*
Feigenbaum and Feldman: *Computers and Thought*
Gear: *Computer Organization and Programming*
Givone: *Introduction to Switching Circuit Theory*
Goodman and Hedetniemi: *Introduction to the Design and Analysis of Algorithms*
Hamacher, Vranesic, and Zaky: *Computer Organization*
Hamming: *Introduction to Applied Numerical Analysis*
Hayes: *Computer Architecture and Organization*
Hellerman: *Digital Computer System Principles*
Hellerman and Conroy: *Computer System Performance*
Kain: *Automata Theory: Machines and Languages*
Katzan: *Microprogramming Primer*
Kohavi: *Switching and Finite Automate Theory*
Liu: *Elements of Discrete Mathematics*
Liu: *Introduction to Combinatorial Mathematics*
MacEwen: *Introduction to Computer Systems: Using the PDP-11 and Pascal*
Madnick and Donovan: *Operating Systems*
Manna: *Mathematical Theory of Computation*
Newman and Sproull: *Principles of Interactive Computer Graphics*
Nilsson: *Problem-Solving Methods in Artificial Intelligence*
Rosen: *Programming Systems and Languages*

McGraw-Hill Advanced Computer Science Series

INTRODUCTION TO
COMPUTER SYSTEMS
Using the PDP-11 and Pascal

Glenn H. MacEwen

Associate Professor of Computing and Information Science
Queen's University, Kingston

McGraw-Hill Book Company

New York   St. Louis   San Francisco   Auckland   Bogotá   Hamburg
Johannesburg   London   Madrid   Mexico   Montreal   New Delhi   Panama
Paris   São Paulo   Singapore   Sydney   Tokyo   Toronto

INTRODUCTION TO COMPUTER SYSTEMS
Using the PDP-11 and Pascal

4567890 HDHD 898765432

This book was set in Times Roman by Progressive Typographers.
The editors were Charles E. Stewart and Frances A. Neal;
the production supervisor was Richard A. Ausburn.
The drawings were done by Burmar.

Library of Congress Cataloging in Publication Data

MacEwen, Glenn H
    Introduction to computer systems.

    (McGraw-Hill computer science series)
    Bibliography: p.
    Includes index.
    1. PDP-11 (Computer) 2. Pascal (Computer program
language) I. Title.
QA76.8.P2M3   001.6'4   79-22646
ISBN 0-07-044350-5

To Jane, Kevin, and Marie

CONTENTS

Read Someday

PREFACE

This text provides an introduction to the internal logical structure of computers and the techniques of machine-level programming. It is intended to give the student an understanding of the basic structure and functioning of conventional computer systems.

The student should possess a programming ability in some high-level language as the necessary background. The level of competence required is that obtainable from one full course of study in programming and applications.

On completion of the course described in this text the student should have the ability to read the documentation of a conventional computer system and be able to understand the basic functioning of the machine as well as the services provided by the operating system. For example, the documents commonly called "Principles of Operation" and "System Programmer's Guide" should be understandable.

Basic computer structure is taught in the context of a particular machine, the Digital Equipment Corporation PDP-11. At first, assembly-language programming is used to provide an understanding of machine functioning. High-level system programming languages are then introduced as a vehicle for programming in the remainder of the text. Various architectural and programming topics are taught in the context of two particular PDP-11 operating systems, RT-11 and UNIX,[1] although each topic is generalized as much as possible in accompanying discussion.

Data structures are not treated as a separate topic but are introduced in the context of particular applications. This is very specifically done on the assumption that most students will probably receive a complete treatment of data structures in another course.

This text has been used in a course at the second-year level of a computer science program and has also provided the basis for a graduate half course in

[1] UNIX is a trademark of Bell Laboratories.

electrical engineering. Although the text assumes a good exposure to programming in a well-structured high-level programming language, it may be that not all students will have this preparation. It is usually necessary, therefore, to supplement the chapters on the languages Pascal and C with some tutorial material. Pascal, particularly, should be introduced early if sufficient familiarity has not been attained, since many algorithms early in the text are expressed in Pascal-like notation.

All material required for the curriculum of course CS-3, Assembly Language Programming, prepared by the ACM Committee on Curriculum in Computer Sciences, is included. Specifically, parts of Chapter 1, Chapters 2 through 9, and Chapter 14 provide a basis for this course with sufficient optional material to give the instructor some flexibility. In addition, Chapter 0 gives a preview of some material so that the student can begin to apply, almost immediately, what he or she will learn in more detail later. It is recommended, also, that some material on number systems from Chapter 1 be included in any version of CS-3 to be offered from this text.

The text provides an excellent basis for further study in computer architecture and operating systems. The approach taken here is to present some of the mechanisms that will be encountered in the study of operating systems without attempting to introduce many of the abstractions that are useful in designing operating systems. In this way the student will be well prepared to study these abstractions, having seen examples of the problems they are intended to solve. The text is, therefore, essentially a bottom-up approach to systems programming, since the author feels that students must understand examples before they are ready to fully understand abstractions. To this end the advanced material stops just short of the issues and complexity that are more properly studied with the abstractions of operating systems theory.

Material has been carefully sequenced to avoid forward references and to present only sufficient information for the reader to progress in relatively modest steps. The major exception to this is Chapter 0, in which a bit of a preview is given so that the student can begin to program immediately. This is intended to avoid making the early material too dry while the groundwork is laid for programming topics.

Chapter 1 contains the necessary introduction to number systems. Where this material has already been covered in another course, one can start with Chapter 2, which discusses the basic components of a computer in general terms. Chapter 3 gives a partial view of the PDP-11; the intent here is to avoid becoming involved in a discussion of the unique way that addressing is accomplished in the PDP-11. Consequently, students can move on quickly to programming in Chapter 4 without getting stuck on these details, which are covered in Chapter 5.

Chapter 6 comprises some elementary topics concerned with structuring programs. Macros, however, are left to Chapter 7 where they are treated rather extensively. It is important to include at least the basic material on macros in order to understand the material that follows.

Chapter 8 fulfills two major objectives. First, it explains the basic algorithms of an assembler so that the translation process is made clear to the student. Second, it uses the symbol table as an example within which to discuss the topic of sorting and searching. This, of course, follows the policy of treating data structures only in the context of particular applications. Much of the material in this chapter can, however, be omitted without affecting comprehension of following material.

Chapter 9 brings together all considerations of how a program is transformed from assembly-language form into its final machine-language form. Chapter 10 introduces concurrency, which was carefully omitted from the introduction to I/O in Chapter 5. Is is not until this point that interrupts are introduced, so that the student has a rather solid foundation before having to cope with this difficult area. Chapter 11 introduces the supervisor as a program that makes the machine more reliable and more convenient to use. Traps and interrupt handling services are covered here.

Chapters 12 through 17 constitute a set of special topics that can be selected according to the needs of a specific curriculum. In our course at Queen's approximately 25 percent of the time is spent on these topics. However, since some features of Pascal that do not appear in earlier chapters are used in these chapters, a review is included in Chapter 12. The description of the language is not complete and is given rather informally so that a language text or manual is necessary if programming is to be assigned. The language C is also included here as an example of another system language and to enable those with access to UNIX system documentation to read programs.

Although Chapters 13 through 17 may be selected as desired, I would expect Chapter 15 on multiprogramming to be given priority because of its central importance to the subject of systems programming. Chapter 17 is rather ambitious, attempting to introduce methods of systematic software system design. The material here derives largely from the work of D. L. Parnas and J. F. Guttag. I must, however, take responsibility for attempting to properly interpret their work.

Finally, Chapter 18 describes the structure of a moderately large program that was designed according to a disciplined method. There are several ways to use it. Portions can be introduced throughout the course and given as programming assignments so that a student has a complete program at the end of the course. (This is the way that I have used it.) It can be used as an exercise in group programming. It can simply be studied as an exercise in design principles. Whichever route is chosen, this project provides exposure to large software system design, something that is not often gained by students.

A particularly difficult aspect of producing a book is deciding when to stop. One is never quite satisfied with the work nor completely confident that errors do not lurk in hidden places. But at some point it is necessary to say "this is it" and to send it off to the publisher. I therefore take full responsibility for deficiencies or errors that are found and would appreciate hearing about them quickly.

The manuscript was prepared in the Department of Computing and Information Science at Queen's University and partly in the Department of Electrical Engineering at Royal Military College of Canada, to both of which I am grateful for the facilities to do this. The former made available the computing facilities with which the manuscript was prepared using a text editor written by I. A. Macleod and D. G. Ross. Appreciation is due to many people who contributed typing, editing, and reading of the manuscript. To attempt to list all would risk omissions; those involved are aware of their contribution. Particular mention, however, is due to T. P. Martin, who did the original design of the MITE system described in Chapter 18. His M.Sc. thesis work, which included the design, was supported by a grant from the National Research Council of Canada. Finally, I wish to acknowledge the tolerance of those to whom I made work commitments that were somewhat neglected as book writing tended to swallow the available time.

Glenn H. MacEwen

INTRODUCTION

The power of a digital computer derives from its ability to store a large quantity of information, in a way permitting ready access, and to process that information. In the following chapters we first consider methods of representing information for computer storage. These methods reflect the fact that the physical devices used for storage, called *memory devices,* consist essentially of a set of switches, each switch being in one of two states: on or off. All information to be stored must, then, be transformed into a representation that can be mirrored by a set of switches.

Having a basic understanding of information representation, we will move on to consider the basic mechanisms within a computer that enable the machine to process information. These mechanisms form a set of basic operations which may then be combined to form an algorithm. Algorithms, based on the operations provided by the machine, are specified by writing a program in machine language. A computer can execute a program expressed in machine language in a way analogous to that of a person carrying out the actions expressed in a list of instructions printed on a piece of paper. An interesting feature of most computers is that machine-language programs are stored in memory devices in exactly the same way as the data to be processed.

A programmer need not write programs in machine language; it is a very tedious process to specify an algorithm by setting a vast number of switches. Most computer manufacturers supply customers with a program called an *assembler* that translates programs written in a symbolic programming language into machine language. Such symbolic languages, called *assembly languages,* mirror the internal structure of the computer in their design. Assembly language is used in situations where a programmer needs precise control over the internal functioning of a computer and the programs are small enough to be manageable without more elaborate languages. In our case, assembly-language programming provides an excellent means of gaining an understanding of the internal functioning of computers. The basic hardware computer, manifested by circuits and wires, needs a vast amount of program, its software, to transform it from an executor of machine instructions into an executor of commands by human users. It is primarily with this large amount of software that this text is concerned. Along the way of course it is necessary to understand the various hardware structures that exist in support of the software.

Although assembly language is a useful vehicle for explaining the details of hardware structure, it is not convenient for writing software. For writing well-structured, reliable software it is not at all suitable.

A class of high-level languages called *systems languages* are more appropriate for writing large programs. If necessary, assembly language can be used in critical parts of the software. Systems languages allow precise control over the hardware while encouraging the programmer to use well-structured design in the programs. Most newer software systems are now written in systems languages.

As we proceed in the study of hardware and software structures, there will be much preoccupation with detail, especially with regard to our example system, the PDP-11. The reader should try to remember that this detail will vary somewhat from machine to machine and that our primary purpose is to study fundamental concepts. Computing is a subject in which one can learn concepts well only by doing a lot of computing, and for this one needs an example system.

0-1 ALGORITHMS AND LANGUAGES

Computers exist primarily to facilitate the construction and execution of algorithms. The study of computers is then largely a study of algorithms and of the machine structures that support their implementation. An *algorithm* is a precise set of unambiguous instructions that can be followed and carried out by some execution mechanism (a computer) such that the execution eventually terminates. The language used to express the instructions of an algorithm will vary with the intended use. In our case we wish to describe algorithms for the purpose of reading and understanding them. It follows, then, that some language close to English will be most comfortable for doing this. Unfortunately, English itself is a very ambiguous medium for communicating precise meaning. On the other hand, the language used to describe instructions directly to a computer is far too detailed for easy reading. Besides, one objective here is to explain machine language, so we can hardly use it as a vehicle of explanation.

The compromise commonly adopted to informally explain algorithms is what can be called *structured English:* Ordinary English statements are imbedded in statements of a high-level programming language, and thus we obtain the readability of English with the precision of a programming language. On the assumption that the reader has been exposed to at least one high-level programming language, the following chapters present algorithms based on a particular language, Pascal, without detailed explanation of the meaning of the statements involved. Pascal is a readable enough language that experience with programming in another language should yield sufficient understanding.

To illustrate structured English, here is a set of instructions for reading this text.

```
VAR i,j: INTEGER;
① IF  you have no programming background THEN
        take a course in programming;
② FOR i := 1 TO 18 DO BEGIN
        WHILE chapter i is not fully understood DO
            read chapter i;
        FOR j := 1 TO number of exercises in chapter i DO
            complete exercise i-j END
```

simple st:

compound statement

English statements are written in lowercase, as are program-variable names. In this program, i and j are declared in the first line to be integer variables. As can be seen, Pascal keywords are written in uppercase. The semicolon character (;) is used to separate statements to be executed sequentially. In this program, for example, there are, following the single declaration, two statements. There may appear to be more than two statements, but this is because a compound statement can be formed by enclosing a sequence of statements with a BEGIN . . . END pair of keywords. Such a compound statement can be used in a program wherever a simple statement can appear. The first statement starts with IF and the second with FOR. Notice that the indentation is carefully done to indicate the statement structure.

The first statement is a *conditional* with the meaning that the reader without a background of programming should obtain this background before attempting the material in the text. The semantics of this form of the IF statement are simply that the statement following the THEN is executed only if the condition following the IF is true.

The second statement is an *iteration* to be carried out 18 times. That is, the statement following the DO is carried out once for each one of a set of values to be assigned, in sequence, to i. The statement which is to be repeated is, in this example, a compound statement itself comprising two statements.

The first of these nested statements is an *indefinite iteration,* that is, a loop to be repeated an indefinite number of times depending on some specified condition. The WHILE is an indefinite iteration in which the looping condition is evaluated before each execution. Thus, if the condition is true, then the governed statement is executed; if it is false, looping terminates and execution proceeds to the statement following the WHILE statement. Obviously, execution of the statement governed by the WHILE had better affect the result of evaluating the condition or the iteration will never terminate!

The second nested statement is another FOR in which the number of iterations varies with the value of i determined in the outer loop.

Although there are many other kinds of statements in Pascal, this example illustrates three fundamental kinds of control structures required to express algorithms: sequential execution, indefinite iteration, and conditional execution. In the case of conditional execution, we have actually shown only a special case of the general conditional structure, the IF . . . THEN . . . ELSE. To illustrate this general form, a slightly different set of instructions than those above for reading this text are

```
IF   you have no programming background THEN
       take a programming course
ELSE proceed with this text as indicated above
```

The difference here is that the statement following the THEN is executed if the condition is true and the statement following the ELSE is executed if it is false. In either case control passes to the following statement if one is supplied. The reader without a background, therefore, does not get to read the text even if the required background is obtained!

It is not the intention to teach Pascal in detail here. Various features will be introduced and used throughout, and a later chapter will summarize the language. Enough information will be given to enable the reader to read the text, but if programs are to be written in Pascal then a language manual for the system in use is required.

0-2 ASSEMBLY LANGUAGE

Machine-level programming in assembly language is characterized by very simple, primitive operations. In general, much more effort is required of the assembly-language programmer to accomplish a task than would be required using a high-level language. More significant, however, is the fact that assembly language gives the programmer much less assistance in detecting errors and thereby increasing reliability. Consequently, much greater care and discipline are required in using assembly language.

Although later chapters explore assembly language in more detail, we can preview some of what is to come by looking at some simple cases. With the reader's appetite satisfied somewhat, we can then progress more systematically.

One of the primitive data types available in assembly language is the *character*. Much assembly-language programming deals with character manipulation. A character value is stored in a memory cell which can be given a name, much as a high-level language variable has a programmer-assigned name that is associated with its value. In the case of character storage let us just take as an illustration the following statement:

```
Q:      .ASCII  /?/
```

This statement specifies that there is to be a cell named Q containing the character value "question mark." The cell could have been given a longer name, up to six letters. At the moment the particular reason for the letters ASCII is not important. The significant point is simply that the programmer can define a named cell and give it an initial value.

Having defined some data, the programmer can manipulate it via program statements. The simplest such statement is that which copies a value from one cell to another, as follows:

MOVB   Q,X

The effect of this statement, in a program also containing the above definition of Q, is to copy the character value from Q and store it in another cell X, which must also be similarly defined such as in

X: .ASCII / /

where X is initialized to contain a blank character. The significance of the B in MOVB is that cells containing characters are called *bytes;* MOVB is read, then, as "move byte." The MOVB statement behaves much like the familiar assignment statement which in Pascal would be written

x := q

where x and q are declared to be character variables. So instead of thinking in terms of variables and their values, one thinks in terms of cells and their contents.

Perhaps the greatest difference between assembly and high-level languages concerns the names of cells. In simple terms, it is quite usual in assembly language to treat names of cells as values and to store and manipulate these values. The names are not stored as characters, however, but as numbers. When a programmer defines a cell with its associated name, this name then represents a number, which was permanently associated with the cell when the machine was built. The significant thing is that the programmer can then define a cell containing that number. For example, having defined Q above, one can define another cell whose contents are the number represented by the name Q, called the *address* of Q. Numbers, however, are not usually stored in the same type of cell as are characters. As an example, in the machine that we will be using, the PDP-11, cells containing numbers are called *words.*

To define a word containing the address of Q, one simply writes

ADDR: .WORD   Q

where ADDR could be any six-letter sequence. This same statement can be used to define a word containing any representable number by writing the number in place of Q. For example,

Z: .WORD   5.

defines a word initially containing the value five. Note that the number includes an explicit decimal point.

There is a different set of program statements to operate on words rather than bytes. For example, the version of the move statement to operate on words is MOV.

Let us conduct the rest of this preview in terms of a specific program. The following algorithm takes a stored sequence of characters, terminated by a hash character (#), and writes it on an output device ignoring blanks.

```
addr := address of the first character;
WHILE character addressed by addr is not hash DO BEGIN
    IF character addressed by addr is not blank THEN write it;
    addr := addr + 1 END
```

One can readily see that it has been assumed that the sequence of characters has numerically ascending addresses. This can easily be arranged by defining the characters in a single statement, such as

```
TEXT:    .ASCII  /HERE IS THE EXAMPLE LINE OF TEXT/
```

Furthermore, any character cells defined in statements immediately following each other will be assigned to cells with ascending addresses. The use of this can be seen in the following assembly-language version of the algorithm in which the terminating hash character is defined in a separate statement:

```
LOOP:  CMPB    HASH,@ADDR      ;comments can go
       BEQ     DONE            ;here after a
       CMPB    BLANK,@ADDR     ;semicolon
       BEQ     L
       OUTB    @ADDR           ;not directly available
L:     ADD     #1.,ADDR
       BR      LOOP
DONE:  HALT
ADDR:  .WORD   TEXT
TEXT:  .ASCII  /HERE IS THE EXAMPLE LINE OF TEXT/
HASH:  .ASCII  /#/
BLANK: .ASCII  / /
       .END
```

First notice that program statements can contain labels that resemble the names of data cells. In this case these labels are used in branch statements to alter the flow of control, which otherwise starts at the beginning and proceeds sequentially. For example, the program starts at the statement labeled LOOP and the outer iteration is implemented by the statement BR LOOP, meaning "branch to LOOP." The BR statement, in other words, is the familiar "goto" from high-level languages.

The first program statement is a *compare byte* which simply carries out a comparison of the contents of the two specified cells. (A different compare, CMP, is used for words.) The notation @ADDR means "the address stored in ADDR." Since ADDR initially contains the address represented by TEXT, the first statement, then, initially means the same as CMPB HASH,TEXT. As seen in the algorithm given previously, however, the contents of ADDR are altered, so in general this first statement means "compare the contents of HASH with the contents of the cell whose address is found in ADDR."

Following the compare is a conditional branch statement, BEQ, which causes a branch to label DONE if the result of the previous compare determined that the two values specified are equal. Following this conditional branch is a similar pair of statements that cause a branch to L if the character addressed by ADDR is blank. If this character survives both tests, it is written out by the statement OUTB @ADDR. Finally, whether or not the character is written, the statement at L adds the value one to the contents of ADDR, thus causing ADDR to address the succeeding character.

The value to be added in this ADD statement is a constant which, in assembly language, is simply expressed as the number (with explicit decimal point) preceded by a hash character. The value to be added in the ADD need not be a constant, however, and can be a word name. For example, the program could have been coded ADD ONE,ADDR where ONE is defined by ONE: .WORD 1.

Finally, the program is terminated by a HALT statement which does just that: it halts the computer. Other statements can be discovered by looking ahead to the list of machine instructions given in App. B. It should then be possible to write some simple programs. A good practice, before becoming more familiar with the language, is to place program statements first followed by word definitions and then by character definitions. All programs must be terminated by the .END statement.

One stumbling block has been obscured as implied in the comments; the OUTB statement is not directly available. However, it can be made available relatively easily [1]

0-3 GETTING STARTED

You are undoubtedly anxious to start working on the system that is available to you. Although there probably will be some initial frustration as you get used to unfamiliar technicalities, you will quickly feel at ease with the machine so that you can get on with discovering its capabilities. By starting early to experiment with the facilities you will be able to apply the material covered in the following

---

[1] The OUTB statement can be provided by substituting the appropriate statements dependent on the particular system in use. One way to do this, which will work in the majority of cases where a small PDP-11 system is being used on a stand-alone basis, is to precede the program with the following statements which will cause output to the console:

```
     .MACRO   OUTB,A
1$:  TSTB     @#177564        → ck. device #s
     BPL      1$
     MOVB     A,@#177566
     .ENDM
```

It is recommended that the reader check with an instructor or other experienced person to determine the most appropriate way to provide OUTB.

chapters as you learn it. Since installations differ in many ways, however, it is not possible to give detailed information on just how you should go about getting started. Consequently, it is necessary that you have an instructor or other experienced person to assist you. All details needed should be available to you in manuals provided by the manufacturer or your local computing facility. Your first task should be to locate such manuals, or perhaps to obtain your own copies, although this should not normally be necessary.

0-3.1 Machine Access

The primary requirement is access to a PDP-11 computer. There are many models of this machine, each with somewhat different characteristics, and there are various ways in which access may be available. Three of the most probable kinds of access are time-sharing, batch, and stand-alone.

A *time-sharing* facility allows access via an input-output terminal, either hard copy or display screen, with the machine itself not being physically accessible. In fact, it may be some distance from the terminal. All communication with the system must pass through the terminal, although there will probably be a facility to print on a high-speed printer. Time-sharing is characterized by the fact that the computer, although shared among many operators, provides interactive facilities to each of them. It thus appears to be dedicated to each operator at a terminal.

Batch access is via an input device which may, for example, be a card reader. In this case, the facility does not appear to be dedicated, and after presenting the input device with a program to be processed one must wait until the system gets around to completing its work before output is received back, usually on a high-speed printer associated with the input device.

A *stand-alone* facility is one that is physically accessible and dedicated to the operator. It may provide either interactive facilities similar to those in a time-sharing system or batch facilities. In the latter case, of course, there is a minimal delay. In several ways, a stand-alone facility is most appropriate for use with this text. It enables one to become much more intimate with the machine, thus dispelling much of the mystique that often surrounds the use of a computer.

The control panel is accessible to the user of a stand-alone facility. Consequently, direct and complete control over the machine is possible. The control panel may appear in one of two forms, depending on the machine. It may be physically on the front of the computer with a set of switches and dials giving direct control over the operation of the machine. Alternatively, there may be few switches on the front of the computer, with direct control available via a console input-output terminal which is directly controlled by the computer hardware. In the latter case, the console terminal does "double duty," since some of the time it is under the control of programs running on the machine. When not under program control, however, the console always reverts to acting as the system control panel.

0-3.2 Files

The prime function of most computer systems is to store information and to process that information. The most common aggregate of information storage is the file, and computer systems can be viewed as manipulators of files. For our purposes, a *file* can be thought of as simply a sequence of characters. Thus, interaction with a computer system takes the form of entering strings of characters into files, invoking operations on these stored files, and obtaining strings of characters as output.

One of the characteristics of a system of which you will first become aware is its treatment of files. In particular, if you have physical access to a machine (whether it be stand-alone or not) you will see a file-storage device. In the smaller models this is very likely to be a "floppy disk" device. You may be given your own storage medium, a conveniently sized disk, on which your private files can be stored and removed from the system. In the case of a time-sharing system your files will be stored on your behalf in a larger file-storage device not accessible to you. Such files can then be retrieved by supplying a file name assigned when the file was created.

0-3.3 The Operating System

With stand-alone operation the system can be controlled locally. Additionally, one can retrieve the operating system from the file system device. (Normally one particular device contains the operating system.) The operating system is simply a collection of programs that takes over control of the machine and through which the operator communicates with the system. Thus, in a stand-alone system with a console terminal control panel the console is taken over by the operating system when it is loaded.

A time-sharing system or a batch system is probably under the control of an operator who will already have loaded the operating system by the time you are able to communicate through your terminal or input device. It is therefore the operating system rather than the hardware machine itself that largely determines the appearance of a system to a user. Even in the case of a stand-alone system, a user will spend far more time communicating with the operating system than with the hardware. Consequently, a user must first become familiar with the operating system available.

0-3.4 Systems Programs

Creating files, modifying files, processing (such as assembling) files, and retrieving files are accomplished by invoking systems programs. Once having created some of your own programs via the systems programs, of course, you will be able to invoke these user programs to do similar functions.

The first systems program that one must use in an interactive system (i.e., not a batch system) is the text editor. This is the program by which you create files. The very first thing you will probably do is to enter a small example program like the one given in Sec. 0-2. More than any other aspect of the available system, the characteristics of the text editor can ease or hinder your use of the facilities. If you are fortunate, there will be available a screen editor enabling you to type data into files from a display screen terminal in such a way that an entire screenful of data can be modified simply by moving a cursor mark to the data to be modified. Less convenient are line editors (designed for use with hard-copy typewriter terminals but also used with display screen terminals) through which only one line can be referenced at one time.

Other systems programs with which you will become familiar are the *assembler*, for translating an assembly-language program into machine code, the *linker*, for preparing one or more programs for execution, the *loader*, which takes such a prepared machine-language program stored in a file and places it into memory for execution, and the *debugger*, which provides a way of monitoring the progress of a program as it executes.

EXERCISES

0-1 Explain precisely what distinguishes a computer from other machines such as a sewing machine, mechanical calculator, automobile, or television set.

0-2 On what grounds does the first set of statements in Sec. 0-1, describing how to read the text, fail to meet the definition of an algorithm as given in the discussion?

0-3 Rewrite the first set of statements in Sec. 0-1 to conform to the definition of an algorithm.

0-4 Write an algorithm for starting a car including a consideration of possible mechanical failures.

0-5 Obtain a manual of instructions for gaining access to your available system. What kind of access is provided? Briefly describe the facilities available.

0-6 Obtain a manual for the text editor that you will be using (if this is the case) and create and retrieve a file containing your name, address, and phone number.

0-7 Enter the example program from Sec. 0-2 into a file and assemble, link, and execute it.

0-8 Write and test a program that outputs a string in reverse order. You may need the statement for subtract, denoted SUB, which subtracts the first operand from the second.

REFERENCES

Goldstine (1972) is an excellent review of the history of digital computers by an author who was directly involved. Also, Rosen (1969) provides a more concise survey of the computer's history.

There are several good texts on introductory programming using Pascal. In particular, Wirth (1973) presents a concise and rigorous approach. The standard reference document for Pascal is Jensen (1974).

The appropriate machine and operating system manuals will depend very much on the particular facilities available. For smaller PDP-11 installations, however, "Microcomputer Handbook" (Digital, 1976) is a useful reference encompassing a great deal of information regarding the hardware and software in one compact reference.

CHAPTER ONE

REPRESENTATION OF NUMBERS AND DATA

We have mentioned that a computer memory consists essentially of a large set of two-position switches. These switches are electronic with a variety of ways in which switch position is determined. For example, the on/off position can be indicated by the presence or absence of charge on a capacitor, the direction of flow of current in a transistor, or the value of voltage in a transistor circuit. Some kinds of memory (such as magnetic tape) employ a ferro-magnetic material that is magnetized in one of two possible orientations. This technology leads us to represent numbers by using only two digits, 0 and 1. One direction of current, value of voltage, orientation of magnetization, or amount of charge stores a 0, while the other stores a 1 (Fig. 1-1).

A number system using two digits is called a *binary number system*. Such a system and related systems form the basis of number representation in a computer.

1-1 GENERAL

Using decimal notation, the number 435 means

$$4 \cdot 10^2 + 3 \cdot 10^1 + 5 \cdot 10^0$$

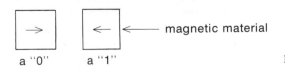

a "0"   a "1"   magnetic material

Figure 1-1 Storage of digits in memory.

11

Generally, we can denote any number by a sequence of digits:

$$d_n d_{n-1} \cdots d_2 d_1 d_0$$

The value is determined by calculating the sum

$$d_n b^n + d_{n-1} b^{n-1} + \cdots + d_2 b^2 + d_1 b^1 + d_0 b^0$$

where b is the base or radix of the number system and is implicitly understood in writing any number. Often, if the base is not known or is not obvious, it is included in the number as a subscript. For example, 435_{10} is a base ten number.

The d's are the digits of a number. There are b distinct digits necessary to express numbers in base b. For example, some systems of particular interest are:

System	Base b	Digits
Hexadecimal	Sixteen	0,1,2,3,4,5,6,7,8,9,A,B,C,D,E,F
Decimal	Ten	0,1,2,3,4,5,6,7,8,9
Octal	Eight	0,1,2,3,4,5,6,7
Binary	Two	0,1

Note that in the hexadecimal system we have exhausted our 10 decimal digits so we have chosen to use A through F as digits representing the values ten through fifteen. Some different ways to express the value twenty-three are 23_{10}, 27_8, 17_{16}, and 10111_2.

In addition to integer values we wish to represent fractional values. We can do this by using the more general form of expressing values:

$$d_n d_{n-1} \cdots d_2 d_1 d_0 . d_{-1} d_{-2} d_{-3} \cdots$$

where the point following d_0 is called the *radix point* and the value is determined by

$$d_n b^n + d_{n-1} b^{n-1} + \cdots + d_2 b^2 + d_1 b^1 + d_0 b^0 + d_{-1} b^{-1}$$

$$+ d_{-2} b^{-2} + d_{-3} b^{-3} \cdots$$

Some different ways to express the value one and three eighths ($1\frac{3}{8}$) are 1.375_{10}, 1.3_8, 1.6_{16}, and 1.011_2.

1-2 ARITHMETIC IN NONDECIMAL BASES

Arithmetic in bases other than decimal is performed in the usual way, although it may feel awkward at first. Readers should attain some familiarity at this point with performing simple integer arithmetic operations in bases other then ten. In particular, the ability to do simple operations in binary and octal is useful. Binary arithmetic is quite easy: Since only two digits are involved, the arithmetic tables are easily memorized. Octal is not so easily memorized since there are eight digits and the tables, although smaller than the decimal arithmetic tables, are not small. The best way to familiarize oneself with binary and octal numbers is simply to practice a bit. For example:

$$4_8 + 17_8 + 4_8 \times 31_8 = 4_8 + 17_8 + 144_8 = 167_8$$

and

$$1101_2 + 10001_2 \times 110_2 = 1001_2 + 1100110_2 = 1101111_2$$

1-3 CONVERSION OF NUMBERS BETWEEN BASES

We shall find that it is often necessary to convert between bases. In particular, many computers store numbers in nondecimal representations. Programmers, however, prefer to prepare data for input or to read output data in decimal. Some conversions are therefore necessary.

Consider the problem of converting an integer number x from base s to base t. The value of the representation that we are seeking can be expressed by

$$d_n t^n + d_{n-1} t^{n-1} + \cdots + d_1 t^1 + d_0 t^0$$

In other words, the representation of the value x in base t is

$$d_n d_{n-1} \cdots d_1 d_0$$

so that the digits in this representation are what we need to find. Suppose that we divide the value of x by the value of t. (To actually perform this division we will first express t in base s.) The value that we obtain can be expressed by

$$d_n t^{n-1} + d_{n-1} t^{n-2} + \cdots + d_1 + \frac{d_0}{t}$$

Notice that the remainder of this division is the least significant digit of the representation sought. Simply taking the remainder then yields the least significant digit. Furthermore, the next most significant digit can be obtained by dividing the quotient by t and taking the remainder in the same way. Repeating the procedure yields each digit of x in base t. For example:

Convert 167_{10} into octal First we express eight in decimal, which is simply 8. Then we repeatedly divide 167_{10} by 8_{10}.

Destination base	Source value	Remainder digits
8	167	$7 = d_0$
	20	$4 = d_1$
	2	$2 = d_2$
	0	

Therefore, $167_{10} = 247_8$.

Convert 119₁₀ into binary → *Convert 119_{10} into binary*

2	119	$1 = d_0$
	59	$1 = d_1$
	29	$1 = d_2$
	14	$0 = d_3$
	7	$1 = d_4$
	3	$1 = d_5$
	1	$1 = d_6$
	0	

2^6	2^5	2^4	2^3	2^2	2^1	2^0
64	32	16	8	4	2	1
1	1	1	0	1	1	1

$$64$$
$$32$$
$$16$$
$$4$$
$$2$$
$$1$$
$$\overline{119}$$

Therefore, $119_{10} = 1110111_2$.

Convert 121_8 into base five

5	121₈	$1 = d_0$
	20₈	$1 = d_1$
	3	$3 = d_2$
	0	

This calculation is performed using octal numbers. (For convenience we have omitted the subscript.) Therefore,

$$121_8 = 311_5$$

Consider now the problem of converting a fractional number x from base s to base t. The representation that we seek is

$$d_{-1}t^{-1} + d_{-2}t^{-2} + \cdots + d_{-m}t^{-m}$$

Suppose that we multiply the value of x by the value of t. (To actually perform this multiplication we will first express t in base s.) The value that we obtain can be expressed by

$$d_{-1}t^0 + d_{-2}t^{-1} + \cdots + d_{-m}t^{-m+1}$$

This number consists of a fraction and an integer part which is the most significant digit of the number that we seek. The next digit can be obtained by subtracting off the first and again multiplying by t:

$$d_{-2}t^0 + d_{-3}t^{-1} + \cdots + d_{-m}t^{-m+2}$$

Repeating the procedure yields each digit of x in base t. For example:

Convert 0.167_{10} into octal to three places Repeatedly multiply 0.167_{10} by 8_{10}.

Integer digits	Source value	Destination base
	0.167	8
$d_{-1} = 1 +$	0.336	
$d_{-2} = 2$	0.688	
$d_{-3} = 5$	0.504	
$d_{-4} = 4$	0.032	

$.167 \times 8 = 1.336$

$.336 \times 8 = 2.688$

$.688 \times 8 = 5.504$

$.504 \times 8 = 4.032$

$\frac{3}{64}$
$\frac{8}{512}$

Therefore, $0.167_{10} = 0.125_8.$ $= 1 \times 8^{-1} + 2 \times 8^{-2} + 5 \times 8^{-3} = \frac{1}{8} + \frac{2}{64} + \frac{5}{512} = .1660$

Convert 0.125_{10} into binary Repeatedly multiply 0.125_{10} by 2_{10}.

	0.125	2
$d_{-1} = 0$	0.250	
$d_{-2} = 0$	0.500	
$d_{-3} = 1$	0.000	

Therefore, $0.125_{10} = 0.001_2$. Note that, in this case, the procedure terminated with a zero fractional part since 0.125 decimal is exactly representable in binary.

1-4 REPRESENTATION OF NEGATIVE NUMBERS

The usual way of representing negative numbers is called *signed-magnitude*: one represents a number by a magnitude (distance from zero) and a sign (direction from zero). The example of an automobile odometer illustrates a technical problem with signed-magnitude representation. Moving an odometer backward one obtains

0003, 0002, 0001, 0000, 9999, 9998, etc.

The desired sequence, for the analogous mechanism in a computer, is

0003, 0002, 0001, 0000, -0001, -0002, etc.

To implement this sequence on an odometer the wheels must reverse direction on reaching zero and a sign indicator must be set. Similar technical problems exist using signed-magnitude in a computer. This system is, nevertheless, widely used.

Two other systems of representing negative numbers are commonly used in computers as well. First, note that an odometer has a fixed number of digits. Numbers in computers are also represented in some fixed number of digits. If a representation has n digits to the base b, then there are b^n distinct representable "states." For example, the four-digit odometer above can display one of $10^4 = 10,000$ positions.

We can represent the value of a *negative* number x by $x' = b^n - |x|$ where x' is the n digit representation of x. This is called the *b's complement*. For example, using 10's complement representation, a three-digit counter represents numbers as follows:

x'	Value represented
499	+499
498	+498
.	.
.	.
.	.
002	+2
001	+1
000	0
999	−1
998	−2
.	.
.	.
.	.
501	−499
500	−500

Note that negative numbers are detectable in the sequence by a leftmost digit that is greater than or equal to 5.

We can represent the value of a negative number x by $x' = b^n - 1 - |x|$. This is called the *(b − 1)'s complement*. For example, using 9's complement representation, a three-digit counter represents numbers as follows:

x'	Value represented
499	+499
498	+498
.	.
.	.
.	.
002	+2
001	+1
000	+0
999	−0
998	−1
997	−2
.	.
.	.
.	.
500	−499

In this case negative numbers are also easily detectable. However, note the double zero obtained with $(b-1)$'s complement.

Using this three-digit counter for signed-magnitude representation we can represent only positive values from 000 to 999. To represent negative numbers we would have to add a fourth position to indicate sign.

Since numbers in computers are most often encountered in binary, we shall be most interested in the *2's complement* and the *1's complement* systems, as well as binary *signed-magnitude*. It is convenient in signed-magnitude to use the most significant binary digit (*bit*) to signify the sign. Most commonly, 0 denotes positive and 1 denotes negative. This leaves $n-1$ bits to represent the magnitude. Take for example numbers with $n=4$. Then

$$4_{10} = 0100_2 \qquad -5_{10} = 1101_2 \qquad \text{and} \qquad -1_{10} = 1001_2$$

(We shall drop the subscripts in the text following since the meaning is usually clear.)

Using 4 bits there are $2^4 = 16$ possible representations. Each number system, signed-magnitude, 2's complement, and 1's complement, assigns values to representations in a different way. This can be illustrated by writing the sequence of representations on the circumference of a circle as shown in Fig. 1-2.

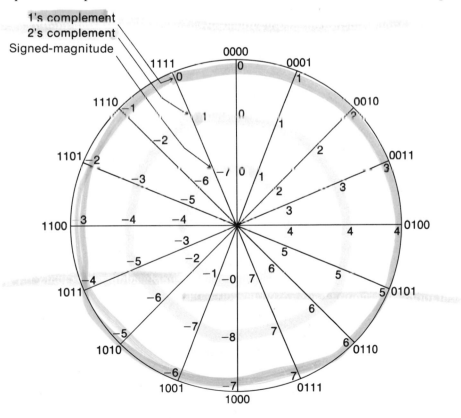

Figure 1-2 A number representation comparison.

The values assigned by each of the three number systems are also shown, each value labeling the "spoke" of the corresponding representation.

Signed-magnitude. The signed-magnitude system includes values from -7 to $+7$. It contains a double zero, which wastes one representation as well as being computationally incorrect, since a signed zero is meaningless. Signed-magnitude does not "wrap around" as one counts down through zero by subtracting 1's from the binary representation.

2's complement. The 2's complement system eliminates the double zero and possesses the desirable wraparound property. In addition, negative numbers are easily detectable by a 1 in the leftmost bit.

The most important advantage of 2's complement, however, is the ease with which arithmetic can be performed. Recall that a negative number is the 2's complement of its positive counterpart. That is, a negative number x is represented by $x' = 2^n - |x|$. For example, if $n = 4$,

$$-5 \text{ is } 2^n - (5)$$
$$= 10000 - 0101$$
$$= 1011$$

The 2's complement can also be found by *inverting the bits and adding 1*. Inverting the bits means changing 0's to 1's and 1's to 0's. For example, the 2's complement of $5 = 0101$ can be formed as follows:

5 is	0101
Invert bits	1010
Add 1	1011 which represents -5

Positive numbers are also the 2's complement of their negative counterparts. For example, the 2's complement of $-7 = 1001$ can be formed as follows:

-7 is	1001
Invert bits	0110
Add 1	0111 which represents 7

It follows that one can invert the sign of a number (multiply by -1) by taking its 2's complement, regardless of its original sign.

Addition of 2's complement numbers can be performed without regard to the sign of the numbers involved. This is done by simply adding the binary representations and ignoring any resulting carry bit. For example,

$$-7 + 5 = \quad 1001$$
$$+ \underline{0101}$$
$$1110 = -2$$

and

$$-4 + 3 = \quad 1100$$
$$+ \underline{0011}$$
$$1111 = -1$$

and
$$(-5) + (-2) = \begin{array}{r} 1011 \\ +\,1110 \\ \hline 11001 \end{array} = -7 \quad \text{(carry ignored)}$$

Subtraction of 2's complement numbers is performed by inverting the sign of the subtrahend and adding. The sign inversion, of course, can be simply done by taking the 2's complement. That is, given $A - B$, form $-B$, and add $A + (-B)$. For example,

$$\begin{aligned} 4 - (-2) &= (0100) - (1110) \\ &= (0100) + (0010) \\ &= 0110 \\ &= 6 \end{aligned}$$

and
$$\begin{aligned} 7 - 3 &= (0111) - (0011) \\ &= (0111) + (1101) \\ &= 10100 \\ &= 4 \quad\quad\quad\quad\quad \text{(carry ignored)} \end{aligned}$$

1's complement. The 1's complement system possesses the desirable wrap around property, and negative numbers are easily detectable by a 1 in the leftmost bit. Although the undesirable double zero is present as in signed-magnitude, 1's complement offers the advantage of a very simple complementing operation. A negative number x is represented by $x' = 2^n - 1 - |x|$.

$$\begin{aligned} -5 \text{ is } 2^n - 1 - (5) \\ = 1111 - 0101 \\ = 1010 \end{aligned}$$

The 1's complement can also be formed by *inverting the bits.* As seen above, the 1's complement of $5 = 0101$ is simply 1010.

Positive numbers are the 1's complement of their negative counterparts. As in 2's complement, one inverts the sign of a number by taking its 1's complement, regardless of its original sign.

Addition of 1's complement numbers can be performed without regard to the sign of the numbers involved. This is done by adding the binary representations and then *adding one if a carry occurred.* For example,

$$-7 + 5 = \begin{array}{r} 1000 \\ 0101 \\ \hline 1101 \end{array} = -2 \quad \textit{no carry}$$

and
$$-1 + 6 = \begin{array}{r} 1110 \\ 0110 \\ \hline 10100 \\ +\,1 \\ \hline 0101 \end{array} = 5 \quad \textit{carry, add!}$$

and
$$(-2) + (-3) = \begin{array}{r} 1101 \\ 1100 \\ \hline 11001 \\ 1 \\ \hline 1010 = -5 \end{array}$$

The addition of 1 is an adjustment required when the addition operation wraps around through zero. The double zero occupies two representations and necessitates the adjustment. A wraparound through zero is detected by a carry.

To see graphically why the adjustment is necessary, start at the -1 spoke on the circle shown previously. Count clockwise six spokes, thus performing $-1 + 6$. You should end up at the 0100 spoke. Since you counted twice for zero (at the 1111 spoke and the 0000 spoke), you must count for one additional spoke, thus ending up finally at 0101.

Remember that the foregoing discussion is valid for numbers of any length, although we chose only 4-bit numbers in the examples.

1-5 OVERFLOW

We have been very careful in all the examples to choose numbers which, when added, yield a result within our range of representable numbers. It is possible to add two numbers and obtain a result that is a valid representation of some number but which is incorrect. For example, consider 2's complement numbers with $n = 4$:

$$6 + 4 = \begin{array}{r} 0110 \\ 0100 \\ \hline 1010 = -6 \end{array}$$

The correct result is 10, but that is outside our representable range using only 4 bits. A similar phenomenon occurs with large negative results:

$$-(-5) + (-4) = \begin{array}{r} 1011 \\ 1100 \\ \hline 10111 = 7 \end{array} \quad \text{(carry ignored)}$$

The correct result is -9, but again, that is outside our representable range.

2's complement. A systematic method for detecting overflow is needed. Such a method can be devised for 2's complement if we note that negative numbers can be filled out with leading 1's in the same way that positive numbers can be filled out with leading 0's. Doing so does not alter the value of the number.

Take all the numbers representable in 4 bits and add a leading digit: 0 for positive numbers and zero, and 1 for negative numbers. Notice that all valid numbers now have either two leading 1's or two leading 0's. That is, any 5-bit binary number whose leftmost two bits are 01 or 10 is not representable in 4 bits. This leads directly to the algorithm for overflow detection, which is

1. Before adding two n-bit 2's complement numbers, fill out each number with a leading digit identical to its leftmost bit.
2. Perform the addition using $n + 1$ bit arithmetic, ignoring a carry into the $n + 2$d bit.
3. Examine the $n + 1$ bit result. Overflow has occurred if the leftmost two digits are not identical.

For example, $n = 4,$ 2's comp.

$$
\begin{aligned}
-7 + 5 = \quad &1 \quad 1001 \\
&0 \quad 0101 \\
\hline
&1 \quad 1110 = -2 \quad \text{(correct)}
\end{aligned}
$$

n + 2d bit carry ignored

$$
\begin{aligned}
-5 + (-2) = \quad &1 \quad 1011 \\
&1 \quad 1110 \\
\hline
&(1)1 \quad 1001 = -7 \quad \text{(correct, carry ignored)}
\end{aligned}
$$

$$
\begin{aligned}
6 + 4 = \quad &0 \quad 0110 \\
&0 \quad 0100 \\
\hline
&0 \quad 1010 = \text{invalid overflow result}
\end{aligned}
$$

$$
\begin{aligned}
-5 + (-4) = \quad &1 \quad 1011 \\
&1 \quad 1100 \\
\hline
&11 \quad 0111 = \text{invalid overflow result (carry ignored)}
\end{aligned}
$$

1's complement. Overflow detection in the 1's complement system is identical to the 2's complement method except that one adds in any carry resulting from the $n + 1$ bit addition. For example,

$$
\begin{aligned}
5 + 6 = \quad &0 \quad 0101 \\
&0 \quad 0110 \\
\hline
&0 \quad 1011 = \text{invalid overflow result}
\end{aligned}
$$

$$
\begin{aligned}
5 + 2 = \quad &0 \quad 0101 \\
&0 \quad 0010 \\
\hline
&0 \quad 0111 = 7 \quad \text{(correct)}
\end{aligned}
$$

$$
\begin{aligned}
-5 + (-2) = \quad &1 \quad 1010 \\
&1 \quad 1101 \\
\hline
&11 \quad 0111 \\
&1 \qquad \text{(add carry out of sign bit)} \\
\hline
&1 \quad 1000 = -7 \quad \text{(correct)}
\end{aligned}
$$

$$
\begin{aligned}
-5 + (-4) = \quad &1 \quad 1010 \\
&1 \quad 1011 \\
\hline
&11 \quad 0101 \\
&1 \qquad \text{(add carry out of sign bit)} \\
\hline
&1 \quad 0110 = \text{invalid overflow result}
\end{aligned}
$$

Signed-magnitude. The $n - 1$ bit magnitude portion of an n-bit signed-magnitude number is in the range 0 to $2^{n-1} - 1$ since $n - 1$ bits can represent 2^{n-1} distinct values. Overflow occurs if an arithmetic operation on the $n - 1$ bit magnitude yields a result greater than 2^{n-1}.

Overflow can be detected simply by checking for a carry out of the leftmost bit when adding or subtracting magnitudes.

1-6 FRACTIONAL NUMBERS

Fractional numbers can be represented in any of the three systems discussed here. The algorithms for addition, subtraction, and overflow detection remain the same except that the rule Add 1 is interpreted as "add 1 to the least significant bit position." For example, using $n = 4$ and 2's complement we may choose to represent numbers in the range $-2, -1\frac{3}{4}, -1\frac{1}{2}, \ldots, 1\frac{1}{2}, 1\frac{3}{4}$. The binary representations are:

$$
\begin{array}{ll}
10.00 & -2 \\
10.01 & -1\frac{3}{4} \\
10.10 & -1\frac{1}{2} \\
\quad \cdot & \quad \cdot \\
\quad \cdot & \quad \cdot \\
\quad \cdot & \quad \cdot \\
11.11 & -\frac{1}{4} \\
00.00 & 00.00 \\
00.01 & +\frac{1}{4} \\
\quad \cdot & \quad \cdot \\
\quad \cdot & \quad \cdot \\
\quad \cdot & \quad \cdot \\
01.11 & +1\frac{3}{4}
\end{array}
$$

The representation for $1\frac{3}{4}$ is complemented by:

$1\frac{3}{4}$ is	01.11
Invert bits	10.00
Add 1 to least significant bit	1
$-1\frac{3}{4}$ is	10.01

Note that many fractions are not representable with our 4 bits. As with any base, the binary system can only approximate certain fractions. For example $\frac{7}{16} = .0111$ must be represented by 00.10. By increasing n, the number of bits we use to represent numbers, we may approximate fractions to a higher accuracy.

ASCII

24

1-7 ALPHANUMERIC DATA REPRESENTATION

Much of the information processed in computers is not represented ... form but as sequences of characters. A company's employee records, for example, contains such information as names, titles, and addresses. Each item can be stored as a sequence of characters. A further reason for representing information in character form is that printed output to be read by humans must appear as a sequence of characters.

Characters are stored in *coded* form; that is, each character is associated with a unique binary number. Codes are often constructed using 8-bit binary numbers, since this provides $2^8 = 256$ unique character codes, more than

Bit 5 of letters = 0 (6th bit)

Table 1-1   ASCII codes

Octal code	Character	Octal code	Character	Octal code	Character
040	BLANK	100	@	140	`
041	!	101	A	141	a
042	"	102	B	142	b
043	#	103	C	143	c
044	$	104	D	144	d
045	%	105	E	145	e
046	&	106	F	146	f
047	'	107	G	147	g
050	(	110	H	150	h
051	)	111	I	151	i
052	*	112	J	152	j
053	+	113	K	153	k
054	,	114	L	154	l
055	−	115	M	155	m
056	.	116	N	156	n
057	/	117	O	157	o
060	0	120	P	160	p
061	1	121	Q	161	q
062	2	122	R	162	r
063	3	123	S	163	s
064	4	124	T	164	t
065	5	125	U	165	u
066	6	126	V	166	v
067	7	127	W	167	w
070	8	130	X	170	x
071	9	131	Y	171	y
072	:	132	Z	172	z
073	;	133	[	173	{
074	<	134	\	174		
075	=	135	]	175	}
076	>	136	∧	176	~
077	?	137	—	177	DEL

CR = 15

LF = 12

01000001 = A = 101   ∅ = 060

01011010 = Z = 132   9 = 71

enough for most applications. A grouping of 8 bits is often called a *byte*. One can, therefore, speak of storing a character in a byte.

There is a standard set of 7-bit character codes called the *American Standard Code for Information Interchange* (ASCII). It is shown in Table 1-1 with each individual code represented in octal. For our purposes this code can be converted to an 8-bit code by adding a leading zero.[1]

We shall frequently use octal notation in representing binary numbers since it is less tedious than writing out long sequences of 0's and 1's. Since every 3-bit sequence is uniquely representable by a single octal digit, it is very easy to convert from binary to octal and vice versa. For example, the character W is coded in ASCII as 01010111, which can directly be written in octal as 127. Note that in converting from octal back to binary it is necessary to remove a leading 0 so that the result has only 8 bits. For example:

1. A blank is coded as $00100000 = 040_8$. (Blanks must be explicitly represented.)
2. A period is coded as $00101110 = 056_8$.
3. A character "3" is coded as $00110011 = 063_8$.

Note that *numeric characters* are quite different from *numbers* represented in a system such as 2's complement. The binary number five is represented in 8 bits by 00000101. The character "5" is represented in the 8-bit ASCII code by 00110101. This distinction will become clearer after the reader has written some programs to process alphanumeric data.

EXERCISES

1-1 Complete the addition, subtraction, and multiplication tables for the binary and octal number systems.

1-2 Convert the following decimal numbers into binary, octal, and hexadecimal: 369, 27, 255, 64.

1-3 Convert the following values into decimal: 436 octal, 101101 binary, AF3E hexadecimal, 312 base five.

1-4 Express the following values, using 8 bits, in each of the three number systems: binary signed-magnitude, 1's complement, and 2's complement.

Number	Base
17	Eight
−13	Ten
−13	Sixteen
−43	Five
−35	Eight

[1] The leading bit can be used for error detection by giving it a value dependent on the number of 1's in the remaining 7 bits. This method, called *parity checking*, is quite often carried out automatically in hardware.

1-5 For each of the three number systems in Exercise 1-4, add the five values together using that number system and showing the steps involved.

1-6 Express the following values using 8 bits, 2's complement representation, and 4 bits of the 8 for a fractional part: 7.0625, -5.9, -4.5, 7.4, -0.125 (all values are expressed in decimal).

1-7 Show that binary numbers can be converted to octal simply by grouping the bits in threes starting from the binary point and replacing each group by its corresponding octal digit.

1-8 Given a 2's complement 8-bit number system with 4 bits of fractional part, what are the representation and the value of: (*a*) the largest positive number, (*b*) the largest number in magnitude, (*c*) the smallest positive number, (*d*) the smallest negative number?

1-9 What is represented by each of the following 8-bit groups, which are expressed in octal, when interpreted as 1's complement integers, 2's complement integers, signed-magnitude integers, and ASCII characters?

$$040 \qquad 077 \qquad 111 \qquad 134$$

1-10 Explain the rule for detecting overflow in the 10's complement number system.

REFERENCES

The outstanding reference in the area of representation of numerical values is undoubtedly Knuth (1973). For a discussion of the implementation of arithmetic operations in digital circuitry, Hellerman (1967) provides an excellent treatment.

TWO

BASIC COMPUTER STRUCTURE

This chapter contains a discussion of some basic mechanisms common to most computers. These mechanisms are described without reference to any particular computer so that the concepts involved will not be obscured by the details which necessarily arise when considering an actual machine. Chapter 3 will describe a particular computer, the PDP-11.

2-1 MEMORY

Data in a computer are stored as a sequence of bits called a *cell*. All cells, of which there may be thousands or millions, are of the same length and are arranged in a sequence forming a computer's *memory*. Figure 2-1 shows a memory of m cells where each cell is n bits long.

The relative location of a cell within memory serves to identify the cell. Thus we refer to a cell by giving its relative location, or *address*. One must remember to distinguish between the *contents* of a cell (the stored data) and the *address* of the cell.

It is often necessary to store memory addresses as data. One may for example store a number in cell 15 and wish to remember in which cell the number is stored. The address 15 can then be recorded by storing it in some other prearranged cell.

Addresses are usually represented in binary. The number of bits required to hold any arbitrary address is directly related to the size of memory. For a

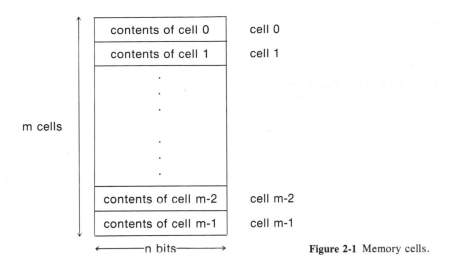

Figure 2-1 Memory cells.

memory of m cells, addresses occupy A bits where $2^A = m$. It is necessary that $n \geq A$ if we are to store addresses in a memory of m cells.

As well as cells, the memory includes some mechanisms to place data into cells and to retrieve data. These are described in the next section.

2-2 THE PROCESSOR

A simple computer may be viewed as having two basic components: a *memory* to store data and a *processor* to process the data. For the moment we view the processor as a "black box" and just describe its characteristics as viewed externally. We shall add components to our basic processor as we expose the need for such additions.

The processor is connected to memory in a way permitting two kinds of processor-memory interactions (see Fig. 2-2):

1. The processor can *store* data into a specified cell of memory. Storing data into a cell destroys the previous contents of the cell.
2. The processor can *fetch* data from a specified cell of memory. Fetching data from a cell leaves the contents of the cell unaltered. That is, a *copy* of the stored data is moved into the processor.

Storing and fetching are accomplished via the three components of the "interface" between the processor and memory, the *store-fetch switch* (SFS) and two special cells called the *memory data register* (MDR) and the *memory address register* (MAR).

The name *register* is usually applied to any cell in a computer other than a normal memory cell. For example, cells in the processor (to be described later) are called registers.

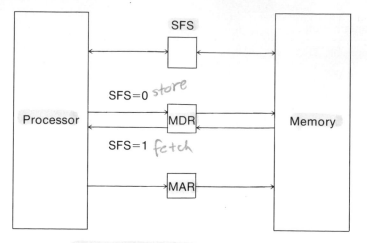

Figure 2-2 Processor-memory communication.

The SFS, a 2-bit register, is an indicator of the interaction to be performed; zero (00) indicates a store, one (01) indicates a fetch, and two (10) indicates no interaction or the completion of an interaction.

The MDR has a capacity of n bits and acts as a temporary resting place for data moving to or from memory.

The MAR has a capacity of A bits (recall $2^A = m$ or $A = \log_2 m$) and during an interaction holds the address of the memory cell involved.

A fetch proceeds as follows:

1. The processor places an address a in the MAR and sets SFS to 1.
2. The memory obtains a copy of the contents of cell a, places the copy in the MDR, and sets SFS to 2. $= 10$
3. The processor removes the data from the MDR.

A store proceeds as follows:

1. The processor places an address a in the MAR, places some data in the MDR, and sets SFS to 0.
2. The memory removes the data from the MDR, places them in cell a, and sets SFS to 2.

The algorithms for storing and fetching, as implemented in the processor and in memory, are described below using structured English and Pascal programs. In a computer these algorithms are implemented using circuitry of course and not a programming language.

In the processor we have:

CONST maxaddr = largest address { m − 1};
    maxvalue = largest number { 2∗∗ n − 1 };

TYPE addr = 0..maxaddr;
    value = 0..maxvalue;

FUNCTION fetch (a:addr):value;
    BEGIN
        wait until memory has finished any previous operation;
        transmit address and signal memory;
        wait until memory signals completion of fetch;
        receive data from memory;
        return function value
    END;

FUNCTION store (data: value; a:addr);
    BEGIN
        wait until memory has finished any previous operation;
        transmit address and data and signal memory
    END

Expressing these algorithms in Pascal:

FUNCTION fetch (a:addr):value;
    BEGIN
        WHILE sfs <>2 DO   ;
        mar :− a;
        sfs := 1;
        WHILE sfs <> 2 DO   ;
        fetch := mdr
    END;

PROCEDURE store (data: value; a:addr);
    BEGIN
        WHILE sfs <> 2 DO   ;
        mar := a;
        mdr := data;
        sfs   := 0
    END

First, notice that the WHILE statements simply implement a delay until the memory is not busy; the dummy statement following DO is executed repeatedly until SFS is set equal to 2 by the memory.

Notice also that the processor must wait until any previous interactions have been completed (SFS = 2) before initiating another. Note in addition that the processor need not wait for a store (SFS = 0) to finish but must of course wait for a fetch (SFS = 1), since it presumably needs the data before it can proceed.

In the memory we have an endless loop that services the fetch and store requests from the processor as they are signaled. In reading this algorithm remember that the processor and the memory operate concurrently because the processor does not wait for a store to finish before proceeding to do something else. Furthermore they operate independent of each other's internal timing. The function of the SFS register is to synchronize this concurrent activity.

The memory operates as follows:

```
WHILE TRUE DO BEGIN
    wait for a request from the processor;
    IF   request is a store THEN BEGIN
        receive data and place in memory cell;
        signal completion END
    ELSE BEGIN
        transmit data to processor;
        signal completion END
END
```

Expressing this in Pascal we have:

```
VAR a:addr; mem: ARRAY [addr] OF value ;
WHILE TRUE DO BEGIN
    WHILE sfs =2 DO    ;
    IF   sfs=0 THEN BEGIN
        a := mar;
        mem[a] := mdr;
        sfs   := 2 END
    ELSE BEGIN
        a := mar;
        mdr := mem[a];
        sfs   := 2 END
END
```

2-3 REPRESENTATION OF PROGRAMS

Algorithms, as you know, can be expressed in some high-level programming language such as ALGOL, FORTRAN, Pascal, or PL/I. The reason for expressing such algorithms is, of course, to permit a computer to examine the program and carry out or *execute* the precise operations specified therein.

One can conceive of storing a Pascal program in memory, one character per cell perhaps, and designing a processor to execute the program. It would be perfectly feasible to do this, but there would be two problems:

1. The processor would be very complex and therefore expensive.
2. The computer would be capable of executing only Pascal.

Rather than building a Pascal processor, one normally *translates* the program into a language that can be executed by a very simple processor.[1] The primitive operations of such a language will, of course, be much less powerful than the primitive operations of Pascal. Nevertheless, any algorithm expressible in Pascal can be expressed in a language with a suitable set of simpler primitives. Such languages are called *machine languages*.

Programs in machine language consist of a sequence of *instructions*. Each instruction is simply a sequence of bits. Often a single instruction is stored in one memory cell but, as we shall see later, an instruction may occupy several cells. For the moment, assume that an instruction occupies one cell. A program then is stored as a sequence of instructions, each occupying a memory cell.

2-3.1 Three-Address Machines

The processor executes a program by repeatedly fetching instructions and carrying out the operation specified in each. To understand this process let us first consider a very simple kind of processor that executes instructions appearing in the format shown below.

c	a1	a2	a3

The instruction contains three addresses: a1, a2, and a3. The remaining $n - 3A$ bits contain a binary number c called the *operation code* representing some primitive operation of the processor (e.g., an arithmetic operation such as addition). The addresses a1 and a2 specify cells *the contents of which* are to be the operands of the operation specified by the operation code c. The result (of applying the operation to the contents of cells a1 and a2) is to be placed in cell a3.

The processor locates each instruction in a sequence of instructions by means of an internal register, called the *program counter*, which is used to contain the address of the next instruction to be executed. Figure 2-3 shows such a simple processor, usually called a *three-address processor* because of the number of address fields in each instruction.

[1] Recently a Pascal processor has been built to execute a special intermediate language into which Pascal programs are translated.

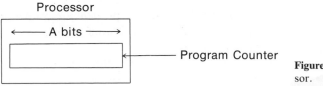

Figure 2-3 A three-address processor.

Suppose that $n = 32$ and $A = 9$. Memory then contains a maximum of $m = 2^A = 2^9 = 512$ cells. The processor can be constructed to recognize $2^5 = 32$ different operations. Operations provided usually include the normal arithmetic ones such as add, subtract, multiply, etc.

The algorithm followed by the processor in executing a stored program is called its *execution cycle*. The Pascal program below describes the execution cycle for a three-address processor. The program counter must be initialized with the address of the program's first instruction; thus the algorithm is expressed as a procedure with one argument supplying this initial address. To ensure that the program counter (PC) contains the correct address, the processor adds 1 to its contents each time an instruction is executed.

```
PROCEDURE execute (a:addr);
    BEGIN
        pc := a;
        WHILE machine not halted DO  BEGIN
            fetch instruction from cell given by pc;
            pc := pc+1 ;
            decode operation;
          4 fetch operand #1 from cell a1;
          5 fetch operand #2 from cell a2;
            carry out operation;
          7 store result in cell a3 END
    END
```

Figure 2-4 shows a three-address processor and a program to calculate the result of $R := (X + Y - Z)/X$.

A three-address processor as we have defined it can execute only sequential programs. That is, we cannot for example program an iteration. This is remedied by ensuring that one of the operation codes defines a JUMP operation that enables the programmer to alter the sequential execution of the program. A JUMP instruction requires only one address field and might appear as

JUMP	a1	a2	a3

$\longleftarrow$ unused $\longrightarrow$

The JUMP operation is carried out in the processor by *placing the address a3 in the PC,* thus causing the next instruction to be fetched from some cell other than the one immediately following the current instruction. The previous contents of the PC are destroyed.

In the previous example we might place the data after the program and jump around them (since errors would result if the processor attempted to execute data). Figure 2-5 shows such a program.

The fourth, fifth, and seventh lines in the inner block of the execution cycle

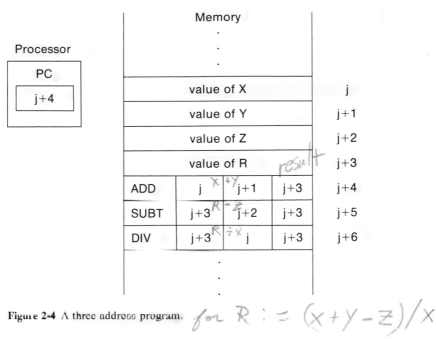

Figure 2-4 A three address program. for $R := (x+y-z)/x$

Memory

Processor				
PC				
j

ADD	j+4	j+5	j+7	j
SUBT	j+7	j+6	j+7	j+1
DIV	j+7	J+4	j+7	j+2
JUMP	—	—	j+8	j+3
value of X				j+4
value of Y				j+5
value of Z				j+6
value of R				j+7
				j+8

Figure 2-5 The JUMP instruction.

are not required for JUMP instructions. To be correct, then, we should modify these lines by changing them to

Fourth: fetch operand #1 from cell a1 if required; *of - p.³²*
Fifth: fetch operand #2 from cell a2 if required;
Seventh: store result in cell a3 if required;

2-3.2 Single-Address Machines

One can reduce the number of addresses required in an instruction. Notice that in the example program above we used a cell in memory to hold temporary values during the expression evaluation. A register can be provided within the processor to hold temporary values. By making the contents of such a register an *implicit operand of every instruction,* we reduce to one the number of addresses required in each instruction.

The register that we are describing is usually called an *accumulator* (AC) and may hold a source operand or a result operand depending on the operation. The typical instruction in a single-address machine does both by taking one operand from the accumulator and leaving the result there. An accumulator contains at least n bits, as indicated in Fig. 2-6.

A 32-bit single-address instruction may be formatted as:

←————8————→	←————————————24————————————→
c	a1

With $A = 24$, $m = 2^{24} > 16$ million cells. Also the number of possible operation codes is $2^8 = 256$.

Some operations of a single-address processor exist only for the purpose of placing data into or removing data from the accumulator. Two such operations are the LOAD and the STORE. These are defined as:

Operation

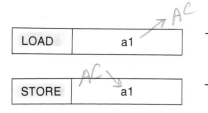

LOAD	a1

—place the contents of cell a1 in the accumulator destroying the previous contents.

STORE	a1

—copy the contents of the accumulator into cell a1. The contents of the accumulator remain unchanged.

Most operations in a single-address processor take the AC and another cell as source operands and place the results back in the AC. For example:

Operation

ADD	a1

—add the contents of cell a1 to the contents of the AC and place the result in the AC.

Processor

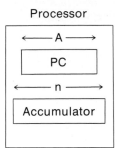

Figure 2-6 A single-address processor.

The execution cycle for a single-address processor is:

```
PROCEDURE execute (a:addr);
    BEGIN
        pc := a;
        WHILE machine not halted DO BEGIN
            fetch instruction from cell given by pc;
            pc := pc+1;
            decode operation;
            fetch operand from cell a1 if required;
            carry out operation;
            store result in cell a1 if required END
    END
```

cf. p. 32

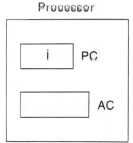

Memory

LOAD	j+6 X	j
ADD	j+7 y	j+1
SUBT	j+8 Z	j+2
DIV	j+6 X	j+3
STORE	j+9 R	j+4
JUMP	j+10	j+5
value of X		j+6
value of Y		j+7
value of Z		j+8
value of R		j+9

Figure 2-7 A single-address program.

cf. p. 33   R := (X+Y-Z)/X

The example in Fig. 2-7 shows a program for a single-address processor to calculate $R = (X + Y - Z)/X$.

2-3.3 Stack Machines

Some processors are designed to be able to execute instructions having no explicit operand addresses. Such zero-address processors have a peculiar type of accumulator called a *stack* accumulator. A stack has the property that placing data in it does not destroy the previous contents. Instead, the previous contents are pushed down into the stack. As an analogy, think of the racks for holding trays in a cafeteria. At any time only the top one or two trays are accessible. Placing additional trays on the rack pushes the contents down so that only the newest top trays are accessible. Removing the top tray pops the contents up so that another tray replaces the tray that was removed. This type of stack is often called a last-in–first-out (LIFO) stack.

In a zero-address processor or "stack machine" some instructions take as implicit operands the contents of the cells at the top of the stack. Such instructions are, of course, zero-address instructions. For example, ADD and SUBT may function as follows:

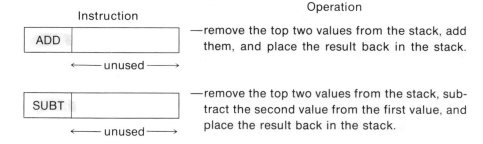

Figure 2-8 illustrates how ADD and SUBT operate on the stack. Of course, stack processors need some one-address instructions so that data can be moved to and from the stack and memory. The two instructions that perform these moves are the POP and PUSH:

Instruction		Operation
PUSH	a1	—place the contents of cell a1 into the stack (pushing down the previous contents).
POP	a1	—remove the top value from the stack (popping up the stack) and place it in cell a1.

Stacks are useful for a number of applications including the evaluation of expressions. The program in Fig. 2-9 calculates $R := (R + Y)/(A + B)$.

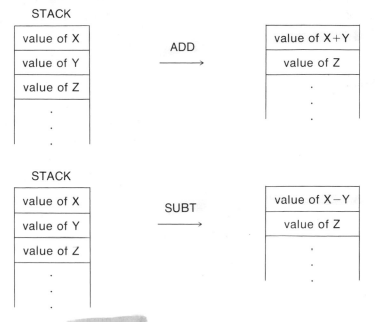

Figure 2-8 Stack operations.

2-3.4 Practical Processors

Most processors are designed to execute a mixture of instruction types with three, two, one, or zero addresses. As a result, many computers have an instruction format that varies in length depending on the particular operation and the number of addresses required. The processor must be able to recognize the type of an instruction and fetch from a sufficient number of cells to obtain a complete instruction. Updating the PC then is accomplished by adding the length of the current instruction. Some newer machines even have an instruction format that varies dynamically so that the processor may fetch only the part of an instruction needed for a particular execution of it.

2-4 INTERNAL PROCESSOR STRUCTURE

To introduce the notion of a stored program, it is useful to treat the processor as a "black box" with certain describable behavior. However, mystery inevitably arises. A discussion of the internal structure of a processor can dispel some of the mystery. Figure 2-10 shows some of the major components of a simple single-address processor. The program counter (PC) and the accumulator (AC)

Processor

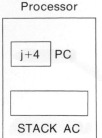

	Memory	
	.	
	.	
	.	
	value of R	j
	value of Y	j+1
	value of A	j+2
	value of B	j+3
PUSH	j+2 *A*	j+4
PUSH	j+3 *β*	j+5
ADD	*A+B on top*	j+6
PUSH	j+1 *Y*	j+7
PUSH	j *R*	j+8
ADD	*Y+R on top*	j+9
DIV	*Y+R/A+B on top*	j+10
POP	j *R*	j+11
	.	
	.	
	.	

$R := (R + Y)/(A + B)$

Figure 2-9 A stack program.

have already been introduced. The memory address and memory data registers (MAR and MDR) discussed earlier are shown as being part of the processor rather than being somewhere external as implied before. The lines between the various components show data flow paths. What is shown then is only part of the processor organization since there must be other connections to control the operation of the various components. None of these control connections are shown in order to keep the diagram simple. In addition the processor-memory signaling connections are also omitted.

The box labeled *control* represents the circuitry that controls the data flow in the processor. Each of the data paths can be, in effect, "opened" by this control, thus enabling data to flow along the path in the direction indicated. The operation of the processor is therefore determined by the sequence of openings of data paths by the control.

If the control of the processor is the brain, then the heart is the arithmetic logic unit (ALU). This component carries out the arithmetic operations such as add or subtract. The lines indicate that this simple processor can transmit the

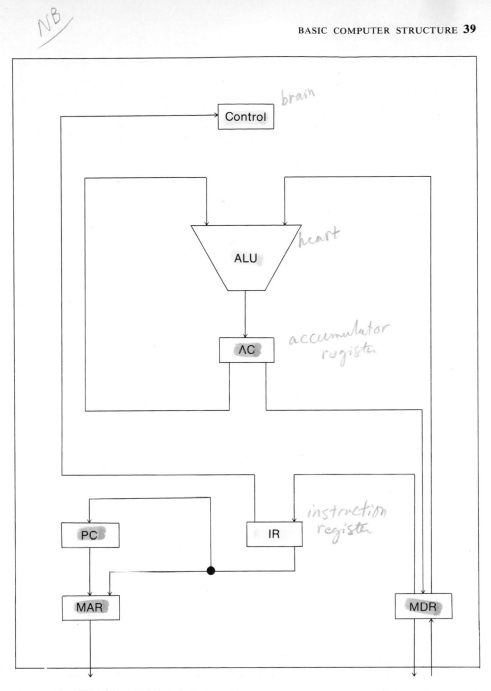

Figure 2-10 Internal processor data flow.

contents of the AC and the MDR to the inputs of the ALU with the output being sent back to the AC. An operand fetched from memory and available in the MDR can therefore be added, for example, to the contents of the AC with the results being stored in the AC. In order to be able to store the contents of the AC there is also a path from the AC to the MDR.

Instructions fetched for execution are temporarily stored in a register called the *instruction register* (IR). From here the operation code can be sent to the control for decoding. The instruction address field can be sent either to the PC in the case of a Jump instruction, or to the MAR in the case of an operand fetch or store being required.

2-5 PROGRAM AND DATA SEPARATION

The computer model discussed in this chapter, which is largely followed in the rest of the text, is known as the *von Neumann machine* (named after one of the early pioneers of computing) because it was von Neumann who suggested that program instructions and data be stored in a linear memory in exactly the same way. Although this yields a fairly simple structure for engineers to construct, there are difficulties for the programmer. First of all, all data and programs must be organized so that a linear storage is appropriate, even though some other organization may be more convenient. Second, errors in a program could result in the program being written into and therefore changed. While a discussion of alternatives to the von Neumann machine is beyond our scope at the present time, it is important to realize that the linear memory storing both programs and data is not an inherent concept for computing but one which is with us for largely historical reasons. In a later chapter we shall describe a technique for separating program instructions and data from each other.

EXERCISES

2-1 A small hypothetical single-address computer has 32 memory cells, an accumulator AC, and a program counter PC. Each instruction contains a 5-bit address A in the rightmost field and a 3-bit operation code in the leftmost field. Arithmetic is 2's complement. The operation codes are:

Name	Binary code	Meaning
LOAD	000	Load the contents of A into AC
STO	001	Store the contents of AC into A
ADD	010	Add the contents of A to the contents of AC and place the result in AC
SUB	011	Subtract the contents of A from the contents of AC and place the result in AC
JMP	100	Jump to A if AC contains a nonzero number; otherwise do nothing
HLT	101	Halt the processor

(*a*) Describe in Pascal the execution cycle of the processor.

(*b*) Assume that memory is initialized with the following program and the program counter is initialized to 3. Describe the action of each instruction as it is executed.

Address	Contents
0	00001101
1	00001100
2	00000001
3	00000000
4	01100010
5	00100000
6	01100001
7	10000011
8	10100000

2-2 Augment the processor of Exercise 2-1 with Multiply and Divide instructions and write a program for your modified machine to evaluate $[(X + Y)(Z) - A]/X$.

2-3 Suggest a way of informing the program of an overflow in the processor of Exercise 2-1. You may need to add a new instruction to do this.

2-4 In Exercise 2-2 the Multiply instruction that you added can overflow in a different way than the Add and Subtract instructions. Suggest a modification to the basic processor that would eliminate the possibility of overflow in a multiply operation and allow temporary results of a computation to exceed the 8-bit limit of memory.

2-5 The Jump instruction in the simple processor of Exercise 2-1 is called a *conditional* jump because of the dependence on a stored value. How would you program an *unconditional* jump on this machine?

2-6 Modify the processor of Exercise 2-1, by altering the set of instructions, to make it into a stack machine. You may assume that the stack size is unbounded.

2-7 Write a program for the processor of Exercise 2-6 to evaluate $[(X + Y)(Z) - A]/X$.

2-8 Show the internal data flow paths for the stack machine of Exercise 2-6.

2-9 Show the internal data flow paths for a modified version of the processor of Exercise 2-1 in which there are two memories, one for program code and one for data only. Explain clearly how addresses for each memory are treated differently.

2-10 Describe in Pascal the execution cycle for the processor of Exercise 2-9.

REFERENCES

Other introductory texts in the area of computer systems include Gear (1974), Eckhouse (1975), Stone (1975), Katzan (1976), and Graham (1975). For those interested in more detail regarding the internal organization of digital systems, Mano (1976) is a very readable text requiring about the same background as this text.

THREE

THE PDP-11: A SIMPLIFIED VIEW

The PDP-11 is a small general-purpose computer of a type sometimes referred to as *minicomputer*. This term is misleading, however, in that computers such as the PDP-11 have many, if not most, features found in larger computers.[1] The PDP-11 in particular contains many interesting features, making it an excellent machine for study.

In this chapter, we describe only those features of the PDP-11 that are sufficient for writing reasonably interesting programs. See Chap. 5 or the PDP-11 manual for a more complete description of the machine. It is recommended, however, that beginning students restrict their reading to the description given here.

3-1 PDP-11 MEMORY

Memory in a PDP-11 consists of up to 65,536 cells of 8 bits; that is, $n = 8$ and $m = 65,536$. Addresses require $\log_2 65,536 = 16$ bits; that is, $A = 16$. Therefore, two cells are required to store a memory address.

The PDP-11 memory is organized as a sequence of pairs of 8-bit cells, each pair forming a *word* of memory (see Fig. 3-1). Each 8-bit cell is called a *byte*. A memory address, then, can be stored in a single word of memory.

---

[1] The term *minicomputer* usually denotes a 16-bit word length machine, although recently 32-bit versions of such machines have been produced.

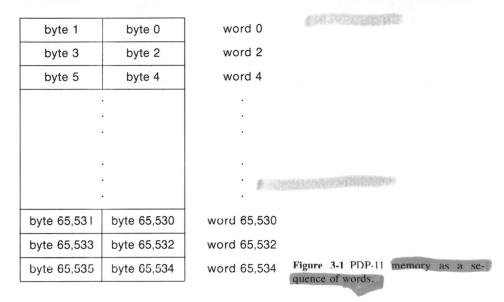

byte 1	byte 0	word 0
byte 3	byte 2	word 2
byte 5	byte 4	word 4
	.	.
	.	.
	.	.
	.	.
	.	.
byte 65,531	byte 65,530	word 65,530
byte 65,533	byte 65,532	word 65,532
byte 65,535	byte 65,534	word 65,534

Figure 3-1 PDP-11 memory as a sequence of words.

Each word in memory can be addressed by specifying the address of its rightmost byte. Sometimes it is convenient for a programmer to think of memory as a sequence of bytes rather than words, in which case one of the representations shown in Fig. 3-2 is more appropriate.

It is important to remember that word addresses are always *even* integers, while byte addresses may be either even or odd.

word 0 {	byte 0
	byte 1
word 2 {	byte 2
	byte 3
	.
	.
	.
	byte 65,533
word 65,534 {	byte 65,534
	byte 65,535

byte 65,535	byte 65,534	⋯	byte 1	byte 0

Figure 3-2 PDP-11 memory as a sequence of bytes.

3-2 PDP-11 PROCESSOR

The PDP-11 processor, shown in Fig. 3-3, has eight 16-bit *general registers:* R0, R1, R2, R3, R4, R5, R6, and R7. All are identical except that their intended use differs as follows:

R0 through R5 are used as *accumulators* (as well as having additional uses to be introduced later).

R6 has a special purpose to be discussed later.

R7 is used as the *program counter* PC.

The PDP-11 processor executes zero-, one-, and two-address instructions. The format of one-address instructions is shown below:

```
15                    6 5           0
┌──────────────────┬─────────────┐
│   10 bits        │   6 bits    │   mode
└──────────────────┴─────────────┘
  operation code    address field a1
```

The operation code occupies bits 6 through 15 and the operand address occupies bits 0 through 5. Note that bits are numbered by convention from right to left within each word. The format of two-address instructions is shown below:

```
15 ←─ 12 11 ←── 6 5 ←──── 0
┌────────┬─────────┬─────────┐
│ 4 bits │ 6 bits  │ 6 bits  │   mode
└────────┴─────────┴─────────┘
 operation  address   address
  code      field a1  field a2

  OPC        SS        DD
```

Figure 3-3 PDP-11 processor.

The operation code occupies bits 12 through 15 and the operand addresses occupy bits 0 through 5 and 6 through 11.

It would appear that operand addresses are only 6 bits in length, although PDP-11 addresses occupy 16 bits! In fact, the operand addresses themselves are stored in words immediately following the instruction. The address field contains a code indicating the *mode* of the operand address. To understand address modes let us look, in a simplified way, at some of the different modes that are possible. Following this simplified view, the full details of PDP-11 addressing will be exposed in Chap. 5.

3-3 DIRECT ADDRESSING

absolute

Direct addressing corresponds exactly with addressing as discussed in Chap. 2. That is, an operand address specifies a memory cell, the content of which is the actual operand. This is often called *absolute* addressing. To review, recall the LOAD instruction for a single-address accumulator machine. It can have the following form:

LOAD	a $\rightarrow$ AC

Example: LOAD with a direct address

This means that the contents of cell *a* are to be stored into the (implicitly addressed) accumulator register.

In the case of the PDP-11 we can take the Move instruction, a two-address instruction denoted by the mnemonic MOV, as a representative instruction. It causes the contents of one word to be placed in another word but leaves the first word unchanged. The format of a MOV instruction is shown in the following example:

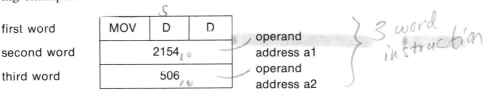

first word	MOV	D	D
second word	2154₁₀		operand address a1
third word	506₁₀		operand address a2

3 word instruction

The operation code for the instruction is denoted by MOV (the actual PDP-11 code is 0001 binary). The direct-mode code is denoted by D (the actual direct-mode code is 011111 binary). Binary addresses are shown in decimal for convenience. One can see now why instructions in the PDP-11 can be longer than one word. The MOV instruction shown above occupies three words and causes the contents of word 2154 to be placed in word 506. We shall adopt the following notation for describing PDP-11 instructions:

mnemonic   a1,a2

a1 is called the *source* (src) operand and a2 is called the *destination* (dst) operand. For example, the MOV instruction shown above is described by:

MOV 2154.,506.

The period after each operand is used to denote a base ten number. We shall always do this when using this notation since addresses are sometimes expressed in octal. In addition, we shall see that this notation is similar to assembly language.

An instruction similar to MOV is the Move Byte instruction, denoted MOVB. The instruction MOVB 503., 8194. is stored as:

MOVB	D	D
503		
8194		

3 word instruc.

MOVB causes the contents of a byte to be placed in another byte.

In describing the operation of instructions we shall use Cw(a) to denote the "contents of word *a*" and Cb(a) to denote the "contents of byte *a*." For example MOV and MOVB have the following operations, respectively:

Instruction	Operation
MOV src,dst	Cw(src) –> dst
MOVB src,dst	Cb(src) –> dst

Another PDP-11 instruction and its operation are:

3 - word

ADD src,dst	Cw(src) + Cw(dst) –> dst

In other words, ADD causes the source operand to be added to the destination operand and the result placed in the destination word. ADD occupies three words as does MOV and MOVB. There is no Add Byte instruction. The operand addresses of an ADD instruction must, then, always be even. The same, of course, is true of MOV.

With only a few basic instructions one can write reasonably interesting programs. While the remaining sections of this chapter formally explain individual instructions in detail we can informally introduce just the essentials of some of these basic instructions at this point. In this way the reader can focus on how programs are constructed as the chapter proceeds.

A minimal set of instructions might include ADD and MOV as well as the following:

subtract   SUB   src,dst   similar to ADD but subtracts the src from the dst

(handwritten: A, B) *(handwritten: $\} dst - src$ $B - A!$)*

compare   CMP   src,dst   compares the src and the dst without affecting either

branch on
greater than   BGT   dst   a conditional jump that sends control to the instruction on the line specified by dst if the result of an immediately preceding compare indicated that its src was greater than its dst

branch   BR   dst   an unconditional jump

To make programs more easily readable, line numbers will sometimes be used as instruction operands in place of addresses. A line number used in this way represents the address occupied by the instruction on the line specified. Also, words containing data rather than instructions will be shown as

.WORD   contents

With these few notational additions the machine code below

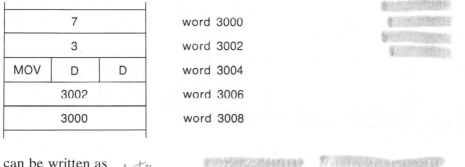

7			word 3000
3			word 3002
MOV	D	D	word 3004
3002			word 3006
3000			word 3008

can be written as   *(handwritten: data)*

```
1  .WORD  7
2  .WORD  3
3  MOV    2,1
```
(handwritten: line #5 = Mov #3 → loc. 3000)

The two basic program structures, other than sequential execution, are the conditional and the loop. Consider first the following simple example of a conditional.

IF x <= y THEN z := 0 ELSE z := 1

An equivalent machine code program might look like the following (the initial values of x, y, and z on entry to this code are shown symbolically in the .WORD statements).

A 1 .WORD   x
B 2 .WORD   y
C 3 .WORD   z
D 4 .WORD   0
E 5 .WORD   1
If 6 CMP   1,2   *x, y*
7 BGT   10   *if x > y, go to line 10, so 1 → z*
then 8 MOV   4,3   *0 → z*   *H:*
else 9 BR   11   *skip line 10*
10 MOV   5,3
11

CMP A,B
BGT G
MOV 0,C
F: BR H
G: MOV E,C

where execution is assumed to enter the program at line 6.

    As shown in this example, a very common way for CMP and BGT to be used is as a pair to construct a test followed by a transfer of control.

    The following example loop structure

WHILE y <= 10 DO y := y + 1

could be written as

1 .WORD   y
2 .WORD   10
3 .WORD   1
4 CMP   1,2   *y, 10*
5 BGT   8   *if y > 10, then halt*
6 ADD   3,1   *else   = 1 + y → y*
7 BR   4   *repeat*
8 HALT

where execution is assumed to enter the program at line 4.

    Again, CMP and BGT combine to construct the test and transfer control.

3-4 REGISTER-MODE ADDRESSING

For machines with several general registers rather than just one accumulator it is necessary for instructions to explicitly reference an operand that is in a register. Going back to the LOAD instruction, suppose that the single-address machine used in previous examples is modified to have several general registers that can be used in the same way as an accumulator. Then the LOAD instruction may have the following form:

LOAD	r	a

Example: LOAD with a register address

where the field denoted r contains a register number designating the register to be loaded from memory. Although the machine would probably still be referred to as a single-address machine, since each instruction contains at most one memory address, instructions of the above format actually contain two addresses: one for memory and one for the registers. Consequently, the term *register address* is used to describe a register operand designation in an instruction.

In the PDP-11, as stated earlier, the general registers, R0 through R5, are used as accumulators (among other things). When used as an accumulator a general register is addressed explicitly within the instruction. *Register mode* is the term used for such register addresses. For example, MOV R1,R3 is stored as:

MOV	R	001	R	011

and has the operation:

$$Cw(R1) \quad -> \quad R3$$

Note that the register designation is stored in a 3-bit field as part of the mode code (the actual code for R is 000 binary). In general, a register may appear as an operand of any instruction.

Address modes may be mixed, the length of an instruction being determined by the mode of the operands. For example:

Instruction	Operation	Length in words
MOV R2,656.	Cw(R2) -> 656.	2
ADD 1076.,R1	Cw(1076.)+Cw(R1) -> R1	2
ADD R3,R0	Cw(R3)+Cw(R0) -> R0	1
MOVB R5,1096.	Cb(R5) -> 1096.	2

The last instruction shown above contains a register-mode operand in a byte instruction. In this case, the processor always takes as the operand the contents of the *rightmost* byte in the register.

Registers, of course, need not be defined in a program along with the definitions of memory words since they are in the processor not in memory. In a sense, they constitute predefined program storage locations. A common usage for registers is to hold temporary values such as the control variable for a loop.

In this way locations for temporary values need not occupy space in memory but can be allocated from the available register set as required. The program shown below:

```
z := 0;
FOR i := 1 TO 16 DO z := z + i
```

could be written, using R0 to store i, as

```
1   .WORD  0
2   .WORD  1
3   .WORD  16
4   .WORD  z
5   MOV    1,4
6   MOV    1,R0
7   ADD    2,R0
8   CMP    R0,3
9   BGT    12
10  ADD    R0,4
11  BR     7
12
```

[handwritten annotations: $0 \to z$; $0 \to R0$; $1 + 0 \to R0$; if i (in R0) > 16, go to 12 + halt; else $z = R0(i) + z$; repeat increment + test]

where execution is assumed to enter the program at line 5.

3-5 IMMEDIATE ADDRESSING

Often, as seen in the examples of the previous sections, a programmer needs to store a constant in his program. This can be done by storing the constant in a word and simply addressing it with direct addressing. For example, a PDP-11 instruction to load a constant, say 3, into R1 might be stored as:

MOV	D	R	001
	3156		
	.		
	.		
	.		
	3		word 3156

Since the constant 3 never changes, we are really wasting a word by using direct-mode addressing. Immediate addressing allows the programmer to store such a constant *within the instruction*. In the case of the load operation in a single-address machine this can be provided by defining a special version of the LOAD instruction with a different operation code meaning "load immediate."

The Load Immediate instruction can have the form:

LOADM	r	data

with the meaning that the constant, denoted *data,* is to be loaded into register r.

In the case of the PDP-11, immediate mode is provided by defining an address mode with that meaning. Using immediate mode, denoted IM, the MOV instruction can be stored as:

MOV	IM	R	001
3			
. . .			

(The actual code for IM is 010111 binary.) The instruction shown above is denoted by:

MOV #3.,Π1

and has the operation:

3. -> R1

(That is, place the constant 3 into R1.)

Some examples of immediate-mode addressing are:

Instruction	Operation	Length
ADD #153.,68.	153.+Cw(68.) -> 68.	3
MOV #157.,R1	157. -> R1	2

Note that for instructions of length 2 the extra word may be associated with either the source or the destination operand. For instructions of length 3, the first extra word is associated with the source and the second extra word is associated with the destination.

It should be pointed out here that the progammer is rarely concerned about details such as the actual code for immediate-mode addressing, the operation codes, or the length of instructions. Consequently, we shall be mainly concerned not with how instructions are stored but with the notation for describing instructions.

The short program described below carries out the computation repre-

sented by the Pascal statement "r := x + y + 3" if we assume that the values
of r, x, and y are stored in words 224, 226, and 228, respectively.

MOV   226.,224. $C(226) = X \longrightarrow 224 = r$ that is, $X \rightarrow r$

ADD   228.,224. $y + r \rightarrow r$ (now $r = x+y$)

ADD   #3.,224. $3 + r \rightarrow r$ (now $r = x+y+3$)

Note that word 224 is used as a temporary location to store intermediate
values during expression evaluation as well as to store the final value of r.

Alternatively we could have used R0 as a temporary location and written:

MOV   226.,R0 $X \rightarrow R\emptyset$

ADD   228.,R0 $y + R\emptyset \rightarrow R\emptyset$ $(R\emptyset = X+y)$

ADD   #3.,R0 $3 + R\emptyset \rightarrow R\emptyset$ $R\emptyset = X+y+3$

MOV   R0,224. $3 \rightarrow r$

The latter program could be stored as shown in Fig. 3-4. In order to execute
this program the PC must be initialized to contain the address of the first instruction, shown as word i in the diagram.

MOV	D		R	000	word i
	226				
ADD	D		R	000	
	228				
ADD	IM		R	000	
	3				
MOV	R	000		D	
	224				

value of r	word 224
value of x	word 226
value of y	word 228

Figure 3-4 Immediate mode.

Using the extended notation this program might be written

```
1  MOV      21,R0
2  ADD      22,R0
3  ADD      #3.,R0
4  MOV      R0,20
   .
   .

   .
20 .WORD  r
21 .WORD  x
22 .WORD  y
```

where the data is arbitrarily assumed to appear on line 20 of the program.

3-6 INDEXED-MODE ADDRESSING

Direct mode, register mode, and immediate mode are inconvenient for certain types of programming. To illustrate, consider the problem of initializing an array of words to zero. One could write a program that moves a zero into each array element, each move using a separate MOV instruction. Such a program is shown in Fig. 3-5, where the array to be initialized has five elements in words 428 through 436. The program is stored beginning at word 438. To execute the program the PC must be initialized to contain 438. The program first moves a zero into R2 via immediate-mode addressing. This is done so that the remaining five MOV instructions can address the operand zero with register-mode addressing, thus saving one word of instruction length. (Can you think of another reason for using R2 in this way?)

This program is very inefficient in its use of storage space however; five of the instructions are identical except for an address a2 that varies from 428 to 436 by increments of 2. In fact, this programming method is similar to writing, in Pascal,

```
VAR a1,a2,a3,a4,a5: INTEGER;
a1 := 0;
a2 := 0;
a3 := 0;
a4 := 0;
a5 := 0;
etc.
```

A way of systematically altering an operand address would enable us to use the same instruction repeatedly. In other words, we need to be able to imple-

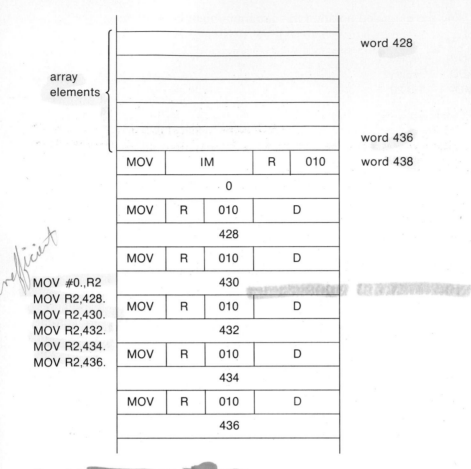

array elements

MOV	IM		R	010
		0		
MOV	R	010		D
		428		
MOV	R	010		D
		430		
MOV	R	010		D
		432		
MOV	R	010		D
		434		
MOV	R	010		D
		436		

word 428

word 436
word 438

inefficient

MOV #0.,R2
MOV R2,428.
MOV R2,430.
MOV R2,432.
MOV R2,434.
MOV R2,436.

Figure 3-5 Array initialization without looping.

ment the Pascal array structure so that we can implement the equivalent code to

```
VAR a: ARRAY[1..5] OF INTEGER;
FOR i := 1 TO 5 DO a[i] := 0;
etc.
```

In addition to altering the address we would, of course, need an instruction to allow us to program an iteration or loop.

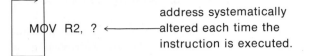

MOV R2, ? ←————————altered each time the
address systematically
instruction is executed.

Indexed-mode addressing, or simply *indexing,* enables a programmer to alter the address of an operand and thereby use an instruction repeatedly but with a different operand each time. An operand address in indexed mode is altered, each time the operand is referenced, by *adding to the address the contents of a specified index register.* Although some machines have index registers used only for this purpose, many machines allow the general registers to be used as index registers. For example, a single-address machine with general registers might have a Load Indexed instruction having the following format:

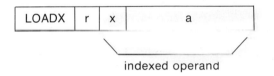

indexed operand

with the meaning that the register r is to be loaded from the cell whose address is formed by adding the contents of register x to a.

The PDP-11 MOV instruction below contains a source operand in indexed mode and a destination address in register mode.

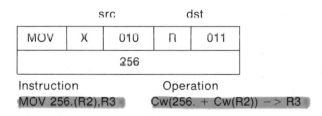

Instruction	Operation
MOV 256.(R2),R3	Cw(256. + Cw(R2)) –> R3

The indexed mode code is denoted by X (the actual code is 110 binary) in the diagram of the stored instruction. The rightmost 3 bits in the mode field specify the register to be involved in the indexing operation. The operand address to be indexed is stored in a word following the first instruction word, as are direct-mode addresses and immediate-mode operands.

The notation we shall use for describing indexed mode is an address followed by a register designator in parentheses. Thus the source operand above is denoted by 256.(R2). Before fetching this operand the processor adds the contents of R2 to the address 256. The result of the addition is used as the address of the operand to be fetched. The operation of the MOV instruction, of course, simply places the operand in the destination address, R3 in this case.

Note that indexing is performed by the processor just prior to a fetch or store if the address involved is in indexed mode.

Before we can rewrite our array initialization program we need an instruction to facilitate iteration. The PDP-11 has a collection of one-address Conditional Jump instructions called *Branch* instructions. One of these is the Branch on Plus instruction, denoted BPL:

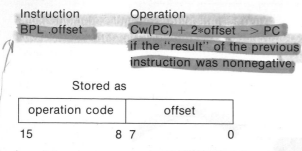

Instruction	Operation
BPL .offset	Cw(PC) + 2*offset —> PC
	if the "result" of the previous
	instruction was nonnegative.

Stored as

operation code	offset

15   8 7   0

The single operand of BPL is an 8-bit 2's complement number called the *offset*. The dot (.) preceding the offset is used to indicate that the operand is a relative location rather than an actual address. The BPL operation consists of the following:

1. Check the result of the previous instruction's execution. (In many cases this involves checking the value of the destination operand.)
2. If the result was negative, do nothing.
3. If the result was nonnegative, multiply the offset by 2, add the result to the contents of the PC, and store the final result into the PC.

The BPL instruction changes the contents of the PC depending on the result of executing the previous instruction. Note that *the execution cycle has already incremented the PC* so that it contains the address of the following instruction. Changing the PC of course causes the next instruction to be fetched from a (possibly) nonsequential location. Thus a Conditional Jump or Branch is effected.

The BPL instruction can now be used in conjunction with indexing to rewrite the array initialization program as shown in Fig. 3-6.

It is convenient to describe the execution of this program with a *trace table* containing a column for each location involved in the computation and a row for each instance of instruction execution (see Fig. 3-7). Entries in each row show the values contained in each location on *completion* of the execution of the instruction. For example, the entry in the first row corresponding to the PC would be 442. A dash (—) indicates an unknown value.

Instructions 1 and 2 initialize R1 and R2 with 8 and zero, respectively. The *first time* instruction 3 is executed, a zero (from R2) is stored into word 428 + 8 = word 436. Instruction 4 subtracts 2 from R1, leaving 8 − 2 = 6. In-

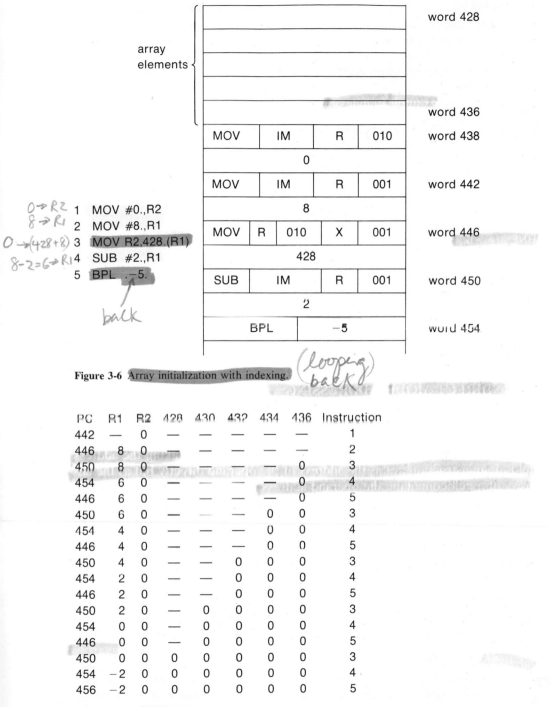

Figure 3-6 Array initialization with indexing.

PC	R1	R2	428	430	432	434	436	Instruction
442	—	0	—	—	—	—	—	1
446	8	0	—	—	—	—	—	2
450	8	0	—	—	—	—	0	3
454	6	0	—	—	—	—	0	4
446	6	0	—	—	—	—	0	5
450	6	0	—	—	—	0	0	3
454	4	0	—	—	—	0	0	4
446	4	0	—	—	—	0	0	5
450	4	0	—	—	0	0	0	3
454	2	0	—	—	0	0	0	4
446	2	0	—	—	0	0	0	5
450	2	0	—	0	0	0	0	3
454	0	0	—	0	0	0	0	4
446	0	0	—	0	0	0	0	5
450	0	0	0	0	0	0	0	3
454	−2	0	0	0	0	0	0	4
456	−2	0	0	0	0	0	0	5

Figure 3-7 A trace table.

struction 5 causes a branch back five words to instruction 3. The *second time* instruction 3 is executed, a zero (from R2) is stored into word 428 + 6 = word 434. Instruction 4 subtracts 2 from R1 leaving 6 − 2 = 4. Execution continues as indicated in the trace table until finally instruction 4 subtracts 2 from 0, leaving − 2, whereupon the branch does not take place and execution continues at word 456.

As a further example of indexing, consider the following problem. An array of 32 bytes is stored in locations 600 through 631. A piece of program is required to locate the first blank character in this array and leave its index in R1. A blank constant is stored in location 640. The coding necessary to do this job is made easier if a blank can be stored in location 632. Doing this, one can write:

```
MOV     #−1.,R1        −1 → R1
ADD     #1.,R1         R1 + 1 → R1 = ∅ → R1
CMPB    640.,600.(R1)  If C(640) ≠ C(600 + c(R1)),
BNE     .−6.           then branch back 6 bytes ?
```

Note the newly introduced conditional branch BNE, Branch on Not Equal to Zero. The subtraction of any two unequal operands thus yields a nonzero result and causes the loop to execute again.

3-7 INDIRECT-MODE ADDRESSING

A fourth addressing mode, *indirect,* is similar to indexing in that it is used as a way of altering the operand address of an instruction so that the instruction can be used to operate on different operands. This is done by taking the address field in an instruction not as the address of the operand directly but as the address of a cell containing the operand address. Thus, this stored operand address can be altered without altering the instruction itself. A Load Indirect instruction in a single-address general register machine might have a format as shown below:

LOADD	r	a

with the meaning that the register r is to be loaded from the cell whose address is stored in cell a. In the PDP-11, indirect-mode addressing comes in several varieties, two of which are *indirect register* and *indirect indexed.* Let us first examine indirect-register mode which, in PDP-11 terminology, is called *register deferred.*

Using indirect addressing the operand address field in an instruction does not contain the operand address itself. Rather, it contains the address of a location containing the operand address. Indirect-mode addresses, as shown below, are denoted by @. For example,

Instruction   Operation
MOV R0,@R1   Cw(R0) –> Cw(R1)

register deferred (indirect register)

Stored as

MOV	R	000	IR	001

The instruction MOV R0,@R1 causes the contents of R0 to be placed in the word whose address is found in R1. The code for indirect-register mode is denoted by IR in the stored instruction (the actual code is 001 binary). The rightmost 3 bits in the address field specify the register containing the operand address.

Before rewriting our array initialization program we need an instruction to compare the contents of two locations. The PDP-11 has the Compare instruction, which was informally introduced earlier.

Instruction	Operation
CMP src,dst	Cw(src) – Cw(dst)

CMP S–D
of SUB S,D = D–S

The operation of the CMP instruction forms the result of subtracting the destination operand from the source operand. This result is not stored anywhere; it is simply retained (in a way we shall see later) to be examined by a subsequent instruction such as a Branch instruction.

The new array initialization program in shown in Fig. 3-8.

Note the new instruction BNE, Branch on Not Equal to Zero. This instruction causes a branch if the result of the previous instruction's execution was not zero; otherwise no branch occurs.

This program uses indirect addressing through R1 to address array elements (instruction 3). Each time through the iteration the address in R1 is decremented by 2 (instruction 4). Instruction 5 checks to see if the array element just initialized was the last to be done, namely, word 428. Since the decrementing of R1 is done in instruction 4, R1 will contain the value 426 immediately after word 428 is initialized by instruction 3. The CMP instruction (5) must therefore check to see if R1 contains the value 426 by subtracting 426 from R1. After the fifth iteration R1 will contain 426 and the result of Cw(R1) − 426 will be zero. Therefore, the branch will not be taken.

Indirect indexed-mode addressing, called *index deferred* in PDP-11 terminology, works in a similar way except that indexing is used to locate the

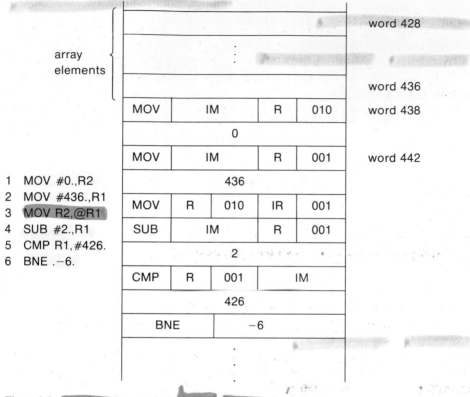

1 MOV #0.,R2
2 MOV #436.,R1
3 MOV R2,@R1
4 SUB #2.,R1
5 CMP R1,#426.
6 BNE .−6.

Figure 3-8 Array initialization with indirect addressing.

operand address. For example,

Instruction   Operation
MOV @6.(R2),R3   Cw(Cw(6+Cw(R2))) −> R3

                    Stored as

MOV	IX	010	R	011
		6		

The actual code for indirect indexed (IX) is 110 binary.

Recall the following simple array search program shown at the end of the previous section.

```
MOV    #−1.,R1
ADD    #1.,R1
CMPB   640.,600.(R1)
BNE    .−6.
```

If it is required to leave in R1 the address of the blank found rather than its index, with a zero indicating that none was found, then the following code using indirection is appropriate:

```
MOV    #599.,R1
ADD    #1.,R1
CMPB   640.,@R1
BNE    .-5.
CMP    R1,#632.
BNE    .+2.
MOV    #0.,R1
```

The offset in the BNE is shown with an explicit plus sign to emphasize that it is a forward branch.

3-8 SINGLE-ADDRESS INSTRUCTIONS   2 words

Although the PDP-11 is basically a two-address machine, it does have a number of single-address instructions of which Branch instructions are a special case. The remaining single-address instructions have a 10-bit operation code and a 6-bit operand field. A good example is the Clear instruction, some examples of which are shown below.

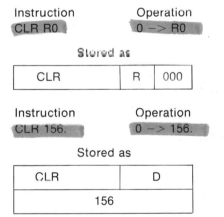

Instruction   Operation
CLR R0   0 -> R0

Stored as

CLR	R	000

Instruction   Operation
CLR 156.   0 -> 156.

Stored as

CLR	D
156	

As indicated, CLR stores a zero in the operand.

It should be evident at this point that we can formulate a general rule for instruction length: *An instruction contains one word plus one word for each operand not in register or indirect-register mode.*

As we shall see in the next chapter, however, a programmer need not always be concerned about instruction formats, lengths, or actual memory addresses. We have presented these details only to enable the reader to gain an understanding of how a processor executes instructions.

EXERCISES

3-1 A small hypothetical computer has 64 memory cells, one index register X, an accumulator AC, and a program counter PC. The processor executes instructions in the following format:

Bits	0–5	Address field
Bit	6	Index bit; a one indicates indexing of the operand address
Bits	7–10	Operation code

The operation codes and their meanings are given below. A refers to the address field. Instructions marked with an asterisk can be indexed.

0000	STX	Store the contents of X into A
0001	LDX	Load the contents of A into X
0010	ADX	Add the contents of A to the contents of X and place the result in X
0011	SBX	Subtract the contents of A from the contents of X and place the result in X
0100	*LOAD	Load the contents of A into AC
0101	*STO	Store the contents of AC into A
0110	*ADD	Add the contents of A to the contents of AC and place the result in AC
0111	*SUB	Subtract the contents of A from the contents of AC and place the result in AC
1000	BNZ	Branch to A if X contains a nonzero value
1001	HLT	Halt

Describe in Pascal the execution cycle of the processor in this machine. Assume that memory is initialized with the program shown below and that the program counter is initialized to zero. Provide a trace of the program's execution.

Address	Contents
0	00010001101
1	00110001110
2	01001000111
3	01101001010
4	01011000111
5	10000000001
6	10010000000
7	00000010011
8	00000001111
9	00000010110
10	00000000001
11	00000001110
12	00000011001
13	00000000011
14	00000000001

3-2 Describe the algorithm for the execution cycle of the simplified PDP-11 described in this chapter.

3-3 Why does MOVB replicate the leftmost bit of the source operand in all bits of the leftmost byte of a register destination?

3-4 Explain how two levels of indirection can be obtained in the PDP-11?

3-5 Show a trace of the example program given at the end of Sec. 3-6.

3-6 Show a trace of the example programs shown at the end of Sec. 3-7.

3-7 Explain the savings in time and memory space yielded by using CLR rather than MOV #0., etc., in clearing a memory location.

REFERENCES

Eckhouse (1975), Gear (1974), and Stone (1975) all contain material on the PDP-11. (The first is based entirely on the PDP-11, as is this text.) An early description of the PDP-11 can be found in Bell (1970), which puts some perspective on the design of this machine in the context of the time at which it was designed. Although each PDP-11 model has its own manual, a good general reference for the student who has access to the PDP-11/03 (based on the LSI-11 processor) is "Microcomputer Handbook" (Digital, 1976), which contains a variety of useful information including software descriptions and a comparison of the different models.

The reader should not forget that for practical reasons we are ignoring many other minicomputers. Truly interested students are encouraged to seek out and read machine manuals for other minicomputers, which are simply too numerous to list.

CHAPTER FOUR

ASSEMBLY LANGUAGE

Programmers need not construct programs in machine language. Most manufacturers provide a programming language, usually called an *assembly language,* that can be used to write programs for their machines. An assembly language reflects the detailed structure of the computer for which it is designed. In fact, one statement in assembly language usually corresponds directly to one machine instruction.

Manufacturers supply a program, called an *assembler,* that translates assembly-language programs into machine language. In this chapter, we describe the assembly language for the PDP-11. As we shall see, it is very similar to the notation for describing instructions developed in the previous chapter.

4-1 ASSEMBLY TIME VERSUS EXECUTION TIME

One of the reasons for discussing assembly language in a separate chapter is to emphasize the distinction between actions carried out by the assembler in translating a program and actions carried out by the processor in executing a program. Through experience with beginning students, we have found that one cannot repeat this point too often. It must become quite clear what actions take place during translation and what actions take place, normally much later, at execution time. If one can get this distinction clearly in mind early, then many conceptual problems are avoided.

Assembly language statements are of two kinds: *assembler directives* and *machine operations.* The former are commands from the programmer to the assembler to carry out some action during translation. The sorts of commands possible include memory reservation and initialization, definition of symbols, etc. Machine operations are translated directly into instructions so that their meaning is carried out at execution time.

4-2 STATEMENTS

Most statements are machine operations and so are translated directly into machine instructions. For example, the following are valid statements:

Statement	Operation
MOV #20.,R1	20. -> R1
SUB #2,R1	Cw(R1) - 2 -> R1
MOV R1,R0	Cw(R1) -> R0

Decimal constants (e.g., #20.) defining immediate-mode operands are denoted by adding a decimal point to the number as in the notation used previously. Constants without a point are assumed to be in octal. Note that it is never necessary to write #2. since 2 octal = 2 decimal.

Statements are typed one to a line and must be preceded by at least one blank column. The two components of a statement, the *operation field* (e.g., MOV, SUB) and the *operand fields* (e.g., #2,R1), must be separated by at least one blank. Comments may be added to a statement by typing a semicolon (;) anywhere to the right of the operand fields and following it with the comment

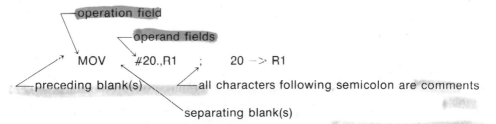

As each statement is translated, the assembler reserves memory words for the corresponding instruction and stores the instruction therein.

4-3 LABELS

A statement can be labeled by a character string of up to six characters, starting with a letter in or after column 1 and terminated by a colon (:). The programmer may use such labels in place of the offset in a branch statement. For example, the Branch on Result Not Equal to Zero in the program below

```
LOOP:  SUB   #2,R1
       MOV   R1,R0
         .
         .              }  other statements
         .
       BNE   LOOP
```

causes control to transfer to the Subtract instruction. The assembler automatically constructs the proper offset when it translates the BNE instruction. Thus, a programmer need not be concerned with offsets.[1]

4-4 RESERVING AND INITIALIZING MEMORY

Three assembler directive statements, .WORD, .BYTE, and .ASCII, allow the programmer to reserve cells of memory for data and to initialize those cells.

The statement .WORD includes as operands a list of integers. The assembler reserves one word of memory space for each integer in the list and initializes it with the integer value. For example,

```
.WORD   -15.,17.,285.,5
```

reserves and initializes four words as follows:

−15	←——first word following machine
17	language translation of
285	statement preceding .WORD
5	

.BYTE is similar to .WORD; the integer operands are stored in successive bytes. For example,

```
.BYTE   -15.,17.,285.,5
```

reserves and initializes four bytes as follows:

17	−15
5	285

---

[1] Since offsets are limited to the range −128 through +127, the destination of a Branch instruction must be within a restricted range.

.ASCII is similar to .BYTE in that it reserves a sequence of bytes. The operand list, however, is a sequence of characters delineated by any nonblank character and not separated by commas. Each byte is initialized to the ASCII code for the corresponding character. For example,

.ASCII   /SOME DATA./

reserves and initializes 10 bytes as follows:

O	S
E	M
D	"blank"
T	A
.	A

Of course it is more convenient when dealing with a character string to represent memory as a sequence of bytes:

···	S	O	M	E		D	A	T	A	.	···

increasing byte addresses ⟶

Labels can be used on the memory reservation statements .WORD, .BYTE, and .ASCII. Labeling a statement defines the label as representing the address of the first byte (word) reserved by the statement. For example,

ARRAY: .WORD 0,0,0

reserves three words, initializes them to contain zero, and defines ARRAY as the address of the first word. The label ARRAY may be used as an operand of a statement. Thus

MOV   ARRAY,R0

moves the contents of the first word reserved above into R0.

An address represented by a label may, of course, be altered through indexing. The two statements

MOV   #2,R1
MOV   ARRAY(R1),R0

move the contents of the second word of ARRAY into R0. Note that a constant 2 was placed in R1 since we are dealing with word data.

4-5 EXAMPLE PROGRAM 1

Consider a piece of program to initialize an array arr, of length 10, so that arr[i] = i − 1, 1 ≤ i ≤ 10. The following would do the job in Pascal:

```
VAR arr: ARRAY[1..10] OF INTEGER;
     i: INTEGER;
FOR i := 1 TO 10 DO arr[i] := i − 1
```

A complete assembly-language program to accomplish an equivalent task is:

```
1.  GO:    MOV    #20.,R1          ; 20 -> R1
2.  LOOP:  SUB    #2,R1            ; Cw(R1) - 2 -> R1        18 -> R1
3.         MOV    R1,R0            ; Cw(R1) -> R0            18 -> R0
4.         ASR    R0               ; Cw(R0)/2 -> R0          9 -> R0
5.         MOV    R0,ARR(R1)       ; i -> i-1st element
6.         BNE    LOOP             ; branch if result not zero
7.         HALT                    ; execution halts
8.  ARR:   .WORD  0,0,0,0,0,0,0,0,0,0  ; a 10-word array
9.         .END   GO               ; execution is to start at GO
```

Example Program 1

This program contains three new statements. The HALT on line 7 translates into a Halt instruction; this instruction causes the processor to stop executing. The statement .END GO on line 9 is directive to the assembler to stop translating. The operand GO indicates to the assembler where execution is to start. The assembler then ensures that the PC is initialized with the address represented by GO before the program starts execution.

The statement ASR R0 on line 4 represents a single operand Arithmetic Shift Right instruction defined by:

Instruction	Operation
ASR dst	The destination is shifted 1 bit to the right. Bit 0 is lost. Bit 14 is replicated in bit 15.

For example, MOV #6,R0 places 0000000000000110 into R0. Executing ASR R0 immediately afterward changes the contents of R0 to 0000000000000011. Observe that shifting an even binary number 1 bit to the right effectively divides the number by 2.

The assembler program shown above creates, during translation, an array of 10 words called ARR and initializes each word to zero. Again, it is emphasized that these actions occur during translation, or *assembly* as it is often called. During execution, the program places the value i − 1 in the ith word.

Execution proceeds as follows: R1 is initialized to 20 (line 1). Subtracting 2 from R1 leaves 18 (line 2). The value 18 is moved into R0 (line 3). The value 18 is divided by 2 leaving 9 in R0 (line 4). The value 9 is stored in the tenth word of ARR (line 5); this is accomplished by adding 18 to the address ARR through indexing. The BNE statement on line 6 sends control back to LOOP if a non-zero value has been stored in ARR. Subsequent iterations store the values 8,7,6, etc., in successive array elements. On the final iteration a 0 is stored in first word of ARR. Consequently, the branch does not occur and HALT is executed.

Lines 1 through 7 are machine operations, or simply "instructions." Lines 8 and 9 are assembler directives. As exemplified here, some directives (such as .WORD) cause the machine code being generated to be affected and others (such as .END) do not.

The alert reader will probably have noticed that the initialization in program 1 could have been accomplished at assembly time with the single statement

ARR: .WORD   0,1,2,3,4,5,6,7,8.,9.

4-6 EXAMPLE PROGRAM 2

Searching for and comparing character strings occurs often in systems programs. Typically, strings of characters are searched for substrings that are identical to some stored string. The algorithm below searches a character string c for an occurrence of two successive periods (..). If found, the index of the first of these is placed in variable i.

```
VAR i: INTEGER;
    s,f: BOOLEAN;
        c: ARRAY[0..15] OF CHAR;
CONST p - '.';
s := TRUE;      success if S = FALSE
f := TRUE;      failure
initialize c;
i := 0;
WHILE s AND f DO BEGIN
    IF c[i] = p AND c[i+1] = p THEN s := FALSE;
    IF i = 14 THEN f := FALSE
            ELSE i := i+1 END
{ At this point s = FALSE indicates success. }
```

There are two approaches to implementing an algorithm in assembler given its description in a high-level language form. The first is to translate directly, creating an assembler variable to represent each high-level language variable and reproducing the control flow exactly. In this case the direct translation is followed by an optimization in which advantage is taken of the close machine control yielded by assembler programming. The second approach is to optimize as one is translating, thus using the high-level language as only a guide to understanding the algorithm. While the former approach is necessary for large programs because of the possibility of error if nonsystematic methods are used, the latter is perhaps better for small programs. Taking the second approach, then, we might produce the following program:

```
I:       .WORD   -1              ; result variable
P:       .ASCII  /./             ; character sought
C:       .ASCII  /a bcde .. fghijklb/ ; 15 characters
LASTC:   .ASCII  /x/             ; last of 16 characters
GO:      MOV     #C,R0           ; use indirect addressing via R0
         SUB     #1,R0           ; prepare R0 for incrementing
LOOP:    ADD     #1,R0           ; advance to next substring
         CMP     R0,#LASTC       ; last character in C?    Does R0 have X in it?
         BEQ     DONE            ; stop if yes
         CMPB    @R0,P           ; check first character
         BNE     LOOP            ; branch if not period
         ADD     #1,R0           ; advance to second character
         CMPB    @R0,P           ; check second character
         BNE     LOOP            ; branch if not period
         SUB     #1,R0           ; reset R0 to first character
         MOV     R0,I            ; store address in I
DONE:    HALT                    ; I positive means success
         .END    GO
```

Example Program 2

The result variable I is initialized to -1 so that a positive value can be used to indicate a successful search. For illustration purposes the program uses indirect addressing rather than indexing, so the result is to be stored in I as an address. The program begins by placing the address of the string C into R0 in preparation for using R0 to scan through the string via indirect addressing. In the body of the loop R0 is incremented by 1, so initially it is decremented by 1 so that the scan will commence at the first character. Notice that the SUB #1,R0 would be unnecessary if R0 had been initialized with P rather than C. This would have produced obscure, hard-to-read code, however, and would also have made the code dependent on the relative positions of P and C, an invitation to error if the code is modified. We have therefore chosen clarity over efficiency.

The loop in the program examines each pair of adjacent characters in turn, branching back to LOOP if either is not identical to the period stored in P. If neither branch back to LOOP is taken, R0 is decremented to reference the first character in the pair of periods just found, and this result is stored into I.

..

NUM. DATA, BIN → CHAR.

4-7 EXAMPLE PROGRAM 3

see p. 125, 175

Another common task in programming at the assembly-language level is the conversion of numeric data from binary to character representation. Example program 3 shows an algorithm that converts a positive binary integer, stored in variable b, into the appropriate character string in the character array c.

```
VAR b: 0..32767; r: 0..9; i: 0..4 ;
    c:  ARRAY[0..4] OF CHAR;
        initialize b and c ;
        i := 4 ;
        REPEAT
            b := quotient of b/10 and r := remainder of b/10 ;
            convert r into character form ;
            c[i] := r ;
            i := i − 1
        UNTIL b=0
```

Example Program 3: Algorithm

This algorithm works by repeatedly dividing the binary integer b by 10 and subtracting off the fractional part each time. Such a sequence of divisions produces the decimal digits of b starting with the units digit and working to the most significant digit. The quotient is stored back into b to be divided again, and the remainder is stored into r as a binary integer. The binary value r must then be converted into an ASCII character, a task which is best described in assembly language. As shown, the digits are stored into c until a zero quotient indicates that the last remainder obtained was the most significant digit.

Assembly-language code for this conversion program is shown below. In this example, B is initialized to 569, C is initialized to five blanks, and no output is performed, so one must examine the memory after execution to observe the results.

```
       R0 = %0
       R2 = %2
       R3 = %3
  B:   .WORD 569.
  C:   .ASCII /     /  ; 5 characters
       .EVEN
 GO:   MOV   #4, R0    ; index into array C
       MOV   B,R3      ; get ready to divide    NuM → R3
LOOP:  CLR   R2        ; clear leading zeros
       DIV   #10.,R2   ; R2 = quotient, R3 = remainder
       ADD   #48.,R3   ; insert bits 4 and 5    ASCII offset
       MOVB  R3,C(R0)  ; put digit into C
       SUB   #1,R0     ; and reduce index
```

```
MOV    R2,R3        ; get ready to divide
BNE    LOOP         ; stop if quotient is zero
HALT
.END   GO
```

Example Program 3: Assembly-language code

There are several new items in this program. First, the symbols for the registers are redefined from the %n expected by the assembler to a more readable Rn, where n may be any value from 0 to 7. Any statement containing = is something like an assignment statement to be executed during assembly. Thus %2 always means "register 2," and the statement R2 = %2 assigns to the symbol R2 the same value.

While translating a program that assembler maintains a variable, the *location counter*, whose value equals the next relative address in the program being generated into which code can be placed. In other words, taking the first byte of code generated as byte 0, if i bytes of code have been generated by the assembler then the location counter would equal i. After the values of B and C have been assembled in the program above, the location counter contains a byte address. Since the statement following is an instruction, it must be assembled into a word. The assembler directive .EVEN simply causes the location counter to be adjusted to the next highest even (word) address.

The string C needs only five character positions since the largest integer possible using 16 bits can be expressed in five decimal digits. R0 is used to index C from right to left, so it is initialized to 4. The division is performed at the beginning of the loop. The division instruction requires the destination operand to be an even register. It then takes the dividend to be the 32-bit binary integer formed by concatenating that register with the following odd-numbered one. In our program, therefore, the dividend is the contents of registers R2 and R3. Since the value of the dividend is taken from a memory word, it is stored into R3 and the leading 16 bits in R2 are cleared.

As indicated by the comments in the program, DIV places the result quotient into the even-numbered register and the remainder into the odd register. Thus, the contents of R3 can be taken as the digit value, converted to ASCII by inserting bits 4 and 5 (see the ASCII chart given earlier), and stored into C. The quotient is then moved into R3 and the program loops to divide again.

The DIV instruction may not be available on smaller PDP-11 models. Notice also that an ADD instruction is used to insert the required bits into the remainder for the conversion to ASCII. In the next chapter we shall see a clearer way of performing this operation.

EXERCISES

4-1 Rewrite Example Program 3 using indirect addressing instead of indexing.
4-2 Rewrite Example Program 2 using indirect addressing instead of indexing.

4-3 Design the algorithm for, and code, a program that reverses the order of a character string. Use indexing to reference the string.

4-4 Repeat Exercise 4-3 using indirect addressing.

4-5 Rewrite Example Program 1 to use indirect addressing instead of indexing.

4-6 Rewrite the algorithm for, and recode, Example Program 2 to search for a substring of periods of some arbitrary given length.

4-7 Show how to implement a multiplication by 10 in assembly language assuming that you have no multiply instruction available. *Hint:* A companion instruction to ASR is the Arithmetic Shift Left described as:

Instruction	Operation
ASL dst	The destination is shifted 1 bit to the left. Bit 15 is lost. Bit 0 becomes zero.

4-8 Design the algorithm for, and code, a program to convert a five-digit ASCII-coded decimal number to binary. You may make reasonable assumptions regarding the input data to your program where you feel these are necessary. The Multiply instruction functions as follows:

Instruction	Operation
MUL src,Rn	$Cw(src) \cdot Cw(Rn) \rightarrow Rn$ where n is odd (Only the least significant 16 bits are stored). $Cw(src) \cdot Cw(Rn) \rightarrow Rn:Rn+1$ where n is even (The notation $Rn:Rn+1$ means that the complete 32-bit product is stored in Rn and the successively numbered register, with the most significant bits in Rn).

4-9 Repeat Exercise 4-8 with the assumption that you do not have a Multiply instruction available.

4-10 Rewrite Example Program 3 for the case of binary-to-octal conversion rather than binary-to-decimal.

4-11 Repeat Exercise 4-10 with the assumption that you do not have a Divide instruction.

REFERENCES

Barron (1969) discusses assemblers in some detail. For a machine-independent treatment see Knuth (1968), in which a hypothetical machine and its assembly language, called MIX, are used to illustrate a large number of important algorithms.

FIVE

THE PDP-11: A MORE DETAILED VIEW

The previous chapters have described a portion of the PDP-11 and its assembly language sufficient for interesting programs to be written. There remain, however, many important topics. In this chapter we describe the PDP-11 addressing method in detail, condition codes and branching, overflow detection, bit addressing instructions, and simple input-output. Although not complete, these topics, when supplemented with the various PDP-11 manuals supplied by the manufacturer, provide enough background to reasonably utilize the PDP-11.

5-1 ADDRESSING MODES

We have discussed six ways of specifying operand addresses:

1. Register
2. Indexed
3. Indirect register (register deferred)
4. Indirect indexed (index deferred)
5. Immediate
6. Direct (absolute)

Actually, only the first four of these represent primitive addressing modes of the PDP-11. These modes are summarized in Table 5-1.

The remaining two methods of addressing already discussed, immediate and direct (absolute), are conventional methods that one commonly sees on other machines. However, in the PDP-11 these are actually composed from

Table 5-1 Four primitive addressing modes

Binary code	Name	Assembler symbol	Meaning
000	Register	Rn	Register contains operand
001	Register deferred	@Rn or (Rn)	Register contains operand address
110	Indexed	X(Rn)	X+Cw(Rn) equals operand address
111	Index deferred	@X(Rn)	X+Cw(Rn) equals address of word containing operand address

other, more elementary addressing modes. We will now describe these elementary modes.

The four remaining elementary addressing modes, in addition to those in Table 5-1, involve an automatic change in the operand address either just before or just after it is referenced. This can be very convenient where a sequence of locations is to be accessed. Consider, for example, the array initialization program described earlier in connection with indirect addressing. This program, along with another version using *autodecrement-mode addressing*, is shown in Fig. 5-1.

In line 3 the symbol – (R1) means that R1 will be decremented by 2 and the resulting contents used as the operand address. R1, then, is initialized to 438 since the decrementing takes place before the operand is referenced. The destination operand of the CMP is also adjusted accordingly and, of course, the SUB instruction is not needed. Notice also the more efficient way of clearing R2; the CLR instruction requires only one word.

Autodecrement-mode addresses are, in general, denoted by – (Rn). For example,

Instruction	Operation
MOV R0,–(R1)	Cw(R1)–2 –> R1 *decrement before*
	Cw(R0) –> Cw(R1) *move*

Stored as

MOV	R	000	AD	001

The actual code for autodecrement (AD) is 100 binary. Although autodecrement is described above as subtracting 2 from the designated register, this is true only for word instructions. In the case of a byte instruction the register is decremented by 1. For example,

Instruction	Operation
MOVB R0,–(R1)	Cw(R1)–1 –> R1
	Cb(R0) –> Cb(R1)

Stored as

MOVB	R0	000	AD	001

```
1.          MOV #0,R2              CLR R2
2.          MOV #436.,R1           MOV #438.,R1
3.   L0:    MOV R2,@R1        L0:  MOV R2,-(R1)
4.          SUB #2,R1              CMP R1,#428.
5.          CMP R1,#426.           BNE L0
6.          BNE L0
            Using indirection      Using autodecrement
```

no SUB needed
start w/clear

Figure 5-1 Array initialization.

Suppose that for some reason the programmer of the array initialization code wanted to scan the array in increasing address order. The following would do the job:

```
        MOV #428.,R1
L0:     CLR (R1)+
        CMP R1,#438.
        BNE L0
```

auto inc.

We have further improved our method by using a CLR directly to store a zero into successive array locations. This time the *autoincrement mode* is used. In this case the contents of R1 are used as the operand address, and after the operand is referenced R1 is incremented by 2.

Autoincrement-mode addresses are, in general, denoted by (Rn)+. For example,

Instruction	Operation
MOV 2(R0),(R1)+	Cw(Cw(R0)+2) --> Cw(R1)
	Cw(R1)+2 --> R1

move
increment after

Stored as

MOV	X	000	AI	001
2				

The actual code for AI is 010 binary. As with autodecrement, 1 is added in the case of byte instructions rather than 2 as for word instructions. Now consider a similar but slightly more complex programming task. Suppose that the words to be initialized to zero do not constitute an array but are scattered throughout memory. Then the addresses of these words can be placed in an array and *autodecrement-deferred-mode* addressing used to scan the list of addresses and set the designated words to zero. If we assume that the addresses are stored in locations 428 through 436, then the following code will do the job:

```
        MOV #438.,R1
L0:     CLR @-(R1)
        CMP R1,#428.
        BNE L0
```

Here the operand $-(R1)$ is prefixed with a @, which simply adds one level of indirection to the operand reference. In general, autodecrement-deferred-mode addresses are denoted by $@-(Rn)$. For example,

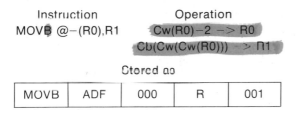

Instruction	Operation
MOV Z(R3),@−(R2)	Cw(R2)−2 −> R2
	Cw(Cw(R3)+Z) −> Cw(Cw(R2))

decrement before

Stored as

MOV	X	011	ADF	010
Z				

The actual code for autodecrement deferred (ADF) is 101 binary. Since the register involved contains the address of an address, whether or not the instruction is a byte or word instruction, the decrementing operation is always by 2. For example, the following shows a byte instruction using ADF:

Instruction	Operation
MOVB @−(R0),R1	Cw(R0)−2 −> R0
	Cb(Cw(Cw(R0))) −> R1

Stored as

MOVB	ADF	000	R	001

Notice in the operation that it is only when the data are retrieved that a byte fetch is performed. Its address, of course, requires a word fetch.

Of course the final addressing mode is *autoincrement deferred*, which allows the same task to be performed in order of increasing addresses within the list of addresses. For example:

```
      MOV  #428.,R1
L0:   CLR  @(R1)+
      CMP  R1,#438.
      BNE  L0
```

As with autoincrement mode the register involved is incremented after the operand has been referenced. In general, autoincrement-deferred-mode addresses are denoted by $@(Rn)+$. For example,

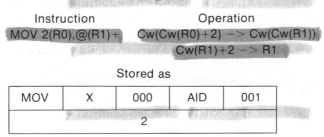

Instruction	Operation
MOV 2(R0),@(R1)+	Cw(Cw(R0)+2) −> Cw(Cw(R1))
	Cw(R1)+2 −> R1

Stored as

MOV	X	000	AID	001
2				

The actual code for autoincrement deferred (AID) is 011 binary.

Table 5-2 Remaining four primitive addressing modes

Binary code	Name	Assembler symbol	Meaning
010	Autoincrement	(Rn)+	Operand referenced by address in register before register incremented
011	Autoincrement deferred	@(Rn)+	Operand referenced indirectly by address in register before register incremented
100	Autodecrement	−(Rn)	Register decremented before operand referenced by address in register
101	Autodecrement deferred	@−(Rn)	Register decremented before operand referenced indirectly by address in register

We have now described all eight PDP-11 addressing modes. These last four are summarized in Table 5-2.

To illustrate the machine code produced by an assembly, a source listing is shown below. The assembled code does not represent an algorithm but simply provides examples of each addressing mode. Notice that the assembler provides the machine-code listing, in octal, to the left of the corresponding source code. The relative location (from the beginning of the program) of each data word or instruction of machine code is shown immediately to the left of this octal code. On the extreme left are the source-code line numbers.

This listing should be studied to observe the correspondence between assembly language and machine code. Only three items require comment. First, the assembler lists the value of symbols defined using the equal sign (=) although no code is generated; Thus, one sees 000001 beside R1 = %1. Second, the assembler lists the value of the parameter on a .END statement although, also, no code is generated. Third, the meaning of the prime character (') beside some of the octal code words will be explained in a later chapter.

```
1              000000          R0=%0
2              000001          R1=%1
3  000000      000000   X:     .WORD      0,0,0,0
   000002      000000
   000004      000000
   000006      000000
4  000010      010001   GO:    MOV        R0,R1    ;REGISTER
5  000012      010011          MOV        R0,@R1 ;REGISTER DEFERRED
6  000014      010061          MOV        R0,4(R1);INDEXED BY CONSTANT
   000004
7  000020      010061          MOV        R0,X(R1);INDEXED BY LABEL
   000000'
8  000024      010071          MOV        R0,@4(R1);INDEX DEFERRED
   000004
9  000030      010071          MOV        R0,@X(R1);INDEX DEFERRED
   000000'
10 00034       010021          MOV        R0,(R1)+  ;AUTO INCREMENT
```

```
11 00036   010031        MOV      R0,@(R1)+;AUTO INCREMENT DEFERRED
12 00040   010041        MOV      R0,-(R1)  ;AUTO DECREMENT
13 00042   010051        MOV      R0,@-(R1);AUTO DECREMENT DEFERRED
14         000010'       .END     GO
```

Example: Assembler listing

5-2 PROGRAM-COUNTER ADDRESSING

Most computers do not allow a programmer to reference the program counter. Referencing is there in the processor controlling the flow of the program but, except for implicit referencing via branch instructions, a program cannot explicitly change its contents. In the PDP-11, the PC is simply one of eight addressable registers and, as such, can be referenced in exactly the same way as can the other registers. The PC is different in only one respect: the processor uses it to fetch the first word of successive instructions from memory and, after doing so, it increments the PC by 2.

The reader may have noticed that the only addressing modes that make use of words following the first instruction word are indexed and index deferred. The remaining six modes refer only to registers.

The question now is: How are immediate and absolute addressing performed? The answer is simply that one uses the PC, since it always contains the address of the word following the last instruction fetched by the processor.

We now see the significance of the code for immediate addressing: 010111 $= 27_8$ binary. An immediate-mode operand is actually an *autoincrement on the PC*. The assembler accepts the symbol #n as meaning "autoincrement using R7"; it is simpler, of course, for the programmer just to view it as an immediate operand.

We also see the significance of the code for absolute addressing: 011111 $= 37_8$ binary. An absolute-address operand is actually an *autoincrement deferred on the PC*. The assembler accepts the symbol @#A as meaning "autoincrement deferred using R7," where A can be an integer or an assembly-language symbol representing an address.

5-2.1 Immediate and Absolute Addressing

Consider again, as an illustration, the array initializing problem. Suppose that the array begins at ARRBEG and ends at ARREND. Then the following code will initialize the array to zero:

```
ARRBEG:   .WORD 0
          .=.+60
ARREND:   .WORD 0
          .
          .
          .
```

```
        MOV        #ARRBEG,R0
        MOV        #ARREND+2,R1
LO:     CLR        (R0)+
        CMP        R0,R1
        BNE        LO
```

Before examining the machine instructions notice the assembly time assignment statement

$$.=. + 60 \quad \rightarrow LC = LC + 60$$

Here we have introduced the special dot symbol (.) which denotes the current value of the assembler's location counter. Recall that this assembly time variable contains the location (relative to the beginning of the program being assembled) of the next cell into which generated machine code will be placed. This assignment, then, simply gives the location counter a new value, namely, 60 octal more than its value when the assignment is encountered by the assembler. The effect is to reserve space for an array of 52 decimal bytes.

The use of expressions is also illustrated in this program with the first such use occurring in the assignment. The first address of the array, ARRBEG, is placed in R0 using immediate addressing, and an ending address is placed in R1. The address assembled in the latter case is, however, that of the word following ARREND, since the expression ARREND + 2 is specified. Notice that this program is now independent of the length of the array; that is, the program can be reassembled with another expression for array size such as .=. + 100.

If the programmer wished to have the size of the array available during execution, then it could be defined as a symbol and referenced as follows:

```
           ARRLEN = 52.
ARRBEG:    .WORD 0
           .=.+ARRLEN-2
ARREND:    .WORD 0
LENGTH:    .WORD ARRLEN
           .
           .
           .
           MOV    @#LENGTH,R0  ;  52. -> R0
```

The MOV instruction uses absolute addressing to place the length of the array, stored in LENGTH, into R0. Now the program can be reassembled with a different array length by merely changing the assignment statement ARRLEN = n.

While on the subject of the assignment statement, let us review the notion of assembly time variables. These variables behave, during assembly, much like program variables do during execution. That is, they can be assigned values and these values can be referenced. There are two ways of giving a value to an assembly time variable (called simply a *symbol* for brevity): it may appear in a label field, or it may appear on the left of the equals character (=) in an assignment.

In the code above, for example, there are five symbols that are given values: ARRLEN, ARRBEG, ARREND, LENGTH, and the dot character (.). The first four are *defined* in this code; that is, they are named and given an initial value. The dot character, of course, is predefined by the assembler, initialized before assembly begins, and incremented each time some code is assembled.

Finally, any properly defined symbol can be referenced in an expression, as are the dot character (.) and ARRLEN in the code above. Expressions can appear almost anywhere in a statement, as can a symbol. It is important to remember that expressions are evaluated during assembly.

5-2.2 Relative Addressing

For reasons that will be explored later we would like to be able to easily move a program from one part of memory to another. The code above would not ease this operation since the MOV instruction contains an absolute address. If the machine-language program were moved, a new address for LENGTH would have to be calculated and placed into the MOV instruction. To ease the operation of moving programs, the PDP-11 assembler recognizes another form of addressing, *relative addressing*, in which the location of the operand, relative to the instruction index word associated with the operand, is placed in that index word. The address mode used is *indexing on the PC*. The assembler accepts any simple symbolic name, such as A, to mean "indexing using R7," with the relative address of A to be used as the index. For example,

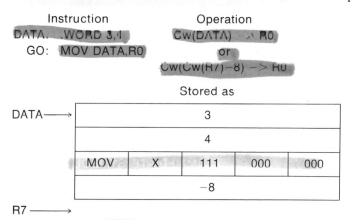

```
        Instruction              Operation
DATA:   .WORD 3,4               Cw(DATA) -> R0
   GO:  MOV DATA,R0                  or
                              Cw(Cw(R7)-8) -> R0

                           Stored as
DATA--->  ┌──────────────────────────────────┐
          │                 3                 │
          ├──────────────────────────────────┤
          │                 4                 │
          ├──────┬──────┬──────┬──────┬───────┤
          │ MOV  │  X   │ 111  │ 000  │  000  │
          ├──────┴──────┴──────┴──────┴───────┤
          │                -8                 │
          └──────────────────────────────────┘
R7 --->
```

Now, why is the value −8 assembled here? Recall, in the discussion regarding the processor execution cycle, that the program counter is advanced when an instruction has been fetched. In the case of the PDP-11 this is also true when an index word has been fetched. Thus, when the index word above is fetched, R7 is incremented by 2 to address the word following. Consequently, a value of -8 is required so that, when added to the contents of R7, the word containing 3 is referenced.

If the reader looks back at Example Program 3 (Chap. 4) an example of relative addressing occurs there in the instruction MOV B,R3. As we will discuss later, relative addressing is preferred over absolute addressing unless absolute is needed for a particular reason such as the fact that the program and the data are not treated as a single unit of code.

Finally, the assembler accepts the notation @A to mean "relative deferred addressing." *The actual mode used is index deferred on the PC.* An example is shown below.

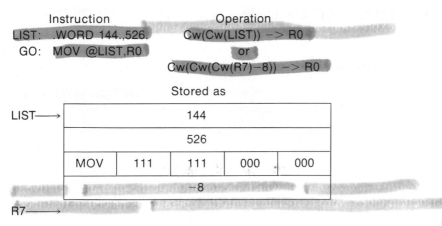

	Instruction	Operation
LIST:	.WORD 144.,526.	Cw(Cw(LIST)) –> R0
GO:	MOV @LIST,R0	or
		Cw(Cw(Cw(R7)−8)) –> R0

Stored as

LIST⟶	144			
	526			
MOV	111	111	000	000
	−8			

R7⟶

Table 5-3 summarizes PC addressing recognized by the assembler.[1]

An illustration of generated machine code for program counter addressing is shown in the listing below.

```
1              000000      R0=%0
2              000001      R1=%1
3 000000   000000 X:     .WORD   0,0,0,0
  000002   000000
  000004   000000
  000006   000000
4 000010   012700 GO:    MOV     #4,R0      ;IMMEDIATE CONSTANT
           000004
5 000014   012700        MOV     #X,R0      ;IMMEDIATE SYMBOL
           000000'
6 000020   012700        MOV     #X+4,R0   ;IMMEDIATE EXPRESSION
           000004'
7 000024   010037        MOV     R0,@#4    ;ABSOLUTE CONSTANT
           000004
```

[1] The meaning of an integer operand, such as in MOV 100,R0, depends on the assembler. It usually means "relative" but can mean "absolute" similar to the instruction notation used in Chap. 3.

8 000030	010037	MOV	R0,@#X	;ABSOLUTE SYMBOL
	000000'			
9 000034	010067	MOV	R0,X	;RELATIVE SYMBOL
	177740			
10 00040	010077	MOV	R0,@X	;RELATIVE DEFERRED SYMBOL
	177734			
11	000010'	.END	GO	

Example: Assembler listing of program counter addressing

5-3 CONDITION CODES AND BRANCHING

This section introduces the way in which Branch instructions detect the result of the previous instruction's execution. The mechanism is related to overflow detection as discussed in Chap. 1.

The PDP-11 processor contains, in addition to the eight general registers, a ninth register called the *program status* (PS) register. Bits 0, 1, 2, and 3 of this 16-bit register comprise the processor *condition codes* and are called respectively the C, V, Z, and N bits.

Program Status Register

Following the execution of each instruction, the condition codes are assigned values, recording information about the "result" of executing the instruction. How an instruction affects the condition codes can only be determined by looking at the definition of the instruction in the PDP-11 manual. Generally, however, they have meanings as shown on page 84.

The "result" is usually the final value of the destination operand. For example, in line 5 of Example Program 1 (Chap. 4) the instruction MOV R0, ARRAY(R1) sets the condition codes according to the value stored in the array element. Storing the values 9, 8, 7, . . . , 2, 1 causes the codes to be set as

Table 5-3 PC addressing modes

Binary code	Name	Assembler symbol	Meaning
010111	Immediate	#n	Operand follows instruction
011111	Absolute	@#A	Address of operand follows instruction
110111	Relative	A	Relative address of operand follows instruction
111111	Relative deferred	@A	Relative address of location containing operand address follows instruction

$27 = $
$37 = $
$67 = $
$77 = $

Bit	Value	Meaning
N	0	Result was nonnegative
	1	Result was negative
Z	0	Result was nonzero
	1	Result was zero
C	0	No carry out of bit $n-1$ of result
	1	Carry out of bit $n-1$ of result
V	0	No overflow occurred
	1	Overflow occurred

follows: $N = 0$, $Z = 0$, $C = 0$, $V = 0$. Storing the value 0 causes the codes to be set as follows: $N = 0$, $Z = 1$, $C = 0$, $V = 0$.

The instructions MOV, SUB, ADD, and ASR all set the codes according to the final value of the destination operand.

Branch instructions function by checking the condition codes. The branch is taken on the occurrence of a specified value in one or more codes. For example, BNE causes a branch if $Z = 0$. Thus, in line 6 of Example Program 1, the execution will iterate about label LOOP until Z is set to 1 as a zero is stored into the first array element. The definitions of four useful Branch instructions are summarized below.

Instruction	Condition for branching
BNE (Branch on Not Equal to Zero)	Z=0
BEQ (Branch on Equal to Zero)	Z=1
BPL (Branch on Plus)	N=0
BMI (Branch on Minus)	N=1

In Example Program 1 the MOV instruction in line 5 conveniently set the condition codes for the BNE instruction to check. Many times, however, it is necessary for the programmer to insert an instruction in the program solely for the purpose of setting the codes. There are two instructions available for this purpose: Compare (which was introduced in Sec. 3-7) and Test. Both instructions have a word and a byte version.

Instruction	Operation
CMP(B) src,dst	Computes src-dst and sets N,Z,C,V according to result. *Does not alter operand values.*
TST(B) dst	Sets N,Z according to operand value. Sets V and C to zero.

The Compare instruction computes the value of the source minus the destination. This value is used to determine the setting of N, Z, V, and C. Neither of the operands is altered. After the condition codes are set, the result value is discarded by the processor.

The Test instruction has only one operand, called the *destination*. The N and Z bits are set according to the value of the destination. Since no carry or overflow can occur, the C and V bits are set to zero. The operand is not altered.

A common use of CMP occurs where a string of characters is being processed. Consider the following portion of a program:

```
1.              MOV    #STRING,R0
2. LOOP:         .                            ;instructions to
                 .                            ;process data
                 .
3.              MOVB   (R0),R1     register def.
                 .
                 .
                 .
4.              ADD    #1,R0
5.              CMP    #ENDSTR,R0
6.              BPL    LOOP
                 .
                 .
                 .
7. STRING:   .ASCII  /SOME DATA HER/
8. ENDSTR:   .ASCII  /E/
```

The two statements labeled STRING and ENDSTR cause a string of characters to be constructed by the assembler. The last character in the string is defined in a separate .ASCII statement so that it may be referenced directly by its address, ENDSTR.

S	O	M	E		D	A	T	A		H	E	R	E

STRING   ENDSTR

At execution time the address represented by STRING is stored into R0. The character string can be examined character by character simply by repeatedly adding 1 to R0 as shown in line 4. Line 3 shows how a character may be referenced within the loop by using indirect addressing with R0. The end of the string is detected by the CMP in line 5; as long as R0 contains an address that is less than or equal to the address represented by ENDSTR, the branch to LOOP will occur because $\#ENDSTR - Cw(R0) \geq 0$. The branch will not occur after the last character has been processed and N is set to 1 because $\#ENDSTR - Cw(R0) < 0$.

The example just discussed can be rewritten using indexing instead of indirect addressing.

```
1.              MOV    #13.,R0
2.  LOOP:        .                          ;instructions to
                 .                          ;process the data
                 .
3.              MOVB   STRING(R0),R1
                 .

                 .
4.              SUB    #1,R0
5.              BPL    LOOP
                 .

                 .
6.  STRING:  .ASCII  /SOME DATA HERE/
```

In this program the characters are processed in order of decreasing address since it is easy to detect, using BPL, when the contents of R0 become negative.

Programmer taste and constraints imposed by the requirements of the algorithm determine whether indexing or indirect addressing should be used in a particular situation.

5-4 USING THE CONDITION CODES

Recall the algorithm for detecting overflow in n-bit arithmetic as described in Sec. 1-5. The operation is carried out using $n + 1$ bits, each operand having one extra leading digit. Overflow is signaled by the result having differing values in bits n and $n - 1$. The PDP-11 handles overflow detection in a similar way.

In the case of the arithmetic instruction ADD, for example, the N bit is simply set equal to bit $n - 1$ (bit 15) of the result. The C bit is set equal to bit n (bit 16) of the result. The V bit is set to 0 if N and C are equal, or to 1 if N and C are not equal. The V bit, therefore, carries no extra information in this case. Its value can be determined directly from the N and C bits.

A special branch instruction exists for overflow detection: Branch on Overflow Set.

Instruction	Operation
BVS dst	Branch to dst if V=1

Overflow can be checked by inserting BVS immediately following an arithmetic operation. For example:

```
        .
        .
        .
ADD   NUM1,NUM2
BVS   ERROR          ; branch to error recovery
   −                 ; continue
        .
        .
        .
```

It is important to remember that CMP and CMPB are arithmetic instructions just like ADD or SUB. Consequently overflow is possible when using these instructions. In general, it could be checked. For example:

```
CMP   NUM1,NUM2   ; compare two signed values
BVS   ERROR       ; branch if overflow
BPL   LABEL1      ; branch if NUM1 >= NUM2  to LABEL 1
   −              ; here if NUM1<NUM2  otherwise
```

This example illustrates the fact that Branch instructions do not affect the condition codes. We can use a sequence of branches to detect different conditions. More important here, this example implies that a programmer must treat as a potential error the result of a perfectly normal compare operation!

Suppose that NUM1 and NUM2 contain values such that an overflow condition occurs. Let us do a sample calculation using 4 bits to illustrate what is happening. Suppose that

$$\text{NUM1} = -7. = -1001 \text{ binary}$$
$$\text{NUM2} = 6. = 0110 \text{ binary}$$

The subtraction carried out by the CMP instruction can be described, using the algorithm of Sec. 1-5, as follows:

$$-7-(6) = (1001) - (0110)$$
$$= (1001) + (1010)$$
$$= (11001) + (11010)$$
$$= (1)10011$$

$$\text{ignored} \underline{\quad}$$

Overflow has occurred since bit 3 and bit 4 are not equal. The N bit will be taken from bit 3 and, of course, the V bit is also set. If the programmer had coded

```
CMP   NUM1,NUM2
BPL   LABEL1
```

on the hope that the branch would be taken only in the event that

NUMI ≥ NUM2, then the programmer would have been incorrect, since BPL checks only the N bit, which in the example above is 0.

The point here is that the programmer's algorithm did not try to compute an invalid value; rather, the PDP-11 hardware, in doing a compare, does a subtraction and therefore causes an overflow. For this reason, the branch instructions BMI and BPL are called *simple* conditional branches and should not be used with 2's complement operands unless one is quite sure that overflow cannot occur. To this point we have seen four simple conditional branches, BEQ, BNE, BMI, and BPL.

To avoid the problem of overflow occurring during the execution of the CMP (or CMPB) instruction, the PDP-11 instruction set includes four *signed* conditional branches. These instructions examine the V, N, and Z bits to take appropriate action as summarized below.

Instruction *SIGNED*	Condition for branching
BLT (Branch on Less Than)	N XOR V = 1
BLE (Branch on Less Than or Equal)	Z OR (N XOR V) = 1
BGT (Branch on Greater Than)	Z OR (N XOR V) = 0
BGE (Branch on Greater Than or Equal)	N XOR V = 0

The logical binary operator XOR is the *exclusive or,* defined as follows

XOR	0	1
0	0	1
1	1	0

$0 \text{ XOR } 1 = 1$

$1 \text{ XOR } 0 = 1$

The result of applying XOR is a 1 if and only if either, but not both, operands are 1.

The logical binary operator OR is the more common *or,* defined as follows:

OR	0	1
0	0	1
1	1	1

$0 \text{ V } 0 = 0$

The result of applying OR to two operands is a 1 if either is 1 and 0 only if both are 0.

The third branch, BGE, provides the solution to the problem presented above. It will always cause a branch if preceded by a CMP in which the 2's complement source is strictly greater than or equal to the 2's complement destination. It will cause a branch if either of the following occur:

1. src − dst is positive and no overflow   N = 0   V = 0
2. src − dst overflows positively   N = 1   V = 1

Notice that it will not cause a branch where src-dst overflows negatively, that is, where src is negative and src-dst overflows, setting N = 0 and V = 1.

Similarly the other three signed conditional branches BLE, BLT, and BGE will work correctly when preceded by a CMP with 2's complement operands. The reader should verify for himself that the branch conditions shown are correct.

The reader will have noticed that we have been avoiding mention of the C bit. If the C bit is always set according to our overflow algorithm of Sec. 1-5, that is, directly from bit 16 of the 17-bit computed result, then it would be redundant; knowing V and N would yield C, and knowing N and C would yield V. By using a different criterion to set C, however, the PDP-11 gives the programmer some added convenience. The ADD instruction, then, which does follow the overflow algorithm, is not representative of arithmetic instructions.

The C bit is set by CMP to enable the comparison of unsigned 16-bit integers such as PDP-11 memory addresses. To do this there are four unsigned conditional branch instructions as summarized below.

Instruction *UNSIGNED*	Condition for branching
BHI (Branch on Higher)	C = 0 AND Z = 0
BCC BHIS (Branch on Higher or Same)	C = 0
BCS BLO (Branch on Lower)	C = 1
BLOS (Branch on Lower or Same)	C OR Z = 1

Let us look at a sample calculation using 4 bits to illustrate what will happen if one attempts to use one of the previously described branches on unsigned integers. Suppose one compares the 4-bit unsigned values 2 and 9 using CMP, which of course performs a subtraction *using the 2's complement rules*.

2. − 9. = (0010 binary) − (1001 binary)
      − (0010 binary) + (0111 binary)   unsigned 9 appears like 2's complement −7
      = 1001 binary

The V and N bits are set according to our overflow algorithm, and therefore V = 1 and N = 1. If, for example, BLT was used in an attempt to cause a branch (since 2 is less than 9), it would not happen since BLT does not branch if both V and N are 1. Notice that, according to the overflow algorithm, C would be 0. Notice also that one wants the branch to occur if the result is negative or if it overflows negatively. To provide this ability CMP and SUB set the C bit to 1 if there is no carry out of bit 15. (This is not bit 16 of a 17-bit result of a 17-bit computation as in our overflow algorithm.) Thus C = 1 if the result is negative and C = 0 if the result is zero or positive. Thus BLO, which branches on C = 1, can be used to perform the comparison in this example.

To see why a carry never appears when the result is negative, consider the comparison

CMP   X,Y

where X and Y are unsigned 16-bit integers. Assume that $X < Y$ is true. The compare operation will yield the computation

X + Y′

where Y′ is the result of the complementing operation on Y. If we look at the largest possible values for X and Y′ and see that no carry can occur, then that shows that no carry can ever occur. The largest possible value for X, given that $X < Y$ is true, is

$$X_{max} = Y - 1$$

Also,

$$Y' = 2^{16} - |Y|$$
$$= 2^{16} - Y$$

therefore, the maximum value of X + Y′ is

$$(X + Y')_{max} = X_{max} + 2^{16} - Y$$
$$= Y - 1 + 2^{16} - Y$$
$$= 2^{16} - 1$$

regardless of the value of Y. In other words the result of the addition is $2^{16} - 1$ or less and thus cannot produce a carry.

Since, then, a carry implies that the result is nonnegative, i.e., zero or positive, CMP sets C = 0 and BHIS provides the complementary comparison to BLO.

Similarly the other three unsigned conditional branches BHI, BHIS, and BLOS will work correctly when preceded by a CMP with 16-bit unsigned operands. The reader again should verify that the branch conditions shown are correct.

There are, then, three groups of branches: simple, signed, and unsigned. The remaining simple branches not already introduced are summarized below for completeness.

Instruction MORE SIMPLE	Condition for branching
BCC (Branch on Carry Clear)	C=0
BCS (Branch on Carry Set)	C=1
BVC (Branch on Overflow Clear)	V=0
BVS (Branch on Overflow Set)	V=1

(BHIS)
(BLO)

The simple branches allow individual condition codes to be tested. As can be seen BHIS and BLO are equivalent to BCC and BCS respectively. The dual mnemonics are provided purely for programmer convenience.

Another use for 16-bit unsigned arithmetic arises in the common situation that 16 bits of integer accuracy are insufficient. For example, one may want to use a fixed-point representation with a 20-bit fraction part and 12-bit integer part with sign forming a 32-bit 2's complement representation. It is then necessary for the programmer to code arithmetic operations on 32-bit operands using the available PDP-11 instructions. Two additional instructions are provided to assist in this regard: Add Carry and Subtract Carry.

Instruction	Operation
ADC dst	Cw(dst)+C −> dst
SBC dst	Cw(dst)−C −> dst

There are also byte versions: ADCB and SBCB.

Assuming that the pairs X1,X2 and Y1,Y2 contain double precision operands (X1 and Y1 are the most significant components), an add operation is coded as

```
ADD   X2,Y2
ADC   Y1
ADD   X1,Y1
```

To subtract, one needs to complement and add. Complementing can be accomplished with the NEG instruction which operates on a 2's complement operand.

Instruction	Operation
NEG(B) dst	−Cw(dst) −> dst
	or
	−Cb(dst) −> dst

If one simply complements both components of Y as in

```
NEG   Y2
NEG   Y1
```

then, according to our complementing algorithm, one has inverted the bits and added 1 to both components. If, however, on inverting the bits of the complete double precision operand and adding 1 into the least significant bit there would not have resulted a carry out of the least significant component Y2 into Y1, then one must subtract a 1 from Y1 to compensate.

When does a 1 have to be subtracted from Y1? Just in the case that Y2 is nonzero after complementing, because a carry can only appear after adding 1 if Y2 will yield a zero result. The definition of NEG indicates that the C bit is set if the result is nonzero and cleared if it is zero. Thus the following code complements Y:

```
NEG  Y1    LEFT
NEG  Y2    RIGHT
SBC  Y1    LEFT
```

and the following code subtracts Y from X:

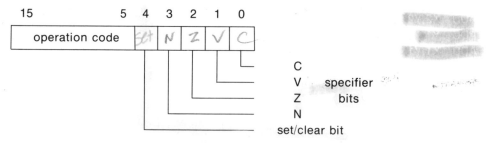

$$\boxed{X1 \mid X2} - \boxed{Y1 \mid Y2}$$

```
NEG  Y1      LEFT
NEG  Y2      R
SBC  Y1      L
ADD  X2,Y2   XR + YR
ADC  Y1      L
ADD  X1,Y1   XL + YL
```

Finally, to complete our discussion of condition codes we note that some instructions do not affect the codes. It is occasionally necessary therefore to explicitly alter the codes. This is accomplished via an instruction that has the following format:

```
15                5 4 3 2 1 0
┌───────────────┬──┬──┬──┬──┬──┐
│ operation code│Set│N │Z │V │C │
└───────────────┴──┴──┴──┴──┴──┘
                              │  C
                              │  V   specifier
                              │  Z   bits
                              │  N
                              │  set/clear bit
```

The set-clear bit indicates whether the codes are to be set or cleared. The specifier bits indicate the codes to be affected by specifying a 1 for those affected. This instruction is represented in assembly language by a collection of mnemonics, each representing a different combination of bits 0 through 4. These mnemonics are described in the PDP-11 handbook.

5-5 THE JUMP INSTRUCTION

The Branch instructions in the PDP-11 are restrictive to the programmer in two important ways. First, a branch is possible only to a word within -127 or $+128$ words of the Branch instruction. Second, because of the way offsets are used, the operand may only be a label (or an actual offset). These restrictions are adopted to produce a short instruction; a Branch instruction occupies only one word.

The single operand Jump instruction provides a mechanism to transfer control to any word. Furthermore, the destination operand can be specified in any mode except register.

Instruction	Operation
JMP dst	dst -> PC

Some examples of JMP statements are:

```
JMP   LABEL1        ; relative
JMP   @LABEL1       ; relative deferred
JMP   @R3           ; indirect register
JMP   LABEL1(R2)    ; indexed mode
```

No JMP R3!

5-6 EXAMPLE PROGRAM 4

The program shown below introduces a new instruction, INC. It is defined by:

Instruction	Operation
INC dst	Cw(dst)+1 -> dst

In other words, INC increments the operand by 1.

```
 1    GO:      MOV      #TEXT,R0
 2    L0:      CMPB     @R0,CHAR
 3             BNE      L1
 4             INC      TOTAL
 5    L1:      INC      R0
 6             CMP      R0,#END
 7             BEQ      STOP
 8             CMPB     @R0,#040
 9             BNE      L1
10    L2:      INC      R0
11             CMP      R0,#END
12             BEQ      STOP
13             CMPB     @R0,#040
14             BEQ      L2
15             JMP      L0
```

```
16    STOP:      HALT
17    TOTAL:     .WORD   0
18    TEXT:      .ASCII    /HERE IS THE DATA TO BE PROCESSED/
19    END:       .ASCII    / /
20    CHAR:      .ASCII    /T /
21               .END    GO
```

The program is intended to illustrate how a string of characters can be scanned by storing the *address* of a character in a register, in this case R0. The program scans the characters stored beginning at TEXT and looks for words beginning with the character stored at CHAR, in this case T. The total number of such words is to be stored in TOTAL.

The program begins by placing the address represented by TEXT into R0. The statement CMPB @R0, CHAR examines the first character in the string to see if it matches the character in CHAR. If it does match, TOTAL is incremented; if it does not, a branch to L1 is taken. The five statements beginning at L1 scan through the word just examined looking for either the end of the string or a blank. The end of the string is detected by the CMP following L1. A blank is detected by the following CMPB. If neither is detected, the branch back to L1 is taken to continue the scan by incrementing R0.

The five statements beginning at L2 scan through the blanks separating words (we allow more than one). When the next word is reached the JMP to L0 is taken.

5-7 LOGICAL OPERATIONS: BIT ADDRESSING

A programmer often needs to examine the value of a particular bit in a byte (or word). Similarly it is necessary to be able to set an individual bit to a particular value while the other bits in the byte (or word) are left undisturbed. Several *logical instructions* are provided for this purpose.

The functioning of the logical instructions is based on three mathematical operators,[1] which we now discuss. One of these, OR, was introduced in Sec. 5-4.

The first operator is the AND, denoted $\wedge$. It is a binary operator, thus taking two operands. The operand values are restricted to 0 and 1. The result of evaluating a $\wedge$ b is defined in the following table:

	b	
$\wedge$	0	1
a 0	0	0
a 1	0	1

$/ \wedge / = /$ only T when both T

---

[1] These operators are the familiar AND, OR, and NOT encountered in using logical expressions in high level languages. The values TRUE and FALSE will correspond here to the values 1 and 0 respectively.

Thus the value of a ∧ b is 1 if a = b = 1 and 0 otherwise. That is, the value is 1 if a and b are 1.

The second operator is the OR, denoted ∨. It is also a binary operator whose operands are restricted to the values 0 and 1. The result of evaluating a ∨ b is defined in the following table, which we repeat from Sec. 5-4.

	b	
∨	0	1
a 0	0	1
1	1	1

$0 \lor 0 = 0$ only F if both are F

Thus the value of a ∨ b is 0 if a = b = 0 and 1 otherwise. That is, the value is 1 if a *or* b is 1.*

The third operator is the NOT, denoted ~. It is a unary operator, thus taking one operand, whose value is 0 or 1. The result of evaluating ~a is defined in the following table:

		a
~	0	1
	1	0

Thus the value of ~a is simply 0 if a = 1, and 1 if a = 0.

The logical operators may be applied to strings of bits as well as individual bits. Where the operands of ∧ or ∨ are strings of bits, the operator is applied to pairs of corresponding bits from each operand. In the case of ~ the operator is simply applied to each individual bit. For example,

0101 ∨ 0010 = 0111   ,
0101 ∨ 0011 – 0111   ,
1110 ∨ 1100 = 1110   ,
1111 ∧ 0100 = 0100   ,
0010 ∧ 0100 = 0000   ,
1100 ∧ 1001 = 1000   ,
  ~ 1011 = 0100   .

$\lor \begin{matrix} 0101 \\ 0010 \\ \hline 0111 \end{matrix}$ $\land \begin{matrix} 0100 \\ 0100 \\ \hline 0100 \end{matrix}$

~(1011)
 0100

The Bit Set instruction, denoted BIS or BISB, enables the programmer to assign the value 1 to specified bits in a word or byte respectively. Assigning the value 1 to a bit is usually called *setting* the bit. The Bit Set Instruction is defined as follows:

src ∨ dst → dst

Instruction	Operation
BIS src,dst	Cw(src)∨Cw(dst) –> dst
BISB src,dst	Cb(src) ∨ Cb(dst) –> dst

* This is the inclusive OR operator since it includes the case of a = b = 1.

For example,

100000

BISB	#040,L1	sets bit 5 in byte L1	
BISB	#377,L1	sets all bits in byte L1	*111 111 111*
BIS	#060,L1	sets bits 4 and 5 in word L1	*000 110 000*
BIS	#48.,L1	sets bits 4 and 5 in word L1	

The Bit Clear instruction, denoted BIC or BICB, enables the programmer to assign the value 0 to specified bits in a word or byte respectively. Assigning the value 0 to a bit is usually called *clearing* the bit. The Bit Clear instruction is defined as follows:

Instruction	Operation
BIC src,dst	~Cw(src)∧Cw(dst) −> dst
BICB src,dst	~Cb(src)∧Cb(dst) −> dst

~s ∧ d → d

For example,

BICB	#040,L1	clears bit 5 in byte L1
BIC	#060,L1	clears bits 4 and 5 in word L1

The Bit Test instruction, denoted BIT or BITB, enables the programmer to examine the value of specified bits in a word or byte respectively. The Bit Test instruction is defined as follows:

Instruction	Operation
BIT src,dst	Cw(src)∧Cw(dst)†
BITB src,dst	Cb(src)∧Cb(dst)†

s ∧ d

† The result is used to set the condition codes and is then discarded.

For example,

BITB	#040,L1	
BNE	L2	Scr branches to L2 if bit 5 has the value 1.

5-8 INPUT-OUTPUT

The PDP-11 programs shown in previous chapters define data through the .ASCII, .BYTE, or .WORD statements. All input data to these programs must, therefore, be stored in memory before the program begins execution. There is no way to reduce memory requirements by transferring data into memory during program execution. No output is produced by these programs. Consequently, there is no way to conveniently observe the result of the processing. In this chapter we consider how two particular devices can be used by the programmer to move data into and out of memory during program execution.

Data can be stored externally (that is, not in memory) on paper tape, magnetic tape, cards, or other storage media. An *input device* is used to transfer data from one such storage medium into memory. In addition, other input devices transfer newly produced data from sources such as a teletypewriter keyboard. An *output device* is used to transfer data from memory to one of the storage media listed above, to output paper, or to some form of display such as an alphanumeric CRT screen. Visual output is, of course, the most convenient for people to read.

As well as transferring data between memory and an external storage medium, an input device or output device may also convert the coded representation of the data from one form to another. Take for example card input data. The character A is stored as a 12-1 punch in a card column; that is, rows 12 and 1 of the card contain perforations in that column. The character A is stored in memory as the ASCII code 101 octal. A card input device, on reading an A from a card column, will convert the representation from its card code to its ASCII code before transferring it into memory. An output device, such as a card punch, performs the opposite conversion, changing each internal ASCII code into the corresponding external card code before punching a card column.

Input-output (I/O) devices can, respectively, store data into memory and fetch data from memory in the same way as can the processor. The processor, however, controls when, and what, data are transferred by an I/O device.

In the PDP-11, processor control over I/O devices is exercised via special device control words in memory. These words, accessible to both processor and I/O devices, are illustrated in Fig. 5-2.

We shall consider only paper-tape I/O to illustrate the principles involved. We therefore assume that all input data are stored on paper tape and all output data are produced by punching paper tape.

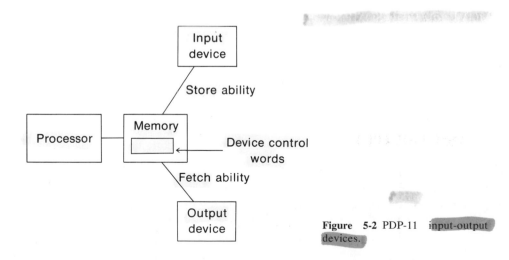

Figure **5-2** PDP-11 input-output devices.

5-9 INPUT WITH THE PAPER-TAPE READER

Four device control words provide communication between the PDP-11 processor and the paper-tape reader and punch. Two words, shown below, are associated with the reader and two with the punch.

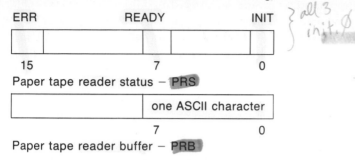

Example: Paper-tape-reader control words

The paper-tape-reader *status word* is located at a fixed address which we will refer to here with the implicitly defined label PRS. The label PRS will not be used for any other purposes. Similarly, the paper-tape-reader *buffer word*[1] is located at a fixed address and will be referenced by the implicitly defined label PRB.

The PRB and PRS function as follows: Bits 0, 7, and 15 of the PRS, called respectively INIT, READY, and ERR, are initially zero. The reader is positioned ready to read a character of data. The INIT bit is set to 1 under program control; this can be accomplished with INCB @#PRS. Setting INIT to 1 causes the reader to transfer the next character in the input stream into memory. The character is transferred into memory and stored, in ASCII, in the rightmost byte of the PRB. The READY bit becomes 1 and INIT is cleared to signal the completion of the transfer. Once READY has become 1, the transferred character can be removed from the buffer; this can be accomplished with MOVB @#PRB, SOMEBYTE. A fetch from the PRB clears READY.

The ERR bit becomes 1 at the same time as the READY bit if an error occurred during the transfer. Generally, this will occur only if no next character exists, that is, if the program has read all the available data, or if an invalid ASCII character is read. Occurrence of an error causes all subsequent read operations to fail and the PRB to contain zero.

Suppose we wish to read 10 characters into memory. These characters may, for example, be decimal digits with leading blanks, and the processing to be accomplished may be a decimal-to-binary conversion. The portion of program shown below reads the first 10 characters of input data.

---

[1] The term *buffer* usually refers to a storage area used for passing data between devices with differing processing speeds. In this case the processor is much faster than the paper-tape I/O devices.

```
1.   ARRAY:    .BYTE    0,0,0,0,0,0,0,0,0,0
2.   GO:       CLR      R1
3.   LOOP:     INCB     @#PRS
4.   WAIT:     TSTB     @#PRS
5.             BPL      WAIT
6.             TST      @#PRS
7.             BMI      ERROR
8.             MOVB     @#PRB,ARRAY(R1)
9.             INC      R1
10.            CMP      #10.,R1
11.            BNE      LOOP
12.              .
```

        <code to process the data>

The .BYTE statement labeled ARRAY reserves 10 bytes of memory and initializes them to zero. The CLR statement on line 2 initializes R1 to contain zero. A read operation is initiated by the statement INCB @#PRS on line 3. The first character to be transferred into memory will be that under the tape read head. Subsequent read operations transfer data from successive characters.

A read operation takes some time to complete. Consequently, the program, if it needs the next character before further processing, must cause a delay until the character arrives. The arrival is signaled by READY switching from 0 to 1. The statements on lines 4 and 5 constitute a *wait loop*; execution will loop about WAIT until READY becomes 1. The statement TSTB @#PRS sets the condition codes. The N bit is simply set equal to bit 7 of the PRS; that is, N is set equal to READY. The branch BPL WAIT will be taken if N = 0. As soon as N = 1, execution will continue at line 6.

Lines 6 and 7 check for an error condition and branch to ERROR (not shown) if such a condition is detected. The value of ERR is detected by using TST to set the N bit; since TST is a word instruction, the N bit is simply given the value of bit 15 of the operand, namely, ERR. The programmer should *always* check for errors and never assume that the data are correct.

Line 8 removes the newly arrived character from the PRB and stores it, using indexed-mode addressing, in the character string ARRAY. Finally, R1 is incremented by 1 (line 9) and if R1 contains 9 or less (see line 10) a branch is taken back to LOOP to read another character.

Input data sometimes appear in the form of *card images* of 80-character blocks. Within such card images, data may appear as only a few characters per block, leaving most of the block blank. In order that it not be necessary to scan through all these blanks each time a block is read, a simple mechanism can be devised to skip to a new block. A special character called a *newline* can be used to separate blocks. Thus, following the read of a newline, the *next* character to be read will come from the following block. Short blocks can then simply be terminated with a newline rather than be filled out with blanks. Of course, it is necessary for the input program to detect and remove the newline characters from the data. In the following, we assume that 012 octal is used as the newline character.

The portion of program shown below could be part of a larger program that reads data from card images as a continuous stream. This code, using R1 as a temporary location for characters, ignores newline characters by simply reading another character when a newline is detected.

```
LOOP:   INCB    @#PRS
WAIT:   TSTB    @#PRS
        BPL     WAIT
        TST     @#PRS
        BMI     ERROR
        MOVB    @#PRB,R1
        CMPB    #012,R1        ;check for newline
        BEQ     LOOP           ;branch if found
```

5-10 OUTPUT WITH THE PAPER-TAPE PUNCH

Two control words, shown below, are associated with the PDP-11 paper tape punch.

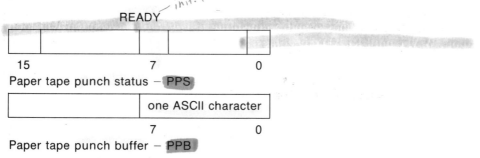

Paper tape punch status — PPS

Paper tape punch buffer — PPB

Example: Paper-tape-punch control words

The paper-tape-punch status word is located at a fixed address but will be referenced here with the implicitly defined label PPS. The label PPS will not be used for any other purpose. Similarly, the paper-tape-punch buffer word is located at a fixed address and will be referenced by the implicitly defined label PPB.

The PPB and PPS function as follows: Bit 7 of the PPS, called READY, is initially 1. Storing a character into byte 0 of the PPB causes the character to be printed and READY to be cleared. No further punch operations can be performed until READY becomes 1; any character stored into PPB while READY = 0 has no effect.

If blocks of data (similar to the blocks of input data,) are to be produced on output, then the newline character can also be used as a separator.

Recall the portion of program, previously shown in Sec. 5-9, that reads 10 characters. An extended example, shown below, augments this program with code to punch the data after processing.

```
 1.  ARRAY:   .BYTE    0,0,0,0,0,0,0,0,0,0
 2.  GO:      CLR      R1
 3.  LOOP:    INCB     @#PRS
 4.  WAIT:    TSTB     @#PRS
 5.           BPL      WAIT
 6.           TST      @#PRS
 7.           BMI      ERROR
 8.           MOVB     #PRB,ARRAY(R1)
 9.           INC      R1
10.           CMP      #10.,R1
11.           BNE      LOOP
12.              .
                 .
                 .
        <code to process the data>
                 .
                 .
                 .
13.           CLR      R1
14.  LOOP1:   MOVB     ARRAY(R1),@#PPB
15.  WAIT1:   TSTB     @#PPS
16.           BPL      WAIT1
17.           INC      R1
18.           CMP      #10.,R1
19.           BNE      LOOP1
20.           HALT
21.           .END     GO
```

The statement on line 14 initiates a punch operation by storing a character into PPB. Lines 15 and 16 comprise a wait loop. Program execution will loop about WAIT1 until READY = 1. This condition is detected by TSTB @#PPS, as this instruction causes N to be assigned the value of bit 7 (READY) of the operand (PPS). The statement BPL WAIT1 causes control to branch to WAIT1 if N = 0; that is, if READY = 0.

5-11 EXAMPLE PROGRAM 5

The program listed below reads and lists (i.e., it echoes) uppercase English text consisting of words separated by blanks, punctuation, or both. After reading and listing the input, it extracts the individual words and writes them to the output device with a separating character.[1] The text is assumed to terminate with a hash character (#).

First, following good documentation practice, we show the algorithm followed by the assembly listing of an implementation of this algorithm.

```
CONST hash = '#';
VAR c,j: INTEGER;
      text: ARRAY[0..2000] OF CHAR;
c := 0;
REPEAT
    read a character into text[c];
    IF text[c] <> hash THEN BEGIN
      echo character;
      c := c + 1 END
UNTIL text[c] = hash OR c = 2000;
j := 0;
WHILE j < c DO BEGIN
    WHILE text[j]>='A' AND text[j]<='Z' DO BEGIN
      write new-line character;
      REPEAT
          write text[j];
          j := j+1;
          IF j = c THEN GOTO 999
      UNTIL text[j]<'A' OR text[j] > 'Z'END
    j := j+1 END
999:
```

Notice in the implementation below that the redundant test on leaving the inner REPEAT loop has been eliminated and that the programmer has chosen to increase j at the beginning of the outer WHILE loop rather than at the end.

```
1              000000          R0=%0
2              000001          R1=%1
3              177550          RS=177550   Reader Status
4              177552          RB=177552   R. Buffer
5              177554          WS=177554   Writer Status
6              177556          WB=177556   W. Buffer
7  000000     043   HASH:     .ASCII  /#/
8  000001     000   TEXT:     .BYTE   0
9              003722'         .=.+2000.
10                            .EVEN
11 03722   005000   START:    CLR     R0      ;R0 COUNTS CHARACTERS
12 03724   105737   L1:       TSTB    @#WS    ;ENSURE WRITER READY
           177554
13 03730   100375             BPL     L1
```

---

[1] If the output device were a printer, two separating characters would be needed, a *line feed* (012 octal) followed by a *carriage return* (013 octal).

```
14 03732  005237  MORE:  INC    @#RS      ;READ NEXT CHARACTER
           177550
15 03736  105737  L2:    TSTB   @#RS      ;WAIT FOR IT
           177550
16 03742  100375         BPL    L2
17 03744  113760         MOVB   @#RB,TEXT(R0)  ;STORE CHARACTER
           177552
           000001'
18 03752  126760         CMPB   HASH,TEXT(R0)  ;CHECK FOR END OF
           174022                             ;INPUT
           000001'
19 03760  001413         BEQ    EOT       ;BRANCH IF END OF INPUT
20 03762  116767         MOVB   RB,WB     ;ECHO WRITE CHARACTER
           177552'
           177556'
21 03770  105767  L3:    TSTB   WS        ;WAIT FOR IT TO COMPLETE
           177554'
22 03774  100375         BPL    L3
23 03776  005200         INC    R0        ;INCREASE CHARACTER COUNT
24 04000  020027         CMP    R0,#2000  ;CHECK FOR FULL TEXT BUFFER
           003720
25 04004  001401         BEQ    EOT       ;IGNORE INPUT IF IT IS FULL
26 04006  000751         BR     MORE      ;LOOP TO READ NEXT CHARACTER
27                ;
28                ;      THE TEXT HAS NOW BEEN READ AND LISTED.
29                ;      R0 CONTAINS A COUNT OF THE NUMBER OF
30                ;                          CHARACTERS
31 04010  012701  EOT:   MOV    #-1,R1    ;INCREMENTING INITIALIZES
           177777                         ;R1 TO ZERO
32 04014  005201  SKIP:  INC    R1        ;R1 INDEXES TEXT
33 04016  020001         CMP    R0,R1     ;CHECK IF ALL TEXT SCANNED
34 04020  001440         BEQ    FINI      ;BRANCH IF FINISHED
35 04022  126127         CMPB   TEXT(R1),#101  ;CHECK IF CHARACTER
           000001'                             ;LESS THAN 'A'
           000101
36 04030  100771         BMI    SKIP      ;SKIP NON-ALPHABETIC CHARACTER
37 04032  122761         CPMB   #132,TEXT(R1)  ;CHECK IF CHARACTER
           000132                             ;GREATER THAN 'Z'
           000001'
38 04040  100765         BMI    SKIP      ;SKIP NON-ALPHABETIC CHARACTER
39 04042  112737         MOVB   #012,@#WB      ;WRITE A NEW-LINE
           000012                             ;CHARACTER
           177556
40 04050  105737  L4:    TSTB   @#WS      ;WAIT FOR IT TO COMPLETE
           177554
41 04054  100375         BPL    L4
```

```
42 04056 116137  LIST:   MOVB  TEXT(R1),@#WB  ;PRINT ALPHABETIC
          000001'                             ;CHARACTER
          177556
43 04064 105737  L5:     TSTB  @#WS  ;WAIT FOR IT TO COMPLETE
          177554
44 04070 100375          BPL   L5
45 04072 005201          INC   R1        ;ADVANCE TEXT INDEX
46 04074 020001          CMP   R0,R1     ;CHECK IF ALL TEXT SCANNED
47 04076 001411          BEQ   FINI      ;BRANCH IF FINISHED
48 04100 126127          CMPB  TEXT(R1),#101  ;CONTINUE LISTING UNTIL
          000001'
          000101
49 04106 100742          BMI   SKIP      ;A NON-ALPHABETIC CHARACTER
50 04110 122761          CMPB  #132,TEXT(R1)  ;IS ENCOUNTERED
          000132
          000001'
51 04116 100736          BMI   SKIP
52 04120 000756          BR    LIST
53 04122 000000  FINI:   HALT
54        003722'        .END  START
```

SYMBOL TABLE

EOT	004010R	FINI	004122R	HASH	000000R
LIST	004056R	L1	003724R	L2	003736R
L3	003770R	L4	004050R	L5	004064R
MORE	003732R	RB =	177552	RS =	177550
R0	=%000000	R1	=%000001	SKIP	004014R
START	003722R	TEXT	000001R	WB =	177556
WS =	177554				
. ABS.	000000	000			
	004124	001			

ERRORS DETECTED: 0
FREE CORE: 18309. WORDS

Example: Input-output programming

EXERCISES

5-1 Write a text compaction program that, given a character string, replaces all substrings of contiguous blanks with a single blank. Assume that the text is terminated with a hash character (#). Use autoincrement mode.

5-2 Write a program to reverse the order of a given character string. Use autoincrement and autodecrement mode.

5-3 Run a program, on the assembler available to you, to see what it does with the first operand of

MOV 600,R0 (or any constant other than 600). Does it produce an expected result? If not, wha. would you expect it to do?

5-4 Show that the following branch conditions are correct for the instructions given.

Instruction	Operands of preceding CMP	Condition
BLT (Branch on Less Than)	Signed 2's complement integers	N XOR V = 1
BHI (Branch on Higher)	Unsigned 16-bit integers	C=0 AND Z=0

where XOR is the exclusive or, defined by:

XOR	0	1
0	0	1
1	1	0

5-5 The following algorithm initializes an n by n array arr so that arr[i,j]=i+j :

```
FOR i := 1 TO n DO
    FOR j := 1 TO n DO
        arr[i,j] := i+j
```

Write an assembly-language program that does the same thing. Your program should work for any given value of n. Arrays can be stored by rows. For example, a 3 by 3 array arr could be stored as follows:

arr[1,1]
arr[1,2]
arr[1,3]
arr[2,1]
arr[2,2]
arr[2,3]
arr[3,1]
arr[3,2]
arr[3,3]

5-6 A table of words with an associated uninitialized value, for example

Word	Value
THE	—
HAT	—
PROGRAM	—
WHICH	—

is given along with several lines of English text. Design and code a program that searches in the text for the first occurrence of each given word and places the line number of this occurrence in the value field for the word. Assume that lines of text are separated by a single 012 octal character. Decisions as to the method of storing the table are left for you.

5-7 Augment your program of Exercise 5-6 by adding, at the beginning, a piece of program that initializes that text at execution time and, at the end, a piece of program that prints the word table.

5-8 Modify Example Program 5 as follows: Assume that the input includes 012 octal characters that separate the text into lines. Amend the program so that, as well as printing individual words, it also prints, on the same line, the line number of the line which originally contained the word.

5-9 Repeat Exercise 5-5 for 48-bit 2's complement integers as array elements.

5-10 Design and code a program that reads lines of text separated by a single 012 octal character. Each line contains a valid assembly-language statement. The program writes each line after formatting it so that all fields start in the same character position.

REFERENCES

The PDP-11 has a rather unique architecture, especially regarding its addressing method. To see another common architecture it would be useful for the student to look at the IBM System/370 since this series of machines is widely used. Katzan (1971) and Donovan (1972) can provide an exposure to this system. Of course, as pointed out earlier, the serious student is urged to find and read as many articles and manuals as possible that describe other machines.

SIX

PROGRAM SEGMENTATION

The reader should already be familiar with the notion of a *subroutine*, or *procedure*, as it is often called. If the same sequence of instructions is needed in several places in a program, it is often wasteful of memory space simply to include these instructions in each place. Rather, one would prefer to supply only one copy of the instruction sequence, called a subroutine, and use this copy at several places in the program. To do this, the programmer inserts, at each point in his program where the sequence is needed, code to transfer control to the subroutine. The code constituting the subroutine must be designed to transfer control back to the point from where it received control. A transfer of control to a subroutine is often referred to as a *call*; the subsequent return transfer is called a *return*. A subroutine return usually transfers control to the location following the instructions constituting the call.

Inserting an instruction sequence directly in a program is called *in-line* coding. The difference between in-line and subroutine coding is illustrated in Fig. 6-1. In this chapter we describe the PDP-11 subroutine mechanism as well as discuss other topics related to constructing programs that are useful in as general an environment as possible. Such programs are often called *modules* and their construction, *modular programming*.

6-1 THE SYSTEM STACK

In our description of the PDP-11 processor we stated that R6 has a special purpose. This purpose is to provide a stack mechanism, of which one important use is to implement subroutine calls and returns.

PUSH +
POP
below

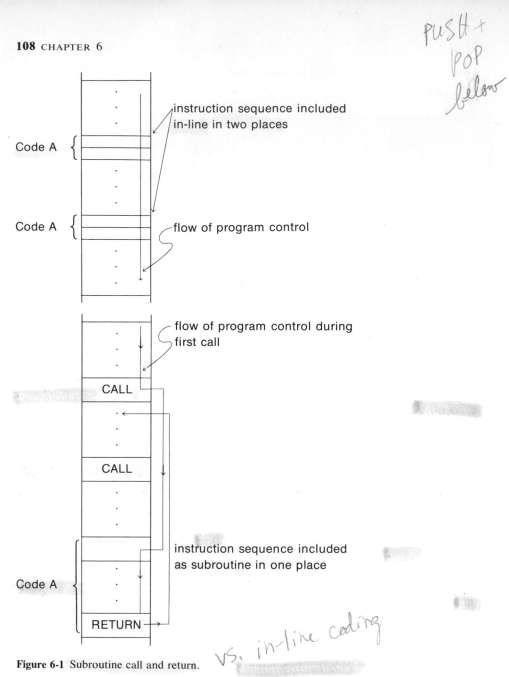

Code A {

instruction sequence included
in-line in two places

Code A {

flow of program control

flow of program control during
first call

CALL

CALL

instruction sequence included
as subroutine in one place

Code A {

RETURN

Figure 6-1 Subroutine call and return.

vs. in-line coding

R6 contains the address of the top word of a stack in memory. As a program begins executing, its stack is empty and R6 should contain an address which is 2 greater than that of the bottom word of the memory area reserved for the stack. Figure 6-2 shows an empty stack.

Placing a word of data into the stack (PUSH) is accomplished by subtract-

PUSH ↓ = MOV #X, -(SP) = MOV #X, -(R6)

POP ↑ = MOV (SP)+, X = MOV (R6)+, X

SP pts. to addr. of top word of stack

R6 o

↑osp

↑.0.S.

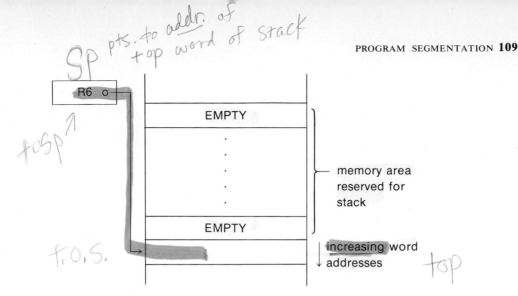

EMPTY

.
.
.
.

EMPTY

memory area
reserved for
stack

increasing word
addresses

top

Figure 6-2 An empty stack.

ing 2 from R6 and storing the data in the word addressed by R6. We shall use
the notation ↓ (stack) to denote a PUSH operation.

Removing a word of data from the stack (POP) is accomplished by fetching
the data from the word addressed by R6 and adding 2 to R6. We shall use the
notation ↑ (stack) to denote a POP operation.

As seen in Figs. 6-2 to 6-4, the PDP-11 stack is implemented in memory and
not in the processor. Also, there is some maximum size to which the stack can
grow.

The programmer need not be concerned with the stack. However, if the
stack is to be used by a program, it is the responsibility of the programmer to
initialize R6. Thus the programmer can decide where in memory the stack is to
be placed. Since the subroutine mechanisms to be described require the stack,
it will be necessary to initialize R6 whenever subroutines are used. A conve-

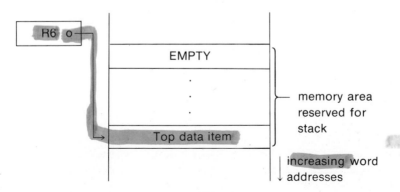

R6 o

EMPTY

.
.
.

Top data item

memory area
reserved for
stack

increasing word
addresses

Figure 6-3 Stack containing one word of data.

never use MOVB ← SP

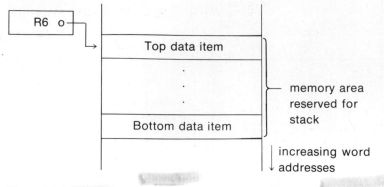

Figure 6-4 A full stack.

nient way to initialize the stack is to place it immediately in front of the program, as shown in Fig. 6-5. The initialization of R6 is then accomplished with:

```
        .=.+100
GO:     MOV   #GO,R6
        .
        .
        remainder of program
        .
        .
        .END  GO
```

The MOV statement simply places the address represented by GO into R6. The stack, therefore, will grow from address #GO−2 toward smaller addresses. Having thus initialized R6, the program can use the stack either explicitly via R6 or implicitly via certain instructions that use R6 (see Sec. 6-2). Below, for

Figure 6-5 Stack initialization.

example, is a piece of program that reads a string of unknown length and writes it in reverse order by storing it in the stack.

```
        .=.+100                  ; maximum stack size is 100        > init, stack
GO:     MOV  #GO,R6
        .
        .
        .
        MOV   #012,-(R6)         ; push a newline   LF
LOOPR:INCB    @#PRS             ; read a character  set go
WAITR:TSTB    @#PRS             ; wait for it
        BPL   WAITR                 if not done?
        MOVB  @#PRB,-(R6)        ; push it   char
        CMPB  #012,(R6)          ; check for newline
        BNE   LOOPR                 if not LF, get next char
        ADD   #2,R6              ; pop newline
LOOPW:MOVB    +(R6),@#PPB        ; pop and write a character
WAITW:TSTB    @#PPS             ; wait for it to go
        BPL   WAITW                 if not done
        CMPB  #012,(R6)          ; check for newline
        BNE   LOOPW                 if not LF, print next char
        MOVB  +(R6),@#PPB        ; pop and write newline  LF
        .
        .
        .

        FND   GO
```

Example: Explicit use of the stack

This example also illustrates an aspect of the autodecrement and autoincrement modes: When the register involved is R6, the decrementing or incrementing is always by 2, even for byte operands. Thus, the stack is maintained as a word stack and R6 always contains an even address. Otherwise, pushing a byte followed by a word would yield an addressing error.

Although R6 is assumed to contain the stack address, by certain PDP-11 instructions the programmer can create stacks using any of the other registers R0 through R5. This usage of the registers is described in detail later. For the moment, then, we are only concerned with the special way that R6 is used. To distinguish between the R6 stack and other possible stacks we will refer to R6 as the *stack pointer* (SP) and the SP stack as the *system stack*.

It is appropriate at this point to describe a restriction on PDP-11 memory usage. The programmer is not allowed to use memory words 0 through 255 decimal (377 octal). These words have special uses, discussed in a later chapter. The effect of this restriction in the example above is that the memory area reserved for the stack is bounded by words 377 octal and #GO.

6-2 SUBROUTINE INSTRUCTIONS

The PDP-11 includes two special instructions for implementing subroutines, one for a call and one for a return. They can be defined as follows:

Instruction	Operation
JSR R7,dst	Cw(R7)—> ↓ (stack)
	dst —> R7
RTS R7	↑ (stack) —> R7

[handwritten: push old PC → stack → new PC; subr addr → new PC; pop old PC → new PC]

(A more detailed and complete definition is given in this section.)

The Jump to Subroutine instruction, JSR, performs a call. The source operand used here is R7 although we shall see shortly that other possibilities exist. Its action is to

1. Save the PC in the stack.
2. Transfer control to the destination address. *(start of SUBR)*

Code for the subroutine, starting at the destination address, has as its final instruction RTS R7, a Return from Subroutine.

The subroutine return, RTS R7, functions by removing the saved address from the stack and replacing it in the PC. Thus control is transferred to the instruction following the JSR instruction that called the subroutine.

The example program in Fig. 6-6 contains a subroutine to add two num-

```
1.              .=.+100
2.      GO:   MOV   #GO,R6        init. SP
3.            MOV   #33,R0
4.            MOV   #44,R1
5.            JSR   R7,SUB
                                   77₈ → R₁
6.            JSR   R7,SUB
                                   132₈ → R₁
7.            HALT
8.      SUB:  ADD   R0,R1       } subr. to add R0 + R1
9.            RTS   R7
10.           .END  GO
```

[handwritten margin notes: 1ST, 2ND; 77₈, 32₈, 132]

Figure 6-6 A subroutine example.

[handwritten: result R0 = 33₈ ? R1 = 132₈]

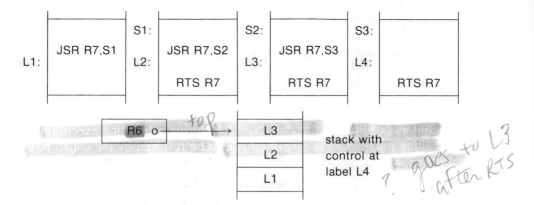

top

stack with
control at
label L4

? goes to L3 after RTS

Figure 6-7 Nested subroutine calls.

bers. This is a very simple subroutine consisting of only one instruction, ADD. It is coded on the assumption that the numbers to be added are stored in R0 and R1.

First, note that R6 is initialized on line 2. The subroutine, called SUB, is called from two locations, lines 5 and 6. Lines 3 and 4 contain code to load two values to be added into R0 and R1. The first time SUB is called (line 5), the RTS R7 will transfer control to the instruction on the line following 5. The second time SUB is called (line 6), control will return to the instruction on the line following 6.

Subroutines can call other subroutines. A sequence of subroutine calls simply creates a stack full of return addresses. Each time RTS R7 is executed the PC is loaded with the *most recent* return address. Figure 6-7 illustrates a sequence of three subroutine calls. The stack, when execution is at label L4, is shown (labels are used in the stack to represent the word addresses actually stored).

Although using R7 as the source operand in a JSR instruction provides a convenient subroutine mechanism, there is no restriction on which of the eight registers can be used. In fact, using a register other than R7 provides a more general mechanism due to the way in which JSR and RTS are actually implemented. The complete definitions of JSR and RTS are given below.

Instruction	Operation
JSR Rn,dst	dst —> temporary
	Cw(Rn) —> ↓(stack)
	Cw(R7) —> Rn
	temporary —> R7
RTS Rn	Cw(Rn) —> R7
	↑(stack) --> Rn

hold new addr (of subr start)
push Reg → stack
old pc → Reg
new addr c(PC) → PC

The reader can see that using R7 means that these definitions simply reduce to those given previously.

The complete definition of JSR and RTS is given here for completeness, but we shall now defer an explanation of the full significance of the mechanism until parameter passing is discussed. For the moment, the reader should see that

1. The contents of Rn are stored in the stack during subroutine execution.
2. The calling program's PC is saved in Rn to be restored by the called program's return.

6-3 INPUT-OUTPUT SUBROUTINES

Input-output programming is a necessary part of almost all programs that a student will write. It is likely also that I/O will be performed in various parts of a program. Rather than duplicate code for reading or writing each time it is required, I/O subroutines can be constructed.

A subroutine to read one character is shown below. It is called by

```
JSR R7,READCH
```

and on return the newly arrived character is located in byte 0 of R0.

```
READCH:   INCB    @#PRS        set go on reader status
READC1:   TSTB    @#PRS        if not done, keep testing
          BPL     READC1
          TST     @#PRS        error check
          BMI     ERROR
          MOVB    @#PRB,R0     char in reader BUF → R0 itself
          RTS     R7
```

Example: Subroutine to read one character

(In this program, ERROR is an error-recovery label provided in the main program. This violates the principle that a subroutine should never transfer control externally other than via a return. A better method for error return is discussed later.)

A subroutine to write one character is shown below. Before calling the subroutine with JSR R7,WRITCH the character to be written must be loaded into byte 0 of R0.

```
WRITCH:   TSTB    @#PPS
          BPL     WRITCH
          MOVB    R0,@#PPB     ; R0 contains actual char. to be printed
          RTS     R7
```

Example: Subroutine to write one character

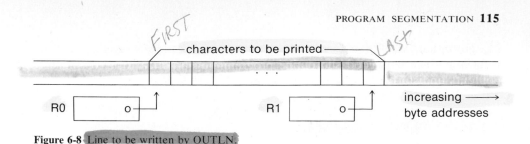

FIRST *LAST*

Figure 6-8 Line to be written by OUTLN.

Note that WRITCH returns control before the character has actually been written. Consequently, subsequent calls to WRITCH must first check that the previous write operation has completed. This is accomplished by the first two statements of the subroutine.

It is often convenient to use a version of WRITCH that is called with the *address* of a character in R0 rather than with the character itself. Such a version is shown below; R0 is simply replaced by @R0.

Addr.

```
WRITCH:    TSTB    @#PPS
           BPL     WRITCH
           MOVB    @R0,@#PPB    ; R0 pts. to addr. that contains char to
           RTS     R7                                    be printed
```

Similarly, a version of READCH, shown below, is coded on the assumption that it is called with an address in R0. The next character read is stored in the byte addressed by R0, and not in R0 itself.

Addr

```
READCH:    INCB    @#PRS
READC1:    TSTB    @#PRS
           BPL     READC1
           TST     @#PRS
           BMI     ERROR
           MOVB    @#PRB,@R0    ; char in BUF → addr. ptd. to by R0
           RTS     R7
```

One can now construct a subroutine that writes a sequence of characters. This subroutine, called OUTLN (for *out line*), is called with two addresses stored in R0 and R1 (see Fig. 6-8). R0 contains the address of the first character to be written, and R1 contains the address of the last character to be written. Clearly, Cw(R1) ≥ Cw(R0) must hold. OUTLN is shown below; note that it calls the version of WRITCH expecting the *address* of a character in R0.

```
OUTLN:     MOV     R0,OUTLN1   ;Save R0
OUTLN2:    JSR     R7,WRITCH   ;Write character  using Addr. WRITCH, above
           INC     R0          ;Next character
           CMP     R1,R0       ;Done?
           BPL     OUTLN2      ;Branch if not
           MOV     OUTLN1,R0   ;Restore R0
           RTS     R7          ;Return
OUTLN1:    .WORD   0           ;Temporary location
```

Note that OUTLN1 must save the contents of R0 and restore them before returning since it is good subroutine programming practice to leave register contents undisturbed.

6-4 EXAMPLE PROGRAM 6

It is important to approach the design of a program with some guiding principles in mind. The remaining sections try to establish some of these principles, remembering that the prime objective is *not* to become an expert assembly-language programmer but to gain an understanding of computer structure and of program structure.

The first step in constructing a program is to understand the algorithm and to describe it in some concise way. Flowcharts can be used to specify the overall structure of algorithms, but we prefer to use the structured English notation. Flowcharts, while having some graphic value, are hard to draw in a disciplined way and hard to modify, and also they tend to be sparse in information content. It is extremely hard to produce a well-structured flowchart in a natural way.

Consider the following problem: A PDP-11 assembly-language program is required to process natural-language text as follows.

A section of text is supplied in the program, beginning at the address designated by TEXT and ending at the address designated by TXTEND. The text consists of English words, where each word is defined as a string of nonblank characters preceded and followed by a blank (except possibly in the case of the initial and final words). Some words may be followed by a period or comma before the blank. The final word is always followed by a period.

The program must scan the text, locating and writing each word which begins with the character found at the address designated by SEARCH. Thus the result should be a list, in successive blocks, of words beginning with a particular letter, in the order they occur in the text. All letters are in uppercase. The only punctuation marks included are commas and periods.

The problem can be described by the self-explanatory algorithm below, which becomes the base on which we build the program. Each line in the algorithm has been numbered for identification.

```
1.    Initialize;
2.    WHILE not at the end of text DO BEGIN
3.        IF first character = Cb(SEARCH) THEN BEGIN
4.            scan to end of word;
5.            write word END
6.        ELSE scan to end of word;
7.        scan to next word or end of text
8.    END
```

Example: Text processing algorithm

Since most programs include some initialization steps, the algorithm starts with line 1 for this purpose; details of initialization are of no concern at this point. The algorithm proceeds by checking whether it has been positioned at TXTEND (perhaps with a null string of text), and if so it terminates. It then examines the first character of a word and acts accordingly. If the first character matches the contents of SEARCH, the word is written; otherwise, the writing is skipped. In either case, the word is scanned to find the delineating blank or punctuation.

Having processed a word, the algorithm scans through any following blanks and punctuation to find either TXTEND or the first character of the next word. If TXTEND is encountered, the algorithm terminates; otherwise, it returns to process the word encountered.

Implement the program following two principles: First, look for tasks that occur in several places and which may be candidates for subroutines. Second, construct the program from the inside out, making assumptions where necessary.

The task of scanning through a word occurs in two places. A subroutine to do this job is created assuming that R1 contains the address of the first character of the word (assumption 1).

```
SCAN:   INC    R1           ;next character
        BITB   #40,@R1      ;bit 5 of letters is 0
        BEQ    SCAN         ;branch if letter
        RTS    R7           ;return
```

Example: Subroutine for lines 4 and 6 of algorithm

The SCAN subroutine increments R1 until it contains the address of the character following the word; this delineating character is detectable by the fact that the blank character, comma character, and period character all have a 1 in bit 5, while letters have a 0 in bit 5 (see the ASCII chart in Sec. 1-7).

Now construct code to write a word (line 5). This code will be entered with R1 pointing to the character following the word. Assume that R0 contains the address of the first character of the word (assumption 2).

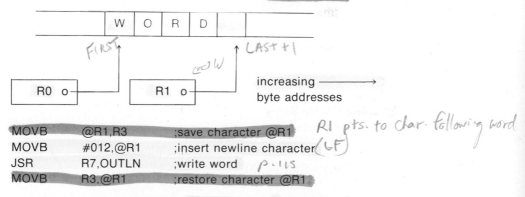

```
MOVB    @R1,R3       ;save character @R1
MOVB    #012,@R1     ;insert newline character
JSR     R7,OUTLN     ;write word
MOVB    R3,@R1       ;restore character @R1
```

Example: Code for line 5 of algorithm

This code assumes that R3 is available to temporarily save the delineating character (assumption 3). A newline is inserted following the word so that the next word written will appear in a new block.

Let's now construct code to implement the WHILE loop (lines 2 and 8).

```
LOOP:    CMP    #TXTEND,R1    ;Cw(R1)=TXTEND?    Are we at end of text
         BEQ    DONE          ;branch if not     If yes, done
         ——                   ;line 3 goes here
         JMP    LOOP                              Else, repeat at LOOP
DONE:    ——                   ;termination of algorithm
```

Example: Code for lines 2 and 8 of algorithm.

Code for line 7 can now be inserted at the end of the loop as follows.

```
NOTLET:  INC    R1            ;next character?
         BITB   #40,@R1       ;bit 5 of letters is 0
         BNE    NOTLET        ;branch if not a letter
         MOV    R1,R0         ;set up R0 for SCAN
         JMP    LOOP          ;loop to process the next word
DONE:
```

Example: Code for line 7 of algorithm

At this point notice that one can place the address of the first character of the next word into R0 as required by assumption 2. If this were not noticed here, then it would be detected after completion of the program, as the assumptions are systematically checked.

Line 3 is implemented by

```
         CMPB   SEARCH,@R1   ;Cb(Cw(R1))=Cw(SEARCH)?
         BNE    NOWRIT       ;branch if not; don't write char
         ——                  ;line 4 goes here
```

where NOWRIT will be the label of line 6. Knowing that line 7 is labeled NOT-LET, put lines 2 through 8 together as shown below.

```
2. LOOP:    CMP    #TXTEND,R1    ;Cw(R1)=TXTEND?
            BEQ    DONE          ;branch if not
3.          CMPB   SEARCH,@R1    ;Cb(Cw(R1))=Cw(SEARCH)?
            BNE    NOWRIT        ;branch if no
4.          JSR    R7,SCAN       ;scan word
5.          MOVB   @R1,R3        ;save character @R1
            MOVB   #012,@R1      ;insert newline character
            JSR    R7,OUTLN      ;write word
            MOVB   R3,@R1        ;restore character at R1
            BR     NOTLET
6. NOWRIT:  JSR    R7,SCAN
```

```
7.  NOTLET:   INC    R1             ;next character
               BITB   #40,@R1        ;bit 5 of letters is 0
               BNE    NOTLET         ;branch if not a letter
               MOV    R1,R0          ;set up R0 for OUTLIN
8.             JMP    LOOP
     DONE:
```

Example Program 6: Partial code

Figure 6-9 shows some test data and the complete program including the initialization required to load R6, R1, and R0. At this point one should systematically check the assumptions to be assured that they are all satisfied. This is left to the reader.

TEXT PROCESSING EX. (NB)

```
         .=.+100
    GO:  MOV    #GO,R6          ; init. SP
         MOV    #TEXT,R1        ; init. R1 to 1st letter of TEXT array
         MOV    R1,R0           ;initialize R0
    LOOP: CMP   #TXTEND,R1      ;Cw(R1)=TXTEND? Are we done?
         BEQ    DONE            ;branch if not
         CMPB   SEARCH,@R1      ;Cb(Cw(R1))=Cw(SEARCH)?  Is this letter we're searching for?
         BNE    NOWRIT          ;branch if no ; don't write it
         JSR    R7,SCAN         ;scan word   else, scan word to find its end
         MOVB   @R1,R3          ;save character @R1   R1 pts. to delimitor
         MOVB   #012,@R1        ;Insert newline character
         JCR    R7,OUTLN        ;write word that begins with letter SEARCH (USING WRITCH + OUTLN)
         MOVB   R3,@R1          ;restore character at R1
         BR     NOTLET
  NOWRIT: JSR   R7,SCAN         Scan word not beginning w SEARCH
  NOTLET: INC   R1              ;next character
         BITB   #40,@R1         ;bit 5 of letters is 0
         BNE    NOTLET          ;branch if not a letter
         MOV    R1,R0           ;set up R0 for OUTLN
         JMP    LOOP
    DONE: HALT
         ;
         ;
         ;
    SCAN: INC   R1              ;next character?
         BITB   #40,@R1         ;bit 5 of letters is 0
         BEQ    SCAN            ;branch if letter
         RTS    R7              ; at end, R1 has NOTLET (delimitor)
  WRITCH: TSTB   @#PPS
         BPL    WRITCH          write char.
         MOVB   @R0,@#PPB       in addr. ptd.  Con't →
         RTS    R7              to by R0
         [PC]
```

Addr. (WRITCH)

} addr. WRITCH (con't)

```
        MOVB    @R0,@#PPB
        RTS     R7
OUTLN:  MOV     R0,OUTL1        ;save contents R0
OUTLN2: JSR     R7,WRITCH       ;write character
        INC     R0              ;next character
        CMP     R1,R0           :done?
        BPL     OUTLN2          ;branch if not
        MOV     OUTL1,R0        ;restore R0
        RTS     R7
OUTL1:  .WORD 0
        ;
        ;
        ;
SEARCH: .ASCII  /T/
TEXT:   .ASCII  /THERE ARE THREE RUNS REQUIRED TO/
        .ASCII  /DEBUG A SMALL PROGRAM. THE FIRST/
        .ASCII  /DETECTS TYPING ERRORS, THE SECOND/
        .ASCII  /DETECTS LOGICAL ERRORS, AND THE THIRD/
        .ASCII  /WORKS/
TXTEND: .ASCII  /./
        .END GO
```

Write a sequence of characters using nested SUBR - WRITCH (eg - writes ea. word beginning with 'T' ea time OUTLN is called.

find + print all words beginning w/ T

data

Figure 6-9 Text processing implementation.

6-5 PARAMETER PASSING

Methods

Although subroutines without parameters are sometimes useful, they are less common than parameterized subroutines. In the I/O examples of Sec. 6-3 we have already seen subroutines with parameters. The two versions of READCH, the subroutine to read a character, as well as WRITCH and OUTLN illustrate a simple technique of passing parameters, namely, to establish an agreement or convention between the caller and subroutine as to where the parameters will be stored.

This can be called the *fixed location* technique. The most elementary form is to place the parameters in a prespecified memory location. Thus a call to a subroutine SUBR requiring two parameters may take the form

```
MOV   VAL1,PARAM1
MOV   VAL2,PARAM2
JSR   R7,SUBR
```

Output parameters can be passed back to the caller in a similar way. Such a method requires that memory locations be reserved solely for parameters, thus requiring an agreement on common labels. To simplify matters one might place the parameters in registers and call SUBR as follows:

```
MOV   VAL1,R0
MOV   VAL2,R1
JSR   R7,SUBR
```

Still, this requires that parameters be moved into special locations before each call. As we have already seen with WRITCH and READCH, a more convenient solution is often to place the address of the parameters into a register, or to arrange the code so that it is already there. Thus

```
MOV   #VAL1,R0
MOV   #VAL2,R1
JSR   R7,SUBR
```

will call SUBR in this way, and SUBR can access the parameters using indirect register addressing, as in

```
SUBR:   MOV   @R0,PAR1   ;get parameter 1
        MOV   @R1,PAR2   ;get parameter 2
```

or they may be operated on directly, as in

```
SUBR:       .



        ADD   @R0,@R1   ;add parameters
        .
        .
        .
```

Fixed-location parameter passing requires an explicit convention for each individual subroutine. It is more general to have a convention that works in all cases. That is, all subroutines expect parameters to be passed in the same way regardless of the identity of the calling program. Therefore, no explicit convention is required for each subroutine.

A very common parameter-passing convention is the *in-line calling sequence* technique. Here, the parameters can be placed within the code of the calling program immediately following the point of the call. For example,

```
            JSR      R7,SUBR
PARAM1:     .WORD    0
PARAM2:     .WORD    0
            .
            .
            .
```

would accomplish such a call. The subroutine could reference the parameters

using: JSR PC, SUBR
JSR PC PARAM1: .WORD 0
PARAM2: .WORD 0

via the saved copy of the caller's PC in the stack as follows:

```
SUBR:   MOV     @SP,R0          ;get caller's PC
        MOV     (R0)+,PAR1      ;get parameter 1        (.WORD follows JSR)
        MOV     (R0)+,PAR2      ;get parameter 2
        MOV     R0,@SP          ;restore caller's PC
          .
          .
          .
        RTS     R7  (PC)
```

Notice how the caller's PC copy is moved into R0 so that autoincrement can be used to fetch the parameters. It is then moved back into the stack so that the subsequent RTS R7 will cause control to go to the instruction immediately following the parameters. In general, however, the caller's PC will not be available at the top of the stack, since the subroutine may use the stack for other purposes such as computing intermediate expression values. The more general form of JSR can then be used to automatically accomplish the moving and restoring of the caller's PC as follows:

```
        JSR     R5,SUBR                      PC not used directly,
PARAM1: .WORD   0                            use Reg. 0-5
PARAM2: .WORD   0
          .
          .
SUBR:   MOV     (R5)+,PAR1      ;get parameter 1    } don't need to
        MOV     (R5)+,PAR2      ;get parameter 2    } get or restore
                                                      caller's PC
          .                                           explicitly
          .
        RTS     R5  gone w
```

Using this version of JSR, the content of R5 is saved on the stack during the call so that R5 can be used to reference the parameters. The caller's PC is restored from R5 so that autoincrement can be used as shown. A variable number of parameters can be passed simply by using the first parameter to specify the number of parameters that follow.

Again, it may be inconvenient to store the parameters themselves within the code. More important, we shall see later that this practice is prohibited in certain circumstances. As with fixed-location parameter passing, one can place the addresses of the parameters in line with the code. The calling sequence and subroutine code might then appear as follows:

```
        JSR     R5,SUBR                PARAD1 = addr. of PARAM1
PARAD1: .WORD   PARAM1
PARAD2: .WORD   PARAM2
```

addr of param.

NOTE ADDR. MODE

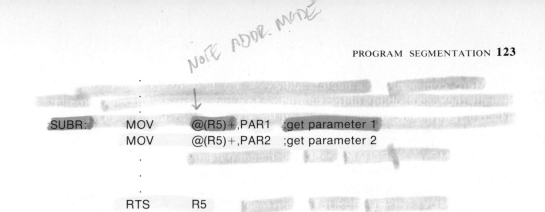

```
SUBR:    MOV      @(R5)+,PAR1   ;get parameter 1
         MOV      @(R5)+,PAR2   ;get parameter 2
              .
              .
              .
         RTS      R5
```

Using in-line parameter passing, every instance of a call (i.e., a JSR) must include a list of parameters or addresses. This is wasteful in either case. If parameter values are used, then they must be moved prior to each call. In both cases a great deal of storage is wasted, since only one parameter list is ever used at any one time. To improve the situation one can use a common area for storing parameter lists. This leads us to a third method for parameter passing.

The *stack calling sequence* technique of parameter passing eliminates the need for duplicate identical parameter lists. Rather than the parameters or their addresses being placed in line, they are placed in the system stack. A calling sequence using parameter values might look as follows:

```
MOV      PARAM2,-(SP)   ;push parameter 2
MOV      PARAM1,-(SP)   ;push parameter 1
JSR      R7,SUBR
MOV      (SP)+,RESULT   ;pop result
```

2ⁿᵈ first

; use PC (push pc → stack)

old PC
P1
P2

```
SUBR:    MOV      (SP)+,R0     ;pop and save PC
         MOV      (SP)+,PAR1   ;pop parameter 1
         MOV      (SP)+,PAR2   ;pop parameter 2
              .
              .
         MOV      RES,-(SP)    ;push result
         MOV      R0,-(SP)     ;restore PC
         RTS      R7
```

; return to pop result

Example: Stack calling sequence using values

There is an inconvenience here in that the caller's PC is placed on top of the parameters in the stack, and it must be saved and restored if the parameters are to be removed by the subroutine. Using the more general form of the JSR will not help the problem, since the register specified rather than the PC will be saved on the stack. This example also shows how an output parameter such as a function value can be conveniently returned via the stack.

CALL BY VALUE (above)

CALL BY REFERENCE

More commonly, parameter addresses are passed via the stack. It is usually the responsibility of the subroutine to remove these addresses, possibly place a return code or result value on the stack, and restore the PC. Such a sequence is shown below.

```
        MOV     #PARAM2,-(SP) ;push addr param 2
        MOV     #PARAM1,-(SP) ;push addr param 1
        JSR     R7,SUBR
        MOV     (SP)+,RESULT    ;pop result
        .
        .
SUBR:   MOV     (SP)+,R0        ;pop and save PC
        MOV     (SP)+,PAR1AD    ;pop addr param 1
        MOV     (SP)+,PAR2AD    ;pop addr param 2
        .
        .
        .
        MOV     RES,-(SP)       ;push result value
        MOV     R0,-(SP)        ;restore PC
        RTS     R7
```

Example: Stack calling sequence using addresses

A complete discussion of the variety of methods of treating parameters is better given in the context of a study of programming languages. At the moment we are mainly interested in the mechanisms involved. Two important classes of parameters however are *call-by-value* and *call-by-reference*. In the former, the subroutine fetches the parameter value immediately following the call, and all subsequent references are to that copy. The caller's copy cannot be altered. In the latter, the subroutine makes all references to the caller's copy of the parameter. Thus the caller's copy can be altered by the subroutine, or it may be changed without the subroutine's knowledge. The reader is referred to a text on high-level languages for a complete discussion of this topic.

Finally, one can identify a fourth method of parameter passing which can be called the *structure reference* technique. Here the parameters may comprise an arbitrary data structure within the caller's program. The data structure, which may be a private stack, for example, is referenced via a single address.

When a structure reference address is placed in R0, the following calling sequence can be used:

```
        MOV     #STRUCT,R0  ; addr. of data struc. → R0
        JSR     R7,SUBR
        PC              (R0 pts. to 1st word)
        .
        .
```

call by VALUE — param. after JSR can't Δ by SUBR

call by REFERENCE — param. CAN Δ in SUBR.

*R0 has
Xaddr.*
(pts → R0)

(R0) 1st word
2 (R0) 2nd
4 (R0) 3rd

```
SUBR:    MOV    6(R0),X        ;get fourth word of structure
           .
           .
           .
         RTS    R7  PC
```

Example: Structure reference parameter passing

The general form of JSR may also be used:

```
         MOV    #STRUCT,R5
         JSR    R5,SUBR
```
{ addr. of STRUC is return location?

```
           .
           .
           .
SUBR:    MOV    @SP,R0         ;copy structure address
         MOV    6(R0),X        ;get fourth word from structure
           .
           .
           .
         RTS    R5
```

Example: Structure reference parameter passing

If a subroutine has only one input parameter, then the general form of JSR as used above yields a convenient way of implementing a stack calling sequence.

As an example of parameter passing consider Example Program 3 from Chap. 4. *(p. 71)* Suppose that this program is to be converted to subroutine form with the freedom to use registers R1, R2, and R3, and with stack parameter passing as described above. The following code would do the job:

*BINARY
→ DEC.
Conversion*

```
BTOD:    MOV    (SP)+,R0      ; save the PC
         MOV    (SP)+,R1      ; address of last significant digit of destination  input
         INC    R1            ; autodecrement will decrease R1
         MOV    (SP)+,R3      ; value to be converted ←          in/out
BTOD1:   CLR    R2            ; same algorithm as previous  p. 71   (variable)
         DIV    #10.,R2
         ADD    #48.,R3       ASCII offset
         MOVB   R3,-(R1)
         MOV    R2,R3
         BNE    BTOD1
         MOV    R0,-(SP)      ; restore the PC
         RTS    R7
```

Example: Subroutine using a stack calling sequence

see p. 71 & 175

Here, the first parameter is passed by *reference* (or, as we shall say, by *address*). That is, the address of the parameter's storage location is passed on the stack. It can therefore be an output parameter which, of course, it is in this example.

The second parameter is passed by *value*. Hence, it can only be an input parameter, which it is here.

6-6 REGISTER SAVING

cf. RE-ENTRANT code

Since subroutines are usually written independently of any particular calling program, it is not possible to establish conventions regarding the use of registers involved in each program. For example, a calling program and subroutine program should not be allocated a disjoint set of registers for their private use. Even where such an agreement is possible, it should not be taken advantage of; a subroutine, for the sake of programming generality, should always be written to be independent of any other program, to the extent that this is possible.

Thus a subroutine must not interfere with the register usage of a calling program. In particular, it is usually the responsibility of a subroutine to save temporarily the contents of any registers that it uses and to restore these contents just before returning to its caller.

The PDP-11 stack is a convenient place in which to save register contents. The calling sequence in Fig. 6-10 shows a standard code sequence that could be used with any subroutine to save and restore all registers. The programmer of such a subroutine would then be free to use any registers. It is more efficient, of

```
reverse     MOV     #PARAM2,-(SP)   ;push addr param 2    → top of stack after dec SP
order       MOV     #PARAM1,-(SP)   ;push addr param 1    → top-2 of stack
            JSR     R7,SUBR
            MOV     (SP)+,RESULT    ;pop result
                                    ;parameter addresses
                .                   ;remain in stack
                .
                .

SUBR:       MOV     R5,-(SP)
            MOV     R4,-(SP)
            MOV     R3,-(SP)        } push/save
            MOV     R2,-(SP)
            MOV     R1,-(SP)
            MOV     R0,-(SP)        } dec. SP, put C(R5) where
                .                     new SP pts.
                .
                .
```

dec. @2.(SP) to @12.(SP) contain reg. contents

NOTE →

```
MOV     @14.(SP),PAR1        ;access parameter 1
MOV     @16.(SP),PAR2        ;access parameter 2
        .
        .
        .

MOV     (SP)+,R0
MOV     (SP)+,R1
MOV     (SP)+,R2
MOV     (SP)+,R3
MOV     (SP)+,R4
MOV     (SP)+,R5
MOV     (SP),-(SP)           ;insert result
MOV     RES,2(SP)            ;value below PC
RTS     R7
```

Copy parameters

pop/restore reverse order

c(SP) → Reg and then SP is inc. for next pop

Figure 6-10 Saving and restoring registers.

course, for a subroutine to save only those registers that it actually uses. It is a good practice, however, to view this improvement as an optimization to be carried out after the subroutine has been thoroughly tested.

Notice that the subroutine has left the parameter addresses on the stack after the return. Whether or not parameters are removed from the stack by the subroutine is established by the rules of the calling sequence. Once a decision is made, all programs and subroutines must follow the convention. Another important aspect of placing parameters on the stack, as shown above, is that they should be copied from the stack just after entry to the subroutine if the stack is going to be used within the subroutine. This prevents possible errors when referencing parameters relative to the top of the stack.

Rather than addressing parameters relative to the top of the stack via indexing, we can employ an additional register with which the parameters can be located. The calling sequence in Fig. 6-11 shows such a technique. The state of the stack after such a call is illustrated in Fig. 6-12.

A place for a return code is always reserved on the stack; it is good practice for a subroutine to have a way of signaling unsuccessful execution to its caller. Next on the stack, the contents of R0 are saved so that R0 can be used as a reference into the stack. As shown, it contains the address of its saved contents, which also happens to be the word below the parameter list. Therefore, the subroutine can easily locate a parameter by indexing on R0. Finally, the address of the saved R0 is also pushed onto the stack so that, on return, the stack is collapsed with a single MOV (SP),SP instruction. This also frees the subroutine to use R0 for other purposes if it wishes to do so.

Notice that the parameters may be addresses or values, and also that the main program is responsible for removing parameters from the stack.

Handwritten margin notes: MAIN (top), TST -(SP) (left), .IRP notes p.56 (left), see notes p.53-56 (right), USING PC, collapse whole stack

```
        SUB   #2,SP          ;make place for return code
        MOV   R0,-(SP)       ;save contents of R0
        MOV   SP,R0          ;note temporarily this point in stack
        MOV   PAR1,-(SP)     ;push parameter 1
        MOV   PAR2,-(SP)     ;push parameter 2
          .
          .
          .
        MOV   PARn,-(SP)     ;push parameter n
        MOV   R0,-(SP)       ;push base address of parameters
        JSR   R7,SUBR        ;call
        MOV   (SP),SP        ;remove parameters from stack
        MOV   (SP)+,R0       ;restore contents of R0
        MOV   (SP)+,RESULT   ;pop return code or result
          .
          .
          .
SUBR:   MOV   R1,-(SP)       ;save
        MOV   R2,-(SP)       ;all
        MOV   R3,-(SP)       ;of
        MOV   R4,-(SP)       ;the
        MOV   R5,-(SP)       ;registers
          .
          .
          .
        MOV   -2(R0),P1      ;access parameter 1
        MOV   -4(R0),P2      ;access parameter 2
          .
          .
          .
        MOV   RES,2(R0)      ;insert return code or result
        MOV   (SP)+,R5       ;restore
        MOV   (SP)+,R4       ;all
        MOV   (SP)+,R3       ;of
        MOV   (SP)+,R2       ;the
        MOV   (SP)+,R1       ;registers
        RTS   R7             ;return
```

Figure 6-11 A general calling sequence.

Handwritten notes at bottom:
```
. MACRO BUILD  p. 56 of notes
    TST
    MOV
    MOV
  . IRP
       MOV
     . ENDR
         MOV  R0,-(SP)
              . ENDM
```

TOP

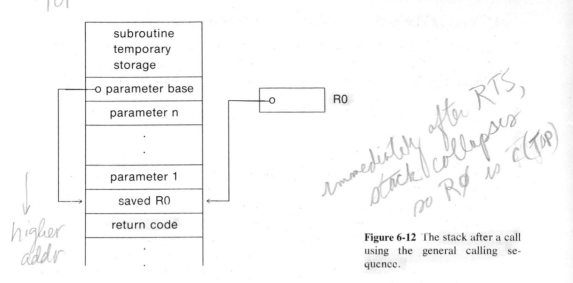

higher addr

*immediately after RTS,
stack collapses
so R0 is C(TOP)*

Figure 6-12 The stack after a call using the general calling sequence.

This calling sequence may differ from instance to instance in

1. The number of parameters
2. The number of registers saved and restored
3. The existence or nonexistence of a return code

Also, the method of treating parameters, whether call-by-value, call-by-reference, or some other method, is independent of this calling sequence. Those considerations depend on whether addresses or values are passed and on the way in which the subroutine accesses the parameters.

pp. 73-75 of notes

6-7 COROUTINES

A subroutine, when called by a main program, always commences execution at some fixed location. The main program, however, on the subroutine's return is entered at the location following the previous call. Figure 6-13 illustrates the flow of control.

This structure places the subroutine in a subordinate position to the main program; it can be called but cannot call. Often, however, it is not clear which of two programs in a program structure is subordinate. Each may be designed in such a way that it invokes the other. The invoking operation in this case is a combination of a call and a return which can be called a *resume*. Programs using resume are called *coroutines*. Figure 6-14 illustrates the flow of control using a resume. In this example, coroutine A starts executing first. Both coroutines are initially entered at a fixed location.

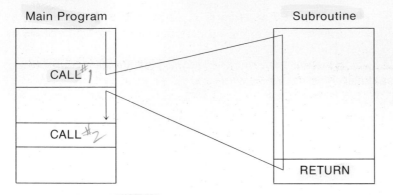

Figure 6-13 Subroutine transfer of control.

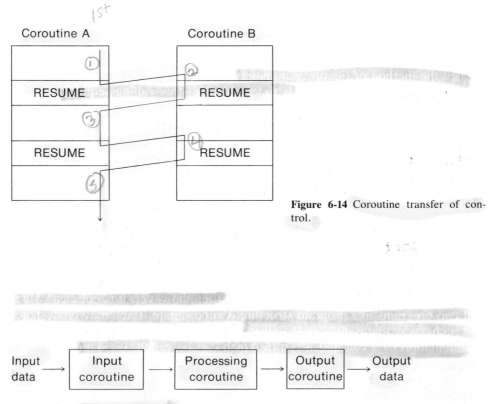

Figure 6-14 Coroutine transfer of control.

Figure 6-15 A coroutine structure.

An example of coroutine usage occurs in processing a stream of data. There may be three coroutines, for input, processing, and output, as shown in Fig. 6-15.

Writing the three programs as coroutines means that the process could be started by entering any one of the three programs. Their algorithms could appear like the following (input, proc, and output are the initial entry points for the resume):

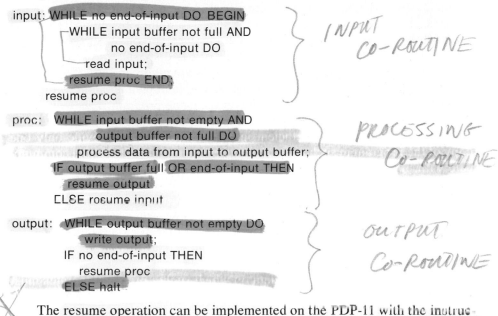

```
input: WHILE no end-of-input DO BEGIN
          WHILE input buffer not full AND
                no end-of-input DO
                read input;
          resume proc END;
       resume proc
```

INPUT CO-ROUTINE

```
proc:  WHILE input buffer not empty AND
                output buffer not full DO
             process data from input to output buffer;
         IF output buffer full OR end-of-input THEN
             resume output
         ELSE resume input
```

PROCESSING CO-ROUTINE

```
output: WHILE output buffer not empty DO
             write output;
          IF no end-of-input THEN
             resume proc
          ELSE halt
```

OUTPUT CO-ROUTINE

The resume operation can be implemented on the PDP-11 with the instruction

```
JSR    R7,@(SP)+
```

Recall the definition of the JSR instruction to see what this accomplishes.

Instruction	Operation	Comment
JSR R7,@(SP)+	@(SP)+ -> temporary	save dst PC
	Cw(R7) -> ↓ (stack)	push own PC
	Cw(R7) -> R7	null
	temporary -> R7	dst PC to R7 PC

In short, JSR R7,@(SP)+ swaps the top of the stack and the current PC. Two coroutines can resume back and forth with this operation. All that is required to initialize the sequence is to store the address of the coroutine to be resumed on the stack of the first coroutine entered.

Parameters can be passed and registers saved in a similar way to that of subroutine calling and returning.

6-8 REENTRANCY

In most modern computer systems it is possible for more than one independent program to coexist in memory. This is called *multiprogramming*. Typically in a single processor system these programs share the processor by switching control from one to another in such a way that over a relatively long period of time each obtains a fair portion of the available processor time for its execution. For example, each program may be communicating with an interactive terminal. Because the actions of a person at a terminal are quite slow compared to the speed of the processor executing the program, each person obtains the appearance of having a dedicated computer at his or her disposal.

Suppose that two persons at such terminals are communicating with identical programs—a text editor, for example. A simple implementation would provide each terminal with a separate copy of the same program. This would be a waste of main memory space, however, since the programs would (at least initially) be identical. A more efficient implementation would provide only one copy of the program in such a way that more than one terminal could communicate with it. (editor)

This imposes some constraints on a program to be used in this fashion. At one moment the program may be in execution by the processor on behalf of terminal A. The processor-sharing switch may then occur, after which the program is in execution by the processor on behalf of terminal B. Of course a different set of data is associated with each terminal. The situation is depicted in Fig. 6-16.

The implication is clear; the data on which such a program operates must

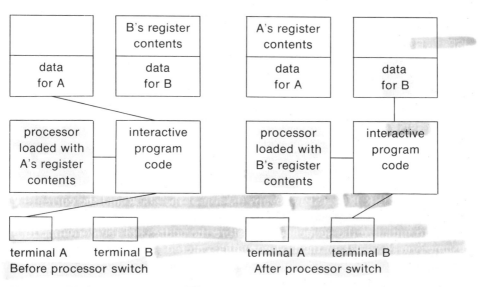

terminal A   terminal B
Before processor switch

terminal A   terminal B
After processor switch

Figure 6-16 Sharing a reentrant program.

be separated from its code. The code itself must be "pure," i.e., non-self-modifying. It may contain constants, of course, but no data that changes in value during execution, and it may not alter its own instructions. Such code is called *reentrant* and a procedure written reentrantly is often called a *pure procedure*.

The processor switch described above will save, in some designated place, the register contents of a suspended computation (including the PS) and then load the registers with a set of contents associated with the computation taking over control of the processor. A reentrant program, then, is free to use the registers in any way. In particular, one register may be used to contain the address of the data associated with the currently executing computation. In a stack machine like the PDP-11 it is convenient to place the data in the system stack which can also be used as a place to save the computation's register contents. A reentrant program, then, can be one in which modifiable data is stored either in registers or in the system stack, or is indirectly addressed via registers or the system stack. Remember also that code must not be modified. (This practice is bad for many other reasons as well!) Figure 6-17 shows how the PDP-11 stack is used to hold data and register contents.

Reentrant code is more generally useful than nonreentrant code. Wherever possible a programmer should write his subroutines reentrantly so that, if necessary, they may be used where reentrancy is required. The mechanism used to carry out processor switching as described above is the subject of a later chapter.

To write a reentrant subroutine simply follow the rule that local data, other than constants, can be stored in registers or in the stack. This means, first, that any temporary values required must be located in the stack, and second, that parameters passed to other subroutines must be located in the stack. The gen-

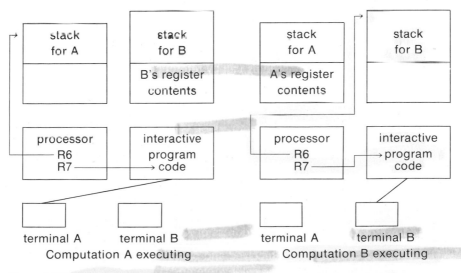

Figure 6-17 Reentrant programs on the PDP-11.

eral stack calling sequence developed in Sec. 6-6 is suitable for reentrant sub-routines.

If a temporary local value is to be passed as a call-by-value parameter, its value is copied to the position on the top of the stack required by the calling sequence. If it is to be passed as call-by-reference, then its address (in the stack) is placed on top of the stack. Parameters having been received into the subroutine as call-by-value are treated in the same way.

Parameters received into the subroutine as call-by-reference can be passed as call-by-value by first making a copy on the stack and then passing that value by recopying it, or by passing that copy directly. They can be passed by call-by-reference by copying the address received onto the top of the stack according to the calling sequence. Figure 6-18 summarizes some of these possibilities.

The essential characteristic of a reentrant program is that it may, at any time, be in a state of execution on behalf of more than one computation. As seen in the example of Fig. 6-19, a multiprogrammed system contains two computations, each periodically using a shareable reentrant subroutine SQRT. A *switcher* system program, part of a collection of programs called the *supervisor*, periodically gains control of the processor, perhaps through a timer mecha-

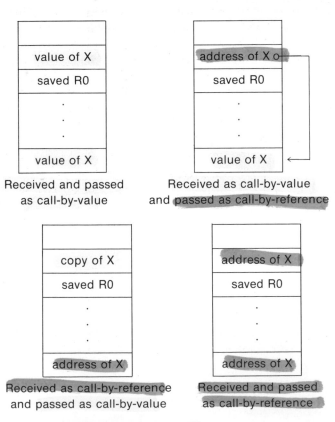

Figure 6-18 Reentrant parameter passing.

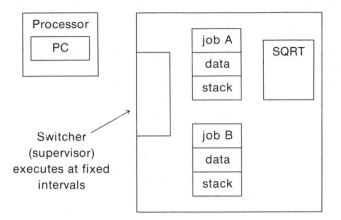

Figure 6-19 A reentrant subroutine.

nism, saves the registers of the executing computation, loads the registers of the inactive computation, and releases control of the processor. Thus, a switch can occur when a computation is in the middle of SQRT.

Since a user's computation cannot always be identified by naming the program it is executing (a reentrant compiler, for example), it has an identity separate from such programs. We therefore refer to a flow of processor execution as a *process*. The concept of a process as a basic component of a computer system is a very important one. Later in this text we discuss it in more detail, but many interesting properties of processes must be left to a course in operating systems. For the present, it is sufficient to define a *process* as a sequence of processor actions, on behalf of a user, usually represented by a set of processor register contents. A process can be executing (the register contents actually loaded into the processor) or not executing (the register contents saved somewhere in memory by the supervisor). It is important to realize that the state of a computation at any time is not affected by its process being taken out of execution.

6-9 RECURSION

Recursion is a special application of reentrancy. Rather than separate computations using the same copy of a program's code, a single computation reuses code by calling a subroutine from within the code of that subroutine. Certain problems are easily described by recursive algorithms. The most common example used to illustrate recursion is the integer factorial function defined (recursively) as:

$$f(0) = 1$$

$$f(x) = \begin{cases} x \cdot f(x-1) & x \geq 1 \\ \text{undefined} & \text{otherwise} \end{cases}$$

The algorithm to calculate the value of this function, given a parameter x, can also be expressed recursively as

```
FUNCTION fact (x:INTEGER; code: BOOLEAN): INTEGER;
    BEGIN code := TRUE;
        IF x<0 THEN code := FALSE
        ELSE IF x=0 THEN fact := 1
            ELSE fact := x*fact(x−1)
    END
```

A recursive algorithm must always contain a conditional statement so that a sequence of calls will eventually terminate, causing a sequence of returns to occur, each corresponding to one of the calls. As we see above, fact is called recursively with x having successive values

$$x', x' - 1, \ldots , 2, 1, 0$$

where x' is the initial value of x. After calling fact with $x = 0$, a sequence of returns occurs causing the following sequence of multiplications to occur:

$$1 \cdot 1 \cdot 2 \cdots (x' - 1) \cdot x'$$

A stack is a convenient place to store the parameters of a recursive procedure. The PDP-11 program in Fig. 6-20 provides an implementation of the integer factorial function. Since it is a very simple algorithm, the procedure does not use an elaborate calling sequence. Also, R1 is assumed to have been reserved for the use of the subroutine.

A recursive procedure is a good example of an occasion where the practice of using only standard calling sequences can be sidestepped. Since a recursive procedure with an elaborate calling sequence can be very inefficient, a specially designed sequence is appropriate.

```
FACT:   TST    2(SP)              ;test value of X
        BPL    FACT1
        RTS    R7                 ;(SP)<0 indicates error on return
FACT1:  BNZ    FACT2
        INC    2(SP)              ;return (SP) = 1   for fact(0)
        RTS    R7
FACT2:  MOV    2(SP),−(SP)
        DEC    (SP)               ;compute X−1 on stack
        JSR    R7,FACT            ;compute fact(X−1)
        MOV    (SP)+,R1           ;move result to R1
        MUL    2(SP),R1           ;compute X·fact(X−1)
        MOV    R1,2(SP)           ;return fact(X)
        RTS    R7                 ;we have assumed result < 32767
```

Figure 6-20 A recursive factorial subroutine.

6-10 POSITION-INDEPENDENT CODE

The interactive system example used to motivate the usefulness of reentrant code also leads to another useful characteristic of program code. In managing the resources of an interactive[1] system [the processor(s), memory, peripheral devices, etc.] the operating system may periodically reallocate these resources among the current computations. We have already discussed how the periodic reallocation of the processor resulted in a requirement for reentrant code.

In an analogous way to processor sharing, computations can share the main memory. Periodically, a program associated with a terminal (or terminals) may lose its portion of main memory and be stored away elsewhere on auxiliary memory to be later reloaded into memory. Because other computations are competing for memory at the same time, however, it may be very difficult to ensure that the program is reloaded into exactly the same memory that it occupied previously. It is very helpful therefore if a program is written so that it can occupy any set of locations in memory. It can then be moved about in memory during its execution without any effect on its computation(s). Such programs are said to be *position independent*.

Before discussing position-independent code (PIC) we should understand the function of a *relocating loader*, the system program that reads a machine-language program from some storage medium such as a tape or disk and stores it into main memory. It can be viewed for the moment as providing two functions:

1. It initializes R7 to contain the correct initial value. This value can be stored with the program by the assembler.
2. It relocates addresses as instructed by the assembler.

The second of these functions is the critical one. Remembering that an implicit initialization . = 0 is done by the assembler, suppose that a program is coded as

```
GO:   MOV     #GO,R6
       .
       .
       .
      MOV     #2,R1
      MOV     X(R1),R0
       .
       .
       .
X:    .WORD   0,0
      .END    GO
```

---

[1] The system need not be interactive in this discussion.

A relocating loader can load this program into memory at any convenient location. If the program is loaded at location 1000 octal, for example, the loader would scan down through the code and relocate addresses where necessary to compensate for the fact that the program was assembled starting at location 0. Thus, within the instruction MOV X(R1),R0 it would add 1000 octal to the address stored in the second word of the instruction. Addresses needing relocating are "tagged" in some way by the assembler.

The program, once loaded, cannot be moved in memory without again relocating all absolute addresses. The problem is that after execution starts, the loader has no way of knowing where such addresses are located. They may have been stored into memory words or they may be located in processor registers. Figure 6-21 shows the demonstration code from Sec. 5-2 if it were to be assembled for loading at location 600 rather than at location zero. As you can see the only changes are in the tagged addresses. These are precisely the addresses that require relocation when a program is loaded into a location other than that for which it was assembled.

Thus, the key to writing PIC is to ensure that locations within the code are not addressed by stored 16-bit addresses—except, of course, by R7. It can be assumed that R7 will be relocated by the loader if the program has been moved.

```
 1          000600        .=.+600                          = not PIC?
 2          000000        R0=%0
 3          000001        R1=%1
 4 000600   000000    X:  .WORD    0,0,0,0
   000602   000000
   000604   000000
   000606   000000
 5 000610   010001    GO: MOV      R0,R1    ;REGISTER
 6 000612   010011        MOV      R0,@R1 ;REGISTER DEFERRED
 7 000614   010061        MOV      R0,4(R1);INDEXED BY CONSTANT
           000004
 8 000620   010061        MOV      R0,X(R1);INDEXED BY LABEL
           000600'
 9 000624   010071        MOV      R0,@4(R1);INDEX DEFERRED   by constant
           000004
10 00630    010071        MOV      R0,@X(R1);INDEX DEFERRED   by label
           000600'
11 00634    010021        MOV      R0,(R1)+   ;AUTO INCREMENT
12 00636    010031        MOV      R0,@(R1)+;AUTO INCREMENT DEFERRED
13 00640    010041        MOV      R0,-(R1)   ;AUTO DECREMENT
14 00642    010051        MOV      R0,@-(R1);AUTO DECREMENT DEFERRED
15          000610'        .END     GO
```

Figure 6-21 Example of an assembler listing.

PIC: (handwritten)

Only two of the addressing modes are always position independent. They are

n must be DATA (handwritten)

#data (handwritten)
A (handwritten)

| #n, | immediate (data only) *(not addr)* (handwritten) |
| A, | relative |

no @# for local data (handwritten)

These modes form the address by using the contents of the PC. Since the loader always ensures that the PC address is valid, the code is PIC. Only data, and not addresses, can be referenced using immediate mode.

BR (handwritten)

Branches are suitable for PIC since the destination is a relative address in the form of an offset.

@# (handwritten)

Locations external to a piece of code that remain fixed can be addressed using absolute addressing in PIC code. For example, the paper-tape control and status registers PRB, PRS, PPB, and PPS are assigned fixed memory locations. In fact, if a program is to be position independent, such fixed external locations *must* be addressed using absolute mode. Otherwise the relative address would need adjusting if the program were moved. For this reason the assembler does not flag absolute addresses as requiring relocation since it is assumed that the programmer will not use absolute addressing for local data.

Let us look at a particular technique which provides a restricted, but useful, form of PIC addressing not otherwise available according to our rules. The idea is to do the relative address calculation, normally done by the assembler during translation, at execution time. Here is an example:

```
L1:     MOV     PC,R0
        ADD     #L2-L1-2,R0
        MOV     @R0,R4
          .
        .EXIT
L2:     .WORD   0
```

NON - AUTOMATIC PIC (handwritten)

This code allows repeated use of the address for L2 calculated in R0 without recomputation of this address before each use. The problem, however, is that the program may be moved at an unpredictable time during execution, rendering the address in R0 invalid. This kind of address calculation can be useful only in certain situations. If the times at which the program is reloaded are known, then the address can be recomputed after each of these times. Another use occurs in the situation where an *absolute loader* is in use and programs, once loaded, are never moved. An absolute loader provides no address relocation; it only relocates the PC. Therefore, loaded programs can relocate themselves by calculating addresses as shown above. Once calculated, these addresses can be used with any addressing mode.

Before leaving position-independent coding, let us summarize how the assembler treats indexed addressing so that any confusion that may have arisen may be clarified.

Any indexed-mode operand containing a single label as the base address will be tagged as requiring relocation. Therefore,

```
MOV      #2,R0
MOV      X(R0),R1      ;relocatable      (not PIC)
```

```
X:      .WORD      0,0,0
```

will result in a relocatable address in the second MOV instruction. This code is not PIC.

Any indexed-mode operand containing an assembler symbol (other than a label), expression, or constant as a base address will not be tagged as requiring relocation. Therefore,

(handwritten annotations: addr (label), not data) *(so not pic)*

```
MOV      #X,R0        ; not PIC )      ; whole not PIC
MOV      2(R0),R1     ; PIC
                                          MOV @#PRB, R0; PIC  also
```

```
X:      .WORD      0,0,0
```

will not result in any relocation tag on the second MOV instruction. Of course #X, the first operand of the first MOV instruction, must be tagged as requiring relocation since it is in fact an address (although it has the form of a data constant). This code is not PIC because of the presence of the #X. The value placed by the assembler in the first MOV instruction for #X will be the value of the location counter at the time X: .WORD 0,0,0 is encountered.

One final observation. Indexed-mode operands using the PC to implement relative addressing are not tagged as requiring relocation. In this code the assembler itself computes the relative address and so this is simply an example of the class of indexed-mode operands having a base that is either an assembler symbol other than a label, an expression, or a constant. To summarize, then, all addressing other than immediate, relative, offsets in branches, and absolute for fixed external locations cannot be used in PIC.

One exception to this rule is system stack addressing. If the system loader relocates the contents of R6 after any move of the program, then any addressing relative to R6 is acceptable. In most cases this is, in fact, likely to be so.   *PIC*

6-11 PROGRAM MODULE INTERFACE SPECIFICATIONS

A *module* is the basic unit of program upon which programming systems are constructed. A software system is usually documented at at least two levels, the intramodule level and the intermodule level. Further levels of description that treat a collection of modules as a single unit (viewed as a single compound module) are also possible.

A module should be the unit of design for a programmer. Given a specification for the module, it is up to the programmer to implement the module according to the specifications and to provide all the intramodule documentation relevant to the module.

A module may contain code only, code and data, or only data. It may or may not coincide with a unit of assembly, although this is often the case. A module containing code may be a program that, once entered, executes until the machine is halted, it may be a subroutine, or it may be of some other flavor of program such as a coroutine. The exact nature of a module must be precisely described in a *module specification*.

There are two parts to a module specification: the module *interface* specification and the module *semantic* specification. The first describes how the module communicates with, or is referenced by, other modules. The second describes in a precise way the operations implemented by the module. At the moment, we are concerned only with interface specification. The semantic specification is more difficult and is the subject of a later chapter.

We are concerned mainly with modules containing code. Basically, the module interface specification must describe every way in which the module interacts with other modules. We are not interested here in describing what the module does, only its paths of communication with other modules. A module specification may take the form of entries in a table similar to Fig. 6-22.

For each module the entry points are listed by name and type, the latter indicating the required calling sequence. For each entry point, the parameters are listed in sequence, giving for each its type: integer value, character value, address, etc. For each entry point the type of the return value is given. Finally, all external references are listed for the module. This may simply be a list of

Module Interface
Specification Sheet

Module name:									
Entry pts		Parameters				Returns	External References		
Name	Type	No.	Type	Ref.	Comment	Type	Reads	Writes	Calls

Figure 6-22 A module interface specification form.

Module name: TABLEMAN (AGER)									
Entry pts		Parameters				Returns	External References		
Name	Type	No.	Type	Ref.	Comment	Type	Reads	Writes	Calls
INSERT	Subr	1	word	value	field 1	word	—	—	STORE
		2	byte	value	field 2				
		3	word	addr	return index				
DELETE	Subr	1	word	value	index	word	—	—	STORE

Figure 6-23 A table manager interface specification.

module names for each type of access, read, write, and call, or it may include for each module the names of the actual data or entry point involved.

The comment field in the parameter description serves to identify the parameter and associate it with a parameter named in the semantic specification. Informal comments on the specification can indicate the actions taken by each entry point. This is merely helpful information, however, and cannot replace a rigorous semantic specification in some other form.

Figure 6-23 shows a table manager module with two entry points for inserting and deleting table entries. The table itself is in another module called STORE which has only one entry point allowing an entry to be stored into a given table position identified by an index.

The reason for producing module interface specifications is not to define the actions of a module but to document its relationships with other modules. It is very important in software systems to know all paths of access between modules. If, for example, a module is modified, all modules that access that module in any way must be checked to verify that their operation is not affected. Such modules can be tracked down by searching the module interface specifications.

6-12 EXAMPLE SOFTWARE SYSTEM

Large programs must, to be manageable, be divided into components, each performing some well-defined portion of the complete processing task. The advantage of organizing a program as a set of such modules is that each module can be constructed and tested individually, perhaps by different programmers.

Thus, a programmer can concentrate attention on a single module at a time without being distracted with details of other modules. In addition, modules may be designed with algorithms that are independent of other modules. Thus, if a piece of code can be improved or needs to be corrected, then this can be done locally to the module without affecting the use of the system.

It is important to define very precisely the way in which program modules interact—that is, how they pass control back and forth—and how data are transmitted. It is extremely important that a programmer *make no assumptions* about the internal workings of another module other than those deriving from the interface specifications. Making assumptions about another module is inviting disaster, because a change in the other module may invalidate the assumption.

The following small case study illustrates some aspects of modular programming. The program to be constructed is to simulate a simple desk calculator as follows:

Input data to the program consist of integer expressions, using only the operators + and −. The = symbol is used to signal the end of an expression. The following are examples of valid expressions:

$$132 + 412 =$$
$$3 - 2 =$$
$$+ 982 - 617 + 4 + 3 + 8 - 1 + 2 =$$
$$- 43 =$$

Expressions are processed one at a time until the end of the input stream is reached, at which time processing halts. The end of the input stream is indicated by a single = symbol not preceded by an expression. Several expressions may appear on a single line, but an expression may not span a line boundary.

The program should compute the result of each expression, proceeding from left to right. Each expression should be printed as input, with the result supplied following the = sign. Thus, if the input consists of the following two lines:

$$8 + 1 =$$
$$- 4 + 47 - 8 -$$

Then the output should be:

$$8 + 1 = 9$$
$$- 4 + 47 - 8 = 35$$

The program can be designed as a set of seven modules.

INIT	initialization module
READ	input module
OPER	arithmetic module
CONV	decimal to binary conversion module
RSLT	result module

SUBR   utility subroutine module
DATA   data storage module

The initialization module, INIT, performs any required initialization and halts if the equal sign signifying the end of the input data is encountered. The input module called READ reads in a portion of an expression called an *element;* each element is either a complete number or an operator: +, −, or =. READ then sends control to a different module for each of three cases:

1. Input of a + or − sends control to the arithmetic module, OPER, which notes the operator for future action after the next number is read.
2. Input of a number sends control to the conversion module, CONV, where the number is converted from decimal to binary form and either added to or subtracted from the intermediate result.
3. Input of an = sends control to the result module, RSLT, where the result is converted from binary to decimal and printed out.

Finally, SUBR contains useful subroutines and DATA contains constants and a temporary storage area.

Except for SUBR, each code module has only one entry point of type program. That is, the entry point is simply a set of instructions; there are no parameters and there is no calling sequence. In addition to the names of the entry points, the interface specifications give the state of the values in the data module after initialization and during execution. It is important that these specifications are invariant at the times that any module is entered or left. Thus, the state of these "global" data must be consistently maintained by each module according to the specifications. These data specifications are given below.

1. A buffer area labeled BUFF, defined as shown, is used to store elements after reading and before writing.

```
BUFF:        .ASCII    /                                    /
ENDBUF:      .ASCII    / /
```

R0 and R1 contain the first and last address of any element stored in BUFF. For example,

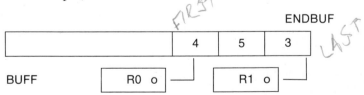

2. The first nonblank in the input data stream following a complete element is stored temporarily in the location NEXT, defined by

```
NEXT:    .BYTE    0
```

3. An operator element is saved in the location OP, defined by

```
OP:    .BYTE    0
```

4. R3 is used to accumulate the result of each calculation.

Each module can be described with an informal semantic specification giving its effect on the data and the flow of program control. These informal semantic specifications are:

1. Initialization
   Entry point: INIT
   Effects: Initialize OP, NEXT, and R3. Stop if = encountered. Branch to READ.

2. Input
   Entry point: READ
   Effects: Read the next element into the buffer, BUFF, and initialize R0 and R1. Place the next nonblank character into NEXT. Branch to one of CONV, OPER, or RSLT as required.

3. Conversion
   Entry point: CONV
   Effects: Convert the number in BUFF into binary. Write the number. Carry out the operation indicated by the contents of OP (R3 <− R3+number). Branch to READ.

4. Result
   Entry point: RSLT
   Effects: Print =. Print sign of Cw(R3) if negative. Convert magnitude of Cw(R3) to character. Print result value terminated by a newline character. Branch to INIT.

5. Arithmetic
   Entry point: OPER
   Effects: Print operator in BUFF. Place operator in OP. Branch to READ.

In addition to the global data invariant specifications, the syntax specifications are needed to complete the system specifications. These are shown in Fig. 6-24.

Since most module entry points are not subroutines and global data are used, rather than parameter passing, the specifications are rather sparse. Notice that the call from OUTLN to WRITCH is internal to the subroutine module and so is not part of the interface specifications.

Also notice that registers R0, R1, and R3 are part of the global data and must be included in the interface specifications.

Module Interface
Specification Sheet

Module name: SUBROUTINES									
Entry pts		Parameters				Returns	External References		
Name	Type	No.	Type	Ref.	Comment	Type	Reads	Writes	Calls
WRITCH	SUBR	1	char	adr	in R0	—	R0		ERROR
READCH	SUBR	1	char	adr	in R0	—	R0		
OUTLN	SUBR	1	char	adr	in R0	—	R0,R1		
		2	char	adr	in R1				

OUTLN makes internal   (a)
call to WRITCH

Module Interface
Specification Sheet

Module name: DATA									
Entry pts		Parameters				Returns	External References		
Name	Type	No.	Type	Ref.	Comment	Type	Reads	Writes	Calls
NEWL	char								
BUFF	char								
ENDBUF	char								
OP	char								
PLUS	char								
NEXT	char								
MIN	char								
EQUAL	char								
TEMP	word								
ERROR	code	—	—	—	—	—	—	—	—

(b)

Module Interface
Specification Sheet

Module name: INITIALIZATION									
Entry pts		Parameters				Returns	External References		
Name	Type	No.	Type	Ref.	Comment	Type	Reads	Writes	Calls
INIT	code	—	—	—	—	—	PLUS	OP	READCH
							NEXT	R0	READ
							NEWL		
							EQUAL		

(c)

Module Interface
Specification Sheet

Module name: INPUT									
Entry pts		Parameters				Returns	External References		
Name	Type	No.	Type	Ref.	Comment	Type	Reads	Writes	Calls
READ	code	—	—	—	—	—	MIN	R0,R1	READCH
							EQUAL	BUFF	RSLT
							PLUS	NEXT	CONV
								TEMP	OPER

(d)

Module Interface
Specification Sheet

Module name: CONVERSION									
Entry pts		Parameters				Returns	External References		
Name	Type	No.	Type	Ref.	Comment	Type	Reads	Writes	Calls
CONV	code	—	—	—	—	—	BUFF	R3	WRITCH
							OP		READ
							R0,R1		

(e)

Module Interface
Specification Sheet

Module name: RESULT									
Entry pts		Parameters				Returns	External References		
Name	Type	No.	Type	Ref.	Comment	Type	Reads	Writes	Calls
RSLT	code	—	—	—	—	—	EQUAL		WRITCH
							R3		INIT
							MIN		
							NEWL		

(f)

Module Interface
Specification Sheet

Module name: ARITHMETIC									
Entry pts		Parameters				Returns	External References		
Name	Type	No.	Type	Ref.	Comment	Type	Reads	Writes	Calls
OPER	code	—	—	—	—	—	R0,R1	OP	WRITCH
							BUFF		READ

(g)

Figure 6-24 Interface specifications for calculator.

An example implementation is shown below, except that CONV and RSLT are left as exercises.

```
;
;
;
;                           INITIALIZATION MODULE
;
;
;
INIT:       MOV     #INIT,R6
            MOVB    PLUS,OP        ; INITIALIZE WITH LEADING +
            CLR     R3             ;INITIALIZE ACCUMULATOR for RESULT
            MOV     #NEXT,R0       ; CURRENT
INIT1:      JSR     R7,READCH      ; READ NEXT CHARACTER
            CMPB    @R0,#040       ; IS IT A BLANK?
            BEQ     INIT1          ; SKIP BLANKS
                                     IF SO, READ NEXT CHAR
                                     ELSE, CK. FOR LF
```

```
        CMPB    @R0,NEWL      ; IS IT #12 (LF)?
        BEQ     INIT1         ;SKIP A NEWLINE CHARACTER
        CMPB    NEXT,EQUAL    ; END OF INPUT INDICATED BY = ALONE
        BNE     READ          ; BRANCH IF MORE INPUT
        HALT                  ; FINISHED
```

;——
;
;
;   INPUT MODULE (ELEMENT IS OPERATOR (+ OR −), NUMBER, OR =)
;
;
;——

```
READ:   MOV     #BUFF,R0      ;INITIALIZE R0   to begin. of storage Buf
        MOV     R0,R1         ;INITIALIZE R1
        CMPB    NEXT,PLUS     ; IF + sign,
        BEQ     READ5         ; move operator
        CMPB    NEXT,MIN      ;BRANCH TO READ5 IF
        BEQ     READ5         ;ELEMENT IS AN OPERATOR
        CMPB    NEXT,EQUAL
        BNE     READ0
        MOVB    NEXT,@R0      ;DO NOT READ AHEAD IF = ENCOUNTERED
        JMP     BRANCH
READ0:  MOVB    NEXT,@R0
READ1:  INC     R0
        JSR     R7,READCH     ;READ NEXT CHARACTER
        CMPB    @R0,#040      ; BLANK?
        BEQ     READ3         ;BRANCH IF BLANK TERMINATES NUMBER
        CMPB    @R0,PLUS
        BEQ     READ2
        CMPB    @R0,MIN       ;BRANCH IF OPERATOR
        BEQ     READ2         ;TERMINATES NUMBER
        CMPB    @R0,EQUAL
        BEQ     READ2
        JMP     READ1         ;LOOP TO READ NEXT DIGIT OF NUMBER
READ2:  MOVB    @R0,NEXT      ;STORE OPERATOR IN NEXT
        MOV     R0,TEMP
        MOV     R0,R1         ;INITIALIZE R0 AND R1 FOR ENTRY TO BRANCH
        MOV     TEMP,R1
        DEC     R1
        JMP     BRANCH
READ3:  MOV     R0,TEMP       ; SAVE R0
        MOV     #NEXT,R0
READ4:  JSR     R7,READCH     ;READ NEXT CHARACTER INTO NEXT
        CMPB    @R0,#040
        BEQ     READ4         ; SKIP BLANKS
        MOV     R1,R0         ;INITIALIZE R0 AND R1 FOR ENTRY TO BRANCH
```

```
            MOV    TEMP,R1
            DEC    R1
            JMP    BRANCH
READ5:      MOVB   NEXT,@R1      ;MOVE OPERATOR INTO BUFFER
            MOV    R0,TEMP       ; SAVE R0
            MOV    #NEXT,R0
READ6:      JSR    R7,READCH     ;READ NEXT CHARACTER INTO NEXT
            CMPB   NEXT,#040
            BEQ    READ6         ;SKIP BLANKS
            MOV    TEMP,R0       ;RESTORE R0
BRANCH:     CMPB   @R0,EQUAL
            BEQ    RSLT          ;BRANCH IF ELEMENT IS A  =
            BITB   #020,@R0      ;BIT 4 OF ASCII DIGITS IS A 1
            BNE    CONV          ;BRANCH IF ELEMENT IS A NUMBER
            JMP    OPER          ;ELEMENT IS AN OPERATOR
;————————————————————————————————————————————————————————————
;
;                    ARITHMETIC MODULE
;
;————————————————————————————————————————————————————————————
;
OPER:       JSR    R7,OUTLN      ;ELEMENT IS AN OPERATOR, PRINT IT
            MOVB   @R0,OP        ;SAVE OPERATOR IN OP
            JMP    READ          ;LOOP TO READ NEXT ELEMENT
```

The reader is left with several tasks. A conversion and a result module are required, with each requiring about 25 instructions. CONV should check for overflow during expression evaluation and character-to-binary conversion. In addition, the reader should modify READ to check for expressions that do not conform to input rules. For example, $5 - - 8 =$ is illegal and should result in an error message. How does the present program treat multiple operators? READ should also detect numbers that are too large to fit into the buffer.

The remaining two modules are shown below. The constant area contains useful character constants, the temporary storage locations, and an Error Halt statement. The reader should note that a branch out of a subroutine (as used here with respect to the label ERROR) is not normally a good practice. It is used only to avoid more complex programming. Normally, subroutines should return to the calling program via an RTS returning an error code if necessary.

```
;————————————————————————————————————————————————————————————
;
;                SUBR – SUBROUTINES FOR I/O
;
;————————————————————————————————————————————————————————————
;
WRITCH:     TSTB   @#PPS
            BPL    WRITCH
```

```
                MOVB   @R0,@#PPB
                RTS    R7
READCH:  INCB   @#PRS
READC1:  TSTB   @#PRS
                BPL    READC1
                TST    @#PRS
                BMI    ERROR
                MOVB   @#PRB,@R0    ; store char in BUFF at addr. ptd. to
                RTS    R7                                        by R0
OUTLN:   MOV    R0,OUTL1
OUTLN2:  JSR    R7,WRITCH    ; WRITE CHAR
                INC    R0            ; NEXT CHAR
                CMP    R1,R0         ; DONE?
                BPL    OUTLN2        ; BRANCH IF NOT
                MOV    OUTL1,R0      ; RESTORE R0
                RTS    R7
OUTL1:       WORD 0
```

;——————————————————————————————————————
;
;
;   DATA — CONSTANTS, TEMPORARY STORAGE, ERROR HALT
;
;
;——————————————————————————————————————

```
NEWL:      .BYTE 012   ; NEWLINE CHAR (LF)
BUFF:      .ASCII /                / ; char. storage
ENDBUF:    .ASCII /  /
UP:        .BYTE 0
PLUS:      .ASCII /+/
NEXT:      .BYTE 0
MIN:       .ASCII /−/
EQUAL:     .ASCII /=/
TEMP:      .WORD 0
ERROR:     HALT
           .END GO
```

6-13 ERROR RETURNS

The example system in the previous section sidesteps an important aspect of modular programming, the problem of error handling. In many cases it is possible for a subroutine to detect, during its execution, that something has gone wrong. It may not know what has happened, but, for example, inconsistencies in data may appear. In the previous example, perhaps, the data invariant $R0 \leq R1$ may be discovered to have been violated.

Our general calling sequence has provided a mechanism to return a code indicating to the caller whether or not the subroutine or function was able to execute successfully. From here on, it will be assumed that the calling sequence specifications require that a return code of zero signals success and a return code of -1 signals failure. The calling program can end its calling sequence with

```
TST    (SP)+
BMI    ERROR
```

where ERROR is the caller's internal error-recovery code. Error recovery is a difficult subject and it is left to a later chapter. However, some of the simpler actions that a module can take when confronted with an unsuccessful return from another module are to (1) return to its caller with a failure signal, (2) retry the call some fixed number of times before returning to its caller with a failure signal, (3) call some alternative module to perform the same or similar function, or (4) halt the machine and request aid from the operator. Which of these or other actions is chosen depends on the particular environment in which the module is expected to run.

Of course, additional information can be passed in the return code. In particular, the calling sequence was designed on the assumption that function subroutines could be implemented with the function value returned on the stack in the place reserved for the return code. In this case, the range of the return value will normally be known and an out of range returned value therefore indicates a failure. If a function is to return a value in the full integer range of the machine, then of course it must be implemented as a subroutine if the return code signal is to be used. This deficiency in the general calling sequence is accepted as a trade-off with either providing a different calling sequence for function subroutines or providing a separate stack word for a returned function value.

EXERCISES

6-1 Write and test a program that reads a line of text from an input device and writes each word (sequence of nonblanks) in reverse order. The words should be written in the same sequence in which they are read.

6-2 Devise a way, without using general registers, of implementing subroutine call and return for a simple machine that does not have a stack or special Call and Return instructions. You may assume indirect addressing is available.

6-3 Write and test a subroutine, INLN, that reads a line of characters in an analogous way to that in which OUTLN writes a line. Your subroutine should "echo" each character as it is read. Assume that INLN is called with R0 containing the address of a line buffer.

6-4 Write and test a program that reads and echoes lines of text using OUTLN and INLN. Each line of input should thus appear twice on the output device, once when echoed by INLN and once when the entire line is echoed.

6-5 Convert the subroutine BTOD from Sec. 6-5 to use the general stack calling sequence shown in Fig. 6-11. Save any registers that are used.

6-6 Write a subroutine DTOB, using the general stack calling sequence, to convert decimal coded integer numbers to binary as a complementary operation to BTOD from Exercise 6-5. What conditions cause a failure signal to be returned?

6-7 Explain why your solution to Exercise 6-2 does or does not allow reentrant code.

6-8 Does the statement MOV #GO,R6 provide position-independent code for initializing the stack? If you do not think so, show a way that is position independent.

6-9 The JSR instruction is not position independent. Show how the same function can be accomplished with position independence. Use this to convert the factorial subroutine in Fig. 6-20 to be position independent.

6-10 Complete and test the example software system from Sec. 6-12.

6-11 Reorganize the example software system from Sec. 6-12 so that the entry points are coroutines. Make any changes that you find are necessary.

REFERENCES

Graham (1975) gives an alternative implementation of many of the mechanisms discussed in this chapter. The first published description of the coroutine structure was in Conway (1963). The serious student is encouraged to read Parnas (December, 1972), which discusses in a very readable way how to go about the task of deciding how to break up a large program into manageable parts.

CHAPTER
SEVEN

MACRO ASSEMBLY

This chapter is concerned with a very powerful facility that is usually available
in assembly-language-level programming: a *macro* language. This facility provides a way for a programmer to define a code sequence that can be conveniently inserted into a program at a later time. Whereas a subroutine is defined
and then effectively inserted in line into a program by coding a subroutine call,
a macro is defined and then actually inserted in line into a program by coding a
macro call. Figure 7-1 illustrates this essential difference between a subroutine
and a macro. Because of this difference, an instruction sequence coded as a
subroutine is sometimes called a *closed* routine. If coded as a macro, it is sometimes called an *open* routine.

A subroutine has two functions: to gain in memory efficiency by providing
one copy of code for a given function, and to improve program understandability and structure. Although a macro can provide improved program understandability in the same way as a subroutine, its prime functions are to ease the
task of programming repetitive sequences of code and to reduce the possibility
of error in such code. Additionally, macro code can be designed to be tailored
at assembly time to suit particular circumstances. Thus, while a subroutine
structure conserves memory space, a macro structure can conserve processor
time by enabling the production of efficient code.

7-1 DEFINING A MACRO

A macro facility provides a means of performing text substitution during program assembly. This basic principle is straightforward, as shown in the following MACRO-11 example:

```
.MACRO CLEAR
CLR X
.ENDM
```

154

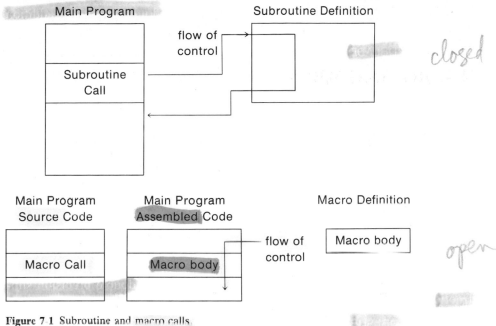

closed

open

Figure 7.1 Subroutine and macro calls.

The .MACRO and .ENDM assembler directives delimit a string of text, in this case CLR X. The .MACRO directive has an associated macro name, in this case CLEAR. The text, called the *macro body,* is substituted for each occurrence of the macro name appearing in the program. This substitution occurs during assembly immediately upon the assembler's detecting the macro name. The *macro definition,* i.e., .MACRO . . . .ENDM, must precede use of the macro name in the program. Thus every occurrence of CLEAR in the program following the definition above will be replaced by CLR X. Immediately following the substitution of the macro body, the assembler continues its translation of the program by processing the text just substituted into the program.

The real power of macros derives from their ability to include parameters with the .MACRO directive. The general form of this directive is

.MACRO␣ name,dummy parameter list   *MACRO HEADER of def.*

where the dummy parameter list is a list of symbols separated by a delimiter such as a comma. The corresponding appearance of the macro name, called a *macro call,* is of the form

name, actual parameter list   *MACRO CALL*

where the actual parameter list is also a list of symbols. The actual parameters are substituted into the macro body with an actual parameter symbol replacing each occurrence of its associated dummy parameter in the macro body. Dummy and actual parameters are associated by their position in the list.

The example below shows the definition of a double precision addition macro.

```
.MACRO    DBLADD,X1,X2,Y1,Y2
ADD       X2,Y2
ADC       Y1
ADD       X1,Y1
.ENDM
```

add least signif halves
add carry bit
add most signif halves

If double precision integers are stored in the register pairs (R0,R1) and (R2, R3), then the following macro call

```
DBLADD    R0,R1,R2,R3
```

would result in the code

```
ADD    R1,R3
ADC    R2
ADD    R0,R2
```

Similarly the following macro definition provides a double precision subtraction.

```
.MACRO    DBLSUB,Y1,Y2,X1,X2
NEG Y1
NEG Y2
SBC Y1
ADD X2,Y2
ADC Y1
ADD X1,Y1
.ENDM
```

The delimiter used in a .MACRO directive or in a macro call can be a blank or a semicolon in addition to a comma. Thus,

```
DBLSUB    Y1  Y2  X1  X2
```

is a valid call on the DBLSUB macro. The use of a blank as a delimiter here provides a very nice way of defining macros that implement user-oriented languages. As we shall see later, one can define elaborate macros that can change the cryptic syntax of normal assembly language into a much more readable syntax.

This is possible since the assembler, unless instructed otherwise, will simply list a macro call as it is coded. Only if explicitly requested by the programmer is the macro expansion listed.

7-2 CONDITIONAL ASSEMBLY

Assembler directives constitute a programming language that is interpreted by the assembler at translation time. In a sense, the programmer can write a program to be executed by the assembler. The reason for doing this is to create a general-purpose program that can be assembled in a variety of ways depending on certain parameters specified to the assembler. As we shall see, the language constituted by assembler directives, like most programming languages, possesses control structures such as definite iteration, indefinite iteration, and conditional execution. Of course, in this case the execution is program assembly and so we are speaking of conditional assembly.

The conditional assembly directives of MACRO-11 can be employed independently of the macro definitional facilities. However, they are extremely useful to use within macro definitions, and for this reason they are included at this point.

The programmer can specify that a piece of code is to be assembled only if certain conditions are satisfied. The following code:

```
.IF      EQ,X
INC      R0
.ENDC
```

If X = 0
then R0 ← R0 + 1

specifies that the code between the .IF and .ENDC directives is to be assembled only if the assembler symbol X has the value of 0. For example, X may have been assigned this value by the directive X = 0.

The general form of the conditional assembly directives is

```
.IF      condition, parameters
.
.
.
.ENDC
```

The condition, of which there are 12 possibilities as described in Table 7-1, is applied to the parameters to determine if it is satisfied. The parameters tagged

.IF EQ, X-5
means
If X = 5

Table 7-1 Conditional assembly operators

Condition symbol	Assembly condition
EQ	Parameter $= 0$
NE	Parameter $\neq 0$
GT	Parameter > 0
GE	Parameter ≥ 0
LT	Parameter < 0
LE	Parameter ≤ 0
B	Parameter * is blank
NB	Parameter * is nonblank
DF	Parameter is a defined assembler symbol
NDF	Parameter is not a defined assembler symbol
IDN	Parameter 1* is identical to parameter 2*
DIF	Parameter 1* is not identical to parameter 2*

} 2 param

* = dummy param, only in MACRO

with an asterisk must be dummy parameters in an enclosing .MACRO directive. The parameters may be assembler symbols or expressions involving assembler symbols, except where noted in the table.

The following macro, for example, removes a condition code from the system stack following a subroutine return and if no branch destination is specified
ignores the value of the code. Otherwise it branches on a nonzero value.

```
.MACRO   TESTCODE,ERROR
TST      (SP)+
.IF      NB,ERROR
BNE      ERROR
.ENDC
.ENDM
```

[handwritten annotations: name; param; pop cond. code from stack; if branch dest. specif. do; if code ≠ 0, BR 'ERROR]

It can be called with either of the following:

```
TESTCODE
TESTCODE   ERR
```

Conditional assembly directives may be nested. Inner .IF conditions are
tested only if all outer .IF conditions are satisfied. In other words a nested .IF
is not substituted into the program unless an enclosing .IF is satisfied; and, of
course, it cannot be tested until the substitution has been performed and assembly continued.

In the TESTCODE macro we can check to see if a JMP is necessary rather
than a branch. The revised macro is shown in Fig. 7-2. This macro is not actually practical, since it will only work for a backward transfer of control, for
two reasons. First, ERROR must have been defined to be used in the expression. Second, the expression assumes that the value of .−ERROR is positive.

Another use of conditional assembly is to provide memory space for a set
of macro calls on the first occurrence of a call. The macro in Figure 7-3 swaps
the contents of two words and thus requires a temporary location. Only one

```
.MACRO   TESTCODE,ERROR
TST      (SP)+
.IF      NB,ERROR
.IF      LT,254−.+ERROR
BEQ      .+4
JMP      ERROR
.ENDC
.IF      GE,254−.+ERROR
BNE      ERROR
.ENDC
.ENDC
.ENDM
```

[handwritten annotation: If ERROR param. IS BLANK, the inner 2 IFs won't be tested]

Figure 7-2 Macro to test a return code.

```
        .MACRO    SWAP,X,Y
        MOV       X,TEMP
        MOV       Y,X
        MOV       TEMP,Y
        .IF       NDF,TEMP          if TEMP not defined
        BR        .+4
TEMP:   .WORD 0
        .ENDC
        .ENDM
```

Figure 7-3 Providing storage for a macro.

such location is provided by the first call on the macro. Subsequent calls on the macro can use the same location.

In the case where only one statement is to be conditionally assembled, a one-line directive is available to make programming a little easier and programs a little more readable. The general format is

.IIF   condition, parameter, statement   IMMEDIATE IF =.IIF

Using this format in TESTCODE we can write

.IIF   GE,254−.+ERROR,BNE ERROR   .IFF or .IIF ?

to replace

```
.IF     GE,254−.+ERROR
BNE     ERROR
.ENDC
```

although it probably does not increase readability very much in this case; .IIF is more useful where a sequence of one-line conditionals occurs.

A label may be placed on the statement or on the line preceding .IIF but not on the .IIF directive itself.

7-3 DEFINITE ITERATION ASSEMBLY

The second control structure available within the MACRO-11 assembler directive language is definite iteration or repetitive assembly. With this facility one can specify that a piece of code is to be assembled repeatedly a specified number of times. There are two general forms, the first of which is

.REPT   expression   ← eval. to # of repetitions
.
.
.
.ENDR

where the expression may involve any assembler symbols and constants. The expression is evaluated and its value used to determine the number of times that the text between .REPT and .ENDR is assembled. Typically, assembler directives within the body of text alter assembler symbol values so that the repeated assembly yields systematically altered code. The following code, for example, produces a string of ASCII characters representing the alphabet:

```
CODE='A
.REPT 26.
.BYTE CODE
CODE=CODE + 1
.ENDR
```

[handwritten: 'A → .BYTE 101 → .ASCII /A/]
[handwritten: "AZ → .WORD 101, 131 → .ASCII /AZ/]

The binary operator single quote (') in an assembler expression produces as a value a single byte containing the ASCII code for its operand, which must be a single character. Thus the symbol CODE is initially assigned a byte value which is the ASCII code for A. (The binary operator double quote (") produces a word value containing two ASCII characters. For example, "AZ yields a word containing the two ASCII characters A and Z.) CODE is systematically altered inside the repeat block so that the .BYTE directive is assembled 26 times with a different value each time. Even though CODE is assigned an ASCII code initially, its value is simply treated as an 8-bit byte so that one can, as is done above, use it in assembler expressions, in which case its value is treated as numeric.

The second general form for definite iteration is   *[handwritten: INDEFINITE REPT.]*

```
.IRP      dummy symbol,<list of symbols>
  .
  .
  .
.ENDR
```

where the list of symbols is any list separated by delimiters.[1]

The code within the .IRP . . . .ENDR block is assembled repeatedly, once for each element in the list. During successive iterations of the assembly the dummy symbol in the .IRP directive is associated with successive elements from the list. Occurrences of the dummy symbol in the macro body are replaced by its currently associated list element. The process is illustrated in the following code, which generates code to save registers on procedure entry:

```
.IRP   REG,<R1,R2,R3,R4,R5>
MOV  REG,-(SP)
.ENDR
```
[handwritten: saves all reg. (push)]

The assembler would expand this to

```
MOV  R1,-(SP)
MOV  R2,-(SP)
```

[1] We shall see later that it may also be a list-valued macro parameter.

[handwritten: restores { .IRP REG, <R5,R4,R3,R2,R1, R0> (pop)
[handwritten: MOV (SP)+, REG
[handwritten: .ENDR]

```
MOV   R3,−(SP)
MOV   R4,−(SP)
MOV   R5,−(SP)
```

7-4 CONCATENATION

The text substitution powers of a macro facility are increased considerably by allowing parts of symbols in code to be altered within a macro. Up to this point we have only seen how to substitute entire lines of code or entire symbols. In other words, the dummy parameters in a macro definition have had to be separated from the rest of the text by some delimiting character, such as a comma or blank. Many times, however, one wants to change only part of a symbol, and so some method of text concatenation is required.

The single quote is also used as a concatenation operator in macro definitions. In the following:

```
      .MACRO  LABEL,X
L'X:  .WORD   0
      .ENDM
```

X is a dummy parameter to be concatenated with L on the left and : on the right. Thus

```
LABEL 3
```

produces

```
L3:    .WORD   0
```

If a blank had been left following the X, a second single quote (') would not have been necessary. Thus

```
      .MACRO  LABEL,X
L'X  : .WORD   0
      .ENDM
```

would yield, when called with LABEL 3,

```
L3:    .WORD   0
```

7-5 NUMERIC-VALUED PARAMETERS

A macro parameter normally represents a character string value identical to the parameter symbol itself. This is quite different from procedure parameters in high-level languages, for example, where a parameter is the name of a value that is not necessarily a character string.

The MACRO-11 definitional facility does allow the inclusion of macro parameters that represent a numeric value rather than their own character

param. as numeric value

string value. To specify that a parameter is to be treated in this way, the actual parameter: (1) is preceded by a backslash character (\ ), and (2), must be a predefined assembler symbol.

In performing the substitution of such a numeric-valued parameter, the assembler obtains its value, as assigned previously in the program, converts the value to an octal character string value, and substitutes this string for the associated dummy parameter.

The following example can be used to restore registers R1 through R5 before a subroutine return.

```
.MACRO   REST,NUM       param
MOV      (SP)+,R'NUM
.ENDM


.MACRO   RESTORE,REG
I=REG
.REPT    REG       expression
REST     \I            ← MOV (SP)+, R numeric value
I=I-1                  convert I to its numeric value
.ENDR
.ENDM
```

Restore Reg. (pop)

When called with

RESTORE 5   ; pops R5 ⟹ R1

the first expansion (of RESTORE) yields

```
I=5
.REPT 5
REST \I
I=I-1
.ENDR
```

and the next five expansions (of REST) yield

```
MOV      (SP)+,R5
MOV      (SP)+,R4
MOV      (SP)+,R3
MOV      (SP)+,R2
MOV      (SP)+,R1
```

Macros to save the registers can be similarly defined:

```
.MACRO   SAV,NUM
MOV      R'NUM,-(SP)
.ENDM


.MACRO   SAVE,REG
I=1
```

Save Reg. (push)

```
.REPT  REG
SAV  \I          macro call reg. for use of \
I=I+1
.ENDR
.ENDM
```

The reason that two macro definitions were used is that the essential process involved in the macro SAVE is to perform arithmetic on the stored binary value of I and then convert this value to character representation before substituting it. The binary operator backslash (\) is really just a binary-to-character-string conversion operator. It can, however, only be involved in a macro call. Therefore SAVE, to employ the backslash for conversion, must call a macro to do so.

The definition of SAV need not precede that of SAVE, but it must be defined before a call is issued to SAVE. In other words no macro call can be expanded and assembled if any of the expanded code contains a call on an undefined macro.

7-6 LIST-VALUED PARAMETERS

It is sometimes necessary to specify an actual parameter that contains delimiter characters. The most common example is a parameter that itself is a list of symbols separated by a delimiter. Suppose one wanted to be able to specify a list of constants to be substituted into a table of values created within a macro. If one tried to define

```
        .MACRO   TABLE,VALUES
TAB:    .WORD    157.,63.,0,VALUES,-16.
        .ENDM
```

                                      call
                              TABLE <10., 23., 119.>
                              to get expansion

to be called with

TABLE   10.,23.,119.   ← No

                              TAB: .WORD 157., 63., 0, 10., 23., 119., -16

intending that the expansion would be

TAB: .WORD   157.,63.,0,10.,23.,119.,-16.

then the expansion would not work correctly, since 10.,23.,119. appears to the assembler as a list of three distinct parameters.

To identify a parameter containing separator characters as a single symbol, it is enclosed in angle brackets < > within the macro call. For example, the problem above could be solved by calling the macro as follows:

TABLE   <10.,23.,119.>

A more realistic situation occurs where one uses a list-valued parameter within a .IRP directive inside a macro definition. This very conveniently allows the definition of macros with a variable number of parameters.

```
.MACRO  CALL  SUB  PARS
TST     -(SP)
.IF     NB,<PARS>
MOV     R0,-(SP)
MOV     SP,R0
.IRP    DUM,<PARS>
MOV     DUM,-(SP)
.ENDR
MOV     R0,-(SP)
.ENDC
JSR     R7,SUB
.IF     NB,<PARS>
MOV     (SP),SP
MOV     (SP)+,R0
.ENDC
.ENDM   CALL
```

(handwritten annotations: name, P', Pv; "If string of list-valued param PARS is NOT BLANK Then"; "push R0"; "pop R0"; "optional macro name")

Figure 7-4 A procedure call macro.

An excellent example can be seen in a macro to implement the call operation. Figure 7-4 shows a call macro which accepts a variable number of word parameters and which always expects a return code or value on the stack. It is the programmer's responsibility to remove the return value after the subroutine has returned.

A typical procedure call might then appear as

```
CALL   SUBR  <PAR1,PAR2,PAR3>
TST    (SP)+
BEQ    ERROR
```

(handwritten: "test remove return value from stack"; "if 0, go to error")

Notice that the .ENDM directive may contain the macro name for program readability and checking by the assembler.

We can also define macros for the procedure entry and return sequences. They may appear as shown in Fig. 7-5.

The macro PROCEDURE first saves a specified number of registers via the previously defined SAVE macro. The remainder of the macro defines a sequence of assembler symbols and assigns to them the values $-2, -4, -6, \ldots$. These assembler symbols are specified in the list parameter <PARMS> and can subsequently be used in conjunction with R0 to reference the procedure's parameters.

For example, the following procedure swaps the values of X and Y, where X and Y are dummy procedure parameters passed by address:

```
SWAP:   PROCEDURE  <X,Y>,1
        MOV  @X(R0),R1
        MOV  @Y(R0),@X(R0)
        MOV  R1,@Y(R0)
        RETURN  #1,1
```

(handwritten annotations: "params", "Reg"; "call M.1"; "call M.2"; "val regs")

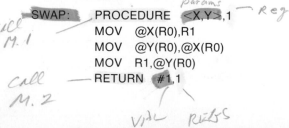

MACRO name

(Writing such a procedure to do this in practice is of course quite inefficient. A macro would be more appropriate.) This procedure could be called by

SUBR   *params*

CALL   SWAP   <#A,#B>   *call by ref./addr.*

To clarify what is happening let us look at the macro expansions. The definition of the procedure SWAP expands to

```
SWAP:    MOV  R1,-(SP)        save
         MOV  @-2(R0),R1
         MOV  @-4(R0),@-2(R0)    } swap + procedure
         MOV  R1,@-4(R0)
         MOV  #1,2(R0)        RETURN
         MOV  (SP)+,R1        RESTORE
         RTS  R7             RETURN
```

and the call to SWAP expands to

```
TST   -(SP)          MACRO 'CALL'
MOV   R0,-(SP)      > since <PARS> is NB (.IF)
MOV   SP,R0
MOV   #A,-(SP)      > (.IRP)
MOV   #B,-(SP)
MOV   R0,-(SP)      (.IF)
JSR   R7,SWAP   -   CALL
MOV   (SP),SP      > .IF NB <PARS)
MOV   (SP)+,R0
```

M.1

```
.MACRO    PROCEDURE    PARMS,REGS
.IF       NB,REGS        If regs are in m.call, save them p.162
SAVE      REGS
.ENDC                  and if parameters exist
.IF    NB,<PARMS>
PINDEX=-2
.IRP  PARDUM,<PARMS>
PARDUM=PINDEX
PINDEX=PINDEX -2
.ENDR
.ENDC
.ENDM  PROCEDURE
```

M.2

```
.MACRO    RETURN  VAL,REGS
MOV   VAL,2(R0)
.IF    NB,REGS
RESTORE  REGS    ; p.162
.ENDC
RTS   R7
.ENDM  RETURN
```

Figure 7-5 Procedure entry and return macros.

using ? LAB and .ENABL LSB

7-7 CREATED SYMBOLS

Since symbols within an assembled program must be unique, any local symbols created during a macro expansion must, of course, also be unique. It is possible for the macro designer to provide for the generation of unique local symbols. This can be done using conditional assembly and the backslash operator ($\setminus$) as in the following outline:

```
        .MACRO  CODE1,NUM
ML'NUM: CLR  R1
        .ENDM
```

unnecessary

```
        .MACRO  CODE2,NUM
        BEQ ML'NUM
        .ENDM


        .MACRO  EXAMPLE,X
           .
           .
           .
        .IF  NDF,L
        L=-1
        .ENDC
        L=L+1
        CODE1  \L
           .
           .
           .
        CODE2  \L
           .
           .
           .
        .ENDM
```

If L is NOT DEFINED) symbol define it
else INC it

   As you can see, this is awkward and difficult to read. Fortunately the assembler has a facility to generate unique symbols within a macro so that devices such as used above are unnecessary. To do this any symbol required to be unique is simply listed with the macro's dummy parameters and is preceded by a question character (?). Any dummy symbol so specified is replaced in the macro expansion by a unique symbol in the range 64$ to 127$. Such symbols are assigned in sequence starting with 64$, and so it is possible to generate up to 64 such symbols in a single assembly.

   For example, the code outline above could be replaced by

```
        .MACRO  EXAMPLE,X,?LAB
           .
           .
           .
```

.ENABL LSB (notes, p.90)

? ⟶ unique symbol

```
LAB:  CLR      R1
       .
       .
       .
      BEQ     LAB
       .
       .
       .
      .ENDM
```

no label

call: EXAMPLE, X

which on expansion as the result of the first call would yield

```
64$:  CLR   R1
       .
       .
       .
      BEQ   64$
```

Finally, an actual parameter can be passed, in a macro call, to a dummy created symbol. If it is not passed (the actual parameter is blank), a symbol is created. If it is passed, then the actual parameter overrides the generation of a created symbol and it is substituted normally. Thus the call

```
EXAMPLE  A,L1
```
← *actual param. overrides ? LAB*

causes L1 to be substituted for LAB.

7-8 SUBCONDITIONALS

.IFF, .IFT, .IFTF w/out .ENDC

Additional flexibility within conditional assembly blocks is provided by three *subconditional* directives. These directives, .IFF, .IFT, and .IFTF, can be used within an enclosing .IF . . . .ENDC construction. Their meaning is

.IFF   All code following this directive up to the next following subconditional or .ENDC is assembled if the condition tested in the enclosing .IF directive was false.
.IFT   The meaning is similar to .IFF with assembly occurring if the condition tested in the enclosing .IF directive was true.
.IFTF   The meaning is similar to .IFF with assembly occurring if the condition tested in the enclosing .IF directive was false or true.

For example,

```
.IF     EQ,X
         .
         .              } assembled if X=0
         .
```

.IF EQ,X [if X=0]

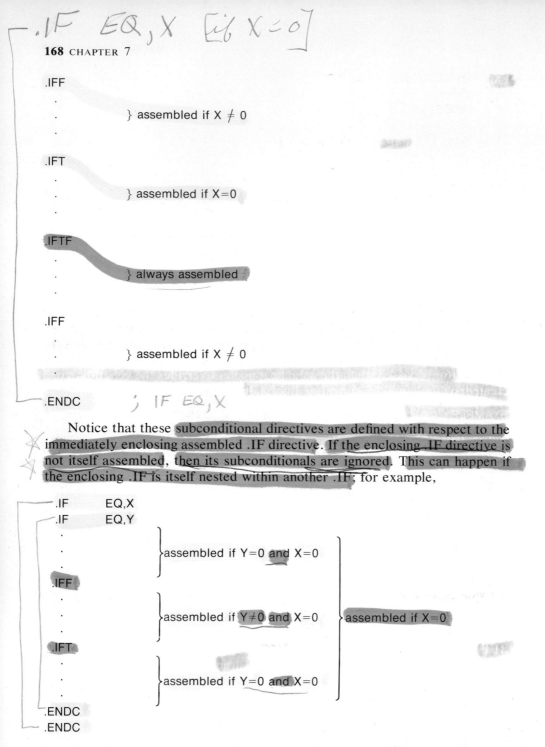

.IFF
.
. } assembled if X ≠ 0
.

.IFT
.
. } assembled if X=0
.

.IFTF
.
. } always assembled
.

.IFF
.
. } assembled if X ≠ 0
.

.ENDC   ; IF EQ,X

Notice that these subconditional directives are defined with respect to the immediately enclosing assembled .IF directive. If the enclosing .IF directive is not itself assembled, then its subconditionals are ignored. This can happen if the enclosing .IF is itself nested within another .IF; for example,

.IF   EQ,X
.IF   EQ,Y
.
.
. } assembled if Y=0 and X=0
.
.IFF
.
. } assembled if Y≠0 and X=0   } assembled if X=0
.
.IFT
.
. } assembled if Y=0 and X=0
.
.ENDC
.ENDC

Subconditionals can be used in the definition for TESTCODE given in Sec. 7-2 and shown in Fig. 7-6.

Although not entirely within the topic of this section it is appropriate to

```
.MACRO   TESTCODE,ERROR
TST   (SP)+
.IF    NB,ERROR
.IF    LT,254-.+ERROR
BNE   .+4
JMP   ERROR
.IFF
BNE   ERROR
.ENDC
.ENDC
.ENDM
```

[handwritten annotations:] If ERROR is passed and 254-.+ERROR < 0 ; BR to ___ if (SP) ≠ 0

Figure 7-6 The TESTCODE macro with subconditionals.

introduce an interesting use of macros at this point since we are discussing nested conditional assembly. This example uses the one-line .IFF directive as well as subconditionals. It is a macro called IF with seven parameters and two created symbols. Shown in Fig. 7-7, it allows the programmer to code an IF . . . THEN . . . ELSE control structure similar to that available in high-level languages.

One is limited to single statements for S1 and S2. Furthermore, statements containing delimiters must be enclosed in angle brackets. This particular defini-

[handwritten: name; P₁ P₂ P₃ opt; T; F; label; NB]

```
.MACRO IF A COND B THEN S1 ELSE S2 ?L  ?M
CINDEX=0
CMPB   A,B
.IRP   DUM,<EQ,LT,NE,GT>
.IF  IDN,COND,DUM
.IIF EQ,CINDEX,BNE L
.IIF EQ,CINDEX-1,BGE L
.IIF EQ,CINDEX-2,BEQ L
.IIF EQ,CINDEX-3,BLE L
.ENDC
CINDEX=CINDEX+1
.ENDR
S1
.IF NB,ELSE
BR  M
L:  S2
M:
.IFF
L:
.ENDC
.ENDM IF
```

[handwritten annotations:] logical opposites → if Cindex = 0 and A ≠ B, BR → L ; if cindex = 3, and A ≤ B, BR → L ; done if 'A cond B' is T ; If ELSE is passed, BRM & skip F statement ; If ELSE not passed (is B) go to L (1st instr outside macro) ; diff symbol created

Figure 7-7 The IF macro.

[handwritten: see notes p. ___ for cell & expansion]

tion restricts A and B to be byte operands. A different application may require word operands.

Another similar pair of macros can be defined to allow a sequence of statements to be conditionally executed.

```
.MACRO IF A COND B THEN GO TO L
    CMPB   A,B
    B'COND L
.ENDM
```

opt.

```
.MACRO  END IF
.ENDM
```

opt.

Both IF macros could not be used in the same assembly, of course, since their names conflict. The first macro might be used, along with END, as

```
    IF LASTCH EQ NEWLIN THEN <INC LINCNT> ELSE <JMP NXT>
        A    cond   B              S1 = T           S2 = F  do
    .    } code to process line of text
    .
NXT:  END IF   call to macro 'END' like NOP?)
```

The second version of IF might be used, assuming the same situation, as

```
    IF LASTCH NE NEWLIN THEN GO TO NXT
    .
    .    } code to process line of text
    .
NXT:  END IF   opt.
      INC LINCNT
```

The IF parameter on the call to END is purely for readability and adds nothing to the meaning of the construction.

7-9 TESTING ARGUMENTS   .NARG, .NCHR, .NTYPE

Three assembler directives enable the programmer to test the nature and number of the parameters supplied to a macro so that the expansion of the macro body can be altered depending on such information. The three directives are explained in turn.

.NARG   symbol   symbol ← #act. param. passed (to macro)

The assembler symbol specified is assigned a value equal to the number of actual parameters passed to the macro definition containing the .NARG directive.

.NCHR   symbol, string   —12345 or <1,2,3,4,5> } → symbol ← 5

symbol ← #char in the param 'string'

The assembler symbol specified is assigned a value equal to the number of characters in the string given as the second parameter of the .NCHR directive. If used within a macro definition the string can be a dummy parameter in which case it is replaced by the corresponding actual parameter before the .NCHR directive is carried out. The assembler, in executing a .NCHR directive, counts characters left to right in the string only up to a delimiter character. Therefore, strings with contained delimiters must be enclosed in angle brackets.

.NTYPE   symbol, parameter   *symbol ← low 6 bits of addr mode of 'param' operand*

The lower-order 6 bits of the assembler symbol specified are assigned a value equal to the addressing mode of the second parameter of the .NTYPE directive. The second parameter must therefore be a valid instruction operand symbol. If used within a macro definition the modes of an actual parameter can be tested by using its corresponding dummy parameter in an .NTYPE directive. Substitution, of course, occurs before the .NTYPE directive is executed.

Argument testing is often used in producing code that is optimized depending on the kind of addressing used. For example, autoincrement and autodecrement addressing can be used only with addresses stored in registers. Consider a character shift right (CSR) macro to take the following form

```
CSR     ADR,LEN
```

where ADR contains the address of the first character of a string of length given by LEN. The effect of calling CSR is to shift the string right one position.

If ADR is a register, we would like to generate something like

```
MOV     LEN,-(SP)        push LENGTH of string
ADD     LEN,ADR
MOVB    -(ADR),1(ADR)
DEC     (SP)
BNE     .-6
ADD     #2,SP            pop LEN
```

On the other hand, if ADR is not a register-mode operand, life is not quite so simple. The following code would be satisfactory for those cases in which another mode is used and it is difficult to determine which registers are in use and therefore unavailable for use in the macro.

```
MOV     R0,-(SP)
MOV     LEN,-(SP)
MOV     ADR,R0
ADD     (SP),R0
MOVB    -(R0),1(R0)
DEC     (SP)
BNE     .-6
ADD     #2,SP
MOV     (SP)+,R0
```

char. shift right macro

A macro definition to generate the two versions of code is

```
.MACRO   CSR,ADR,LEN
.NTYPE   MODE,ADR
.REG=70
.IF      EQ,MODE AND .REG
.IFF
MOV      R0,-(SP)
.IFTF
MOV      LEN,-(SP)
.IFT
ADD      LEN,ADR
MOVB     -(ADR),1(ADR)
.IFF
MOV      ADR,R0
ADD      (SP),R0
MOV      -(R0),1(R0)
.IFTF
DEC      (SP)
BNE      .-6
ADD      #2,SP
.IFF
MOV      (SP)+,R0
.ENDC
.ENDM
```

mode's bits 0-5 ← addr. mode of ADR
? if MODE ∧ 70 = 0, assemble all
if mode and .reg ≠ 0
in any case (always do)
M + R = 0
≠ 0
in any case
≠ 0

7-10 INDEFINITE ITERATION ASSEMBLY

, IF cond [then]
, MEXIT [skip out]

There is no explicit assembler directive for indefinite iteration of the assembly process. The programmer can, however, specify a premature exit from a definite iteration and thereby construct an indefinite iteration. This assembler directive is similar to the "escape" control structure appearing in high-level languages and appears as

`.MEXIT`

GO TO (instr after MACRO) early exit MACRO

It simply causes the assembler to stop expanding the macro body and to return to assembling the program. In other words, it is an "escape" from the macro definition.

7-11 NESTED MACRO DEFINITIONS

A macro definition may contain a macro definition. An inner macro definition, however, is not recognized by the assembler as a valid defined macro until its enclosing macro has been called. This is obviously true if one realizes that a macro body is not assembled until a call to the macro occurs. Any definitions in the macro body, therefore, are not recognized as such by the assembler until the macro body is being assembled.

A situation in which a nested macro definition might be useful occurs where a set of macros have been written but their names conflict with other symbols in a program in which they are to be used. The names of the macros can be conveniently changed without altering their coding. This might be done as follows:

```
.MACRO   MNAMES,N1,N2,---
.MACRO  N1,---
    .
    .
    .
.ENDM

.MACRO   N2,---
    .
    .
    .
.ENDM
    .
    .
    .
.ENDM
```

where the call

```
MNAMES   MAC1,MAC2,---
```

defines the macros with the new list of names specified.

7-12 RECURSIVE MACRO CALLS

Macros can be recursive; a macro definition can contain a call on itself. Care must be taken, of course, to ensure that the expansion of the macro body eventually terminates. This can be accomplished with a conditional assembly directive.

7-13 SYSTEM MACROS AND LISTING CONTROL

A library of predefined macros is usually available with an operating system. In order to make these stored macro definitions available to one's program, it is necessary to list all such macros within the .MCALL directive. Thus

```
.MCALL  .READ,.WRITE, .EXIT, .PRINT,
```

makes the two system macros .READ and .WRITE available. System macros in the PDP-11 RT-11 operating system all begin with a dot character (.) to avoid conflicts with user defined macros. For this reason programmers should avoid defining macros that start with the dot character.

Two directives permit programmer control of program listing. The .NLIST directive causes all specified aspects of listing to be suppressed. For example,

.NLIST ME,CND   *Don't list*

causes macro expansions (ME) and unsatisfied conditional code with .IF and .END directives (CND) to be suppressed. The .LIST directive causes all speci-fied aspects of listing to appear with the listing. For example

.LIST ME,CND   *List macro expansions*

causes macro expansions and unsatisfied conditional code to be listed.

There are many possible parameters for .LIST and .NLIST. The MACRO-11 manual should be consulted for a complete list and detailed explanations.

7-14 MACROS AND SUBROUTINES *see p. 71 + 125*

In Sec. 6-5 a binary-to-decimal conversion subroutine called BTOD was de-scribed. Then, in Exercise 6-5, it was coded using the general calling sequence. Suppose now that in the interest of speeding up calls on the conversion opera-tion it is to be coded as a macro. The listing below shows a possible definition where B contains the binary value and D contains the address of the last character position for the result: *ADR?*

BIN → DEC macro

```
1     000006    SP=%6
2     000002    R2=%2
3     000003    R3=%3
4     000004    R4=%4
5              ;
6              ;   THE FOLLOWING IS A BINARY TO DECIMAL
7              ;   CONVERSION MACRO DEFINITION
8              ;
9                  .MACRO  BTOD   BIN,ADR,?L
10                 MOV     R2,-(SP)      ;SAVE R2
11                 MOV     R3,-(SP)      ;SAVE R3
12                 MOV     BIN,R3        ; Store binary # → R3
13          L:     CLR     R2            ? R2÷10 → R2
14                 DIV     #10.,R2
15                 ADD     #48.,R3       offset = 60 octal
16                 MOVB    R3,@ADR
17                 DEC     ADR
```

```
18              ↗          MOV     R2,R3
19              ↙          BNE     L            If R3 ≠ 0, go to L?
20                         MOV     (SP)+,R3
21                         MOV     (SP)+,R2
22                         .ENDM
23                   ;
24                   ;  WHICH CAN BE CALLED BY THE FOLLOWING
25                   ;                                  44 → R4 → ADR
26 00000 012704            MOV     #A+4,R4
         000050'                         BIN #      ← no label passed
27 00004                   BTOD    X,R4          ADR
28                   ;
29                   ;  WITH THE FOLLOWING DEFINITIONS
30                   ;
31 00042 000000    X:  .WORD   0
32 00044     040   A:  .ASCII   /         /
   00045     040
   00046     040
   00047     040
   00050     040
33         000001'     .END
```

Example: A binary-to-decimal conversion macro

For comparison, the listing below shows the subroutine version of BTOD coded using the procedure entry and return macros which simply provide the correct code sequence for these operations.

```
1        000006           SP=%6        BIN → DEC   Subroutine
2        000000           R0=%0
3        000001           R1=%1                       ↓
4        000002           R2=%2
5        000003           R3=%3
6        000007           R7=%7
7                   ;                                    lines
8                         .MACRO    PROCEDURE PARMS,REGS
9                         .IF  :    NB,REGS
10                        SAVE      REGS      (macro call nested) (62-68)
11                        .ENDC
12                        .IF       NB,<PARMS>
13                        PINDEX=-2
14                        .IRP      PARDUM,<PARMS>
15                        PARDUM=PINDEX
16                        PINDEX=PINDEX-2
17                        .ENDR
                          .ENDC
                          .ENDM
```

Con't →

```
18                      .ENDC
19                      .ENDM     PROCEDURE
20           ;
21                      .MACRO    RETURN VAL,REGS
22                      MOV       VAL,2(R0)
23                      .IF       NB,REGS            (50-56)
24                      RESTORE   REGS
25                      .ENDC
26                      RTS       R7
27                      .ENDM     RETURN
28           ;
29                      .MACRO    CALL  SUB,PARS
30                      TST       -(SP)
31                      .IF       NB,<PARS>
32                      MOV       R0,-(SP)
33                      MOV       SP,R0
34                      .IRP      DUM,<PARS>
35                      MOV       DUM,-(SP)
36                      .ENDR
37                      MOV       R0,-(SP)
38                      .ENDC
39                      JSR       R7,SUB
40                      .IF       NB,<PARS>
41                      MOV       (SP),SP
42                      MOV       (SP)+,R0
43                      .ENDC
44                      .ENDM     CALL
45           ;
46                      .MACRO    REST,NUM
47                      MOV       (SP)+,R'NUM
48                      .ENDM
49           ;
50                      MACRO     RESTORE,REG
51                      I=REG
52                      .REPT     REG
53                      REST      \I              (46-48)
54                      I=I-1
55                      .ENDR
56                      .ENDM
57           ;
58                      .MACRO    SAV,NUM
59                      MOV       R'NUM,-(SP)
60                      .ENDM
61           ;
```

```
62                              .MACRO    SAVE,REG
63                              I=1
64                              .REPT     REG
65                              SAV       \I        (58-60)
66                              I=I+1
67                              .ENDR
68                              .ENDM
69                   ;                              <PARAMS>, REG
70 00000           BTOD:   PROCEDURE <BIN,ADR>,3    (8-19)
71 00006 016001            MOV       ADR(R0),R1
         177774
72 00012 005201            INC       R1
73 00014 016003            MOV       BIN(R0),R3
         177776
74 00020 005002 BTOD1:     CLR       R2
75 00022 071227            DIV       #10.,R2
         000012
76 00026 062703            ADD       #48.,R3
         000060
77 00032 110341            MOVB      R3,-(R1)
78 00034 010203            MOV       R2,R3
79 00036 001370            BNE       BTOD1
80 00040                   RETURN    0,3
81                 ;
82                 ;        WHICH CAN BE CALLED BY
83                 ;
84 00056                   CALL BTOD <X,#A+4>
85                 ;
86                 ;        WITH THE FOLLOWING DEFINITIONS
87                 ;
88 00106 000000 X:         .WORD     0
89 00110    040 A:         .ASCII    /        /
   00111    040
   00112    040
   00113    040
   00114    040
90       000001'           .END
```

SYMBOL TABLE

A	000110R	ADR	=	177774	BIN	= 177776
BTOD	000000R	BTOD1		000020R	I	= 000000
PINDEX=	177772	R0		=%000000	R1	=%000001

R2	=%000002	R3	=%000003	R7	=%000007
SP	=%000006	X	000106R		

```
. ABS.    000000    000
          000115    001
ERRORS DETECTED: 0
FREE CORE: 17823. WORDS
```

Example: A binary-to-decimal conversion subroutine

A call to the macro BTOD, therefore, assembles the number conversion code during translation. A call to the subroutine BTOD is implemented via a call to the macro CALL which assembles the calling sequence code during translation. The actual subroutine call, of course, occurs later at execution time. Finally, whether the number conversion code is implemented as a subroutine or as a macro the conversion itself is carried out at execution time! The difference in the two methods only involves the way in which the code receives control: in one case by a subroutine call and in the other case by sequential control flow.

Furthermore, whether or not control flow follows a subroutine call or sequential flow is not strictly dependent on the use of macros. One can easily define a macro that creates subroutine code with an associated call on its first expansion, and on subsequent expansions creates a subroutine call to that code. In this way, the user of such a macro may be unaware of the particular kind of code generated.

EXERCISES

7-1 Define macros PUSH, POP, PUSHB, and POPB to push and pop words and bytes respectively to and from the system stack.

7-2 Define a RESUME macro to use in implementing coroutines.

7-3 Define macros to read and write single characters from and to standard I/O devices.

7-4 Define a macro to write a line of output such that it calls the output macro of Exercise 7-3.

7-5 Give the macro definition for a macro MOVC (move characters) that is called with

```
MOVC    SRC,L,DST
```

where SRC is the address of the source operand, L is the length in bytes of the source operand, and DST is the address of the destination operand.

7-6 How many number conversions does the following code cause to occur at assembly time?

```
.MACRO  Z,NUM
MOV     R'NUM,-(SP)
.ENDM
I=1
.REPT   2
Z
I=I-1
.ENDR
```

7-7 If you have not already done so, improve your macro of Exercise 7-5 so that autoincrement mode can be used (without requiring register saving) where SRC and DST happen to be registers.

REFERENCES

This chapter has not attempted in any way to touch on the techniques of building a macro facility or, indeed, on some quite interesting applications of macros in areas other than systems programming. A more general treatment of macros in given in Strachey (1965), Brown (1974), and Mooers (1966). McIlroy (1960) discusses an interesting application of macros in extending high-level languages. The implementation and use of a macro facility for assembly-language programming is discussed in Greenwald (1959) and Kent (1969).

EIGHT

ASSEMBLER CONSTRUCTION

Assembling a program is the first step in transforming an assembly-language program into a form suitable for direct execution by the processor. Figure 8-1 shows the three steps of assembling, linking, and loading.

Assembling is a translation process from a source program into a machine-language program called an *object module*.[1] The source program may be input from cards or some other peripheral storage medium and the object module is usually output onto some internal memory device such as a magnetic tape. These memory devices are described in a later chapter. The object module usually contains a program whose addresses are relative to the beginning of the program. That is, the program is constructed on the assumption that it will occupy main memory locations zero and upward. An object module can also contain references to symbols outside itself. These references, called *external references,* are stored in a table with the object module to be resolved by the *linker*.

The linker accepts as input several object modules and combines them into a single machine-language program called a *load module*. Each unresolved external reference must be defined in one of the object modules of the linking step so that a load module contains no external references.

Finally, the *loader* accepts as input a load module and stores it into main memory. All relative addresses are *relocated* to reflect the actual location of the program in main memory. The location in the load module of addresses requiring relocation must be included with the load module. This information is initially supplied by the assembler.

[1] This module need not correspond to a module of the design specification.

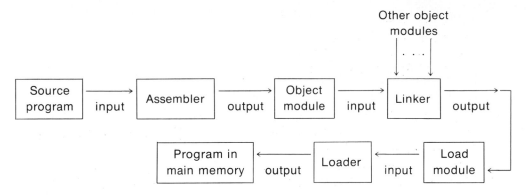

Figure 8-1 Transformations on a program.

A program progresses through four forms, each one being represented by a data structure with certain properties. We have already spent some time describing source programs and machine-language programs loaded in memory. A discussion of object and load modules appears in Chap. 9 on linking and loading. This chapter is concerned with the assembler and its principal internal data structure, the symbol table.

In discussing how to manage the symbol table we shall spend a considerable amount of time describing alternative data structures. Although many texts treat data structures as a separate topic, we have avoided this approach so that data structures are discussed in the context of the particular application. Therefore, since most students encounter data structures in a separate course, the material here should provide a good complement to such study without undue redundancy.

8-1 TWO-PASS ASSEMBLY

The heart of an assembler is its *symbol table* which contains the character string symbols of the program being assembled along with other information such as the types of symbols and their current value. Some of the various types of symbols encountered by the assembler are:

Symbol type	Possible value or other information
Instruction mnemonic	Operation code, instruction format
Assembler directive	Address of routine to carry out
Label	Relative address in program (integer)
Programmer defined	Integer
Register name	Integer
External reference	List of occurrences in program
Macro name	Macro definition

Not all information associated with a symbol is stored in the symbol table, since the different types require differing amounts of information. Usually each entry in the symbol table contains the symbol itself, its type, and a third field used either to store a value or to contain an address pointer to stored information.

In assembling a program a forward reference can be encountered. This is simply the occurrence in the program of an undefined symbol, as in a forward branch such as

        BR   HERE

            .

            .

            .

HERE:

When this happens the assembler cannot construct a relative address for the branch destination. An easy way out of the problem is to process the source program twice, once to fill the symbol table and once to actually translate the program. On the first pass the assembler searches the symbol table for each symbol, and if an entry is not already present, inserts one. On the second pass each statement's operation code is examined by obtaining its symbol table entry and the intended meaning is carried out. Figure 8-2 shows a simple two-pass-assembly algorithm.

```
pass1:  location_counter := 0;
        read first statement;
        WHILE operation is not .END DO BEGIN
            IF label present THEN
                IF label not in symbol table THEN
                    create symbol table entry with
                    value = location_counter
                ELSE flag symbol as multiply defined;
                location_counter := location_counter +
                                    statement length;
            read next statement END;
pass2:  location_counter := 0;
        read first statement;
        WHILE operation is not .END DO BEGIN
            get symbol table entry for operation;
            IF operation not defined THEN flag statement in error
            ELSE call operation procedure;
            { operation procedure carries out meaning
                    of statement and updates location_counter }
            read next statement END;
```

Figure 8-2 Two-pass assembly algorithm.

The algorithm of Fig. 8-2 can be easily modified so that all user-defined symbols rather than just labels are entered into the symbol table on the first pass. This has the advantage that the symbol table is completed before the second pass begins. It is then possible to sort the table before the second pass in order to facilitate searching. Most assemblers, in fact, complete the symbol table during the first pass in this way. In the rest of this chapter it is assumed that a two-pass assembler completes the symbol table after the first pass.

8-2 ONE-PASS ASSEMBLY

A program can be assembled in one pass by placing undefined labels into the symbol table and noting the location of the reference in the object module. When a label subsequently is defined, the assembler can construct the correct relative address at the point of reference. The situation of an undefined label can be depicted as shown in Fig. 8-3.

Since there may be several forward references to an undefined label, the assembler must be able to find all of these occurrences at the time the label is encountered. To do this the address field of the instruction containing the forward reference can be used during assembly to store the location of a previous forward reference to the same label. Thus, a chain of instructions containing forward references is obtained. When an undefined label is encountered in the symbol table, this chain can be followed to construct the proper addresses in the object module. The last instruction will contain a special value (perhaps negative) to indicate the end of the chain. This value is shown as the question mark (?) in Figs. 8-3 and 8-4.

One pass assembly is practical only where the entire object module can be stored in main memory. Otherwise it may be too time consuming to retrieve the

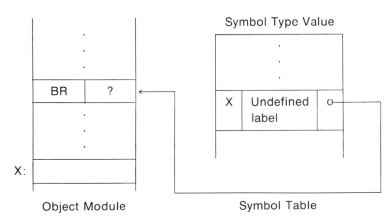

Figure 8-3 An undefined label during assembly.

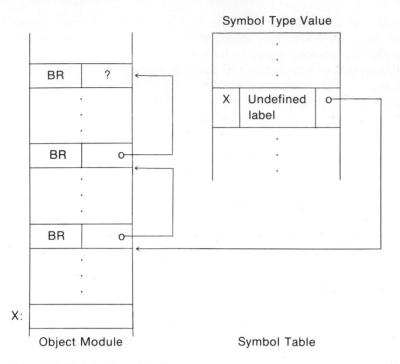

Figure 8-4 Chaining forward references.

program every time a forward reference chain is followed. In certain circumstances, however, a one-pass assembly can be faster than a two-pass assembly.

Figure 8-5 shows a simplified one-pass-assembly algorithm. A one-pass assembler does not, in general, complete the symbol table until assembly is finished. It cannot, therefore, take advantage of a single sort between phases, as can a two-pass assembler.

8-3 DESIGNING AN ASSEMBLER

In this section we will consider the design of a simple assembler. While a general algorithm will be presented and some examples of code written, many details will be left as exercises.

Suppose we are to write an assembler for a simplified version of the PDP-11 assembly language. A statement for our simple language will take one of four forms:

1. A single-address instruction
2. A two-address instruction
3. An assembler directive
4. An assignment

```
location_counter := 0;
read first statement;
WHILE operation is not .END DO BEGIN
    IF label present THEN
      IF label not in symbol table THEN
          create symbol table entry with
          value = location_counter
      ELSE IF label undefined THEN BEGIN
                  flag symbol table entry as defined;
                  save link to forward reference chain;
                  set value = location_counter;
                  insert value into instructions on
                  forward reference chain END
            ELSE flag symbol as multiply defined;
    get symbol table entry for operation;
    IF operation not defined THEN flag statement in error
    ELSE call operation procedure;
            {  The operation procedure carries out the
               meaning of the statement and updates the
               location_counter. Any undefined
               symbols encountered in operand
               fields are entered into the symbol
               table and flagged as undefined.  }
    read next statement END;
```

Figure 8-5 One-pass-assembly algorithm.

Statements of the first three forms may be preceded by a label followed by a colon character (:). Fields are separated by any number of blanks and the only separator required (other than the colon) is a comma between operands of a two-address instruction or assembler directive.

All symbols must be composed of at least one alphabetic character followed by alphanumeric characters up to a maximum of six characters total. Assembler directives all start with a dot character (.) in place of the required alphabetic character. To further simplify matters the location counter will be denoted by the reserved symbol LC. Also, the registers R0 through R7 are predefined symbols.

Allowable operand references will be the following (n and m represent constants):

Type of reference	Example(s)		
Immediate	#X	#n	
Relative	X		
Indexed	X(Rn)	m(Rn)	
Register	Rn		

Expressions will be allowed in assignments only. They will be evaluated from left to right with no parentheses allowed. The operators plus (+) and minus (−) are the only ones allowed.

Since a one-pass assembler is quite easy to write if one can put the entire object program in main memory, this route is chosen for our exercise. Assuming this to be the case, then, we can start with the algorithm seen below. The term *symbol* in the algorithm loosely refers to the primitive strings making up a program: labels, operations, operand addresses, and the separators comma and colon. These are sometimes referred to as *tokens* when translators are discussed:

```
{ one pass assembly algorithm }
initialize source text for reading;
REPEAT
    read next line of source;
    position current character reference at first
        non-blank character;
    IF current character is "." THEN handle directive
    ELSE BEGIN
        scan to character following next symbol;
        IF current character is "=" THEN handle assignment
        ELSE IF current character is not ":" THEN
                handle instruction
            ELSE BEGIN
                handle label;
                scan to non-blank character following ":";
                IF current character is "." THEN
                    handle directive
                ELSE BEGIN
                    scan to character following next symbol;
                    handle instruction END END END
UNTIL a .END directive was just handled;
issue message for any symbols not defined
```

Each of the English statements represents required further refinements in our algorithm. In particular, "scan to character following next symbol" simply examines the character string from the current character on and positions the current character reference to the first nonblank character following a valid symbol. Thus blanks are simply ignored and the syntax of symbols is checked. In the algorithm one can see that there are just three possibilities for this refinement to check: a symbol beginning an assignment, a label, and an instruction mnemonic. All of these must conform to the same syntax rules.

To make the description more precise, assume that the line of source text can be referenced by the array name ln. Also, the index of the current character will be denoted by c. After the advancement of c to the nonblank character following a symbol, the symbol just scanned will be found via the two indices f and l, which reference, respectively, the first and last character of this symbol.

With these additional specifications in mind "scan to character following next symbol" is refined to the following:

```
{ scan to character following next symbol}
f := c;
IF In[c] is not alphabetic THEN  BEGIN
    write "symbol error";
    escape to end of outer repeat loop END
ELSE  BEGIN
    WHILE In[c] is alphanumeric DO c:= c + 1 ;
    IF c <= f + 6 THEN I := c − 1
    ELSE  BEGIN
      I := f + 5;
      write "symbol truncated" END
    WHILE In[c] = blank DO c := c + 1
END
```

Before we proceed with further refinements, the content of the symbol table needs to be considered. In particular, we need to identify the types of entries and their associated values. For these we can choose the following:

Entry type	Code	Value
Instruction mnemonic	6	Binary op code
Directive mnemonic	4	Address of assembler routine
Program defined	2	Integer
Undefined	0	Nil

Entries in the symbol table, then, have three components: a six-character symbol, a type, and a value. The decision as to the type code can be made at this point as shown above, but more-detailed implementation of the table is best left until later.

The necessity of deciding on the content of the symbol table, of course, comes from the requirement for further refinements to the algorithm to access the table. Thus, a reasonable next step is to decide on the operations to be used to do this. Five operations on the symbol table that provide the needed function are: a search of the table for an entry corresponding to a given symbol, an insertion of a newly referenced symbol, a retrieval of a value from a specified entry, an insertion of a new value in a specified entry, and the definition of a forward-referenced symbol.

These five operations can be defined as procedures first, and if they are more naturally functions, then they can be implemented as such later. The first is the table search procedure:

```
search( f,l: INTEGER;
        VAR typ,val,ind: INTEGER) ; . . .
```

which examines the table for the symbol delineated by ln[f] through ln[l] and returns in typ, val, and ind the entry's type, value, and position in the table respectively. A negative value returned in ind indicates that no entry was found.

Second, to enter a new symbol the procedure

```
enter( f,l,type,val: INTEGER;
        VAR ind: INTEGER;
        VAR err: BOOLEAN) ; . . .
```

makes a new entry for the symbol delineated by ln[f] through ln[l] and inserts typ and val into the type and value components. If the symbol was previously referenced by the program (an undefined entry exists in the table), then ind returns the relative location in the object program of the last address in the forward-reference chain; otherwise it returns a negative value. The existence of a defined entry for the symbol causes err to return TRUE; otherwise it returns FALSE.

Next, two procedures

```
getval( i: INTEGER;
        VAR val: INTEGER ) ; . . .
```

and

```
storeval( i,val: INTEGER) ; . . .
```

retrieve a value from the entry at position i and store a new value into entry i respectively.

Finally, to define a symbol that is encountered in a forward reference we have

```
define( i,typ: INTEGER) ; . . .
```

which stores typ into the type component of entry i.

It can be assumed that the symbol table is initialized with entries for each instruction mnemonic and directive mnemonic.

Now with the symbol table sufficiently described, the algorithm can be refined to a greater level of detail. The statement "handle label" uses f and l, which locate the label to be defined, and c, which points to the following colon character (:). These indices are not to be altered by the statement. A possible refinement is

```
{ handle label }
enter(f,l,2,location_counter,ind,err);
IF err THEN write "multiply defined symbol"
ELSE IF ind >= 0 THEN handle forward reference
```

The statement "handle assignment" uses f and l, which locate the symbol to receive a value, and c, which points at the following equal sign (=). Its refinement can become

```
{ handle assignment }
evaluate expression and store in temp;
IF ln[f]='L' AND ln[l]='C' AND l=f+1 THEN
   location_counter := temp
ELSE BEGIN
    search(f,l,typ,val,ind);
    IF ind < 0 THEN enter(f,l,2,temp,ind,err)
    ELSE IF typ = 2 THEN storeval(ind,temp)
          ELSE IF typ = 0 THEN
                   write "cannot assign to label"
          ELSE write "cannot redefine mnemonic"
END
```

Important to notice in this handling of assignments is the fact that a forward reference to a symbol defined via an assignment is assumed to be an error by assigning to a label. In other words, forward references are only allowed to labels. Consequently, the output parameters ind and err (designed to be used for handling labels) are not used in the call to enter as it is called after determining that no entry exists.

Next, the statement "handle directive" starts with c pointing at a dot character (.). Its refinement is

```
{ handle directive }
c := c + 1;
scan to character following next symbol;
search(f,l,typ,val,ind);
IF ind < 0 OR typ < > 4 THEN write "invalid directive"
ELSE branch to directive routine val
```

where the directive routine is entered with c pointing at the first character of the parameters.

Finally, remaining at the first level of refinements is "handle instruction," which starts with f and l delineating the mnemonic and c pointing at the first character of the operand field(s):

```
{ handle instruction }
search(f,l,typ,val,ind);
IF ind < 0 OR typ <> 6 THEN write "invalid instruction"
ELSE BEGIN
    store val into object program;
    { val is a 16-bit integer that is stored in the
      word given by location_counter. The left-most
      bits represent the operation code. }
    IF val is a branch instruction THEN handle branch
    ELSE IF val is a single address instruction THEN
             handle single address
          ELSE handle two address
END
```

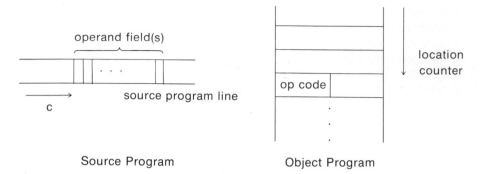

Figure 8-6 Data structures beginning instruction assembly.

All the difficult refinements have now been made to the first level of the assembler algorithm. The other refinements, such as checking at the end for undefined symbols, can easily be taken care of at a later time. In refining this first level it was necessary to design the symbol table structure. Now to further refine the statements that have been created at the second level, we encounter the other major data structure involved, the object program. Figure 8-6 shows the situation at the time that the instruction handling routines in the assembler are entered. The index c points to the first character of the operand field(s) in the source program and location_counter, also an index, references a word in the object program containing a left-adjusted operation code. Since the instructions that are to be supported by this simple assembler have not been specified as yet, we still have some freedom to simplify matters. To minimize the complexity, then, assume that the only instructions to be supported are branches, which have an 8-bit code; single-address instructions, with a 10-bit code; and two-address instructions with a 4-bit code.

The next level of refinement can now begin. Single-address instructions are perhaps the best place to start due to their relative simplicity. Consequently, the statement "handle single address" is next refined. To simplify this and later algorithms the procedure

```
address(c: INTEGER;
        VAR a,x: INTEGER;
        VAR b:BOOLEAN ) ; . . .
```

will be defined to accept an operand string, starting at ln[c], and to return a right-justified 6-bit address in a and, if necessary, a 16-bit index word in x. It will be assumed in address that the index word will immediately follow the location counter in calculating x. A TRUE value in b indicates the presence of the index word; otherwise b is FALSE. The index c will be advanced to the first nonblank character following the operand string. A negative value in a will signal an invalid operand. In this case the procedure will have the responsibility of issuing the error message. With this procedure we have

```
{ handle single address }
address(c,a,x,b);
IF a >= 0 THEN BEGIN
   insert right-most 6 bits of a
      into word given by location_counter;
   IF b THEN BEGIN
      location_counter := location_counter + 2;
      insert x into word given
         by location_counter END END;
   location_counter := location_counter + 2
```

Procedure address is the heart of this assembler. Here an instruction operand is decoded and the proper addressing mode for the instruction created. In our present case this task is not too complex as there are just six possibilities for an operand: immediate constant, immediate symbol, constant indexed, symbol indexed, register, and relative. The general structure for address, then, might be

```
address(c: INTEGER;
        VAR a,x: INTEGER;
        VAR b:BOOLEAN ) ;
BEGIN
   b := FALSE;
   IF ln[c] = '#' THEN
      IF ln[c+1] is a digit THEN      immediate constant
                          ELSE      immediate symbol
   ELSE IF ln[c] is a digit THEN constant indexed
           ELSE BEGIN scan to character
                        following next symbol;
           IF symbol is a register THEN register mode
           ELSE IF ln[c] = '(' THEN     symbol indexed
                        ELSE               relative   END
END
```

For illustration, let us look at the statement "immediate symbol." It could be written as

```
BEGIN
a := autoincrement on the PC code;
b := TRUE;
c := c + 1;
scan to character following next symbol;
search(f,l,typ,val,ind);
IF ind < 0 THEN start a forward reference chain
ELSE IF typ = 6 OR typ = 4 THEN issue error
ELSE IF typ = 0 THEN put on forward reference chain
ELSE x := val
END
```

which could be directly expanded to

```
BEGIN
    a := autoincrement on the PC code;
    b := TRUE;
    c := c + 1;
    scan to character following next symbol;
    search(f,l,typ,val,ind);
    IF ind < 0 THEN  BEGIN
      { start a forward reference chain }
      enter(f,l,0,location_counter+2,ind,err);
      x := 0 END
    ELSE  IF typ = 6 OR typ = 4 THEN  BEGIN
      { issue error }
      write "invalid symbol";
      a := − 1 END
    ELSE  IF typ = 0 THEN  BEGIN
      { put on forward reference chain }
      x := val;
      storeval(ind,location_counter+2) END
    ELSE x := val
END
```

where a zero is used to mark the end of the forward-reference chain.

The remainder of the assembler implementation is left as an exercise. Sufficient detail has been given to make this a reasonable task. What is required is to refine all remaining English statements and then to put all the code together into a well-commented program. Finally, of course, it should be tested. In completing the program, one should not forget the simplifying assumptions that have made it somewhat simpler than an assembler required for practical use. First, as pointed out earlier, we have avoided complications by assuming that the entire object program will fit into main memory. Second, not explicitly mentioned before, this object program is assembled relative to word zero and is not relocatable.

8-4 INTERPRETATION AND TRANSLATION

Assembly-language statements fall into two important categories: those that are *translated* into machine code and those that are *interpreted* by the assembler. The meaning of translated statements is carried out much later by the program as it executes the loaded program. For example,

INC I

causes the contents of the location named by the symbol I to be increased by 1 during execution.

The meaning of interpreted statements is carried out as they are encountered during assembly. For example,

```
I=I+1
```

causes the translation time value of the symbol I to be increased by 1 at the time the assembler encounters this statement.

Statement translation can involve some interpretation of the source program code. A statement such as

```
ADD   #L1−L2−2,R0
```

is translated into a PDP-11 ADD instruction. But before that can be completed, the meaning of the expression #L1−L2−2 must be interpreted. Therefore, the assembler must contain an expression evaluation interpreter that can be invoked by its instruction translation routines.

Conversely, statement interpretation can involve some translation, since not only are assembler actions carried out but object module code may be produced. The simplest case of this is a statement involving the location counter, such as

```
.=.+6
```

which simply adds 6 to its value but which also causes 6 bytes to be reserved in the object module.

8-5 SYMBOL TABLE ORGANIZATION

In designing a data structure to be processed by a known algorithm, one must first examine the operations to be performed on the structure so that it may suit the algorithm. In the case of the assembly algorithm, fairly tough requirements are placed on the symbol table organization.

Consider a one-pass assembler. First, the assembler starts with a symbol table containing the predefined symbols such as the operation codes. It then proceeds to assemble the program during which process it must *search* the symbol table for symbols encountered and, for those symbols not present, it must *insert* a new entry into the table. Searches are necessary both to define a symbol and to find the value of a symbol used as an operand by a statement. In the case of a search to define a symbol, the entire table must be examined to ensure that the symbol is not multiply-defined. Therefore, the time required to search the entire table is of concern, since this occurs very frequently.

Second, the assembler is usually required to list the symbol table along with the program. Such a listing normally contains all user-defined symbols in alphabetical order. Thus, the assembler must *sort* a portion of the symbol table.

In designing a symbol table one is concerned with efficient searching, insertion, and sorting. Certain information about the entries is available which can help in the design process. For example, the instruction operation code mnemonics are referenced most often and could be examined first in a search. The assembler directives could be searched next, followed by system and user-defined macro names. The MACRO-11 assembler, for example, separates user-defined symbols, macro names, and permanent symbols (instruction operand codes and directives).

Since insertions into the table occur very often during assembly, this operation must be relatively fast. This can lead to the conclusion that maintaining a sorted table during assembly is impractical, since inserting entries in a linear sorted table is a time-consuming process. There are, however, other methods than linear of storing table entries. Some of these are examined in the following section. Of course, two-pass assembly is one solution to this problem.

After taking into consideration practical factors such as the separation of the various kinds of symbols, the alternatives that are available for organizing the table for one-pass assembly are:

1. Linear storage with sorting after assembly
2. Nonlinear unsorted storage with sorting after assembly
3. Nonlinear sorted storage with no postsorting required

Each of these is examined in the following sections under the titles of linear storage, hashing, and tree storage, respectively. In these sections it is assumed that the entire symbol table is stored in main memory (the usual case) so that the methods discussed are limited to the so-called "internal" sorting and searching techniques.

Since the two-pass assembler is probably more common than the one-pass, the influence of using two passes on the symbol table organization is discussed under each of the three methods in the following sections.

8-6 LINEAR STORAGE

The simplest way of organizing a symbol table is linear; entries are simply assigned sequential positions in memory, independent of the symbol within the entry.

8-6.1 Linear Insertions

Using linear storage, insertions are trivial. New entries are simply added on to the end of the table. This is the fastest of all insertion methods.

8-6.2 Linear Searching

The only practical way to search a linear unsorted table is by scanning sequentially starting at the first entry (or the last, perhaps). This requires an average of N/2 comparisons for a table of N entries equiprobably positioned. Placing certain highly probable symbols at the beginning can reduce this average considerably, however.

A sequential search is quite efficient for very short tables of unordered entries. For longer tables of the size encountered in a symbol table, however, it is not an efficient method from the point of view of time. From a programming viewpoint it is easy but, of course, assemblers are only implemented once for much repetitive use, so this is not an important factor.

Note also that the number of comparisons required to discover that an entry is not in the table is N, twice the average number required. This is important because such a search occurs quite often in assembly, once for every undefined symbol.

8-6.3 Sorting a Linear Table

A linear unordered symbol table must be sorted for listing. We can store a symbol table as a two-dimensional array, each row corresponding to a symbol and each column corresponding to an item of data. In such a table it is common to refer to the rows as *records* and the columns as *fields*. In the case of the symbol table there may be three fields, the symbol itself, its type, and a value which may simply be a reference to additional data stored elsewhere. We want to order the table on the symbol field. Such a field, on which ordering is based is called the *key*.

The sorting methods presented here are of general interest and are not limited to the context of symbol tables for assemblers. Because of the nature of this text, however, and the importance of sorting as a programmer's tool, it seems appropriate to place a general presentation of sorting at this point.

In sorting a table, records are interchanged and moved about until ordering is achieved. If records are very short, the work involved in moving them may not be great. However, one does not usually wish to move records until their final position is determined, whereupon only one move is required. If an extra POINTER field is added to the table and initialized with the index of the record, then only the POINTER and the key need be moved during the sorting. Once the keys are in order, the remaining fields can be moved into order.

Pointer	Symbol	Type	Value
1	LAB1	Label defined	4
2	LAB2	Label undefined	—
3	COUNT	User symbol	1

In discussing sorting algorithms here, only the key field of each record will be shown. It should not be forgotten that, in general, records may contain several fields. Also, integer-valued keys rather than alphanumeric symbols are used for conciseness.

Performance measures used to describe algorithms do not usually depend on the particular machines which may be used to execute the algorithms. Thus, machine-independent comparisons are possible. In comparing algorithms within the context of a particular machine, other factors may need to be considered. Sorting algorithms are usually analyzed with respect to three performance measures:

1. The number of comparisons required to sort N records
2. The number of extra storage locations required to sort N records
3. The number of data movements required to sort N records

Selection sort. The selection sort proceeds by scanning all N keys to find the smallest key, which is then exchanged with the first key. This procedure is repeated on the remaining $N - 1$ keys, the smallest of the $N - 1$ keys being exchanged with the second key. The process is repeated $N - 1$ times, examining one fewer keys each time. Figure 8-7 shows the order of the keys after each scan.

The number of comparisons performed during each scan is $N - 1, N - 2,$ . . . , 3, 2, 1. Thus the total number of comparisons is

$$\sum_{i=1}^{N-1} i = \frac{N(N-1)}{2}$$

The number of locations required for keys is N, and since two keys are moved on each pass, $2(N - 1)$ data moves are required.

The selection sort always requires $N - 1$ scans because there is no consideration given to the possibility of a partially sorted table. The next sort to be described requires fewer scans if the table is partially sorted.

Bubble sort. The bubble sort proceeds by initializing a flag to 0 and scanning the table, comparing adjacent keys. Each pair of adjacent keys that is not ordered is exchanged. The flag is set to 1 when an exchange occurs. If, on com-

```
99  15  15  15  15  15  15  15  15  15
73  73  16  16  16  16  16  16  16  16
25  25  25  19  19  19  19  19  19  19
45  45  45  45  21  21  21  21  21  21
53  53  53  53  53  25  25  25  25  25
15  99  99  99  99  99  45  45  45  45
21  21  21  21  45  45  99  45  45  45
45  45  45  45  45  45  45  99  53  53
19  19  19  25  25  53  53  53  99  73
16  16  73  73  73  73  73  73  73  99
                                    └─sorted down to here
```

Figure 8-7 Selection sort.

```
99  73  25  25  25  15  15  15  15  15̅
73  25  45  45  15  21  21  19  16  16
25  45  53  15  21  25  19  16  19  19
46  53  15  21  45  19  16  21  21  21
53  15  21  45  19  16  25  25  25  25
15  21  45  19  16  45  45  45  45  45
21  45  19  16  45  45  45  45  45  45
45  19  16  53  53  53  53  53  53  53
19  16  73  73  73  73  73  73  73  73
16  99  99  99  99  99  99  99  99  99
flag ──→1   1   1   1   1   1   1   1   0
sorted up to here
```

Figure 8-8 Bubble sort.

pletion of the scan, the flag is 1 the process is repeated. Otherwise, the sort is completed. The scan is shortened by 1 on each pass as the table becomes ordered from the bottom up. Figure 8-8 shows the order of the keys and the value of the flag after each scan.

In this example $N - 1$ scans are required, because the key 16, the second smallest, was initially in the last position. The last scan may be required to discover that the keys are ordered, but no more than $N - 1$ scans are ever necessary.

Analysis of the bubble sort is difficult because the algorithm depends on the initial ordering of the keys. This is true of any good sorting algorithm, all of which are *adaptive algorithms*. That is, their performance depends on (or adapts to) the data being processed.

In analysing an adaptive sorting algorithm it is important to know the initial distribution of the keys. In the absence of other information, one can assume that all orderings are equally likely; or one can analyze the worst case.

The worst-case analysis for the bubble sort shown above is very easy. At most $N - 1$ scans are required; this will occur if the smallest key is initially in the last position. Each scan requires successively fewer comparisons so that the total number of comparisons is

$$(N-1) + (N-2) + \cdots + 2 + 1 = \frac{N(N-1)}{2}$$

The maximum number of exchanges that can occur on each successive scan is $N - 1, N - 2, \ldots, 2, 1$. Therefore, the total maximum number of data moves is

$$2 \times \sum_{i=0}^{N-1} i = 2\frac{N(N-1)}{2} = N(N-1)$$

Only N storage locations for keys are required.

```
99  73  25  25  25  15  15  15  15  15
73  99  73  45  45  25  21  21  19  16
25  25  99  73  53  45  25  25  21  19
45  45  45  99  73  53  45  45  25  21
53  53  53  53  99  73  53  45  45  25
15  15  15  15  15  99  73  53  45  45
21  21  21  21  21  21  99  73  53  45
45  45  45  45  45  45  45  99  73  53
19  19  19  19  19  19  19  19  99  73
16  16  16  16  16  16  16  16  16  99
```

sorted

Figure 8-9 Improved bubble sort.

The average-case analysis for the bubble sort is more difficult.[1] It can be shown that the average number of comparisons is

$$N^2 - 1.25N^{3/2} - N + 1.25N^{1/2}$$

The bubble sort can be improved as follows: Each time two adjacent keys are found unordered, say, K1 > K2, they are not directly exchanged. Rather, the smaller of the two keys K2 is moved closer to the beginning of the table by successively comparing it with keys above its position until a key, say K3, is found such that K3 ≤ K2. Intervening keys including K1 are moved down and K2 is inserted following K3.

This improved bubble sort is illustrated in Fig. 8-9. Each column shows the table after a single exchange has been performed.

In the worst case the smaller of the two adjacent keys will always be moved into the first position. The number of comparisons required during each exchange is then 2, 3, . . . , $N - 1$, N, which is[2]

$$\sum_{i=2}^{N} i = \frac{(N+2)(N-1)}{2}$$

The maximum number of data moves required on each scan is also

$$2, 3, \ldots, N-1, N = \frac{(N+2)(N-1)}{2}$$

The average-case analysis of the improved bubble sort yields, for the number of comparisons, the expression $(N + 4)(N - 1)/4$.

Notice that the dominant term in all the expressions for the number of com-

---

[1] See Stone (1975), p. 252.
[2] The general formula is

$$\sum_{i=0}^{n} (a + bi) = a(n + 1) + \frac{bn}{2}(n + 1)$$

```
99  45  45  45  45  21  21  19  15  15  15  15  15
73  73  19  19  19  19  19  21  19  16  16  16  16
25  25  25  16  15  15  15  15  21  19  19  19  19
45  45  45  45  45  45  25  25  25  21  21  21  21
53  53  53  53  53  53  53  53  53  25  25  25  25
15  15  15  15  16  16  16  16  16  53  45  45  45
21  21  21  21  21  45  45  45  45  45  53  53  45
45  99  99  99  99  99  99  99  99  99  73  53
19  19  73  73  73  73  73  73  73  73  99  73
16  16  16  25  25  25  45  45  45  45  45  45  99
```

Figure 8-10 Shell sort.

parisons is N^2, although in the average case this term is $N^2/4$ for the improved sort and N^2 for the simple sort. For large tables, then, the improved sort is about four times faster if all orderings of the keys are equally alike.

Shell sort. The shell sort is a modified version of the *improved* bubble sort described previously. The table to be sorted is repeatedly scanned as in the bubble sort, but instead of comparing adjacent keys this algorithm compares keys that are a distance D apart. On comparing two unordered keys K1 and K2 such that K1 > K2, K2 is moved closer to the beginning of the table by successively comparing it with keys in positions D above, $2D$ above, . . . , etc., until a position is found as in the bubble sort. The value of D is decreased on each successive scan.

Values of D can be chosen in several ways. One good way is the following: If Di is the value of D on the ith scan, then make $D1 = 2^{k-1}$ where $2^k < N \leqslant 2^{k+1}$. On successive passes take $Di = (Dj/2)\text{MOD }1$ where $j = i - 1$. In the table used in the previous examples $N = 10$ and therefore $k = 3$. The successive values of D are 7, 3, and 1.

The shell sort is illustrated in Fig. 8-10. Each column shows the table after a single exchange has been performed.

The average number of comparisons required for the shell sort is not known, but experiments show that the number is approximately proportional to $N \log N$ for large N.† The shell sort, therefore, is faster than the sorts described previously, all of which required a number of comparisons proportional to N^2.

Tree sort. This section describes a very interesting, and fast, sorting method. Before describing the algorithm, however, a new data structure is introduced.

Keys stored sequentially in a table can be interpreted as forming a structure called a *tree*. The diagram on the right of Fig. 8-11 shows a tree formed by the keys in the table shown on the left.

A tree is composed of records called *nodes*. Each node in the diagram is

---

† Unless otherwise noted, logarithms are to the base two.

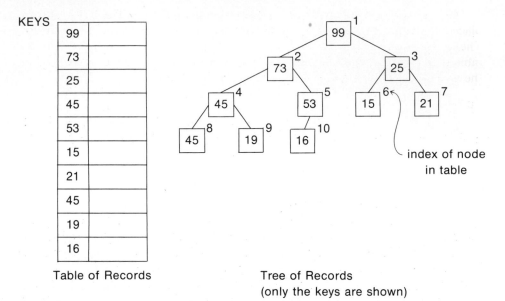

KEYS

99	
73	
25	
45	
53	
15	
21	
45	
19	
16	

Table of Records

Tree of Records
(only the keys are shown)

index of node
in table

Figure 8-11 A tree data structure.

labeled with its corresponding index in the table. Each node in a tree may have a *predecessor* node and one or two *successor* nodes.

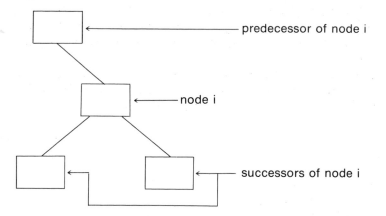

predecessor of node i

node i

successors of node i

The index of the predecessor of node i is $\lfloor i/2 \rfloor$ (where the notation $\lfloor k \rfloor$ denotes the integer part of k). The indices of the successors of node i are $2i$ and $2i + 1$.

For example, the key 45 is stored in node 4. The predecessor of node 4, node $4/2 = 2$, has a value of 73. The successors of node 4, node $2 \cdot 4 = 8$ and node $2 \cdot 4 + 1 = 9$, have values 45 and 19, respectively.

The tree shown has the property that the value of a node is greater than or equal to the value of its successors. Thus, for node 4, $73 \geqslant 45$, $45 \geqslant 45$, and $45 \geqslant 19$ are true. We shall refer to such a tree as a *proper tree*.

Of course not every table of keys forms a proper tree. The keys must be placed so that predecessor and successor nodes have the ordering relationship. The tree sort proceeds in two steps. First, a proper tree is constructed from the table given to be sorted. Second, the table is sorted using a method based on the tree structure. The algorithm is described as follows:

1. Given a table with N records, construct a proper tree such that each node, in key value, is greater than or equal to its successors. That is,

$$KEY[i] \geqslant KEY[2i]$$

and $\qquad KEY[i] \geqslant KEY[2i + 1] \qquad$ for all i

The tree is constructed by adding new nodes one at a time. As each new node is added, its value is compared with that of its predecessor and exchanged with it if necessary. If an exchange occurs, then the new value is compared with that of the predecessor of its current position to see whether another exchange must be made. The process of comparing and exchanging continues until a place is found for the new value at a node within the tree such that it is less than or equal to the value of its predecessor

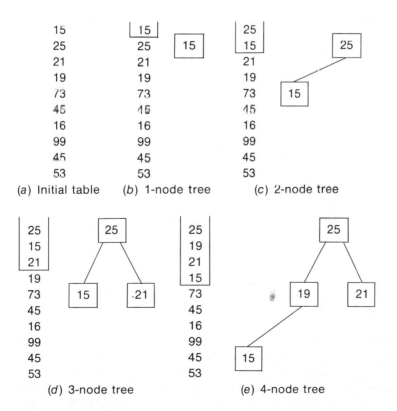

(a) Initial table   (b) 1-node tree   (c) 2-node tree

(d) 3-node tree   (e) 4-node tree

Figure 8-12a to e Tree construction.

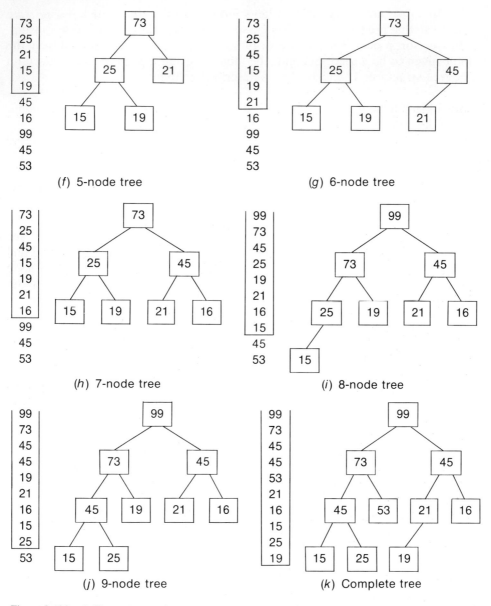

(f) 5-node tree

(g) 6-node tree

(h) 7-node tree

(i) 8-node tree

(j) 9-node tree

(k) Complete tree

Figure 8-12f to k Tree construction.

2. Once the tree has been constructed, the table is sorted by comparing "top down" within the tree as follows: Set I equal to N. The largest key value in the table is KEY[1]. Interchange KEY[1] and KEY[I]. The largest key value is now KEY[I]. Consider the tree consisting of the first $I - 1$ keys in the table. Set TEMP equal to KEY[1]. The larger of KEY[2] and KEY[3] is moved into KEY[1] if it is larger than TEMP. The larger of the two succes-

sors of the KEY just moved is moved into its place if it is greater than TEMP. Successors are moved up in this way until no move takes place, at which time the key in TEMP is moved into the unoccupied node. The process is repeated for $I = N - 1, N - 2, \ldots, 3, 2$.

The tree construction algorithm is illustrated in Fig. 8-12a to k, and the sorting algorithm operating on this tree is shown in Fig. 8-13a to j.

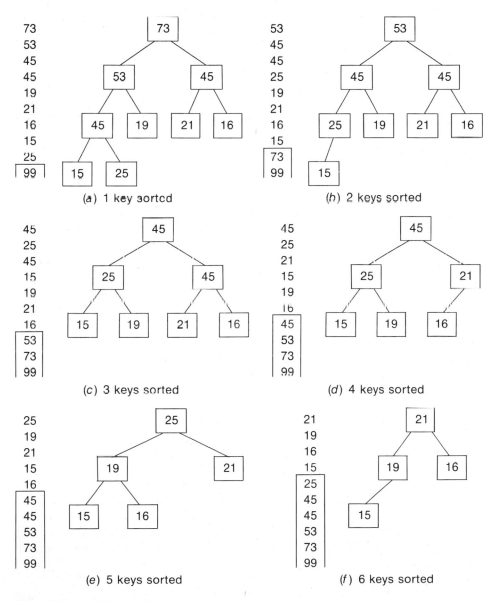

(a) 1 key sorted

(b) 2 keys sorted

(c) 3 keys sorted

(d) 4 keys sorted

(e) 5 keys sorted

(f) 6 keys sorted

Figure 8-13a to f Tree sorting.

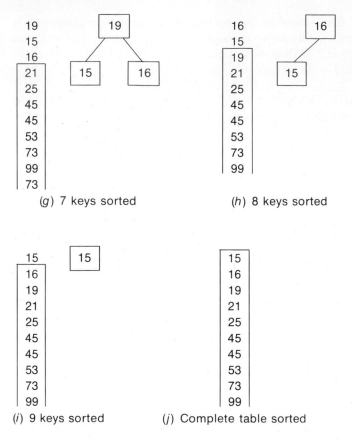

(g) 7 keys sorted   (h) 8 keys sorted

(i) 9 keys sorted   (j) Complete table sorted

Figure 8-13g to *j* Tree sorting.

It can be shown that the maximum number of comparisons in the tree sort is proportional to $N \log N$. That is, this worst-case performance measure for the tree sort is better than the corresponding average-case measure for the improved bubble sort described previously. The number of data moves required for the tree sort is also proportional to $N \log N$. As with the other sorts, only N storage locations are required.

The average-case analysis for the tree sort is unknown.

8-6.4 A Sort Procedure

On the assumption that records are stored in contiguous memory locations with the key field left-justified in each record, we can design a general-purpose sorting procedure as follows:

SORT: PROCEDURE <TBL,KL,RL,N,PTR>,5

where TBL contains the address of the table to be sorted
      KL contains the length of the key field
      RL contains the record length
      N contains the number of table entries
      PTR contains the address of an array of N words

The procedure is to place the key fields in sorted alphanumeric order without moving the data parts. The location of the data part corresponding to sorted key i is returned in word i of PTR. Therefore, the decision as to whether the entire record is to be moved is left to the calling program. An example of SORT that uses the improved bubble-sort algorithm is shown below.

```
SORT:   PROCEDURE     <TBL,KL,RL,N,PTR>,5
;
;           Initialize pointer array.
;
        MOV     PTR(R0),R1      ; Address of array.
        CLR     R2              ; Use R2 as counter.
SRT1:   MOV     R2,(R1)+        ; Store index in array element.
        INC     R2              ; Advance counter.
        CMP     R2,N(R0)        ; Equal to array length?
        BMI     SRT1            ; Branch if not.
;
;           R2 contains address of successive records in outer loop.
;           R3 counts entries processed.
;
        CLR     R3              ; Initialize counter.
        MOV     TBL(R0),R2      ; Initialize record pointer.
        MOV     R2,SRT10        ; Store successor record address
        ADD     RL(R0),SRT10    ;       in location SRT10.
SRT2:   CALL    CMPK <R2,SRT10,KL(R0)>; Compare keys.
        TST     (SP)+           ; Returns zero if ordered or equal.
        BEQ     SRT9            ; Branch if ordered.
        MOV     R3,SRT11        ; SRT11 will hold the address of
        ADD     R3,SRT11        ; the pointer corresponding to the
        ADD     PTR(R0),SRT11   ; key given by SRT10.
        ADD     #2,SRT11        ; Add R3 twice for words.
;
;           This is the inner loop in which
;           R4 is used to scan toward the beginning of
;           the table for the correct position of the
;           record addressed by SRT10.
;
        MOV     R2,R4           ; Initialize R4 to address record
        BR      SRTLP
```

```
SRT3:   SUB     RL(R0),R4         ; preceding that addressed by R2.
        CALL    CMPK <R4,SRT10,KL(R0)>; Compare keys.
        TST     (SP)+             ; Returns zero if ordered or equal.
        BEQ     SRT4              ; Branch to insert if ordered.
SRTLP:  CMP     TBL(R0),R4        ; First record?
        BMI     SRT3              ; Branch if not.
        SUB     RL(R0),R4         ; Following code adds RL.

;
;       At this point all keys from one below that addressed
;       by R4 to that addressed by R2 are shifted down one
;       position. The key addressed by SRT10 is moved to
;       the position below that addressed by R4.
;
;
SRT4:   ADD     RL(R0),R4         ; Adjust R4 down one record.
        MOV     R2,R5             ; Use R5 to scan up table.
        MOV     SRT10,R1          ; Set up here to stack the
        ADD     KL(R0),R1         ; key addressed by SRT10.
        MOV     @SRT11,-(SP)      ; Store pointer which goes with SRT10.
SRT5:   MOVB    -(R1),-(SP)       ; Stack bytes of this key.
        CMP     SRT10,R1          ; Finished stacking?
        BMI     SRT5              ; Branch if not.
SRT6:   MOV     R5,R1             ; Use R1 to address bytes of
        ADD     KL(R0),R1         ; each key as it is moved down.
        MOV     R1,-(SP)          ; Use stack top to address
        ADD     RL(R0),(SP)       ; destination byte.
SRT7:   DEC     (SP)              ; Adjust destination address.
        MOVB    -(R1),@0(SP)      ; Move byte of this key.
        CMP     R5,R1             ; Finished this key?
        BMI     SRT7              ; Branch if not.
        MOV     SRT11,(SP)        ; Use stack to address array element.
        SUB     #2,SRT11          ; Move to previous element of pointers.
        MOV     @SRT11,@0(SP)     ; Shift element down one.
        TST     (SP)+             ; Pop to clear stack.
        SUB     RL(R0),R5         ; Scan to predecessor record.
        CMP     R5,R4             ; Finished moving?
        BPL     SRT6              ; Branch if not.
        MOV     R4,R1             ; Set up here to unstack the key
        ADD     KL(R0),R4         ; to be placed in record addressed
        DEC     R4                ; by R4.
SRT8:   MOVB    (SP)+,(R1)+       ;
        CMP     R4,R1             ; Finished unstacking?
        BPL     SRT8              ; Branch if not.
        MOV     (SP)+,@SRT11      ; Put in pointer to shifted key.
```

```
;
;              The end of the outer loop now advances to the
;              next record, terminating if all records sorted.
;
SRT9:    ADD      RL(R0),R2        ; Next record.
         ADD      RL(R0),SRT10     ; Next successor record.
         INC      R3               ; Count records.
         CMP      R3,N(R0)         ; Last record?
         BMI      SRT2             ; Loop if not.
         RETURN #0,5               ; Keys are ordered.
SRT10:   .WORD 0
SRT11:   .WORD 0
```

Example: A general-purpose sorting procedure

8-6.5 Two-Pass Assembly with Linear Storage

If a two-pass assembly is used, the sorting can be done after the first pass, since the table is complete at that point. The advantage to be gained is that searches of the table during the second pass need not use the sequential scan. Rather, a *binary search* can be performed, since the table is now sorted. This algorithm proceeds by splitting the table in half and determining in which half the SEARCHKEY (the symbol sought) record lies; that half is then split and the comparison repeated. Successively smaller portions of the table are obtained until the SEARCHKEY record is found or until it is determined that no such record exists. The algorithm is shown in Fig. 8-14.

The first comparison, if unsuccessful, is followed by a split of the table into

```
search:  p := 1;
         q := n+1;
         i :- (p+q)/2;
         { integer division }
         found := FALSE;
         WHILE searchkey <> key[i] DO BEGIN
             IF searchkey < key[i] THEN
                 IF q=i THEN escape to out
                 ELSE q := i
             ELSE IF p=i THEN escape to out
                     ELSE p := i;
             i := (p+q)/2 END;
         found := TRUE;
out:     { if found is TRUE then i points to the entry }
```

Figure 8-14 Binary search.

a smaller one of size $N/2$. The second comparison, if also unsuccessful, is followed by a split of the table into one of size $N/4$. Subsequent unsuccessful comparisons are each followed by a split into a table of size $N/8$, $N/16$, etc. The ith split yields a table of size $N/2^i$. If $N = 2^i$, the $i + 1$st comparison determines whether or not the record sought is in the table. In this situation, the maximum number of comparisons is $i + 1$ where $N = 2^i$. Then the maximum number of comparisons $= \log N + 1$.

The equality $N = 2^i$ does not always hold. However, it can be shown that the maximum number of comparisons is either $\log N$ or $\log N + 1$, and the average number of comparisons is $\log N - 1$ for large values of N.

Note that the maximum number of comparisons is only slightly greater than the average number, and also that the binary search is considerably faster than the sequential search for large tables. The price paid for this speed increase is the sorting required.

A general-purpose binary search procedure is shown below. It assumes the same table structure as that of the procedure SORT from the previous section, namely, that records are stored in contiguous memory locations with a left-justified key field.

```
SRCH:    PROCEDURE <ADR,KL,RL,N,KEY>,5
;
;           ADR contains the address of the table.
;           KL   contains the key length.
;           RL   contains the record length.
;           N    contains the number of records.
;           KEY contains the address of the search key.
;           The return code is zero if no record found to
;           equal the search key.
;           Otherwise, the return code contains the address
;           of the record found.
;
            CLR       -(SP)       ; Space for a temporary.
            MOV       #1,R1       ; R1 contains low index P.
            MOV       N(R0),R2    ;
            INC       R2          ; R2 contains high index Q.
            MOV       R2,R3       ; R3 contains middle index I.
            ADD       R1,R3
            ASR       R3          ; I := (P+Q)/2 integer division.
SRCH0:  CLR       (SP)        ; Counter for bytes in key.
            MOV       R3,R5       ; Set up to convert index in R3
            DEC       R5          ; to address in R5.
            MUL       RL(R0),R5   ; Convert to byte index.
            ADD       ADR(R0),R5  ; Convert to address.
            MOV       KEY(R0),R4  ; Use R4 to address search key.
SRCH1:  CMPB      (R5)+,(R4)+ ; Compare characters.
```

```
         BNE      SRCH2        ; Branch with unequal keys.
         INC      (SP)         ; Advance byte counter.
         CMP      (SP),KL(R0)  ; Finished entire key?
         BLT      SRCH1   ; Branch if not.
         SUB      (SP)+,R5; Point R5 at first byte of key.
         BR       SRCH6   ; Exit, record found.
SRCH2:   SUB      (SP),R5 ; Move R5 back to first
         DEC      R5      ; byte of the key.
         MOV      R0,R4   ; R0 cannot be used for nested call
         CALL     CMPK <KEY(R4),R5,KL(R4)>; searchkey < key[I]?
         TST      (SP)+
         BNE      SRCH3   ; Branch if not.
         CMP      R2,R3   ; Q = I?
         BEQ      SRCH5   ; Escape, no record found.
         MOV      R3,R2   ; Q := I
         BR       SRCH4
SRCH3:   CMP      R1,R3   ; P = I?
         BEQ      SRCH5   ; Escape, no record found.
         MOV      R3,R1   ; P := I
SRCH4:   MOV      R2,R3
         ADD      R1,R3
         ASR      R3      ; I := (P+Q)/2 integer division.
         BR       SRCH0   ; Loop back to continue search.
SRCH5:   CLR      R5
         TST      (SP)+   ; Remove temporary space.
SRCH6:   RETURN   R5,5    ; Return address of key found or zero.
```

Example: A general-purpose linear search procedure

8-7 HASHING

One of the most appropriate and often-used symbol table organizations is the hash table. Imagine a table search technique that permits a record to be retrieved directly, without any comparisons. This can be accomplished by reserving a record position for every possible key value such that all positions are in the proper key ordering. A record is positioned in the table at the location reserved for the particular value of the record key. A record is retrieved simply by using the key, or its ordinate in the key sequence, as an index into the table. Figure 8-15 shows an example of such a table. In this example, a 0 is used to denote vacant record positions.

Storing each key value in a unique table position requires a table as large as the range of keys. If only a small proportion of key values is present, then much of the table is wasted. A better way to provide direct retrieval of records is to arrange that certain key values *share* a table position. This sharing provides the

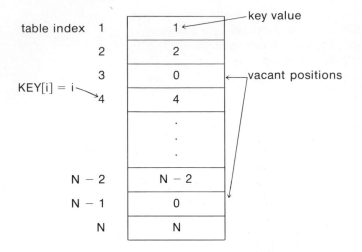

Figure 8-15 An idealized hash table.

essence of hashing. In particular, we shall see that instances of key values actually present in a table cannot, of course, share the space in their allocated position with other instances. This conflict must be resolved somehow.

8-7.1 Insertions with Hashing

Given a range of M possible keys, provide a table with N entries where $N < M$. The position of a particular key value in the table is determined by transforming the key value into an integer in the range 1 to N. The transformation procedure is called *hashing* and a particular transformation is called a *hash function*.

A particularly simple hash function for numeric keys is:

HASH(KEY) = (KEY mod N) + 1

where KEY mod N is the remainder of KEY/N.

Figure 8-16 shows a table constructed using this hash function where $N = 6$ and $M = 36$. Key values are 1 through 36. Vacant positions are denoted by storing a 0 in the key field.

6
0
2
15
22
0

Figure 8-16 A hash table for HASH(KEY) = (KEY mod 4) + 1.

```
i := hash(newkey);
j := i;
WHILE key[i] <> 0 DO BEGIN
    i := IF i=n THEN 1 ELSE i+1;
    IF i=j THEN BEGIN
        tablefull := TRUE;
        escape to end of program END END ;
key[i] := newkey
```

Figure 8-17 Inserting a new record in a hash table.

New records are stored by hashing their key and using the result as an index to determine the proper position in the table. Note that there are only four records present in the table in Fig. 8-16. Suppose the next record to be added to the table has a key of 9. Now, HASH(9) = 4, but position 4 is already occupied by the record with a key of 15. Such an attempt to store two records whose keys hash to the same value is called a *collision*. There are several ways to deal with collisions, but only one is described here.

Collisions can be handled by looking sequentially down the table for the first unoccupied position, and storing the record there. Such a sequential search occurring during a table insertion scans the table in a wraparound fashion, examining entry 1 after entry N, until either a vacant position is found or the entire table has been examined.

It is desirable to minimize the amount of sequential searching performed during table insertions. At the same time, it is desirable to use as small a table as possible. These of course are conflicting objectives. A hash table that becomes nearly full produces a higher number of collisions and consequently requires more sequential searching. On the other hand, a sparsely occupied hash table produces fewer collisions and faster insertion.

The choice of table size and, what is even more important, the hash function critically affects the performance of a hash table. A general discussion of hash functions is, unfortunately, beyond the scope of this text. Figure 8-17 shows the algorithm for inserting a new record in a hash table. NEWKEY refers to the key of a record being inserted.

8-7.2 Searching with Hashing

Records are retrieved from a hash table in a way similar to insertions. Records are sought by first hashing the SEARCHKEY and then using the result as an index to obtain the record; retrieval of a 0 indicates that the desired key is not present in the table. If, however, a nonzero key is retrieved which does not equal SEARCHKEY, then a sequential search is performed starting from the entry just obtained by hashing. If, of course, the key retrieved equals SEARCHKEY, no sequential search is necessary.

A sequential search scans the table in a way similar to insertion searching

```
recordfound := TRUE;
i := hash(searchkey);
j := i;
WHILE searchkey <> key[i] AND recordfound DO BEGIN
    IF key[i] <> 0 THEN BEGIN
        IF i=n THEN i := 1 ELSE i := i+1;
        IF i=j THEN recordfound := FALSE END
    ELSE recordfound := FALSE END;
IF recordfound THEN copy record
```

Figure 8-18 Retrieving a record from a hash table.

until either the desired record is found or the entire table has been examined. If table entries are never removed, the sequential search can be terminated on the discovery of a vacant position. This, of course, is the case with symbol tables, and this fact can be used to shorten the search time for nonexistent entries.

Figure 8-18 shows the retrieval algorithm for a hash table. It assumes that records are never removed. One should remember that this is not true in general.

The example in Fig. 8-19 shows a hash table where $M = 99$ and $N = 11$. The table is constructed using the hash function

HASH(KEY) = (KEY mod N) + 1

The keys inserted in the table, in the order of insertion, are 15, 03, 25, 01, 35, 47, and 87. Sequential search is used to handle collisions.

Keys are often alphanumeric, as in the case of a symbol table, rather than

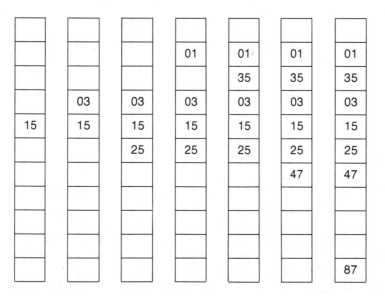

Figure 8-19 Constructing a hash table.

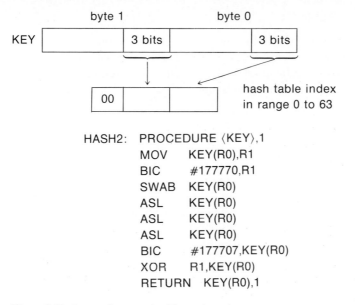

```
HASH2:   PROCEDURE ⟨KEY⟩,1
         MOV     KEY(R0),R1
         BIC     #177770,R1
         SWAB    KEY(R0)
         ASL     KEY(R0)
         ASL     KEY(R0)
         ASL     KEY(R0)
         BIC     #177707,KEY(R0)
         XOR     R1,KEY(R0)
         RETURN  KEY(R0),1
```

Figure 8-20 A two-character hashing subroutine.

numeric. Consider the problem of constructing a hash table for keys composed of two ASCII letters. That is, the range of keys is

AA, AB, AC, . . . , ZX, ZY, ZZ

Assume a table size of $N = 64$. A simple hash function is the following: Concatenate the rightmost three bits of each character of the key. The result is a 6-bit integer that can be used to index the hash table. A PDP-11 subroutine to hash a key passed by value is shown in Fig. 8-20.

A PDP-11 subroutine to hash a six-character key passed by address is shown in Fig. 8-21. In this case the 6 bytes produce the result by exclusive or.

```
HASH6:   PROCEDURE  <KEYADR>, 3
         MOV       #5,R2              ; counter
         MOV       KEYADR(R0),R1      ; get address
         CLR       R3                 ; source of XOR must be register
         CLR       −(SP)              ; space for result
         MOVB      (R1)+,(SP)         ; first character
         MOVB      (R1)+,R3           ; next character
         XOR       R3,(SP)
         DEC       R2
         BNE       .−6
         RETURN    (SP)+,3
```

Figure 8-21 A six-character hashing subroutine.

8-7.3 Sorting a Hash Table

A symbol table organized as a hash table can be sorted for the purpose of listing after the assembly is completed. This destroys the special positioning and the table is, of course, no longer a hash table. In the case of assembling this does not matter because the table is not needed again.

8-7.4 Two-Pass Assembly with Hashing

Using two passes the assembler designer has the option of using hashing for pass 1 and sorting the table between passes so that a binary search can be used in pass 2. Since the sorting is probably going to be performed after the second pass anyway, the decision must be based on the relative performance of searching with a binary search or with hashing. The decision then depends on the performance of the hashing algorithm, the maximum size of the table, and the expected number of entries. The performance of the binary search is well known.

8-8 TREE STORAGE

This section describes a way of storing symbols in a table so that no final sorting is necessary yet insertions and searching are quite fast. The price to be paid for this performance is more storage space for two additional fields in each table entry. As before, only the key field is considered in the examples and discussion.

The tree structure introduced in the discussion of the tree sort was based on the idea that a tree node's position in the tree is determined by its position in the array, i.e., by its array index. A tree structure is also employed in the method to be described now, but in this case there is no fixed relationship between array indices and node position. Rather, the successor links are stored

	KEY	LL	RL
1	JOHN	2	4
2	BILL	8	3
3	HARRY	5	0
4	MARY	7	6
5	GEORGE	0	0
6	ZOLTAN	0	0
7	LAURA	0	0
8	ALBERT	0	0

Figure 8-22a A singly linked tree: physical storage.

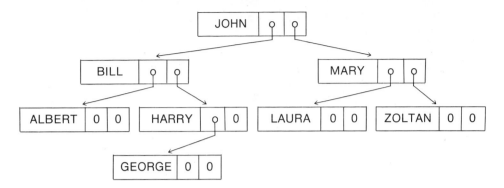

Figure 8-22b A singly linked tree: logical relationships.

explicitly in the array rather than being calculated as before. Such a structure is a *singly linked tree*. An example, in Fig. 8-22, shows the two additional fields, LL (left link) and RL (right link), and how they are used explicitly to store array indices providing successor links from each tree node.

Successors of node i in this singly linked tree satisfy the following relations:

KEY[LL[i]] < KEY[i]

and

KEY[RL [i]] > KEY[i]

In the following, when we refer to a tree this relationship is assumed to hold.

8-8.1 Tree Insertions

Entries into the tree structured table are placed in sequential locations in the order in which they are encountered. Thus, the table will be physically ordered in exactly the same sequence as the linear table discussed previously. The successor links, however, contain the tree ordering information.

To insert a new entry, the record is placed in the next available sequential location. Then a search of the tree is performed starting with the tree root, which is stored in the first table position. The search travels down into the tree comparing node keys with the new key and following the appropriate successor link until a null link is encountered. The table position of the new entry is stored into this null link, thus placing the new entry into the tree. The insertion algorithm is shown in Fig. 8-23.

```
insert:   IF avail <> 0 THEN insert record into record[avail]
          ELSE signal table is full and exit;
          i := 1;
          sw := TRUE;
          WHILE sw DO
            IF newkey = key[i] THEN signal entry present and exit
            ELSE IF newkey < key[i] THEN
                IF ll[i] <> 0 THEN i := ll[i]
                ELSE BEGIN ll[i] := avail ;
                                sw := FALSE END
            ELSE IF rl[i] <> 0 THEN i := rl[i]
                ELSE BEGIN rl[i] := avail
                                sw := FALSE END;
          IF avail = maxsiz THEN avail := 0
                         ELSE avail := avail+1
```

Figure 8-23 Insertion into a singly linked tree.

8-8.2 Tree Searching

Since an insertion involves a search, the search algorithm is similar to the insertion algorithm. Notice the similarity in the structure of the algorithm in Fig. 8-24 and the binary search.

In the case of the binary search tree it was not difficult to estimate the maximum search time. This was true because the tree implicitly defined on the search table by the binary search algorithm is balanced. By this we mean that the depth of the tree from the root to any terminal node (a node with no successors) never differs by more than one. In the singly linked tree, however, the shape of the tree depends not only on the set of keys in the table but also on the order in which they were inserted into the table. An analysis of search time for singly linked trees is beyond our present scope.

```
search:   i := 1 ;
          found := TRUE ;
          WHILE i <> 0 DO
              IF searchkey = key[i] THEN escape to out
              ELSE IF searchkey < key[i] THEN i := ll[i]
                  ELSE i := rl[i];
          found := FALSE;
out:      { if found is TRUE then i points to the entry }
```

Figure 8-24 Searching a singly linked tree.

8-8.3 Sorting a Tree

A table constructed as a singly linked tree could be sorted using any of the sorting algorithms discussed earlier. However, because of the way in which entries are linked together, it is possible to examine the entries in the table in such a way that on a single pass through the table the entries can be copied in sorted order. This copying could simply be an output operation, or the entries could be moved to a fresh area of memory producing a sorted copy of the table. Any scanning of all the tree nodes is called a *tree traversal;* we shall describe, then, the tree traversal algorithm that examines the nodes in sorted order.

Consider any node I in a singly linked tree as shown here.

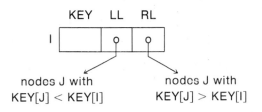

The proper order in which to copy KEY[I] and keys that are successors to node I is the following:

1. IF LL[I] ≠ 0 THEN copy all nodes linked via LL[I],
2. copy node I,
3. IF RL[I] ≠ 0 THEN copy all nodes linked via RL[I].

If I=1, then the entire table is copied in the correct order if these steps are applied recursively to each node in the tree. Restating the algorithm to reflect this recursion we have

To copy KEY[I] in sorted order:
1. IF LL[I] ≠ 0 THEN copy KEY[LL[I]] in sorted order,
2. copy KEY[I],
3. IF RL[I] ≠ 0 THEN copy KEY[RL[I]] in sorted order.

This is still too informal to translate into a programming language. First, let us state the algorithm in a more formal recursive way as shown in Fig. 8-25.

```
PROCEDURE scan (i:0..n);
BEGIN
    IF i <> 0 THEN  BEGIN
        scan( ll[i]);
        copy key[i];
        scan( rl[i]) END
    ELSE copy key[i]
END
```
Figure 8-25 A recursive tree traversal.

```
      i := 1;
1:   WHILE i <> 0 DO BEGIN
         push i;
         i := ll[i];
         GO TO 1;
2:       copy key [i];
         pop i;
         copy key[i];
         i := rl[i] END;
    IF stack is non-empty THEN GO TO 2;
```

Figure 8-26 A nonrecursive tree traversal.

This recursive form of the tree traversal is very easily stated and provides a compact representation. Recursive algorithms tend to be inefficient if implemented directly in a high-level language, so the nonrecursive form in Fig. 8-26 can be used. It requires a stack to save node indices as the scan travels down the tree to terminal nodes.

8-8.4 Two-Pass Assembly with Tree Storage

The situation here is very similar to that of hashing except that the singly linked tree is already in a convenient form for output in sorted order. Therefore the trade-off is between (1) producing a new symbol table by copying and using a binary search during pass 2, and (2) using the tree search during pass 2 and printing the symbol table with the tree traversal scan.

8-9 PACKING SYMBOLS

Although ASCII characters occupy 7 bits and are stored in PDP-11 bytes of 8 bits, it is possible to reduce the memory requirements of a character to less than 6 bits if not all possible $256 = 2^8$ different codes are in use. In assembling a PDP-11 program, for example, the only valid characters in a symbol are a blank, A through Z, 0 through 9, $, and the dot character (.). There are only 39 different characters that may appear in symbols in the symbol table. This fact makes it possible to store a six-character symbol in two PDP-11 words.

A special character code exists for representing the 39 characters named above. This code, called the *Radix-50* code, is given by the following table (codes are in octal):

Character	Radix-50 code
Blank	0
A–Z	1–32
$	33
.	34
0–9	36–47

The name of the code comes from the way in which three Radix-50 characters can be stored into one 16-bit word. The operation required to produce a 16-bit result w, given three Radix-50 characters r1, r2, and r3, is

$$w \quad := [(\text{rl} \cdot 50) + \text{r2}] \cdot 50 + \text{r3}$$

Given a 16-bit word w containing three Radix-50 characters packed in this way, the three characters can be retrieved by

$$
\begin{aligned}
\text{r3} &:= \text{remainder of w/50 ;} \\
\text{w} &:= \text{quotient of w/50 ;} \\
\text{r2} &:= \text{remainder of w/50 ;} \\
\text{r1} &:= \text{quotient of w/50}
\end{aligned}
$$

The reason that 50 (octal) is used here is that it is the smallest integer larger than 47, which is the greatest Radix-50 code. Although one code, 35, is unused and the 39 characters could have been packed into the range 0 to 46, it is convenient to use the range 0 to 47 and multiply by 50 in the packing operation. This is because some PDP-11 computers do not have hardware multiplication (i.e., a MUL instruction) and so multiplication is expensive. The number 50 (40 decimal) has a property that

$$40 = 32 + 8 = 2^5 + 2^3 \quad \text{(using decimal notation)}$$

and so multiplication by 50 octal can be performed by two left-shift operations (multiplication by powers of 2). Thus the multiplication

$$50 \cdot r \quad \text{(octal)}$$

can be performed by

$$32 \cdot r + 8 \cdot r \quad \text{(decimal)}$$

which, as noted, can be done efficiently without multiplication hardware.

The following example gives a symbol packing subroutine. It accepts as input a six-ASCII-character string and produces as output a two-word Radix-50 packed symbol.

```
PACK:     PROCEDURE <ADR,RES>,4
; ADR is the address of the six ASCII character symbol
; RES is the address of the two word RAD50 result
          CLR    R1            ; temporary for character byte
          CLR    R3            ; temporary for RAD50 result
          MOV    #3,R2         ; count for characters of symbol
          MOV    #2,R4         ; count for words of RAD50 symbol
PACK1:    MOVB   @ADR(R0),R1   ; get next ASCII character
          CMPB   R1,#101       ;
          BMI    PACK2         ; not a letter
          CMPB   R1,#133       ;
          BPL    PACK6         ; invalid character
          BIC    #300,R1       ; produce RAD50 A–Z
          BR     PACK5         ;
```

```
PACK2:  CMPB  R1,#60         ;
        BMI   PACK3          ; not a digit
        CMPB  R1,#72         ;
        BPL   PACK6          ; invalid character
        SUB   #18,R1         ; produce RAD50 0-9
        BR    PACK5          ;
PACK3:  CMPB  R1,#56         ;
        BNE   PACK4          ; not a "."
        MOVB  #34,R1         ; produce RAD50 "."
        BR    PACK5          ;
PACK4:  CMPB  R1,#44         ; check for "$"
        BNE   PACK9          ; possible invalid character
        MOVB  #33,R1         ; produce RAD50 "$"
        BR    PACK5
PACK9:  CMPB  R1,#40         ; check for blank
        BNE   PACK6
        CLR   R1             ; RAD50 blank is zero
PACK5:  ADD   R1,R3          ; insert RAD50 character
        INC   ADR(R0)        ; get next ASCII character
        DEC   R2             ; and count characters
        BEQ   PACK8          ; if RAD50 word is full
        MUL   #40.,R3        ; shift RAD50 character
        BR    PACK1          ;
PACK8:  MOV   R3,@RES(R0)    ; store RAD50 word
        DEC   R4             ; and count words
        BEQ   PACK7          ; if symbol converted
        CLR   R3             ; clear for next word
        INC   RES(R0)        ; get next
        INC   RES(R0)        ; RAD50 word
        MOV   #3,R2          ; count for characters of symbol
        BR    PACK1          ;
PACK6:  MOV   #-1,R4         ; 0 indicates error
PACK7:  INC   R4             ; 1 indicates success
        RETURN R4,4
```

EXERCISES

8-1 Design and implement the procedures search, enter, getval, storeval, and define from Sec. 8-6 for a simple unordered linear symbol table. Append new entries to the end of the table and use a simple linear search technique.

8-2 Complete the one-pass assembler designed in Sec. 8-6 using the symbol table implementation from Exercise 8-1. Choose just a few representative instructions and directives to include. Test your assembler by assembling and running some sample programs.

8-3 Design an assembly language for the simple machine described in Exercise 3-1.

8-4 Design and construct a one-pass assembler for the assembly language from Exercise 8-3. You may use the symbol table implementation from Exercise 8-1.

8-5 Design and implement the procedures search, enter, getval, storeval, and define from Sec. 8-6 using a hashing technique. Test these procedures by using them in the assembler from Exercise 8-2.

8-6 Design and construct a two-pass assembler for the assembly language from Exercise 8-3. Use a linear symbol table which is sorted after the first pass using the SORT procedure. Use the procedure SRCH during the second pass. Duplicate symbol table entries should be removed after the sort and an error message issued.

8-7 Modify procedure SORT to use the shell sort. You may test it by using it with the assembler from Exercise 8 6.

8-8 Modify procedure SORT to use the tree sort. You may test it by using it with the assembler from Exercise 8-6. Make any necessary changes to the definition of SORT and to the assembler.

8-9 Modify the assembler of Exercise 8-2 to allow the following additional addressing modes: absolute, relative deferred, index deferred, and register deferred.

8-10 Modify the assembler of Exercise 8 2 to allow the remaining addressing modes.

REFERENCES

A general treatment of assemblers can be found in Barron (1969), and of symbol tables in Batson (1965). There are several excellent texts on the subject of data structures, each of which includes sorting and searching. Some examples are Berziss (1971), Elson (1975), Harrison (1973), and Tremblay (1976). More detailed original material on sorting and searching can be found in Arora (1969), Clampett (1964), Floyd (1964), Heising (1963), Maurer (1968), Patt (1969), and Shell (1959). The foremost summary treatment of searching and sorting is Knuth (1973).

CHAPTER NINE

LINKING, LOADING, AND INTERPRETATION

A program can undergo several transformations before it finally resides in main memory in a machine-language form suitable for execution. As shown in Fig. 9-1, the source program is first translated into an *object module*. Translation itself usually involves many separate transformations. For example, a high-level language may be translated into assembly language and then assembled into an object module. These translation phases are not of concern here, however, and we can regard translation as a single step.

The term *object module* is used to emphasize that a program can consist of several separately translated parts called modules. This usage of the term *module* is quite different from the usage with respect to source program design, however. We shall return to this point later.

More than one object module can be combined in a process called *linking* that produces a single *load module*. The program in load-module form has had all external references resolved. This means that while an object module may contain references to symbols defined in other object modules, a load module may not. A load module, then, is a complete, self-contained program (except that it may require some execution time support from the supervisor).

The load-module form of a program is actually placed into main memory during the *loading* process. This may involve some final transformations of the program to take into consideration the actual memory locations occupied.

Finally, of course, the loaded program is presented as input data to an execution agent. Normally this agent is a hardware processor, and the loader will transfer control to the loaded program, thus causing its execution. In general, however, a hardware processor is just one form of an *interpreter* — any machine, hardware or software, that obeys the statements or instructions of an algorithm causing its meaning to be carried out.

This chapter, then, covers the transformation of a program from the time it is translated from a programming language to the time that it is interpreted. We shall see that the final step, interpretation, can occur at a variety of times.

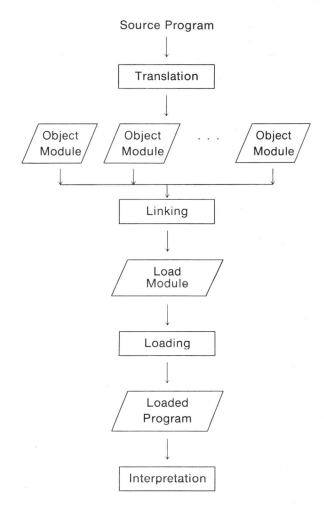

Figure 9-1 Program transformations.

9-1 ABSOLUTE LOADERS

The assembly-language or systems-language programmer usually has the option of specifying the value of the location counter during translation of the program. In MACRO-11, for example, . = 600 at the beginning of the program causes all addresses to be created relative to the first word being word 600. If directly loaded into memory starting at word 600, therefore, no address adjustments are necessary. Such an address adjustment, necessitated by loading a program into memory at a location different from that assumed during translation, is called *relocation*. An absolute loader performs no relocation; it simply loads the load module at a predetermined or otherwise specified address.

A load module presented to an absolute loader needs no descriptive information with it other than its beginning address, which may be predetermined by default. Such a load module is called an *absolute load module*.

A good example of an absolute loader is the *bootstrap,* so called because it is the program that starts up a bare computer having an empty memory. Typically, a bootstrap loader is a very short program that is a special-purpose absolute loader; it loads, from a specific I/O device, the system absolute loader. Once the system loader is in memory, it can load the rest of the supervisor and system software on command from the console, and the system is in operation.

One problem remains. How does the bootstrap loader itself get into memory? There are three common answers. It may be (1) loaded manually via the console switches, (2) permanently stored in memory, or (3) directly incorporated into the processor's internal logic. In the first two cases the bootstrap is invoked by loading the PC via the console with the correct address and starting the processor. In the latter case, there is normally a LOAD button on the console with which the bootstrap is invoked. Additionally, larger machines may have an I/O device select switch allowing the operator to load from different devices.

The PDP-11 uses the second method: the bootstrap is permanently stored in memory. In the PDP-11/03 model, for example, locations 165000 to 165776 and 173000 to 173776 are reserved for the bootstrap, which is stored in a special "read only memory" unit. A processor option is available which causes the processor to start executing at location 173000 when the power is turned on.

The permanent bootstrap loader need not be included in a PDP-11 system and, if not, it must be manually loaded as per the first method above. Since bootstrap loaders are very short for convenient loading, they tend to do clever things at the expense of clarity. It is not, therefore, very productive to look at the actual PDP-11 bootstrap.

A straightforward bootstrap is not difficult to write. For example, assume that a machine is to be bootstrapped from paper tape. Then the tape can be prepunched to contain the following sequence of octal characters:

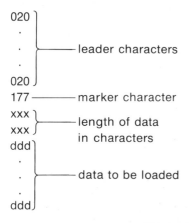

Example: Bootstrap input format

The bootstrap reads the leader, which may be any length, until a 177 character is encountered. It then reads a length from the next two characters and then, into a fixed location, reads the specified number of data characters constituting the loaded program. This loaded program will itself contain an absolute loader for reading into memory the necessary parts of the operating system.

Absolute object programs must be loaded into the locations for which they were assembled, or alternatively, they can be entirely written in position-independent code so that no relocation is necessary. In either case their essential property is that no relocation is possible. A possible absolute load-module format is a sequence of blocks, each of which has the format shown in Fig. 9-2a.

The count of the number of bytes in the block is followed by the address at which the program code is to be loaded. The last word is a *checksum* calculated in a particular way from the contents of the block. On loading the block, errors can be detected by recalculating the checksum and comparing it with the stored value.

The end of an absolute load module, corresponding for example to the assembler directive .END GO, can be indicated by a block with zero byte count as shown in Fig. 9-2b. In the case of this block the loader simply suspends loading and branches to the start address, which corresponds, in the case of MACRO-11, to the operand of the .END directive.

An absolute load-module format comprising separate program sections as described above gives the flexibility to configure a program in memory in a manner dependent on available space. More important, however, it provides a

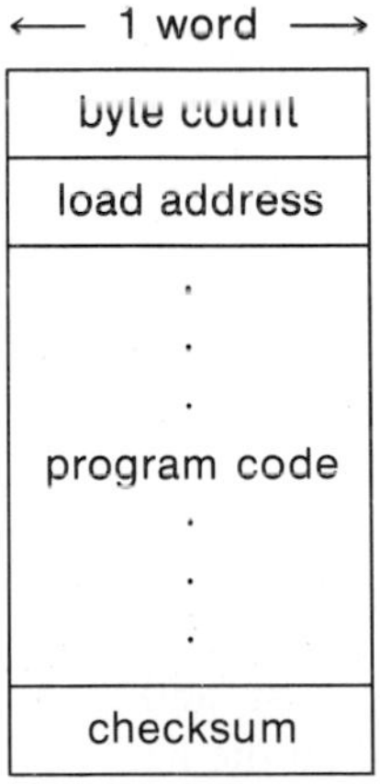

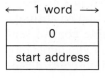

Figure **9-2a** One block of an absolute load module.

Figure **9-2b** Final block of an absolute load module.

mechanism whereby the programmer can be given fairly tight control over the configuration of his loaded program. The next section explores such a facility in more detail.

9-2 RELOCATING LOADERS

A *relocatable object program* need not be loaded into a fixed location because it contains additional descriptive information enabling a *relocating loader* to find and adjust in the program all addresses that were constructed relative to the beginning address. This descriptive information must be included with the program by the *relocating assembler* (as opposed to an absolute assembler, which produces only absolute load modules).

Let's consider for a moment why relocatable object modules are convenient. First of all, the programmer usually does not care from where in memory the program will execute. If absolute references are necessary, then the programmer can specify absolute mode, as we have done with the PDP-11 I/O registers, and these references will be fixed at translation time and left untouched by the loader. Second, modules can be translated separately without concern for the ultimate addressing range to be occupied. Different sets of modules can be linked at different times without retranslation, and generally useful modules can be made public in a program library.

Addresses requiring relocation are those that are relative to the program's beginning address. PIC code requires no relocation. Thus, relative addressing on the PDP-11 is not relocated. Similarly, absolute addresses need no relocation. The assembler usually indicates addresses requiring relocation on the source listing. MACRO-11, for example, puts a prime (') beside such addresses. Immediate operands that are defined as labels and indexed operands (not PC indexed) are prime examples of relocatable addresses.

Relocatable addresses can be described in a *relocation table* placed at the beginning of object program code as shown in Fig. 9-3. Each table entry contains the relative location of one such address along with a reference (an index into the object program code) to all the words that are to contain the address. As seen in the diagram, the words are linked in a list with the last word containing a zero to indicate a null list link.

The relocating loader processes each table entry by adding the actual address at which the code is to be loaded to the relative address given, and then, by following the list, storing the relocated address in each word on the list. The resulting absolute code can then be loaded.

A piece of relocatable contiguous code such as that shown in Fig. 9-3 is called a relocatable *control section*. As seen in the previous section an absolute load module generally consists of more than one nonrelocatable control section, each one being composed of contiguous code and potentially loadable into noncontiguous areas of memory. Configuration of a program into control sections is accomplished via assembler directives (or other translator commands if

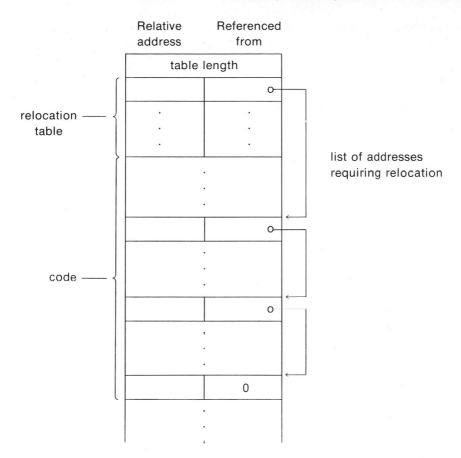

Figure 9-3 Relocation table.

a higher-level language is being used). The programmer can specify which sections of a program are to be loaded into contiguous memory and in some cases which absolute memory locations a section is to occupy.

Where no directives regarding control sections are included in a program, a relocating assembler, as a default, will create a single control section. Optionally, the programmer can specify that others also be created. For example, in MACRO-11, it is possible to specify that up to 253 (decimal) additional control sections be created. Each of these additional control sections can be assigned a symbolic name for identification. The default section is taken to have a null name. Consequently, it is called the *unnamed control section.*

In MACRO-11, the assembler directive .CSECT specifies that the code immediately following is to be assembled in the control section the name of which is given as a parameter. Every program starts with an implicit .CSECT having a null parameter. Thus, the default is to start assembling code into the unnamed section at relative location zero. A subsequent .CSECT with a parameter name causes succeeding code to be assembled, at relative location zero, into a named section as specified by the parameter. The first appearance of a .CSECT parameter in an assembly, then, causes the creation of a new control section whose location counter is initialized to zero.

The assembler maintains a separate location counter for each created control section. In this way a second or subsequent appearance of a .CSECT parameter causes assembly to revert to the specified section with the current value of its location counter.

For example, the following code would create the program configuration shown in Fig. 9-4.

```
.CSECT
        .           ; part #1 of
        .           ; unnamed section
.CSECT  A
        .           ; part #1 of
        .           ; section A
.CSECT  B
        .           ; all of
        .           ; section B
.CSECT  A
        .           ; part #2 of
        .           ; section A
.CSECT
        .           ; part #2 of
        .           ; unnamed section
.END
```

In addition to relocatable control sections, it is normally possible to create *absolute control sections*. These are, as the name implies, nonrelocatable control sections assembled under programmer control for fixed memory locations. For example, MACRO-11 allows one absolute control section to be created via the .ASECT directive.

All code immediately following the first appearance of .ASECT (up to a directive to the contrary) is assembled starting at absolute location zero. The programmer can, of course, alter the absolute section location counter with a .= statement. The code below would cause the absolute section to start at word 800 octal.

```
.CSECT      ; start unnamed section
    .

    .
.ASECT      ; start absolute section
.=800       ; at word 800

    .

    .
.CSECT      ; revert to unnamed section
```

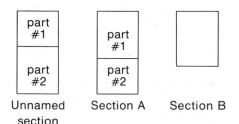

Figure 9-4 Relocatable control sections.

What is the reason for having many named control sections when there is no control over the actual memory locations to be occupied? The answer is that different modules can have matching names for control sections. At linking time these separately assembled control sections are combined so that they share the same memory locations. This then, is the mechanism for modules to share memory. Each module with such a shared control section can reference the shared memory with its own internally defined symbols if that is desirable.

We shall see now that an object module is more complex than might be inferred from Fig. 9-2, which showed only one relocatable control section. Each control section must be described as a separate contiguous piece of code leaving the decision of actual memory configuration to the linker or the loader (except, of course, for any absolute sections). In particular, there must be a separate relocation table for each control section. Not only that, there will be references from one section to another that cannot be entirely resolved by the assembler. For example,

```
    .CSECT
    .
    .

    .WORD X
    .
    .

    .CSECT A
    .
    .

X:  .WORD 0
    .
    .
```

contains a reference from the unnamed section to section A. Although the assembler knows the relative location of X within section A, the location of A relative to the unnamed section is not known. This problem does not occur with references into an absolute section since addresses are absolute, but references out of an absolute section are of this type as well.

To summarize, then, an object module can have more than one control section, and each such control section can contain unresolved references into others. Therefore, in addition to the information shown in the relocation table

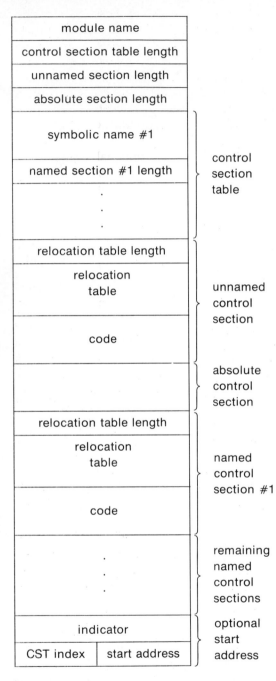

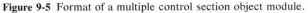

Figure 9-5 Format of a multiple control section object module.

of Fig. 9-3, an object module must contain a description of these inter-section references. Figure 9-5 shows a possible object-module format with a module name at the beginning. This name, required for identifying the module during linking, can be generated by the assembler if not supplied by the programmer. Following the module name is the control-section table listing the name and length of each named control section. Following that table are the unnamed, absolute, and named control sections, each including its relocation table. The inter-section reference information can be placed in the relocation table, modified from Fig. 9-2, for each control section.

Also shown at the end of the object module is an optional start address whose presence is indicated by a special indicator word following the last-named control section. This address, consisting of an index into the control-section table (CST) and a relative address within the specified section, is constructed by the assembler if the .END directive of the module contains the optional starting address parameter.

We have, then, two kinds of relocation required in each control section: for addresses of locations within the same control section, and for addresses of locations within other control sections. In the latter case the only additional information required is an identification of the referenced control section. This identification can be taken to be an index into the CST shown in Fig. 9-5. A possible data structure that the assembler can use in constructing the relocation table to contain this information is shown in Fig. 9-6.

As seen in this diagram, the out-of-section references are separated from the within-section references and an additional field, a control section table index, added to their relocation-table entries. When the time comes it is easy to locate the referenced section via the CST index.

In an absolute section, the within-section portion of the relocation table is

Figure 9-6 Relocation table with inter-section references.

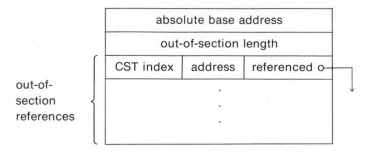

Figure 9-7 Relocation table for absolute section.

not required. An absolute control section does, however, require a base address to be stored, since the loader must be told to which addresses the code has been assembled. Figure 9-7 shows a possible relocation table for an absolute control section.

9-3 LINKERS

The function of a linker is to produce a single relocatable load module from one or more object modules. In doing this it must finish some of the work that the translator was unable to do, that of resolving external references.

These references, to symbols defined in other separately assembled modules, are quite different from the inter-section references discussed in the previous section. In this case of external references, the module containing the symbol's definition and hence its relative location in that module are not known to the assembler.

It is necessary, therefore, for the assembler to include with each control section, in addition to the relocation table, a *global symbol table* (see Fig. 9-8). This table contains a description of all references to symbols not defined within the module containing the control section. Such references cannot be resolved by the assembler and must be left for the linker.

It is not sufficient to describe external references only. The linker must be able to discover, for each external reference, where to find its definition. Consequently, the global symbol table must also contain information describing each symbol that is expected to be referenced from other modules.

A complete control-section format with both relocation table and global symbol table is shown in Fig. 9-8. The global symbol table, which has been simply prefixed to the control-section format examined previously, can be divided into two parts: *entry* symbols and *external* symbols (see Fig. 9-9). Entry symbols are defined in the module and are declared as being available for referencing by other separately translated modules. External symbols are referenced in the module itself but not defined. They are therefore "unresolved" at translation time and must be processed by the linker.

global symbol table length
global symbol table
relocation table length
relocation table
program code

Figure 9-8 Control-section format with relocation and global symbol tables.

Global symbols are usually required to be declared as such by the programmer so that the translator can catch programming errors if symbols are left undefined. Separate declarations for entry and external symbols are often used. Many assemblers have two directives for this purpose, often called ENTRY and EXTERNAL. The former defines its list of parameters as entry symbols, and the latter defines its list as external symbols. MACRO-11, however, employs the .GLOBL directive to declare both symbol types. Those that are defined in the module are assumed to be entry type and others external type. Note that absolute references are not external although they access locations outside the module. They have still been defined inside the module.

An example of how global referencing might be organized is shown in Fig. 9-10. The entry table lists all symbols that were defined to be potential entry addresses. Each symbol is described by its relative location in the control-section code.

The external table contains a list of all external symbols. For each there is a reference (a relative location in the control-section code) to a singly linked chain of addresses to that symbol. This, of course, is the same technique used, in the relocation table, to find all addresses in the code requiring relocation.

The output from a linker can be in relocatable load-module form, object-

global symbol table length
entry table length
entry table
external table

Figure 9-9 Global symbol table.

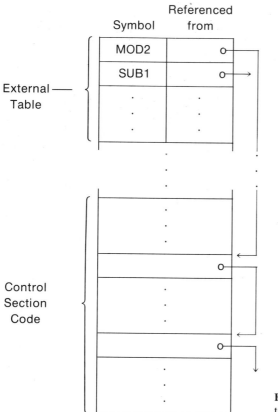

Symbol   Value

SUB1	7104
MOD2	7640

Figure 9-10a Global symbol entry table in a control section of module X.

Referenced

Symbol   from

MOD2	o
SUB1	o

External Table

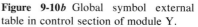

Control Section Code

Figure 9-10b Global symbol external table in control section of module Y.

module form, or absolute load-module form. Circumstances dictate which of these is appropriate at any time.

9-3.1 Relocatable Load-Module Output

A linker producing a relocatable load module has four basic jobs. First, all external references must be resolved and the global symbol table removed from each control section. This means that the addresses in the code that had been linked on a chain from an external table must be converted to some other form.

Second, all like-named control sections must be combined so that they are overlapped in the resulting load module. In other words, like-named control sections share memory locations. As discussed before, this provides a way for separately assembled modules to refer to the same set of memory locations with module-dependent names.

Third, all relocatable control sections (unnamed and named) must be combined into a single contiguous relocatable control section.

Fourth, any absolute control sections that overlap are combined into a single absolute section. Thus memory sharing is a characteristic of absolute sections as well as of named sections. The only difference is that explicit absolute locations rather than symbolic locations are shared.

A possible load-module format is illustrated on the right-hand side of Fig. 9-11. In general, there may be more than one absolute section and a single relocatable section.

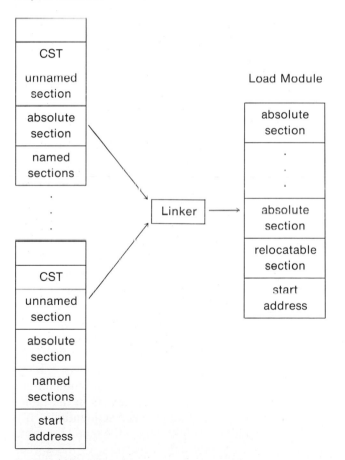

Object Modules

Figure 9-11 Linking for a relocatable load module.

The format of the absolute sections can be compatible with the sections of an absolute load module, as shown in Fig. 9-2a. Likewise, the start address can have the same format as that shown in Figure 9-2b, except that here the starting address is interpreted as a relative location in the relocatable section instead of as an absolute address. It is considered an error if more than one object module contains the optional start address. The relocatable section, which needs only a relocation table, can have the same format as that shown in Fig. 9-3, with the addition of a preceding length field.

A linker can be designed with a two-pass algorithm somewhat analogous to a two-pass assembler. The first pass constructs a table with an entry for each control section involved in the linking. Each table entry gives the location of a specified section; for absolute sections this is its absolute starting address, and for relocatable sections it is its relative starting address in the single load-module relocatable section. The second pass then constructs the load module based on the information in the table, which can be called the *memory map* table. An initial algorithm for a linker is thus:

```
{ linking algorithm }
construct memory map table;
construct load module
```

Entries in the memory map table can contain a module name, control-section name, address, and length fields. The module name is taken from the object module, having been supplied by the programmer or generated by the assembler, and simply serves to identify the module during linking and on the linker output listing. The control-section name identifies the section within the module. For named sections this is obviously the name assigned by the programmer. For unnamed sections this can be taken to be identical to the module name. For absolute sections it can be a string (.ASECT, for example) identifying the entry as absolute.

The address field will contain the absolute starting address for absolute sections and for relocatable sections the relative starting address in the load-module relocatable section. The length is needed by the second pass of the linker.

In forming the memory map table the first pass can examine the absolute sections first. Each is entered into the table. Since there can be overlap among the entries, the linker also creates a list, the *absolute load list,* of nonoverlapping load-module absolute sections. As each entry is made into the table, a check of this list reveals whether the new entry overlaps a section on the list and, if so, the two are combined in the existing list entry. Otherwise a new list entry is created.

Next, the named relocatable sections are examined and each is entered into the table. For each such section a relative address in the load-module relocatable section is assigned. If no other like-named section exists in the table, this address is assigned just by allocating load-module space sequentially. If a matching entry is found, however, the address is taken from the matching table entry. Also, if the length of the new entry is greater than that of the earlier entry, then any following sections must have their addresses increased accordingly.

Finally, each unnamed relocatable section is entered into the table and assigned a load-module address from the next available location. With the complete memory map table, it is now possible to look up any control section and determine its position in the load module. The second pass can now perform all relocation and linking of external references.

The following is an outline of the first-pass algorithm:

```
{ construct memory map table }
FOR each absolute section DO BEGIN
     entertable( module name, .ASECT, address, length);
     IF section overlaps entry on absolute load list THEN
          modify existing entry on absolute load list
     ELSE make new entry on absolute load list END;
FOR each named relocatable section DO BEGIN
     IF matching name not found in table THEN BEGIN
        assign address in load module,
        entertable( module name, section name, address, length) END
     ELSE BEGIN
        assign address from matching entry,
        IF length exceeds existing matching entry THEN
             adjust address for all following sections;
        entertable( module name, section name, address, length) END;
FOR each unnamed relocatable section DO BEGIN
     assign address in load module;
     entertable( module name, section name, address, length) END
```

The second pass now constructs the load module comprising four distinct parts: the absolute sections, the relocation table, the relocatable code, and the starting address. Thus the algorithm can be outlined as follows:

```
{ construct load module }
construct absolute sections;
construct relocation table and perform address relocation;
move relocatable code into load module;
insert starting address
```

Of the four steps, only the second is not straightforward. The first, constructing the absolute sections, consists of building the sections from the absolute load list and then moving the code into place in the load module. The third, moving code into the load module, simply finds the position for each section in the memory map table. The fourth, inserting the starting address, need only check each module to see that no two or more conflicting start addresses are found.

The second step is decomposed into two operations on each relocatable section thus:

```
{ construct relocation table and perform address relocation }
FOR each relocatable section DO BEGIN
    process global symbol table;
    process relocation table END
```

Consider first the global symbol table. For each symbol given in an external table, a search is made of all the entry tables involved in the linking. If no matching entry symbol is found, the reference is treated as an error. If a matching entry symbol is found, then its value component, converted to a relative address in the combined load module, is entered into the relocation table (unless an entry already exists). All words on the list of references to that external are then placed on the reference list for the corresponding relocation-table entry.

Next consider the relocation table. For each out-of-section reference its value is converted to a relative address in the combined load module and an entry is made into the relocation table (unless an entry already exists). All words on the list of references to that out-of-section address are then placed on the reference list for the corresponding relocation-table entry. Each within-section reference is processed identically, except that the address conversion is slightly different. An outline of these operations follows:

```
{ process global symbol table }
FOR each external symbol DO BEGIN
    search all entry tables for a match;
    IF watch not found THEN issue error message
    ELSE BEGIN
        convert entry value to load module address;
        IF no relocation table entry for address THEN
            make new entry in relocation table;
        append list of external references to list of
            relocatable addresses END END;
{ process relocation table }
FOR each out-of-section reference DO BEGIN
    convert value to load module address;
    IF no relocation table entry for address THEN BEGIN
        make new entry in relocation table;
        append list of references to list of
            relocatable addresses END END;
FOR each within-section reference DO BEGIN
    similar to out-of-section references END
```

9-3.2 Absolute Load-Module Output

A *linking loader* produces absolute load modules, thus saving the overhead of relocation during loading, since an absolute loader can then be used. The algorithm is similar to the linker described in the previous section except that the relocatable section is made absolute. Thus, in processing the global symbol table and the relocation table, all relocatable address in the code can be assigned their final value directly without reconstructing the combined relocation table.

Most linking loaders will optionally transfer control directly to the system absolute loader when linking is complete. This simply saves the extra step of explicitly invoking the system absolute loader.

9-3.3 Object-Module Output

In the case that separately assembled modules are always to be used together, then extra overhead required each time the modules are involved in a linking can be eliminated by linking them into a single object module. Figure 9-12 depicts the situation as several object modules are linked to produce a single combined object module.

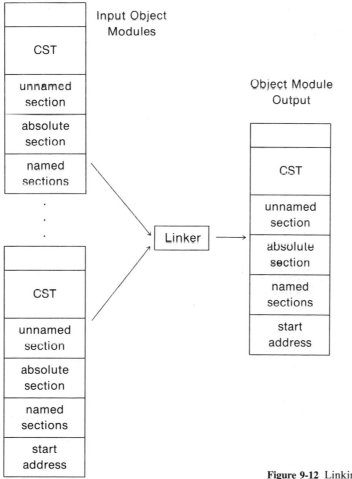

Figure 9-12 Linking for an object module.

Producing an object module rather than a load module is slightly more difficult, because the data structure for the former is more complex. The algorithm, however, is similar. First, a memory map table is constructed to determine the relative location of each section in the output module. All absolute sections and all unnamed sections are combined. Matching named sections are combined. Next, the output absolute section, unnamed section, and named sections are constructed. In doing this, some global references may be transformed into out-of-section references or within-section references. Also, out-of-section references may change according to the memory map produced in the first pass. Finally, within-section references in the unnamed sections will also change as these are combined in a single section. Details of the algorithm are explored in the exercises at the end of the chapter.

9-4 TRANSLATE-AND-GO SYSTEMS

Many times there is a single control section in a single object module to be processed. Student exercises are the most pertinent example of such situations. In this case, much of the mechanism built into the translation and linking phases is unnecessary. Complex global symbol tables and relocation tables are simply not needed at all.

The best way to handle such jobs is to have the assembler generate an absolute load module directly, as was done in the example of Chap. 8. In addition, the assembler can transfer control directly to the system absolute loader, producing a single processing step that takes a program from source form into execution. In most cases it is not necessary to keep a file of the source or absolute programs. Of course, this necessitates retranslation each time the program is to be run. Translate-and-go systems are thus ideal for debugging runs; the final run can be fully assembled to produce a relocatable object module.

9-5 INTERPRETATION

The final step, and the raison d'être, in processing a program is its interpretation, the actual carrying out of the meaning of the program statements. In most cases, this is done by the same hardware system in which the assembler, linker, and loader execute. There are situations, however, where the absolute code produced cannot be, or for good reasons is not, interpreted by the same hardware that produced it.

For example, the target machine, that for which the code is intended, may not be large enough to conveniently run a large translation system. The translation and linking are then done on a large machine and some means is provided to load the code into the smaller machine for interpretation. Translators running on one machine and producing code for another machine are called *cross-translators*.

Another case where a cross-translator is necessary involves writing software for a new machine that does not yet exist. One solution is to write a program that accepts a machine-language program as input and carries out the actions specified as if the program were executing on the hardware processor for which it was intended. Such an interpreted program will "run" very slowly, but the software can be tested to some minimal degree.

Software interpreters have other applications as well. For example, a large class of students learning to program in assembly language for a small machine may not have the hands-on facility available for running their jobs. Here, an assembler-interpreter system can be written to run on a large machine; the assembler feeds the assembled code to the interpreter for execution, and the system appears to the user as a translate-and-go system. Access can be provided via a batch stream or time-sharing for processing of a large volume of jobs.

Another benefit of using an interpreter for execution of student jobs is the ease of providing diagnostic information. Since students will submit jobs with a large number of errors most of the time, it is critical to provide clear helpful error messages. An interpreter can easily diagnose errors and, more important, can easily provide informative messages. Alternatively, with hardware execution, run-time errors arc caught by the hardware, and the information provided to the user via the normal operating system error-recovery facilities is usually very minimal.

Given that a translator is to produce code for a software interpreter rather than for an actual hardware processor, it is not necessary to exactly simulate the hardware. Since the interpreter can be written to interpret whatever the assembler produces, the assembler writer is free to design object code that is most suitable for interpretation. Therefore most translator-interpreter systems are based on a special *intermediate language* designed specifically for its suitability as an output structure for the translator and an input structure for the interpreter. For example, program-variable names may be left in symbolic form so that all run-time error messages are issued with symbolic information.

EXERCISES

9-1 Write and test a bootstrap loader for the system available to you. It should load from a pre-specified device, such as a paper-tape reader, and transfer control to the loaded program.

9-2 Assemble separately the modules of the desk calculator example of Sec. 6-12. Define the ENTRY and EXTERNAL references explicitly. Link and test the system.

9-3 Assemble the modules separately and use the named control-section facility to access the global data in the desk calculator example from Sec. 6-12. Link and test the system.

9-4 Write and test an interpreter for the simple hypothetical machine introduced in Exercise 3-1.

9-5 Write an absolute loader for the simple machine of Exercise 3-1. Test it by loading programs for the interpreter of Exercise 9-4.

9-6 Design a relocatable object-module format for the simple machine.

9-7 Modify the assembler of Exercise 8-4 to produce relocatable object modules.

9-8 Design and program a linker that produces relocatable load modules for the simple machine.

9-9 Design and program a relocating loader for the simple machine.

9-10 Modify the linker of Exercise 9-8 to produce absolute load modules.

9-11 Modify the linker of Exercise 9-8 to produce relocatable object modules.

9-12 Combine your relocating assembler, linking loader, and absolute loader into an assemble-and-go system. Compare its performance with the combination of the absolute assembler and the absolute loader.

REFERENCES

Linkers and loaders are not extensively covered in a tutorial way in the literature, perhaps because they fall into the category of uninteresting but necessary utilities. An exception is the paper by Presser (1972) in *Computing Surveys*. McCarthy (1963) constitutes a very early treatment of linking and will be of historical interest. Finally, Barron (1969) includes the subject in the context of assembly language and so is perhaps the most relevant source for further reading.

CONCURRENT INPUT-OUTPUT

Much of the complexity in systems programming is due to the intricacies of transferring data into and out from main memory. This is first because the devices involved in these transfers differ greatly in their operational characteristics, both among themselves and with the processor. In particular, I/O devices are normally much slower than the processor. Second, and what is more significant than operational differences, is the fact that I/O devices are systems independent of the processor. That is, their timing is controlled internally and any communication with the processor must be carefully synchronized with the processor's internal timing. This has already been seen in Chap. 5, where paper-tape peripherals were described.

The relative slowness of I/O devices, along with their independent timing, forces the recognition of I/O transfers as activities essentially concurrent with processor operation. This chapter explores this concurrency and describes the most common mechanism employed to control it, the *interrupt*.

10-1 I/O INSTRUCTIONS

Many machines have a special set of instructions for performing I/O. A typical set in a small machine might be the following: start_io, read_data, write_data, and read_status; with the following formats and meanings.

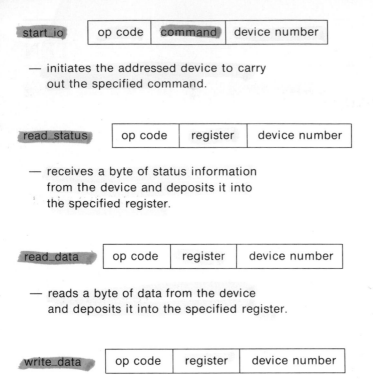

start_io | op code | command | device number

— initiates the addressed device to carry
out the specified command.

read_status | op code | register | device number

— receives a byte of status information
from the device and deposits it into
the specified register.

read_data | op code | register | device number

— reads a byte of data from the device
and deposits it into the specified register.

write_data | op code | register | device number

— writes to the device a byte of data
taken from the specified register.

The key in using such instructions is the condition that the specified device must be prepared to act on the execution of the start_io, read_data, or write_data instruction in order for them to function correctly. This is where the read_status instruction is needed. It can be executed at any time and will return the encoded current status of the device. Suppose that a nonzero status byte means that the device has completed the last I/O instruction executed and is prepared to act on another. Then a character can be read with the sequence (instruction operands are shown in parentheses):

1.   start_io (read,j,);
2.   1: read_status (reg,j);
3.   IF reg = 0 THEN GOTO 1;
4.   read_data (reg,j)

Line 1 starts device j reading. Lines 2 and 3 cause a delay until such time as device j returns a nonzero status, indicating that the read operation has been completed and the next byte is ready to be transmitted. Finally, line 4 receives this byte from device j and deposits it into register reg.

As one can see, this is similar to the algorithm used in the PDP-11, except that special instructions are used here. The use of nonspecialized instructions for I/O is particular to the PDP-11 and results from the design of the architecture in which device registers are addressable as memory words. As seen here, however, the programs for performing I/O are not significantly different.

10-2 BUSY-WAITING I/O

Many peripheral devices on the PDP-11 behave similarly to the paper-tape devices described in Chap. 5. As shown in Fig. 10-1, such devices are represented by four control and status registers (CSRs) in memory, the reader status (RS), reader buffer (RB), writer status (WS), and writer buffer (WB).

Control of these devices has been described in terms of *busy-waiting* loops. That is, the controlling program (i.e., the processor) has to wait in a loop for incoming characters to appear in the RB and for outgoing characters to be removed from the WB. In the former case the character's presence is signaled by the DONE bit going from 0 to 1. In the latter case the character's successful transmittal is signaled by the READY bit going from 0 to 1.

As we recall from previous discussion, the code to read a character might be

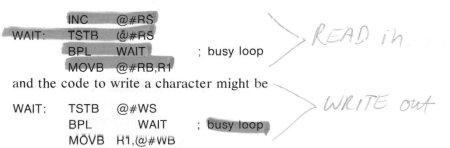

```
          INC     @#RS
WAIT:     TSTB    @#RS
          BPL     WAIT        ; busy loop
          MOVB    @#RB,R1
```

READ in.

and the code to write a character might be

```
WAIT:     TSTB    @#WS
          BPL     WAIT        ; busy loop
          MOVB    R1,@#WB
```

WRITE out

Let's look more closely at the timing of I/O transfers using busy-waiting. In Fig. 10-2 one can see how productive activity in the processor-reader combination is purely sequential as a character is read. The processor, executing a program, is doing (one hopes!) useful work until another input character is needed and INIT is set. While the processor waits in a loop the reader, perhaps very

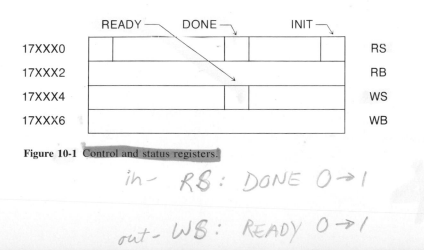

	READY	DONE		INIT			
17XXX0							RS
17XXX2							RB
17XXX4							WS
17XXX6							WB

Figure 10-1 Control and status registers.

in— RS: DONE 0→1

out— WB: READY 0→1

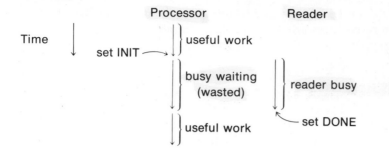

Figure 10-2 Input busy waiting.

slowly,[1] transmits the character. Only when the character arrives can the processor resume executing "useful" code.

All input-output activity need not always be purely sequential if the processor continues to do something else while a device is responding to a signal. For example, many terminals require that characters read be echo-printed so that they appear on the screen or other output mechanism at the terminal. The processor need not wait after writing an echo character; it can proceed to do something else such as reading the next character. Of course, before another character is written, a wait may be necessary. Figure 10-3 shows how processor execution and device operation can be overlapped during echo printing. For the sake of the example, writing has been shown to be faster than reading.

[1] A typical read time from an electromechanical device like a card reader is 3 ms, while a PDP-11/03 processor can execute one instruction in about 3 μs.

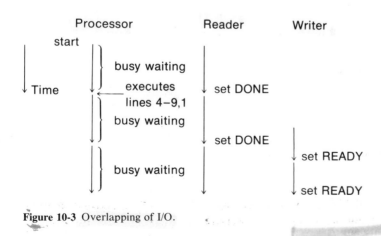

Figure 10-3 Overlapping of I/O.

```
                    ; assume that R1 contains the address
                    ; of a buffer area in memory
1       LOOP :  INC     @#RS                ; read
2       WAITR:  TSTB    @#RS
3               BPL         WAITR
4               MOVB    @#RB,(R1)
5       WAITW:  TSTB    @#WS
6               BPL         WAITW
7               MOVB        (R1),@#WB   ; write
8               CMPB    (R1)+,LAST      ; LAST contains
9               BNE     LOOP            ; terminator character
```

The overlap of reading and writing is clearly shown, but drawing the diagram to a reasonable scale obscures the fact that the processor continues to execute lines 8, 9, 1, 2, and 3 while writing is proceeding. In other words, writing and processor activity (which happens to be control of reading here) overlap. Some processor activity other than reading is also possible, of course, such as in the following:

```
L:      compute result in R1
WAIT:   TSTB    @#WS
        BPL         WAIT
        MOVB        R1,@#WB
        loop to L
```

where results are computed while previously computed results are being written.

Although some overlap of processor execution and I/O device operation is possible with busy waiting, one still needs a better way than using a processor loop to wait for device signals. Specifically, two mechanisms are needed.

1. A way for a program to relinquish processor control while waiting for a device signal.
2. A way for a device to signal such a waiting program in such a way that the program regains processor control.

A discussion of the first requirement is deferred until Chap. 12, but the second requirement is the subject of the following section.

10-3 INTERRUPTS

An *interrupt mechanism* is a facility built into the hardware of a processor. An *interrupt* is a signal from an external device to a processor that causes the processor, after completing its current instruction, to fetch the next instruction from a special location in memory associated with the device. Although other external sources can send interrupts, they normally originate from I/O devices.

The occurrence of an interrupt, then, causes the processor to finish what it is currently doing with its program and then to simply leave that program (i.e., the program execution is interrupted) and begin executing another one. The new program will be one that is waiting for a signal from the device. Its job is to act on the interrupt (this is often called *interrupt handling*) and, when it is ready, to wait again to give control back to the program that was interrupted. Let's now see how this mechanism is implemented on the PDP-11.

For each I/O device on a PDP-11 system there are two permanently as-signed memory words called the device's *interrupt vector.* In the first word of the interrupt vector, the interrupt-handler address for the device is stored. The second word contains a PS word to be loaded at the same time that the PC is loaded from the first word to effect the transfer caused by an interrupt. A reader interrupt vector, RPC and RPS, is shown below.

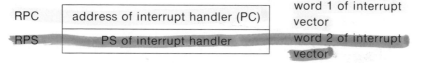

RPC	address of interrupt handler (PC)
RPS	PS of interrupt handler

word 1 of interrupt vector

word 2 of interrupt vector

Since there must be a way to restore the PC and PS of the executing pro-gram, the interrupt mechanism must, of course, save these values before load-ing a new interrupt vector. This can be done by assigning, permanently, a pair of memory words associated with the interrupt vector. An interrupt then stores the old PC-PS pair and loads a new pair. At the conclusion of interrupt handling a special instruction is used to restore the saved pair. Figure 10-4 illustrates the two events, interrupt occurrence and interrupt return.

In the PDP-11, PC-PS saving is done on the system stack, the PS first, fol-lowed by the PC. Specifically, the steps carried out by the PDP-11 processor on the occurrence of an interrupt are:

1. Complete the instruction currently under execution.
2. Save the PC and PS in an internal temporary location.
3. Load the PC and PS from the device interrupt vector.
4. Push the old PS onto the stack.
5. Push the old PC onto the stack.
6. Resume execution, fetching the next instruction as indicated by the PC.

Notice particularly how the PC and PS are pushed onto the stack *after* the interrupt vector has been loaded. Although there is a very good reason for this, it cannot be fully explained until Chap. 12. For the moment, then, the ordering of these steps is not significant. (In fact, on the smaller PDP-11 models it is never significant.)

Before explaining how the saved PC and PS are restored, let's consider the way that a program is designed to use interrupts. Commonly, one describes

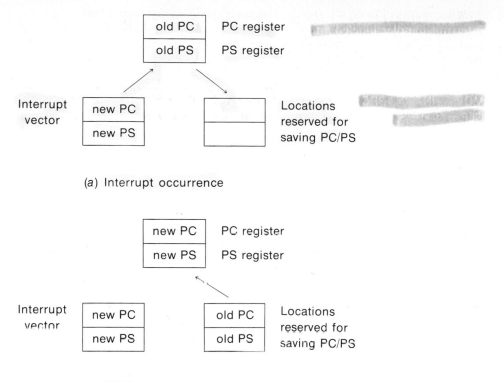

(a) Interrupt occurrence

(b) Interrupt return

Figure 10-4 Saving and restoring of PC-PS pair.

such an I/O program as being *interrupt-driven* since it is activated periodically by interrupts. An outline of an interrupt-driven algorithm is given below.

```
1   start:   initialize interrupt vector;
2            start device reading or writing;
3   loop:   continue execution concurrent with I/O;
             .
             .
             .
            go to loop;

4   resume:  continue execution following completion of I/O;

             .

            terminate;

5   int:    service interrupt (read or write);
6            IF I/O complete  THEN go to resume
7            ELSE  return to interrupted program
```

⎫ interrupt
⎬ handler
⎭

Two segments of code are shown: the main line program labeled *start,* and the interrupt handler labeled *int.* Execution commences at start, where the interrupt vector for the device to be used is initialized. It is important to remember this step, often a source of error when forgotten. The code

```
MOV   #INT, @#RPC
CLR   @#RPS
```

(handwritten annotation:)
```
MOV   #ISR, @#VECTOR    ; new PC
CLR   @#VECTOR+2        ; new PSW
```

would suffice for initialization. The device is started and then the main line program is free to do anything it wishes independent of the I/O, now controlled entirely by the interrupt handler, which will return control to resume when all I/O is completed.

In the interrupt handler, entered at int when an interrupt occurs, the interrupt is serviced; input data are removed from the device buffer or output data are inserted into the device buffer. Control then is returned to the interrupted program, somewhere in line 3 of the main line program, or to resume if the I/O is completed.

Remember that the significance of this design is that the main line program's line 3 can be written almost independently of the I/O going on concurrently. The *almost* is necessary because, of course, the main line program should not interfere with the operation of the interrupt handler by altering its internal data.

10-4 ENABLING AND DISABLING INTERRUPTS

As implied in our descriptions of I/O control using busy-waiting, it is quite possible to control I/O devices without interrupts. This is generally simpler, and in many cases the concurrency provided by interrupts is not needed. Most machines, therefore, provide a way to *disable* the interrupt mechanism and, of course, to *enable* it so that interrupts will occur.

The interrupt enable-disable mechanism way provide device-selectable control, or it may simply disable all interrupts, although the former is more common.

In the PDP-11, the interrupt enable-disable switch for a device is normally located in bit 6 of the device status register as denoted by INTENB in the RS word below. If INTENB is set, an interrupt will occur simultaneously when DONE is set by the device. Recall that reading from the associated RB will clear DONE, thus allowing another interrupt to be recognized.

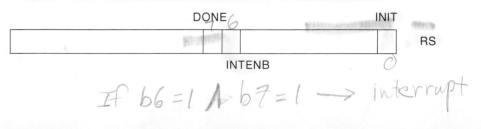

If $b6 = 1 \wedge b7 = 1 \longrightarrow$ interrupt

10-5 INTERRUPT RETURN

To return control to a program that was interrupted, all that is necessary is to restore the saved PC and PS. In the PDP-11 it is easy to see that the interrupt handler can return control to the interrupted program by popping the PS and PC from the stack. The problem with doing this under program control is that it must, for reasons that are more obvious later, be done as a single operation; loading the PC first would transfer control before the PS could be loaded, and loading the PS first would change the status bits for the current program as it loaded the PC. Since there are some important bits in the PS that we have not yet described, the latter sequence is not acceptable.

Most machines provide an instruction to allow loading of the PC and PS as one operation. In the PDP-11 it is the Return from Interrupt (RTI) instruction:

Instruction	Operation
RTI	$\uparrow(SP) \rightarrow PC$
	$\uparrow(SP) \rightarrow PS$

} pops old PC + PSW off stack.

Figure 10-5 shows an example of coding the interrupt-driven I/O. Notice how INTENB and INIT are set with a single Move instruction.

Other things to notice in this program are that absolute addressing is used for locations external to the program, the ADD #4,SP clears the unneeded PC and PS from the stack, and a JMP is used to transfer to RESUME since the offset between these two locations is not known. The reader should be clear as to the reason for removing the PC and PS from the stack. They were pushed there by the interrupt but are not needed if the interrupt handler is to transfer directly to RESUME. No error may be caused by leaving them on the stack, but it would be extremely bad practice to do so; any program should restore the stack to its original state on completing its work.

Finally, some input devices, such as keyboards, transmit a character when initiated from the device itself. This contrasts with a paper-tape reader, for example, which is initiated under program control by setting INIT in its status register. Therefore, with devices such as keyboards it is not necessary to set INIT. When using interrupts, setting INTENB is sufficient to start the device; a character will be transmitted and announced by an interrupt at the same time that the DONE bit is set. In Fig. 10-5, then, the statement INC @#TTY1RS in the interrupt handler could be omitted. Also, INTENB could be initialized with MOV #100,@#TTY1RS.

```
;
; example to read eight characters from device tty1
;
          TTY1RS=17XXX0          ;tty1 control registers are
          TTY1RB=17XXX2          ;at word 17XXX0
          TT1RPC=40              ;tty1 reader interrupt vector is
          TT1RPS=42              ;at word 40
BUFFER:   .BLKB 10               ;buffer for 8 characters
 START:   MOV   #RDRINT,@#TT1RPC ;initialize interrupt vector
          CLR   @#TT1RPS         ;
          MOV   #10,R1           ;R1 is counter for 8 characters
          MOV   #BUFFER,R2       ;R2 addresses next buffer location
          MOV   #101,@#TTY1RS    ;set INTENB and INIT
  WAIT:   BR    WAIT             ;could be useful processing
RESUME:                          ;resume after I/O completed
```

(a) Main line program

```
RDRINT:   MOVB  @#TTY1RB,(R2)+   ;get next character
          DEC   R1               ;decrement counter
          BEQ   END              ;branch if I/O completed
          INC   @#TTY1RS         ;start reader again
          RTI
  END:    ADD   #4,SP            ;remove saved PC and PS
          CLR   @#TTY1RS         ;reset INTENB
          JMP   RESUME           ;resume main line program
```

(b) Interrupt handler

Figure 10-5 Example coding for interrupt handling.

10-6 MASKING INTERRUPTS

It is often necessary to ignore interrupts until a later time when the interrupt handler is prepared to take the required action. A good example of this is the case of a simple program that echoes characters read from a terminal back to the same terminal.[1] Suppose the program is interrupt-driven; a reader interrupt should be handled by restarting the reader and a writer interrupt should be handled by restarting the writer. However, the writer cannot be restarted unless the character to be echoed has already been read. Put another way, the writer interrupt should be ignored until the corresponding reader interrupt has occurred.

[1] A terminal is two I/O devices working together, a keyboard input device and a screen or typewriter output device.

Since it is very clumsy to let an interrupt occur and then ignore it, a mechanism is needed to prevent an interrupt from occurring until the program is ready for it. There are two ways to do this on the PDP-11, one of which, the enable-disable bit, has already been described. If a device is interrupt-disabled, any attempt to interrupt the processor is prevented and the device remains in an *interrupt pending* state. If an instruction sets INTENB for the device, then, on completion of the execution of that instruction, the pending interrupt is recognized by the processor. Thus, a program can ignore interrupts from a device simply by disabling interrupts.

Figure 10-6 shows the algorithm for the echo writing example. For simplicity, the interrupt handlers are symmetrical in that the writer handler enables the reader and vice versa. Thus, the reader does not get ahead of the writer, al-

```
1 start:    initialize interrupt vectors and character counter;
2           read first character;
3           disable writer;
4           start writer;
5           enable reader;
6           start reader;
7 loop:     continue execution concurrent with I/O;
            .
            .
            .
            GO TO loop;
8 resume: continue execution following completion of I/O;
            .
            .
            .
            terminate;
9 rdrint:   disable reader;
10          get character from reader buffer;
11          decrement counter;
12          IF counter > 0 THEN start reader;
13          enable writer;
14          return;

15 wrtint:  disable writer;
16          IF counter > 0 THEN BEGIN
17              put character in writer buffer;
18              start writer;
19              enable reader;
20              return END;
21          ELSE BEGIN
22              write last character;
23              go to resume END
```

Figure 10-6 Interrupt-driven echo writing.

though to do this would be perfectly reasonable. Section 10-11 will discuss the buffering necessary in such situations.

An implementation of the algorithm in Fig. 10-6 is shown in Fig. 10-7. Things to note include the fact that certain tasks that do not appear in the algorithm must be remembered in the implementation. For example, the PC must be removed before resuming the main line program. This is as it should be, since the algorithm designer should be free from implementation details and the

```
        ;
        ;example to read and echo 8 characters from TTY1;
        ;
        TTY1RS=17XXX0            ;tty1 control registers are
        TTY1RB=17XXX2            ;at word 17XXX0
        TTY1WS=17XXX4           ;
        TTY1WB=17XXX6           ;
        TT1RPC =60              ;tty1 interrupt vectors are at
        TT1RPS =62              ;word 60
        TT1WPC =64              ;
        TT1WPS =66              ;
BUFFER: BLKB   10               ;buffer for 8 characters
 START: MOV    #RDRINT,@#TT1RPC   ;initialize interrupt vectors
        CLR    @#TT1RPS
        MOV    #WTRINT,@#TT1WPC
        CLR    @#TT1WPS
        MOV    #10,R1           ;R1 is counter for 8 characters
        MOV    #BUFFER,R2       ;R2 addresses next buffer location
        INC    @#TTY1RS         ;get first character
 WAITR: TSTB   @#TTY1RS         ;and wait
        BPL    WAITR            ;for it
        MOVB   @#TTY1RB,(R2)    ;store it in the buffer
        BIC    #100,@#TTY1WS    ;disable writer
        MOVB   (R2)+,@#TTY1WB   ;start writer
        BIS    #101,@#TTY1RS    ;enable and start reader
  WAIT: BR     WAIT             ;useful work could be done here
RESUME:
```

Figure 10-7a Main line program

```
        BIC    #100,@#TTY1RS    ;disable reader
RDRINT: MOVB   @#TTY1RB,(R2)    ;get character
        DEC    R1               ;count it
        BEQ    ENDRDR           ;if last character
        INC    @#TTY1RS         ;start reader
```

```
ENDRDR:  BIS     #100,@#TTY1WS      ;enable writer
         RTI                        ;return
WTRINT:  BIC     #100,@#TTY1WS      ;disable writer
         TST     R1                 ;test count
         BEQ     ENDWTR             ;if last character
         MOVB    (R2)+,@#TTY1WB     ;start writer
         BIS     #100,@#TTY1RS      ;enable reader
         RTI                        ;return
ENDWTR:  MOVB    (R2),@#TTY1WB      ;start writer and leave R2
WAITW:   TSTB    @#TTY1WS           ;
         BPL     WAITW              ;wait for writer
         ADD     #4,SP              ;pop PC and PS
         JMP     RESUME             ;resume main line program
```

Figure 10-7b Interrupt handlers

Figure 10-7 Example coding for echo writing.

implementor should be free from considering the logic of the algorithm. Both jobs are equally important.

Notice also that explicit starting of the reader has been included for generality. From here on, however, for keyboard devices explicit device initiation will not be performed.

10-7 INTERRUPT PRIORITIES

Interrupt handling becomes complex very quickly as more than two devices are controlled using the enable-disable mechanism for masking interrupts. The main difficulty stems from the need to allow interrupt handlers exclusive processor control without themselves being interrupted. More often, there exist many relationships among interrupt handlers regarding which may be interrupted by which others. Consider just the simple case of three programs, A, B, and C, handling interrupts. Suppose that

A is always interruptible.
B is interruptible only by C.
C is never interruptible.

One can handle such situations with disabling. B simply disables A on entry and enables it before returning. C disables A and B on entry and enables them before returning. There are several problems with this solution, however. The most serious is that it requires each program to be aware of the existence of all others. If an additional program is introduced into the system, then every other program that is uninterruptible must explicitly mask interrupts for the new program's device. This invites errors to occur.

Almost as serious is the fact that it may require several instructions to disable interrupts on entry and during this sequence another interrupt may occur.[1] Since the interrupting program may disable and enable interrupts also, errors can result. In the case of the PDP-11, an undesired interrupt of this sort can mean that during the execution of an interrupt handler the state of the stack is unknown. If the handler is to do a termination cleanup of the stack, then errors can result.

Many machines solve the problem by providing a single instruction with which several interrupts can be masked on entry, and by providing a single instruction to unmask interrupts and return as a single operation. More commonly, however, a priority mechanism is used.

The basic idea in a priority interrupt mechanism is that each device along with its interrupt handler is assigned a numeric priority. *An interrupt handler can be interrupted only by devices with a higher priority.*

In the PDP-11 the priority of the currently executing program is stored in bits 5 to 7 of the PS word and is generally referred to as the *processor priority*. There are, therefore, eight priority levels, 0 to 7.

By placing the processor priority in the PS, an interrupt automatically changes it, because the PS is swapped as already described. An interrupt handler, therefore, is automatically placed in execution at its assigned priority level. The designer of the interrupt handler need not be concerned with devices at lower priority levels, as all are automatically and effectively masked.

The complementary operation of unmasking devices and returning to the interrupted program is of course handled by the RTI instruction, which unstacks the saved priority. As a series of successively higher priority interrupts occur, the PC-PS pair for each is stacked and then unstacked in the proper nested order, each RTI returning control to the interrupted program. Note particularly that the designer of an interrupt handler does not know, in general, to which program control will return. Thus, additional devices and their interrupt handlers can be added without requiring any changes in existing interrupt handlers.

An additional advantage of a priority interrupt mechanism is that the designer of the processor has some basis on which to handle the situation of simultaneous interrupts; the processor simply recognizes the one with the highest

---

[1] Most machines allow an interrupt handler at least one instruction of execution before another interrupt can occur.

Table 10-1 Example PDP-11 device priorities

Priority	Devices
4	Paper tape
	Teletypewriters
	Alphanumeric screen terminals
	Line printer
5	Communications line
	Disk
6	Clock
	Card reader

low

high (nothing can int. dev. w/ priority of 7)

priority. This can be quite important in process control applications where the computer system is handling real-time inputs from a machine tool, for example.

An interrupt masked by the processor's priority will occur immediately following an RTI instruction that lowers the priority sufficiently, provided of course that no other higher-priority interrupt is also pending. Interrupts from devices within the same priority level are recognized by the processor in a fixed order determined by the physical connection of the device to the processor. In fact the connection is done in such a way that the processor sees at most one interrupt pending in each priority level.

Finally, there is flexibility available to the system designer in that the priority level at which a device is connected to the processor need not necessarily be equal to the priority stored in the PS part of the device's interrupt vector. It is the programmer's privilege (and responsibility) to initialize the PS to any priority appropriate to the application. For our purposes it will always be assumed that the device priority and the interrupt handler priority (as stored in the interrupt vector) are equal. Table 10-1 shows some examples of normal PDP-11 device priority assignments. It shows there that alphanumeric screen terminals are connected at priority 4. Figure 10-8 shows a simple priority inter-

```
            TTY1RS=17XXX0        ;tty1 control registers are
            TTY1RB=17XXX2        ;at word 17XXX0
            TT1RPC=40            ;tty1 reader interrupt vector is
            TT1RPS=42            ;at word 40
RDRINT:     MOVB  @#TTY1RB,(R2)+  ;get next character
            DEC   R1             ;decrement counter
            BEQ   END            ;branch if I/O completed
            RTI
   END:     ADD   #4,SP          ;remove saved PC and PS
            CLR   @#TTY1RS       ;reset INTENB
            JMP   RESUME         ;resume main line program
```

Figure 10-8 Priority interrupt handling.

rupt handler for such a device reader. Notice that the unnecessary explicit starting of the keyboard device is omitted.

10-8 NONINTERRUPT SYSTEMS

The complexity of controlling I/O devices can be reduced if the processor-device communication mechanism is modified to eliminate interrupts. The exact nature of such modifications and the trade-offs with the capability for very close control over devices provided by an interrupt mechanism are best discussed in a text on operating systems. The reader is referred to any of the texts in the Bibliography for further reading in this area.

For the purposes of this text, however, it is important to remember that interrupts are presented here as the common method of controlling devices. We feel that a solid understanding of and some practice in these methods provides an excellent base for studying the theory of operating systems and investigating other methods.

10-9 CLASSIFICATION OF DEVICES

Input-output devices exist in many varieties, but their different characteristics can be nicely described with respect to only four basic attributes: data element length, access mode, transfer mode, and storage medium. A clear understanding of these terms makes categorization of devices straightforward.

First, the *data-element length* is commonly the 8-bit byte but may vary from a single bit to much longer words of up to several hundred bits. The data element is the smallest unit of addressability and data transfer.

Second, the *access mode* is either *direct* or *sequential.* A device is direct access if data elements can be referenced by specifying a unique address. Not all data elements in a direct-access device may be referenced in this way, however. A device is sequential access if data elements can be referenced by specifiying simply the "next" data element, that is, the one immediately following, in a fixed sequence, the one previously referenced. We shall see that several common devices provide both access modes in combination. All accessing methods, however, are composed of these two basic methods.

Third, the *transfer mode* is either *block transfer* or *element transfer.* This simply means that in the former case the unit of data transfer is a *block* of one or more data elements in a sequence, and in the latter case it is always a single data element. For byte element devices, the transfer mode is often described as "character transfer."

Fourth, the *storage medium* is classified as either *peripheral* or *auxiliary memory.* This terminology is not as widely accepted as that of the previous three attributes, but it is what we shall adopt here. A peripheral device provides storage external to the computer system. Such devices are either input or out-

Table 10-2 I/O device attributes

Attribute	Typical values
Data element length	From 1 to 128 bits
Access mode	Direct, sequential
Transfer mode	Element, block
Storage medium	Peripheral, auxiliary memory

put devices but not both. The medium onto which data is written may be readable but only after it has been transferred physically to an input peripheral. Thus a peripheral may not be written onto and then read from to obtain the data back again. Examples are paper-tape devices, card readers and punches, printers, data communications devices, teletypewriters, and other terminals.

In contrast, an auxiliary memory device provides storage internal to the computer system. These devices are both input and output so that data can be written and then read back from the same device. Examples are magnetic tape, magnetic disk, semiconductor memory, magnetic core memory, and bubble memory. Table 10-2 summarizes the attributes of I/O devices.

10-10 DIRECT MEMORY ACCESS

All input-output devices described thus far transfer data directly to or from the processor via a single buffer register. In machines with special I/O instructions this buffer is read with a Read Data instruction. In the PDP-11 it appears in the main-memory addressing range and so is read with any instruction in the normal set. As explained before, this particular addressing arrangement is unique to the PDP-11. However, such *direct processor control* of I/O data transfers is common to small machines. That is, the data move into and out of main memory under program control via a device buffer register. In PDP-11 terms, a MOVB instruction must be used to transfer each byte to or from a device. Figure 10-9a illustrates the direct processor control data path. Figure 10-9b shows an alternative method whereby the device has *direct memory access* (DMA).

A DMA connection gives a device the ability to read and write main memory. It communicates with the processor for control (initiation of I/O, interrupts, etc.), but data flow only between the device and memory.

A DMA memory connection is essential for block-transfer devices because these devices transfer a block at a fixed data rate. As each data element becomes available for transfer, it must be read or written or it will be lost. The alternative, using processor-controlled I/O, would mean either that the processor would be dedicated to I/O for the duration of the block or that it would have to respond to individual data-element interrupts at a very high rate. In the former case, the I/O is very expensive in terms of processor time, and in the

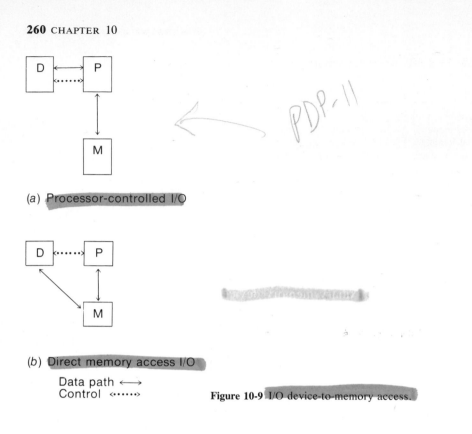

(a) Processor-controlled I/O

(b) Direct memory access I/O

Data path ⟷
Control ⟨······⟩

Figure 10-9 I/O device-to-memory access.

latter case normal block-transfer rates would be too high for the processor to serve several devices without periodically losing data.

A DMA block-transfer device accesses memory concurrently with the processor as it executes programs. Since data can be lost if the I/O device is held up by the memory as it services a reference by the processor, the I/O device is given priority. If, then, both a DMA device and the processor attempt to reference memory simultaneously, the memory will give priority to the I/O device. This arrangement is called *memory cycle stealing* and is an important design consideration. The hardware designer must ensure that cycle stealing does not unduly affect the processor by memory contention.

10-11 BUFFERING

A device buffer register provides a storage area that, with the associated synchronization in the control and status register, matches the different processing rates of the device and the processor. This, of course, is the fundamental reason for buffers. A similar function can be carried out in software by just extending the buffer from a single device register byte to a contiguous area of main memory. Figure 10-10 shows such a *single buffering* program. The

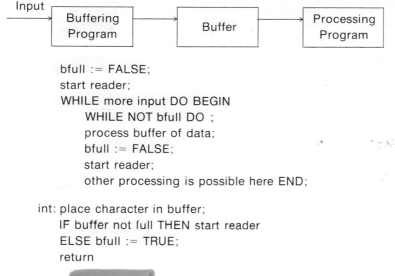

```
bfull := FALSE;
start reader;
WHILE more input DO BEGIN
    WHILE NOT bfull DO ;
    process buffer of data;
    bfull := FALSE;
    start reader;
    other processing is possible here END;

int: place character in buffer;
    IF buffer not full THEN start reader
    ELSE bfull := TRUE;
    return
```

Figure 10-10 Single buffering.

buffering program is simply an interrupt handler that places a character from the device into the next available software buffer position and sets BFULL to TRUE if that action fills the buffer. Otherwise it restarts the reader.

The main line program can now treat the software buffer much like the device buffer; starting the reader initiates the read and BFULL becoming TRUE signals the completion of the complete reading of a buffer of data. Similarly, the program is free to do other processing after the reader has been started. Thus, the software buffer functions much like the device buffer except that a sequence of characters is simultaneously available to the processing program rather than a single character.

Single buffering, as shown here, allows only one of the buffering and processing programs to access the buffer at one time. Therefore, it is not possible to activate the buffering program while the processing program is accessing the data in the buffer. If the processing program has no other processing to do, then no concurrency is possible.

In order to speed up execution time we can extend the buffering mechanism to a double buffering scheme in which input proceeds concurrently with processing of data. As shown in Fig. 10-11, we use two buffers; while the buffering program is filling one the processing program accesses the other. The roles of the buffers are switched under control of the processing program. Notice that the buffering program is almost identical with the single buffering case except that a buffer number i identifies the current input buffer. Now the reader can be kept operating at full speed in the case that processing is faster than the input operation. With single buffering, the reader idles while processing is underway (unless, as we said, other processing is possible).

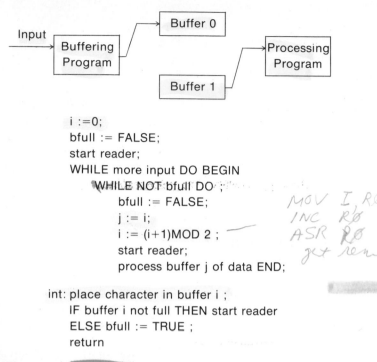

```
i :=0;
bfull := FALSE;
start reader;
WHILE more input DO BEGIN
    WHILE NOT bfull DO ;
        bfull := FALSE;
        j := i;
        i := (i+1)MOD 2 ;
        start reader;
        process buffer j of data END;

int: place character in buffer i ;
    IF buffer i not full THEN start reader
    ELSE bfull := TRUE ;
    return
```

MOV I, RØ
INC RØ
ASR RØ
get ren

Figure 10-11 Double buffering.

These buffering programs are appropriate for an input device requiring pro-
gram-controlled initiation. The case of externally initiated devices like keyboards is more difficult to handle because it is not possible to delay input while
the processing program catches up. Since characters relentlessly appear, sufficient buffer space must be provided in which to store them. Of course, there
must be some limit to this space above which incoming characters are lost. In
the case of a keyboard it is possible to issue a message to the operator when this
limit is reached so at least he or she knows that this has occurred. Other externally initiated devices such as communications lines present a much more
serious problem, since it is not so easy to stop transmission and to recover the
lost data. Some remarks on this problem appear in the section on real-time systems.

The program below shows a double buffering algorithm for an externally
initiated device. The extension to more than two buffers has been left as an
exercise.

```
i := 0;
bfull := FALSE;
enable reader;
WHILE more input DO BEGIN
```

```
WHILE NOT bfull DO ;
     bfull := FALSE;
     j := i;
     i := (i+1)MOD 2 ;
     process buffer j of data END;
```

enable interrupts ——→

i is either 0 or 1 (alternate)

(while more)

```
int:   IF buffer i not full THEN BEGIN
          place character in buffer i;
          IF buffer is full THEN bfull := TRUE END
       ELSE write "input buffer full" to terminal;
```

Example: Buffering an externally initiated device

10-12 INPUT-OUTPUT PROCESSORS

Direct processor control of I/O requires that the processor (under program control) be involved in the transfer, to and from memory, of each data element. As pointed out this has two problems: first, the full computing power of the processor is underworked in doing this task, and second, the processor cannot respond fast enough for many block-transfer devices.

Direct memory access removes the two problems associated with direct processor control but introduces two problems of its own. First, DMA devices are more complex and therefore more expensive. Second, each DMA device requires a connection to memory.[1] Therefore, requiring all devices to be DMA would be excessively expensive because both the devices and memory would be too complex.

The solution found in many systems, most particularly in larger computers, is to place the DMA control function in a separate component that is shared by a collection of devices. Commonly called an *input-output processor* (IOP) or *data channel,* the DMA component was the first example of multiprocessing in computer systems since it is simply an additional processor specialized for I/O work.

Figure 10-12 illustrates the relationship of a typical configuration of processor, memory, and IOP. The design of an IOP can vary considerably; it may execute its program out of its own internal main memory, or it may execute out of the system's main memory. One of the disadvantages of machines with IOP device control is that I/O becomes more complex for the programmer. This is simply because the IOP, in providing facilities for a wide variety of devices, presents a very complex interface to the programmer. The PDP-11, without an IOP architecture, is a more straightforward machine to program for I/O.

---

[1] The following section describes an alternative to multiple connections.

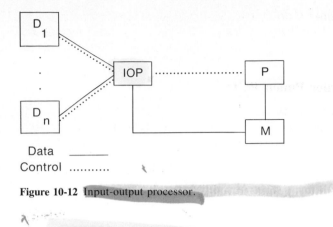

Data ——
Control ....

Figure 10-12 Input-output processor.

10-13 PDP-11 I/O DEVICES

All communication, control and data transfer, between the PDP-11 processor and I/O devices is accomplished via a single set of wires forming a common bus, shown in Fig. 10-13. It is this method of connection that makes device control registers appear as if they are in memory. The processor references memory via the common bus by transmitting a memory address on the bus. If the address transmitted is, in fact a device register address, then it is recognized not by the main memory but by the *device interface,* the digital circuit that provides each device with the logic necessary to conform to the operation of common bus signaling. A MOV into a device register then actually places data into the device register in the interface. The interface, then, determines the format of the device registers and the method of programming I/O operations.

The common bus architecture is, therefore, an alternative to an IOP architecture. A device may be DMA or not and, if not, it does not need complex device-memory data transferring capability. Memory needs only one connection, that to the common bus.

In this section some representative PDP-11 devices and their interfaces are chosen as examples of I/O programming. Not all details of each interface are

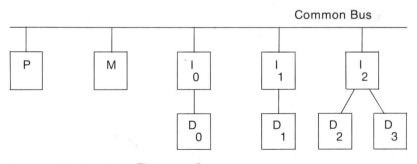

Figure 10-13 The PDP-11 common bus.

given since the reader should refer to the Digital Equipment Corporation Peripherals Handbook for complete and up-to-date reference on device programming.

10-13.1 Paper-Tape Reader-Punch PC11

The PC11 paper-tape reader and punch can read at 300 characters per second and punch at 50 characters per second. Its status and buffer registers are shown below, along with their respective memory addresses.

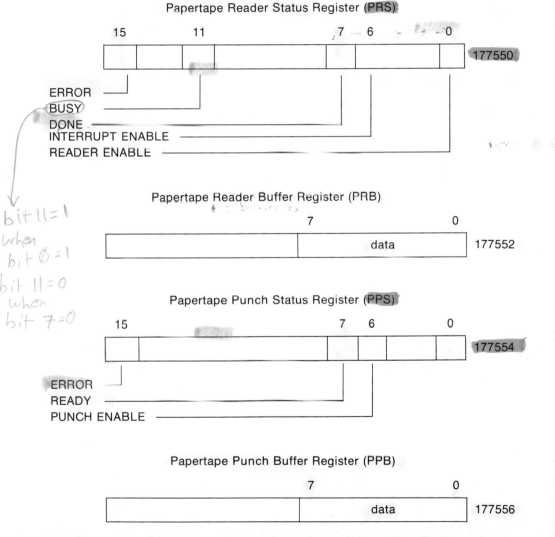

bit 11=1
when
bit 0 =1

bit 11=0
when
bit 7=0

The various bits in the status registers have all been described previously except for the busy bit which is set when **READER ENABLE** is set and cleared when DONE is set. Since READER ENABLE is write-only it is therefore possible to determine the status of the reader.

cf. VT62

10-13.2 Alphanumeric Display-Keyboard VT52

The VT52, or *Decscope,* as it is commonly called, connects to the PDP-11 input-output bus via a serial line unit (a DLV11 on the LSI-11). This unit permits the programmer to read and write characters to a device such as the VT52, which interprets certain characters as commands to execute control functions. Therefore, we shall first describe the DLV11 and then the VT52.

The DLV11 status and buffer registers are shown below. Addresses are shown for the console device.

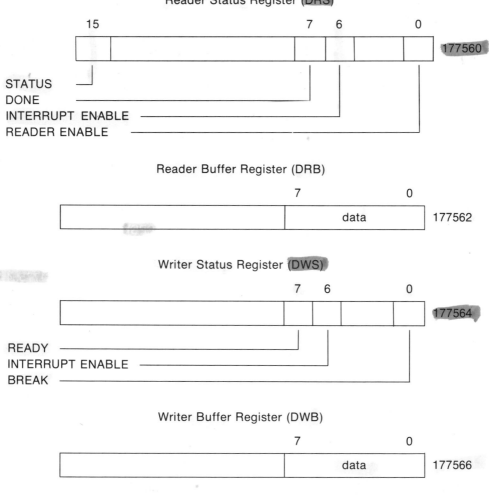

Reader Status Register (DRS)

Reader Buffer Register (DRB)

Writer Status Register (DWS)

Writer Buffer Register (DWB)

The STATUS bit is set when the terminal device is ready to transmit data into the processor. DONE is set when a character is available in the buffer register. READER ENABLE is required to be set by program control when reading from paper tape on a teletypewriter device. It is not necessary to set this bit when reading from a keyboard, since the character transmission is initiated when the key is depressed.

The only other unfamiliar bit function is BREAK, which can be set or reset under program control. When it is set, a continuous space level is transmitted. What this means is that a continuous electrical signal is sent to the device; it does not apply to the VT52.

The VT52 alphanumeric display and keyboard has a standard input device (the keyboard) and a screen capable of displaying 24 lines of 80 characters each in upper- or lowercase. In addition, a cursor (looking like an underscore) is continuously displayed on the screen. Any character written to the VT52 that is to be displayed is written at the position occupied by the cursor.

As an input device, the VT52 simply transmits characters via the serial line unit as they are produced by depressing keyboard keys; the display is not affected. Characters read from the VT52 in this way are of essentially two types: data and control. A data character is simply a printable character such as A, 3, #, or ?. A control character has some other interpretation such as the RETURN, octal code 015, which denotes an end of line.

In order to increase utilization of available keys a large number of control characters can be transmitted from the VT52 with the control (CTRL) key. Depressing a key when CTRL is simultaneously held down produces a unique character code. For example, "control D" (octal code 004) usually means "end of input data stream."

The display is under complete programmer control by writing data and control characters. Data characters, as explained, are displayed at the cursor's current position. The basic cursor control functions are described below as examples of control.

The cursor can be moved one position in any direction, up, down, right, or left, as well as directly to a specified position. To move it one space, a 033 character is transmitted, followed by a 101, 102, 103, or 104 for up, down, right, or left, respectively. The last operation, a backspace, can also be effected by transmitting a single backspace character, 010.

Movement of the cursor to any specified screen position requires four characters. First, the characters 033 and 131 are transmitted in that order. The next two characters are then interpreted as a line number and column number respectively. Lines 0 to 23 are denoted by characters in the range 040 to 067 respectively. Columns 0 to 79 are denoted by characters in the range 040 to 157 respectively.

10-14 REAL-TIME SYSTEMS

Most of our discussion so far in this chapter has ignored a very important consideration. We have implicitly assumed that events external to the computer system occur at a pace sufficiently slow that the computer is able to respond when required. Specifically, it has been assumed that interrupts from input devices do not occur faster than the processor can handle them. In the case of a keyboard device this is reasonable, since a human typist, however fast, cannot generate characters too fast to be handled. There is, however, a very large class of systems in which this assumption of sufficient time is unacceptable. These are called *real-time* systems.

The term *real-time systems* is much misused. In some sense all computer systems are real-time systems, since I/O devices do function in real time. However, there are systems in which an external event, i.e., an interrupt, if not responded to within some specified period of time, results in lost data or damage. It is this criterion of lost data or damage that categorizes real-time systems. Computers used to control physical processes, railway switching equipment, automated machine tools, refineries, assembly lines, aircraft control systems, etc., all fall into this category. Also, data collection systems in which data are read from physical sensors to be stored for later analysis are real-time, since lost data result from inadequate response time. Examples here include satellite data collection, monitoring of laboratory experiments, and recording of the characteristics of an aircraft during test flights.

An adequate treatment of real-time systems is beyond our scope in this text. This is not because the subject is inherently difficult. In fact, there has not been a great deal of theory developed in the area. The subject can best be treated, however, by extensive experience gained by designing actual real-time systems in a laboratory environment. The problem can then be treated as a time-accounting problem. There is just so much computing time available from a given computer system. An analysis of the response requirements of the real-time processes, the method of selecting interrupts for handling, and the frequency of occurrence of events, will reveal whether or not it is possible to guarantee no loss of data or damage to the process being controlled.

EXERCISES

10-1 Write two general purpose subroutines, without using interrupts, to (*a*) write a line on the machine console, and (*b*) read a line from the machine console. (Each character should be echoed as it is typed.)

Test the two subroutines with a main program that calls them in order to read and echo entire lines from the console. Therefore, each line entered will appear twice, once because of echoing characters in the input subroutine and once because of a call on the write subroutine. The main program should halt when it receives a line of input consisting of an asterisk (*) followed by carriage return and line feed. Supply an appropriate parameter design for your subroutines.

10-2 Rewrite the subroutines of Exercise 10-1 to use interrupts. The input subroutine should return after the I/O has been completed. It is called in an identical fashion to the subroutine of Exercise 10-1. The output subroutine should return after the I/O has been started. Its call is modified from that of Exercise 10-1 as follows: An additional parameter is added. The parameter value is required to be nonzero when the subroutine is called. Sometime after the subroutine returns, it will be cleared to signal completion of the I/O. Test your modified subroutines with a suitably modified version of the main program from Exercise 10-1.

10-3 Modify the input subroutine of Exercise 10-2 by artificially making it very slow in responding to an interrupt. This can be done by inserting a short loop that simply iterates some specified number of times. (Interrupts should be masked during this loop.) Run the main program increasing the number of iterations in the loop until you find that input characters are missed. By consulting the table of instruction times in the processor handbook, calculate approximately the speed at which you are typing input.

10-4 If your machine has two (or more) terminals, write a program that reads and echoes characters from each terminal until an asterisk (*) is received, at which time no more characters are echoed on that terminal. The program should terminate when all terminals have transmitted an asterisk. Use a separate interrupt handler for each terminal. Use the priority mechanism available on your machine to make interrupts during interrupt handling. (Smaller PDP-11 models have a less elaborate mechanism than that described in the text.)

10-5 Increase the response time of your interrupt handlers from Exercise 10-4 by inserting an artificial delay loop as was done in Exercise 10-3. Describe the result of increasing the number of iterations in the loop.

10-6 Classify all the devices on the system available to you by consulting the device manuals. Include specifications for relevant parameters of your classification.

10-7 Investigate whether or not there is a DMA device on your system. If so, briefly describe the control interface between the device and the processor.

10-8 Write a single buffering device control program for the console on your machine so that any program receiving input from the console does not communicate with the device directly but only via your control program.

10-9 Modify the device control program of Exercise 10-8 to use double buffering.

10-10 Modify the device control program of Exercise 10-9 to use triple buffering.

10-11 Write a program to read input from the device control program of Exercise 10-8, 10-9, or 10-10 and echo it character by character. Insert an artificial delay in the program with a loop and increase the number of iterations in the loop until you are able to type fast enough to cause lost characters. By consulting a table of instruction timings, calculate the maximum input rate that the program can handle. Does using a control program with more buffers give a higher rate? Explain.

REFERENCES

In this chapter we have been very careful to avoid becoming overly involved in the subject of concurrency. There are some pitfalls that have not been fully explained. To attempt to do so, however, would take us into material more appropriate for a course in operating systems. Rather, the approach here has been to expose the basic mechanisms that are encountered in small computer systems. With an understanding of these mechanisms, more abstract approaches to the study of concurrency are more easily understood.

Two texts specifically devoted to concurrent programming are Brinch-Hansen (1977) and Holt (1978). Other texts on operating systems have extensive treatment of concurrency also. Among these are Brinch-Hansen (1973), Colin (1971, Lister (1975), Madnick (1974), and Shaw (1974). It is highly recommended that one of these references be consulted before you attempt any significant project involving concurrency of any kind.

ELEVEN

SUPERVISORS AND TRAPS

Machine-level programming is tedious and error prone. Already we have suggested that a standard set of I/O subroutines is useful. As the need arises to control more complex devices such as tapes and disks, however, it becomes completely impractical to expect individual programmers to construct their personal library of I/O routines. Another problem is error handling. Typically, a processor, on encountering an error such as an invalid address or an invalid instruction, puts itself into a predefined state and, without software help, halts. It is then the responsibility of the operator to discover what happened. Again, it is completely impractical to expect each programmer to provide the software necessary to recover from such errors, or to provide diagnostic information.

A set of programs that provides the functions of I/O control and error handling is called a *supervisor*.[1] Viewed as a software extension to the hardware that makes programming easier and the machine more reliable, the supervisor is designed to be resident in main memory at all times. Usually, a manufacturer supplies at least a supervisor with each machine sold.

A typical supervisor controls all I/O devices on the machine. A user's program, to carry out I/O, invokes the supervisor, which performs the necessary actions on the user's behalf. Thus I/O, as seen by the user, is simpler, and mechanisms such as interrupts are invisible. This simplification of I/O is absolutely necessary in machines with IOP architectures. This is because the processor-IOP control interface presented to the programmer is usually complex, due to the fact that the IOP is designed to function with a wide variety of devices. Not only must the supervisor assist the programmer in accessing the de-

---

[1] Recently, the term *I/O kernel* has been applied to small supervisors with minimal error handling and with primitive device synchronization only.

vice with which it needs to communicate, it must also protect other devices in the system from inadvertent user errors.

Error handling is the second important supervisor function. Errors discovered by the processor during execution are usually handled by the processor transferring to a fixed location in memory, much like an interrupt mechanism. Supervisor code, of course, is supplied at such locations. This automatic transfer caused by an error, although often implemented exactly like an interrupt, is called a *trap*. The key difference is that an interrupt is caused from a source external to the processor, while a trap is caused by an action of the processor itself. An error trap can, therefore, be viewed as an unscheduled transfer of program control. An interrupt need have no relationship with the executing program, while a trap is caused by the executing program. The reader is cautioned that despite this clear distinction, the terms are often confused.

11-1 ERROR TRAPS

A PDP-11 trap caused by an error occurring during instruction execution is handled by the processor just like an interrupt. Each category of error has an associated *trap vector* which is loaded in the same way as an interrupt vector. The effective priority of these error traps is 8, so that any pending interrupts are not recognized. Some possible errors are shown in Table 11-1 in order of recognition by the processor (the first three are mutually exclusive and are shown with order 0).[1]

Since several kinds of errors may share a trap vector, it is the responsibility of the trap handler to discover the nature of the error. For example, a byte address in an instruction expecting a word operand and a nonexistent address (the machine does not have its full complement of memory) both trap to location 4. Examination of the stacked PC will reveal if either occurred.

Also sharing the trap vector at location 4 are the stack violations. Since locations 0 to 376 are used for interrupt and trap vectors, they are protected from being overwritten by the stack growing toward the low end of memory. Thus a stack warning trap will occur if the contents of R6 go below 420. This gives the trap handler sixteen locations on the stack with which to recover. If the contents of R6 go below 376, then a "fatal" stack violation occurs and the trap handler has less maneuvering room. In the case of an error trap the supervisor's trap handler will not normally return control to the errant program. Rather, it may, for example, print a console message and wait for operator intervention. However, a user handling an error trap could return from a trap with the Return from Trap (RTT) instruction which behaves almost exactly like RTI.[2]

---

[1] Smaller PDP-11 models do not implement some of the error traps. The processor manual should be consulted to determine what traps are included.

[2] See the processor manual for explanation of the trace trap.

RTT

Table 11-1 Error traps

Error	Trap vector	Priority	Order
Odd address	4	8	0
Stack violation	4	8	0
Nonexistent address	4	8	0
Stack warning	4	8	1
Illegal operation code	10	8	2
Power failure	24	8	3

11-2 PROGRAM TRAPS

One of the objectives of the supervisor is to make the system more reliable as well as more convenient to program. It is therefore desirable to protect entry to the supervisor so that it is invoked only at suitable points in its code. In other words the user should not be allowed to transfer in error into the supervisor at an arbitrary address.

A protected entry into the supervisor is commonly provided by a Program Trap instruction. This is simply an instruction whose sole purpose is to cause a trap. In the case of the PDP-11 the instruction is called *Emulator Trap* (EMT). Other machines sometimes refer to this instruction as the *Supervisor Call*. Of course, to provide better protection the trap vector itself should be protected from alteration by a user program. We shall see in a later chapter how this can be done in the larger PDP-11 models.

A side benefit of using a trap for entry into the supervisor is that interrupts can automatically be masked by raising the priority as stored in the trap vector. Since most supervisory functions must run with interrupts masked, this is a convenient way to accomplish this masking.

The EMT instruction, shown below, allows a parameter value in the range 000 octal to 377 octal to be passed to the supervisor.

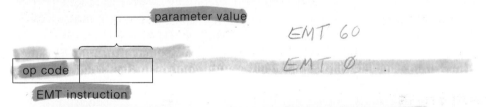

EMT instruction

The parameter value is simply stored in the instruction's low order byte. After the trap occurs (the EMT trap vector is located at word 30), the supervisor's EMT handler can simply fetch the parameter via the PC which was stacked by the trap (Fig. 11-1). This effectively allows up to 256 different supervisory functions to be invoked with the EMT instruction. For example, EMT 60 is the RT-

```
EMTENT:  MOV   (SP),R0 ,        ; fetch PC into R0
         MOV   - (R0),R0        ; fetch EMT instruction into R0
         BIC   #177400,R0       ; zero out EMT op code
         BR    @ADRTAB(R0)      ; index into address table
ADRTAB:  .WORD EMT00            ; function 0
         .WORD EMT02            ; function 2
                .                       .
                .                       .
                .                       .
```

Figure 11-1 Supervisor access to EMT parameter.

11 supervisory function to terminate user program execution and return machine control to the supervisor, which then waits for a command from the console.

MACRO-11 accepts the statement EMT n, where n is an octal number in the range 000 to 377, and constructs an EMT instruction with parameter n. More commonly, however, the programmer uses one of the system library macros to invoke supervisory functions. These macros, of course, include an EMT in their expansion. For example, the system macro

    .EXIT

simply expands to

    EMT 60

System macros, therefore, provide an even more convenient way to invoke supervisory functions. The programmer need not remember individual EMT parameter values since macro names are easier to recall and use. In fact, the EMT parameter is completely invisible to the programmer, who need think only in terms of the macro name.

System macros can have parameters (other than the EMT parameter, which we shall ignore from here on), since most supervisory functions require information from the user program. Figure 11-2 shows how a system macro is used to implement a call on function .SAM with word parameters X and Y. The parameters are simply stacked and the appropriate EMT instruction generated

```
.MACRO  .SAM X Y          ; push add y → stack
MOV   Y,- (SP)            ;   "      "   x   "   "
MOV   X,- (SP)
EMT   0                   ; emulate trap @ vector 0
ADD   #4,SP  ; pop parameters
.ENDM
```

Figure 11-2 Parameterized supervisory functions.

(0 has been chosen arbitrarily) so that the function can be invoked by simply coding

.SAM   PAR1,PAR2

where PAR1 and PAR2 are addresses of word parameters.

As with error traps the supervisor can return from an EMT with RTT. Notice that the macro .SAM removes the parameters after the RTT since it is easier to do it then rather than within the supervisor. It is also better programming practice to push and pop parameters in the same code sequence.

Chapter 12 illustrates some example system macros from the RT-11 operating system.

11-3 INTERRUPT HANDLING

A supervisor normally handles all interrupts for the user programmer. The user however, although it is helpful to let the supervisor handle all the details of interrupts, would still like to have some of the flexibility possible with respect to concurrency. Chapter 10, on I/O, discussed this subject at length. To effect concurrency, then, the supervisor can give the user an option as to how program device synchronization is to occur. For example, suppose there is a supervisor function to write a message on the system console. There might be two versions, .WCON A and .WCONC A, where A is the address of a string of some fixed length. The function .WCON performs the I/O and returns upon completion. The function .WCONC initializes the console interrupt handler appropriately, starts with I/O, and immediately returns to the caller. With .WCON no concurrency is possible, while with .WCONC (write console and continue) the caller can continue executing concurrently with the I/O.

Suppose the caller to .WCONC reaches a point at which it needs to be certain that the console message has been completed. There must be a way then to test for completion of I/O, i.e., a busy-waiting function. This can be provided with a third version of the console writer, .WCONW (write console and wait). This macro requires two parameters A and E, a word in which I/O completion can be signaled. An accompanying macro .WAIT E is used as follows to cause a delay until the I/O initiated with .WCONW is completed.

.WCONW   A,E   ; start I/O

         .   ; execute concurrently

         .

.WAIT   E   ; wait for completion

This is very simply implemented, of course. The function .WCONW gives the address E to the interrupt handler after clearing the addressed word. The interrupt handler then stores a nonzero value in the word when I/O is complete.

The word E, called an *event* word, can then be tested by the .WAIT function in a simple busy-waiting loop.

This .WAIT function is an elementary example of a more general function normally called a *block*. The block operation is one that enables a program to delay continuation of its execution until the occurrence of some specified event, in this case the event word becoming nonzero. The chapter on multiprogramming describes the block operation in detail.

11-4 SUPERVISOR STATE

We have described how a trap instruction can be used to provide some control over entry to the supervisor and also to automatically mask interrupts. This still does not give adequate protection to the supervisor from user program errors. A further barrier is needed to prevent user programs from interfering with supervisory functions. The most common way to do this is to create at least two modes of processor execution: *supervisor mode* and *user mode* (sometimes called *supervisor state* and *user state*). When executing a user program the processor is in user mode and, as such, certain processor instructions and perhaps certain memory areas are not accessible to the executing program. Any attempt to execute such protected instructions or to access protected memory is an error and results in an error trap. I/O instructions in most machines are protected in this way.

In a supervisor-user-mode machine all interrupts and traps automatically switch the processor to supervisor mode, in which there are no restrictions. A trap or interrupt return switches the processor back to user mode (or the mode from which the trap or interrupt occurred). There are then three functions of the trap-interrupt mechanism: automatic interrupt masking, controlled entry to supervisor code, and processor state switching.

In the PDP-11 there are no special I/O instructions so they cannot be protected by supervisor mode. What is necessary is a way to protect the device control and status registers. The mechanism to do this is described in the chapter on memory mapping and protection. The PDP-11 does, however, have a multimode processor. Larger models have, in fact, three modes: *kernel, supervisor,* and *user*. In terms of our previous discussion, PDP-11 kernel mode corresponds to supervisor mode, and PDP-11 supervisor and user modes correspond to a pair of user modes. This can be seen by the fact that there is a separate set of general registers for kernel mode (Fig. 11-3). In kernel mode, all register references are to the kernel set. In user and supervisor mode all references are to the shared set. The only difference is that user and supervisor modes have a separate stack pointer R6. Of course, only one R7 is required. For our purposes we can think of the PDP-11 kernel-user modes as the conventional supervisor-user state structure. The PDP-11 supervisor mode provides a special user mode with its own stack. Supervisor mode on the PDP-11 can be

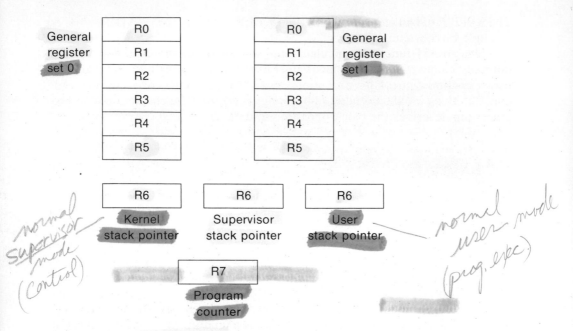

Figure 11-3 The PDP-11 register sets.

used to run supervisory functions that do not require the complete protection of the kernel.

The current processor mode in the PDP-11 is specified in the leftmost 2 bits of the PS, with the next 2 bits indicating the previous mode.

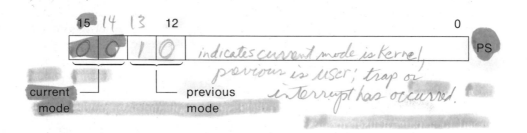

All traps and interrupts set bits 14 and 15 to 00, kernel mode, and store the previous mode into bits 12 and 13, 01 for supervisor and 10 for user. The reason for saving the previous mode, of course, is so the supervisor (i.e., the PDP-11 kernel) can determine from what mode the trap or interrupt originated. The return via an RTI or RTT will automatically reset the mode to that of the PS word restored from the stack.

KERNEL = ∅∅

Supervisor = ∅1

USER = 1∅

11-5 ALTERNATIVE ARCHITECTURES

The supervisor-user state architecture evolved to provide two fundamental characteristics for systems. First, reliability is increased because the supervisor keeps direct control of I/O where user errors are almost inescapable. Second, protection of the system resources, software and hardware, increases because the user is limited in the parts of the system that can be accessed. Supervisor state, with tightly controlled entry, with exclusive access to certain resources such as I/O devices, and with interrupts masked during execution to avoid interference in accessing supervisor data, is the mechanism used to implement this reliability and protection.

As supervisors grew in size to provide more function this reliability and protection decreased somewhat because it was no longer possible to rely on the correctness of such a large program. Also, with larger and slower supervisors it is not practical to mask interrupts for the entire duration of supervisor execution. It was recognized, therefore, that the supervisor-user state architecture was not adequate to satisfy the requirements of more elaborate operating systems, and an alternative was needed.

An alternative architecture should provide two things. First, rather than provide a single monolithic privileged state with complete access to the system, there should be a mechanism to partition all the software, system and user, into modules that can access only those parts of the system that they require. Second, interrupt masking should not be inherent to execution of system functions, since many such functions do not require it.

The larger PDP-11 models provide one example of an alternative, having a supervisor mode in addition to kernel and user modes. Those supervisory functions that do not require interrupt masking and which do not require privileged access to the entire machine can run in supervisor mode.

Another alternative places the responsibility for protection in software rather than hardware. This is done in the Burroughs B6500 series machines which do not have a supervisor state at all. In this system, all programs are written in some high-level language, mostly in a version of Algol. The restrictions on what the program can access are applied by the compiler. Subsequently, the machine code files are protected by the file system in such a way that only properly compiled programs can be run on the system. In addition, the architecture of the machine is designed to directly support many of the features of Algol. The system programs, therefore, run in the same environment as do user programs.

The B6500 does have a special state called *control state,* but this is just the interrupt masked state which can be invoked by system programs that require it. Thus the interrupt masking mechanism is completely separated from the protection mechanism.

A newer alternative architecture is the *capability machine.* Here, the protection mechanism is applied at run time rather than at compile time. The idea is to partition the system into relatively small parts, each of which can be restricted to accessing only that part of the system's resources that it needs at any particular time. This is done through a capability mechanism.

A capability is most easily thought of as an extension of a memory address with two properties. First, while a memory address names a memory location, a capability is a system-wide address that uniquely names a system resource. Thus, any object can be named by a capability: an I/O device, a memory area, a file, a program, etc. Second, capabilities are implemented in such a way that they can be manipulated (passed as parameters, copied, etc.) but not altered. A program is given an initial set of capabilities with which to run. Thereafter, the hardware addressing mechanism enforces the rule that only capability-addressed resources can be accessed by any running program.

Capability machines are largely experimental, although at least one such design appears in a commercial machine, and restricted versions of the capability idea appear in other machines.

EXERCISES

11-1 Consult the processor manual for the system available to you and determine the location of the trap vector for any error condition that you can cause to occur in a program. Write and test a trap handler for this trap condition. It should write a message on the console and either return to the system in use or simply halt the processor.

11-2 Define a macro that provides entry into a program trap handler. The entry should implement an operation to initialize an interrupt vector as follows:

.SETIV   CSR,ADR,PRI

represents a call on the operation where
      CSR is the address of the device control registers
      ADR is the address of the interrupt handler
      PRI is the priority of the interrupt handler

11-3 Write and test a program trap handler and accompanying entry macro to implement an operation to read a line of input from the system console. A call on the operation should appear as

.RCON   ADR

where ADR is the address of a memory area in which the line of input is to be placed.

11-4 Implement, using trap entry macros, the operations .WCON, .WCONC, .WCONW, and .WAIT as described in the chapter text.

REFERENCES

Rosen (1969) gives a good summary of the developments leading to the supervisor-user state architecture. Any text on operating systems describes supervisory functions in more detail, although much of this material is on multiprogramming, which is covered in a later chapter of this text. A look at such references should, therefore, be deferred until later. The B6500 architecture is described in Organick (1973). Several papers on the CAP system, an experimental capability system, can be found in Proceedings of the Sixth Symposium on Operating System Principles (1977).

TWELVE

SYSTEMS LANGUAGES

Assembly language does not assist the programmer in producing readable, well-structured, and reliable programs. For these purposes, a higher-level language is needed. Languages designed for writing systems software, those programs that help to manage the computer system but which are not directly productive in solving users' application problems, have the characteristic that they allow fairly close control over the machine while encouraging well-structured programs. Two such systems languages, Pascal and C, are presented here. They are included in the text to allow algorithms to be expressed in real languages other than assembler and to serve as examples of this class of languages. These particular languages are chosen because of their increasingly wide use, their availability in the two example operating systems to be described later, and their clean structure.

Since it is impractical to define these languages completely in this text, only sufficient information is given so that we can use the languages in later chapters and so that they can be understood by the reader. Of course Pascal has already been employed to explain simple algorithms on the assumption that the reader has a background of high-level language programming and, therefore, simple Pascal should be easily understandable. The reader is referred to the language manuals for complete and authoritative definitions.

12-1 PASCAL

The programming language Pascal was designed by N. Wirth as an improvement upon Algol 60, which is primarily deficient in its capabilities for data structuring. Among high-level languages Pascal has the advantage of particularly elegant data structuring capabilities. Many implementations exist, including several for the PDP-11.

12-1.1 Data Types

Pascal was one of the first languages to allow the definition of types rather than restrict the programmer to several fixed types such as the usual INTEGER, REAL, and BOOLEAN. The notion of defining a new type may be something quite new to the reader. The easiest way to understand what this means is to realize that a type is simply a set of values. Therefore, one can define a new type by listing its values. If there are too many values to list, then some other way of describing the set can be used. Keeping these general comments in mind, then, a type in Pascal is defined by a statement of the form

TYPE t = <definition>

where t represents a programmer-assigned symbol naming the type being defined and <definition> represents the description of the set of values constituting the type. The notation we will use in describing language syntax is as follows: Uppercase words are keywords, lowercase words are program symbols, and words enclosed in angle brackets are metasymbols describing, as a comment, the meaning of the construction that is to be substituted. There are, then, several possible type definitions that can be used in the above specification.

Having defined type t, as above, variables of this type can be declared by

VAR x: t

or

VAR x,y,z: t

Keep in mind that it is the declaration of a variable that causes storage to be allocated for the variable. The type definition merely describes the structure of the storage that will be required for variables of that type.

The type definition can, in some cases, be inserted directly into the declaration, if desired, as follows:

VAR x: <definition>

or

VAR x,y,z: <definition>

Combining the type definition and the variable declaration should not obscure the fact that these are distinct operations.

Before we can look at some examples, we need to show some of the ways in which the set of values constituting a type can be described. The first way is to simply list the values by assigning a name to each and listing these names. Each name is, in itself, a value of the type in the same way that TRUE is a value of the type BOOLEAN and 13 is a value of the type INTEGER. Types defined by listing the values are called *scalar types* and are defined by a statement of the form

TYPE t = (w1, w2, . . . , wn)

where the wi, i =1,n are distinct, ordered elements of the type. One may define, for example,

TYPE color = (red, yellow, blue, green)

so that variables of type color can take on one of these four possible values.

BOOLEAN is a built-in scalar type that has implicitly been defined by

TYPE BOOLEAN = (FALSE, TRUE)

with the usual properties that one would expect.

An example of a scalar type that might be defined in an assembler is

TYPE symboltype = (permanent, macro, user)

so that each symbol in the symbol table has an associated variable of type symboltype describing its category.

A *subrange type* is a specified sequence of consecutive integers defined by a statement of the form

TYPE s – w1..w2

where w1 and w2 are integers such that w1 < w2. Subranges have already been seen in earlier programs, and now one can see that they are just a way of concisely describing a type as being a subset of the type INTEGER. Of course, the type INTEGER is a built-in subrange definition where the range of possible values is determined by the machine in use. Another difference between a scalar type and a subrange type is that the latter is defined in terms of INTEGER, for which the values have particular properties defined by a large body of mathematics. Values of a scalar type have no such implied properties, of course, and any operations on them must be programmed explicitly.

INTEGER variables, as we have seen, can be declared as shown by the following example:

VAR i, count: INTEGER

In most cases INTEGER variables assume values over a known range, and for program readability and reliability these should be declared as subranges.

The built-in type CHAR comprises a finite ordered set of character codes. On the PDP-11 this set will be the ASCII standard described earlier. Two built-in functions can be used to determine ordering in a particular set. These are: ord(c) returning the ordinal number of the character c; and chr(i) returning the character with ordinal number i. Therefore

ord(chr(i)) = i   and   chr(ord(c)) = c

A constant of type CHAR is enclosed in single quotation marks. Thus

```
ch := '$'
```

assigns the code for dollar sign to the CHAR variable ch.

Floating-point data representations (see App. A) are obtained with declarations of the type REAL as in

```
VAR a,b,z: REAL
```

In addition to the scalar types, Pascal allows definitions of compound types, three of which are particularly of interest to the systems programmer: ARRAY, RECORD, and SET. These types have values that are composed from simpler types. That is, each value can have many components, each of which must be of some defined type. Most familiar will be the ARRAY. A value of an ARRAY type is a set of values, of some component type, each of which is associated with a value of some indexing type. The definition of an ARRAY specifies the type of the array elements (the component type) as well as the type of the allowable indexing variables (the indexing type) in the general form

```
TYPE a = ARRAY [<index type>] OF <component type>
```

For example, a REAL ARRAY to be indexed by the subrange $0..9$ could be defined by

```
TYPE realarray = ARRAY [0..9] OF REAL
```

Any other type is allowable as a component type but only scalar and subrange types are allowed as indexing types. For example,

```
TYPE colorswitch = ARRAY [color] OF BOOLEAN;
VAR colorsinstock: colorswitch
```

might be referenced in a piece of code like

```
VAR ordercolor: color;
...
IF colorsinstock[ordercolor] THEN
    proceed with issue
ELSE hold order
```

Each element in an ARRAY value is of the same component type. One may declare ARRAY's of INTEGER, REAL, BOOLEAN, color, or of some other type but mixing them is not permitted. The second kind of compound type remedies this situation somewhat. A RECORD is a nonhomogeneous sequence of variables forming a compound variable. This means that, whereas an ARRAY has components (commonly called *elements,* as we have called them) of the same type, a RECORD has components of different types. The general form of its definition is

```
TYPE r = RECORD <field list> END
```

where the <field list> describes the structure of a RECORD of type r. A familiar example of a RECORD, although it was not previously described as such, is an entry in a table such as the symbol table discussed earlier. Recall that such a table entry comprised several components of different types. One of the types encountered was used as a link in creating a singly linked list. In Pascal, a singly linked list element could be defined as

```
TYPE listelement = RECORD
                    data: REAL;
                    link: ↑ listelement
             END
```

Here, in link, a new type of variable has been introduced, the *pointer*. A variable of type pointer is a reference to variables of a specified type. Thus, if one defines x by

```
TYPE x = RECORD . . . END
```

then pointers to variables of type x can be declared as in

```
VAR p1, p2 : ↑ x
```

Pointer values, for our purposes, can be thought of as memory addresses. Here we see an example of the close control over the machine that is needed for writing systems programs, in that we can create variables with address values.

There is one important difference between variables declared directly and those referenced by pointers. Variables referenced by pointers are not created by declarations, that is, statically. Rather they are created dynamically during program execution. A special procedure, new ( ), is provided for this purpose. Thus, to create a variable of type x one can code new (p1), which reserves storage for a variable of type x and assigns its memory address to p1.

Returning now to RECORDs, individual fields in a RECORD are accessed by giving the name of the RECORD, followed after a dot separator by the field name. If one had declared a variable of type listelement called *element*, then element.data would refer to its data component, a variable of type REAL.

One is often interested in creating lists of records, in which case this dynamic listelement creation is appropriate. The following code creates a singly linked list of n listelements:

```
VAR first,p: ↑ listelement; i: INTEGER; a: REAL;

  .

  .

  .
first := NIL;
FOR i := 1 TO n DO BEGIN
      new(p) ;
      a := next data item for list ;
      p ↑ .link := first ;
      p ↑ .data := a ;
      first := p END
```

Notice that NIL is a constant representing a null memory address. Also, the name p ↑ refers to the variable referenced by p, which is of type listelement.

One of the common kinds of compound variables needed in systems programs is the character string, or simply the string. Although some languages provide a built-in type string, Pascal does not. It is necessary, therefore, to use some other mechanism, the most direct of which is the ARRAY. Strings, then, can be created as an ARRAY [. . .] OF CHAR. This, on some machines, may result in the allocation of one multibyte word per character. To specify that characters are to be allocated to smaller memory units, i.e., bytes, one can code

```
PACKED ARRAY [...] OF CHAR
```

Packed arrays can be costly in accessing overhead, however, and for processing they should be unpacked. Two standard procedures are provided as follows. If one declares

```
VAR a:   ARRAY [m..n] OF type;
VAR z:   PACKED ARRAY [u..v] OF type
```

then pack (a,i,z) packs elements of a into z starting at a[i] and unpack (z,a,i) unpacks elements of z into a starting at a[i].

We come now to the third kind of compound type, the SET. First, think again of a type as a set of possible values from which a variable of that type may take its value. Often, one wishes to ask the question, "Is the value of a certain variable within some specified subset of the possible values of the type?" SETs provide a mechanism to ask such questions. The technique works as follows: Think of a type whose values comprise all the possible subsets of some other specified type. In mathematical terms, such a type is the power set of some other specified type. This type is the SET. Values of a variable of type SET, then, represent subsets of some other type. It is then possible to examine a variable of type SET to see if its value, a subset of a type, contains some value from that type.

SETs can be defined with a statement of the form

```
TYPE s = SET OF <type>
```

which means that variables of type s contain values that are elements of the power set of the specified type. For example, a supervisor might contain the definitions

```
TYPE device = (tty1,tty2, . . . ,ttyn);
TYPE deviceclass = SET OF device
```

and all devices of a particular kind could be identified with

VAR brandxdevice: deviceclass ;

.

.

.

brandxdevice := [tty1,tty3,tty9]

where [. . .] is a constructor of a set containing the specified elements of device. To discover if a particular variable's value is in a set, one codes

IF currentdevice IN brandxdevice THEN ...

where currentdevice is of type device. Other operations on SETs are available, but the reader is referred to the language manual for details of these.

12-1.2 Expressions

For experienced high-level language programmers, the meaning of Pascal expressions is easily understood by reading programs. One significant restriction, however, is that side effects in function calls are forbidden.

12-1.3 Statements and Control Structures

Again, we have been using Pascal control structures on the assumption that readers are familiar with a structured language and can read programs without a detailed explanation of the semantics. It should not, therefore, be necessary to explain most of the Pascal control structures. Consequently, they are simply listed below in their general form. Only two, the WITH and the CASE statements, require some explanation.

The Pascal statement, denoted here by <S>, can be an assignment, which is familiar, a procedure call, which is treated in a later section, or one of the following forms:

```
BEGIN <S1> ; . . . ;<Sn> END
IF <Boolean expression> THEN <S1> ELSE <S2>
IF <Boolean expression> THEN <S>
WHILE <Boolean expression> DO <S>
REPEAT <S> UNTIL <Boolean expression>
CASE <expression> OF <constant list>:<S1>;
                              . . . ;
                <constant list>:<Sn> END
WITH <variable list> DO <S>
GOTO <unsigned integer>
FOR <variable> := <expression> TO <expression> DO <S>
FOR <variable> := <expression> DOWN TO <expression> DO <S>
```

The WITH construct allows the programmer to specify execution of a block with an implicit compound type thus permitting more convenient referencing. For example,

WITH p ↑ DO data := s

accomplishes the same effect as

p ↑ .data := s

In this case, the latter is shorter, but for a large block of statements WITH yields more readable programs.

In the CASE statement the expression is evaluated and that statement having the value included in its associated constant list is executed. If no such statement is found, then no action is taken.

12-1.4 Program Units

Subprograms in Pascal, procedures and functions, are similar to Algol 60 except that the formal parameters are specified within the parameter list. Parameters so specified may be value parameters or reference parameters. For example,

```
PROCEDURE mult( x,y: INTEGER; VAR z : INTEGER);
    BEGIN
        z := 0;
        WHILE x <> 0 DO BEGIN
            IF odd(x) THEN z := z+y ;
            y := 2*y;
            x := x DIV 2 END
    END
```

has two value parameters x and y and one reference parameter z.

Functions are similarly defined. The following is a parametric function outline whose body references a function passed as a parameter:

```
FUNCTION func( a,b: REAL; FUNCTION f: REAL): REAL;
    VAR i,n: INTEGER; x,y: REAL;
    BEGIN
    . . .
    func := value to be returned
    END
```

Notice that the type of func, REAL, is given following the parameter specification, and that local variables can be declared preceding the body of the subprogram. The value to be returned is specified by an assignment to the name of the function as shown.

12-1.5 Pascal Example

The following is a Pascal program which was translated from a C program to be shown in the next section. Since it was originally written in C, this program has some of the flavor of control structure found in C programs. Because of this, it makes a nice comparison when one sees these control structures in Pascal. This is most noticeable in the appearance of GOTOs in Pascal to translate from the BREAK of C.

Some functions used in this program that are not explained in the text include the following: rewrite prepares an output file for writing, read obtains a character from the standard input file, write transmits a character to the standard output file, andfunc is assumed to be a machine-dependent function to perform the logical "and," and rtshiftfunc is assumed to be a machine-dependent function to perform a right shift of the number of bits given by the second operand.

```
PROGRAM compress( input, output, symtab);
{ This program compresses text, found in the input
  file, and writes it to the output file. A word
  table is written to a third file called symtab }

LABEL 788,888,999;

TYPE wordarray = ARRAY[0..31] OF CHAR;
     symbolrec = RECORD
                   lon: INTEGER;
                   alpha: ARRAY[0..31] OF CHAR
                   END;
VAR symtab: FILE OF symbolrec;
    symboloffset: ARRAY [0..4999] OF INTEGER;
    testtable: ARRAY[0..19999] OF CHAR;
    size, lastsymbol: INTEGER;
    ch,c1,c2: CHAR;
    word: ARRAY[0..31] OF CHAR;
    count, location: INTEGER;
    nullchar: CHAR {implementation dependent constant};

FUNCTION andfunc( i,j: INTEGER): CHAR;
{ This function is implementation dependent. }
  BEGIN
  END;

FUNCTION rtshiftfunc( i,j: INTEGER): INTEGER;
{ This function is implementation dependent. }
  BEGIN
  END;

FUNCTION nonalpha( ch: CHAR): BOOLEAN ;
{ This function returns FALSE if the argument is
  an alphanumeric and TRUE otherwise. }
```

```
BEGIN
    IF ch >= '0' AND ch <= '9' OR
        ch >= 'a' AND ch <= 'z' OR
        ch >= 'A' AND ch <= 'Z' THEN nonalpha := FALSE
    ELSE nonalpha := TRUE
END;


FUNCTION lookup( word: wordarray) : INTEGER ;
    { This function searches for the argument in the
      word table and returns either its index as it
      exists in the table or the index of a new entry
      in the table. }
    LABEL 555,666,444,777;
    VAR buf: symbolrec;
        i, n, offset: INTEGER;
    BEGIN
        { Search for a matching entry in the table. The
          number of entries is stored in size. The indices
          of the first character of each variable sized entry
          are stored in the vector symboloffset. }
        FOR n := 0 TO size-1 DO BEGIN
            offset := symboloffset[n];
            { Compare this entry with the input word. }
            FOR i := 0 TO 31 DO BEGIN
                { If not equal, check next entry. }
                IF word[i] <> testtable[offset+i] THEN GOTO 444;
                { If eof then word matches entry. }
                IF word[i] = nullchar THEN GOTO 555 END;
        { Entry found. Return with index. }
          555:lookup := n+1;
                GOTO 777;
        { Entry does not match. Check next entry. }
        444:
        END;
        { No matching entry found. Make new table entry. }
        buf.len := 0;
        WHILE word[buf.len] <> nullchar DO buf.len := buf.len+1;
        symboloffset[size] := lastsymbol;
        FOR i := 0 TO 31 DO BEGIN
            { Move each character of word into new entry. }
            testtable[lastsymbol] := word[i];
            lastsymbol := lastsymbol+1;
            { If word entered escape to write file. }
            IF word[i] = nullchar THEN GOTO 666;
            { Fill buffer to write word table file. }
            buf.alpha[i] := word[i];
```

```
                { Make word vector null for processing next input. }
                word[i] := nullchar END;
  { Write word to word table file and return index of new entry. }
                666:write( symtab, buf);
                      size := size + 1;
                      lookup := size;
                777: ;
      END;
```

```
{ The main program starts here. }
BEGIN
      nullchar := chr(0); { use CTRL SHIFT }
      { Prepare word table file for writing. }
      rewrite( symtab);
      IF eof THEN ch := nullchar
      ELSE read(ch);
      { A null character indicates the end-of-file. }
      IF ch <> nullchar THEN BEGIN
         { This is an indefinite iteration to process each input
           character. }
         WHILE TRUE DO BEGIN
            If ch = ' ' THEN BEGIN
               count := 1;
               IF eof THEN ch := nullchar
               ELSE read( ch);
               WHILE ch = ' ' DO BEGIN
                  { If more than one blank write
                    one blank with a count character. }
                  count := count + 1;
                  IF eof THEN ch := nullchar
                  ELSE read( ch) END;
               IF count > 1 THEN BEGIN
                  write(' ');
                  write( chr(count)) END
               ELSE write( chr(001)) END;
            ELSE BEGIN
               { Nonalphanumerics are just copied. }
               IF nonalpha( ch) THEN BEGIN
                  write( ch);
                  IF eof THEN ch := nullchar
                  ELSE read( ch) END
```

```
            ELSE BEGIN
                { If an alphanumeric read in the complete word. }
                count := 1;
                word[0] := ch;
                WHILE TRUE DO BEGIN
                { This indefinite iteration processes one word. }
                IF eof THEN ch := nullchar
                ELSE read( ch);
                { A nonalphanumeric indicates
                  the end of the word. }
              IF nonalpha( ch) THEN GOTO 788;
              word[count] := ch;
              count := count + 1 END;
              { Now process this input word. }
     788:IF count = 1 THEN BEGIN
                { Single character words are just copied. }
                write( word[0]);
                GOTO 888 END;
          IF count = 2 THEN BEGIN
                { Two character words are just copied. }
                write( word[0]);
                write( word[1]);
                GOTO 888 END;
          IF count = 3 THEN BEGIN
                { 3 character words are just copied. }
                write( word[0]);
                write( word[1]);
                write( word[2]);
                GOTO 888 END;
          { Now search for this word in the word table. }
          word[count] := nullchar;
          location := lookup( word);
          { The special character CTRL < is used to
          indicate that the next entry is an integer reference. }
          write( chr(028));
          c1 := andfunc( location, 127);
          c2 := andfunc( rtshiftfunc( location, 8), 127);
          write( c2);
          write( c1)
        END;
        { End-of-file is indicated by a null character. }
         888:IF ch = nullchar THEN GOTO 999
      END
    END
999:END.
```

12-2 THE LANGUAGE C

The programming language C was designed at Bell Telephone Laboratories as the systems language for the UNIX operating system. It was primarily intended as a PDP-11 language, although other implementations have recently appeared. The reader may find C more unlike other languages than Pascal is. Although we use uppercase letters for language symbols, C normally expects lowercase only.

12-2.1 Data Types

C has four scalar types, INT, CHAR, FLOAT, and DOUBLE, denoting integer, character, single precision floating point, and double precision floating point. In addition, there are two compound types, arrays and structures. Finally, it is possible to create pointers to variables. C does not have type definitions.

Besides its type, each variable has an associated storage class specifying the nature of its memory allocation. The four classes are AUTO, STATIC, EXTERNAL, and REGISTER.

The default storage class is AUTO, in which case the variable is created when the function containing the declaration is called. STATIC specifies that the variable is created only once, at compile time. REGISTER specifies allocation of a register for storage. EXTERNAL means that the identifier is defined outside of the function containing the declaration.

Integers, reals, and characters are declared, respectively, as shown in the following examples:

```
INT i,j,k;
FLOAT a,b,c;
CHAR c1,c2;
```

Arrays are declared by appending the number of array elements n (subscripts are integers in the range 0..n−1) in square brackets, as in

```
INT i,j[3],k[4];
```

where i is a scalar and j and k are arrays, or

```
FLOAT a[4][6];
```

where a is a two-dimensional array—that is, an array of arrays.

Pointers are declared by preceding the identifier with an asterisk, in which case the variable is a pointer to a variable of the declared type, as in

```
INT i, *j, k[4];
```

Here, i is of type integer and j is a pointer to an integer. Any expression of the form k[i], $0 \le i < 3$, is of type integer, but a novel aspect of C is that k, by itself, is a valid expression as well. It is, in fact, of type pointer to an integer, namely the integer k[0]. Multidimensional arrays behave in a similar way. Suppose that one declared

INT k[3][4];

Then k is a pointer to an array of three pointers. Further, k[i] $0 \le i < 2$, is a pointer to an integer k[i][0]. One final point: Indirection is indicated by an asterisk, so that *j = 3 assigns 3 to the integer to which j points. (Assignment is denoted by the equal sign.)

The only type in C that requires a definition, i.e., is not a predefined type, is the structure. The structure is similar in some respects to the record in Pascal. As in Pascal, this type can be defined and given a name, as in the following example:

```
STRUCT listelement {
        FLOAT data ;
        STRUCT listelement *link ;
        } ;
```

which defines the structure listelement to have two components, a real, called *data,* and a pointer to a listelement, called *link.*

The declaration

STRUCT listelement el, *p ;

declares el to be a structure as defined and p to be a pointer to a structure as defined.

Unlike Pascal, instances of a type to be referenced by a pointer are created only via declarations. There must therefore be a way to construct pointer values, i.e., memory addresses, for assignment to pointers. This is done with the & operator. For example,

p = &el ;

assigns the address of el to p.

Individual components of a structure are accessed in one of two ways. First, a notation similar to Pascal allows referencing via a structure name, as in

a = el.data ;

Second, a pointer to a structure, rather than a structure name, can be used, as in

a = p−>data ;

This last statement is equivalent to a = (*p).data since the indirection operator, *, is complementary to &. Notice that the parentheses are required so that the * applies to p only.

To create a list of structures in C it is necessary to declare explicitly an array of structures that is to provide a pool of list elements. The following code creates a singly linked list of n listelements. Compare it with the Pascal code in Sec. 12-1.1.

```
STRUCT listelement space[n], *first, *p;
INT i;
FLOAT a;
    .
    .
    .
first = 0; /* 0 serves as the null pointer */
i = 1;
WHILE (i <=n ) {
        p = &space[i] ;
        a = next data item for list ;
        p->link = first ;
        p->data = a ;
        first = p ;
        i = i+1 ;
        };
```

Since all n elements of space are used without any intervening removals from the list, it is in the same order (reversed) as the array. Comments, as shown, are enclosed in /* ... */. The WHILE should be self-explanatory.

12-2.2 Expressions

C is an expression language. Most statements are expressions; they return a value as well as have the familiar properties of sequential execution. As seen already, an assignment expression has the form

E1 = E2

where E1 is called an lvalue expression yielding a value that is a reference to a storage object. The value of the expression E2 is stored into the referenced object. In graphic terms we have the following situation:

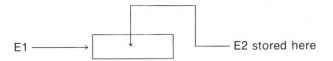

The most common lvalue is an identifier.

The difference between the terms *lvalue* and *pointer* is that a pointer is a stored object, i.e., a variable. An lvalue is C language terminology for the name of a stored object, which may of course be a pointer. The importance of the lvalue is that operators in C are explained in terms of values and lvalues. C is very rich in operators, so rather than give only a few examples we refer the reader to the manual.

12-2.3 Statements and Control Structures

A statement in C is an expression of the form

S;

Statements, mostly assignments and function calls, are executed in the sequence specified in the form

S1; S2; . . . Sn;

Statements can be grouped, making a compound statement, by using braces:

```
{S1;
 S2;
 .
 .
 .
 Sn;
};
```

The forms of the conditional, while, until, for, and case constructs, respectively, are

(a) IF (<expression>) <statement>;

(b) IF (<expression>) <statement>
     ELSE <statement>;

(c) WHILE (<expression>) <statement>;

(d) DO <statement> WHILE (<expression>);

(e) FOR (<expression1; <expression2>; <expression3>){
     <statement>; };

 which is equivalent to

```
              <expression1>;
       WHILE ( <expression2> ) {
                       <statement>;
                       <expression3>;
                       };
```

(f) SWITCH (<expression>) <statement>

 where <statement> is of the form

```
{ CASE <constant1> : <expression1> ;
  CASE <constant2> : <expression2> ;

        .

        .

        .

  CASE <constantn> : <expressionn> ;
  DEFAULT : <expression> ;
}
```

Each CASE alternative is labeled by a constant. The expression is evaluated and its value used to select the alternative labeled with an equal value. The expression given in the alternative is then evaluated. If no such alternative is found, then no action is taken.

In addition to labels, identifiers which may prefix any statement, as in

```
<label> : <statement> ;
```

along with the GOTO <label>; statement, C includes more structured control transfer statements. These allow the programmer to explicitly indicate the destination of the transfer in relation to an enclosing control structure. They are, of course, preferred over the GOTO for increased clarity.

The BREAK terminates the enclosing control structure, WHILE, DO, FOR, or SWITCH, and transfers control to the immediately following expression in sequence. The CONTINUE transfers to the point of loop continuation of the enclosing WHILE, DO, or FOR.

12-2.4 Program Units

All subprograms in C are functions. If an identifier f is declared as

```
<typef> f(...)
```

then f is of type function returning <typef>. Parameters may be specified as shown in the following example:

```
INT max(a,b,c)
INT a,b,c ;
{INT m ;
  m = (a>b) ? a : b ;
  RETURN (m>c ? m : c);
};
```

This completely defined function illustrates the conditional expression as well as the RETURN statement. The RETURN specifies as its parameter the value that is to be returned as the function value. If no parameter is supplied, i.e., RETURN ( ), then a null value is returned.

The conditional expression of the form

<expression1> ? <expression2> : <expression3>

evaluates to <expression2> if <expression1> is nonzero (true) and to <expression3> otherwise.

A complete C program consists of a sequence of external declarations for functions, simple variables, and arrays. Each identifier so declared is of storage class EXTERNAL and of the specified type.

12-2.5 C Example

Here is the same program as that shown in the section on Pascal. Since it was originally written in C, the structure reflects the control facilities of C in that liberal use of the more structured version of the GOTO, the BREAK, is made.

Some of the operators and functions of C which are not described in the text but which appear in this program include the following: The functions exit, creat, open, close, putchar, and getchar perform, respectively, the following: return to the UNIX system, create a file, open a file, close a file, write a character to the standard output, and read a character from the standard input. The operators, ==, \, ++, >>, and & perform, respectively, the following: a test for equality, a conversion of the following string to octal, incrementing, a right shift by the number of bits given in the second operand, and a logical "and."

```
/* This program compresses text, found in the input file
   and writes it to the output file. A word table is written
   into a third file. */
INT symboloffset[5000];
CHAR testtable[20000];
INT size;
INT lastsymbol;
INT file;

MAIN()
{
CHAR ch, c1, c2, ccount, word[32];
INT count, location;
INT i;
/* A byte of zeros indicates end-of-file.
   Read the first character and check this. */
IF((ch = getchar())==0)exit(0);
/* Create a file for the word table. */
creat("./symtab",0666);
file = open("./symtab",2);
```

```
/* This is an indefinite iteration to process
   each character from the input stream. */
FOR(;;)
{
SWITCH(ch)
        {
        CASE '040':
                /* Count sequence of blanks. */
                count = 1;
                WHILE((ch = getchar()) = = '040')count++;
                /* If more than one, write one blank
                   with a count character. */
                IF(count>1)
                    {
                    putchar('040');
                    putchar(count);
                    }
                ELSE putchar('001');
                /* Process next character. */
                BREAK;
        DEFAULT:
                /* Punctuation characters are just copied. */
                IF(nonalpha(ch))
                    {
                    putchar(ch);
                    ch = getchar();
                    /* Process next character. */
                    BREAK;
                    }
                /* Text word must be read and entered into
                   the word table if not already there. */
                count=1;
                word[0] = ch;
                /* This is an indefinite iteration to read
                   in each character of the text word. */
                FOR(;;)
                    {
                    ch = getchar();
                    /* Any nonalphanumeric character indicates
                       the end of the word. */
                    IF(nonalpha(ch))BREAK;
                        {
                        word[count]=ch;
                        count++;
                        }
                    }
```

```
                    /* Single character words are just copied. */
                    IF(count == 1)
                        {
                        putchar(word[0]);
                        /* Process next character. */
                        BREAK;
                        }
                    /* Two character words are just copied. */
                    IF(count == 2)
                        {
                        putchar(word[0]);
                        putchar(word[1]);
                        /* Process next character. */
                        BREAK;
                        }
                    /* Process the multicharacter word.
                       First, append an eof character. */
                    word[count] = 0;
                    /* Search for word in the word table. */
                    location = -lookup(word);
                    /* Construct a two character reference to the
                       word in the table and write these to the
                       output file. Since the index was negated,
                       the first character, c1, will have a 1 in
                       bit 7 thus being easily detectable as a
                       reference character in the decompress program. */
                    c1 = location & 000377;
                    c2 = (location >> 8) & 000377;
                    putchar(c2);
                    putchar(c1);
                    /* Process next character. */
                    BREAK;
                    }
        IF(ch==0)
            {
            /* Finished, close the word table file and terminate. */
            close(file);
            exit(0);
            }
        }
    }
```

```
/*The following function searches the word table and returns either the location
   of the word as it exists in the table or the location of a new entry for it.*/
lookup(word)
CHAR *word;
{
 /* This is a buffer for the word table file. */
  STRUCT{
            INT len;
            CHAR alpha[32];
            }buf;
  INT i, n, offset;
  /* Search the word table. The number of entries is
     stored in size. The indices of each variable
     length entry are stored in the vector symboloffset. */
  FOR(n = 0;n <= size-1; n++)
      {
        offset = symboloffset[n];
        FOR(i = 0;i < 32;i++)
            {
              /* Compare the input word with the table entry.
                  If not equal examine next table entry. */
              IF(word[i] != testtable[offset+i])GOTO nomatch;
              /* If eof reached word has matched and function
                  returns the table index. */
              IF(word[i] == 0) BREAK;
            }
        /* Return table index. */
        RETURN(n+1);
/* Examine next table entry. */
nomatch:;
      }
/* Make new entry in the word table. */
buf.len = 0;
WHILE(word[buf.len])buf.len++;
symboloffset[size] = lastsymbol;
FOR(i=0;i<32;i++)
      {
        /* Move next character of word into table. */
        testtable[lastsymbol] = word[i];
        lastsymbol++;
        /* If word entered escape iteration. */
        IF(word[i] == 0)BREAK;
        /* Move character into buf to write file. */
        buf.alpha[i] = word[i];
        /* Zero vector word for next input processing. */
        word[i] = 0;
      }
```

```
/* Write to word table file, increment size, and
   return the table index of the new entry. */
write(file,&buf,buf.len+2);
size++;
RETURN(size);
}
/* The following function returns a zero if
   the argument is alphanumeric and one otherwise.*/
nonalpha(ch)
CHAR ch;
{
IF((ch >= '0' && ch <= '9')||
   (ch >= 'a' && ch <= 'z')||
   (ch >= 'A' && ch <= 'Z')) RETURN(0);
RETURN(1);
}
```

EXERCISES

12-1 Suggest a systematic scheme for implementing Pascal scalar types in assembly language. Is there any run-time checking required to ensure that values are valid? (Run-time checks are required where the type compatibility checks done by the compiler, or by the programmer doing hand translation, are insufficient.) Justify your answer.

12-2 Suggest a scheme for implementing Pascal boolean types in assembly language. Is any run-time checking required?

12-3 Suggest a scheme for implementing Pascal subranges in assembly language. Is any run-time checking required? Explain your answer.

12-4 Implement ord(c) and chr(i) in assembly language.

12-5 Suggest a scheme for implementing Pascal arrays in assembly language. Is any run-time checking required? Explain.

12-6 Suggest a scheme for implementing Pascal records in assembly language. Is any run-time checking required? Explain.

12-7 Suggest a scheme for implementing Pascal pointers in assembly language. Is any run-time checking required? Explain.

12-8 Implement new(p) in assembly language based on the suggestions of Exercises 12-6 and 12-7.

12-9 Suggest a scheme for implementing Pascal sets in assembly language. Show how the operator IN can be translated into assembly language.

12-10 Describe a systematic method of translating the Pascal CASE statement into assembly language.

12-11 Describe how you would translate into assembly language the meaning of the C descriptors AUTO, STATIC, and EXTERNAL.

12-12 Suggest a scheme for implementing C arrays in assembly language.

12-13 Suggest a scheme for implementing C structures in assembly language. How is this different from the scheme for Pascal records?

12-14 Translate the text compression example program into assembly language and test it.

REFERENCES

Standard Pascal as defined by Wirth is described in Jensen (1974). Two implementations are described in Joy (1977) and Bowles (1978), the former being only a reference manual while the latter is a textbook for beginning programmers. Other introductory Pascal texts include Webster (1976), Keiburtz (1978), and Wirth (1976). The only textbook on C is Kernighan (1978), but it is described in UNIX software references, Ritchie (a manual) and Kernighan (a tutorial).

THIRTEEN

OPERATING SYSTEMS

A supervisor is the heart of a collection of programs that have no directly useful function except to make the computer system more convenient, secure, and reliable for users. These systems programs constitute the *operating system* and in addition to the supervisor include assemblers, compilers, memory management routines, linkers, command-language interpreters, file management utilities, and many others. Operating systems can be special-purpose, providing real-time process control, program development, data communications services, file management services, etc., or they can be general-purpose, providing a wide range of services for a varied user population such as a university community. Nevertheless, the basic mechanisms and concepts involved in operating systems design do not vary greatly from one system to another.

In this chapter we will present two widely used PDP-11 operating systems: RT-11 and the UNIX system. RT-11 is a relatively simple operating system designed to run on the smallest PDP-11 systems. As such, it is an excellent example to start with, since it is easy to understand. The UNIX system, on the other hand, is a much more complex operating system designed primarily to run on larger PDP-11 systems.[1] Its primary advantage as an example is its very clean design. In addition, of course, it can be used as an example of some of the more complex operating system functions.

A basic classification scheme for operating systems functions can help put

---

[1] A single-user version of the UNIX system runs on the LSI-11.

some perspective on our discussion. Operating systems can provide *batch or interactive* service or both. Batch service means that a user's job is submitted in some way to the system, it executes to completion, and the user obtains the results, typically from a line printer. Interactive service means that a user logs on to a terminal and, by typing in commands and receiving responses, carries on a conversation with the operating system. The user is able to carry out the job in small steps, or the user may elect to submit the job to the batch service and sign off to receive the batch output from the line printer.

The collection of programs that provide either batch or interactive service is usually called the *monitor*. Usually resident in memory with the supervisor, the monitor is in charge of allocating the resources of the system (processor, memory, auxiliary memory, and peripherals) to users. In the case of batch service, allocation is often in a sequential order, while for interactive service more than one user may concurrently share resources.

Besides the batch-interactive distinction there are other properties of operating systems that are purely internal, not greatly affecting a single user's view of the system. For example, service may be *local,* i.e., close to the computer, or *remote,* i.e., at a great distance. Also, a system can be *multiaccess,* allowing more than one terminal to access the system concurrently, or *single access.*

Time sharing is the term used to describe multiaccess interactive computing. It may of course be local or remote. Remote job entry (RJE) is the term used to describe remote batch service. Again, it may be single access or multiaccess. An RJE system may in fact be implemented in such a way that users share the machine concurrently but access is still one at a time and job output appears one at a time, although not necessarily in the same order as the jobs were submitted. Such internal resource sharing is the subject of a later chapter.

In addition to the supervisor, which makes the bare hardware more convenient to use, and the monitor, which allocates the resources of the system, there are many other operating system programs available to a user. Usage of these programs is generally under the control of the monitor and is requested of the monitor by users via the system's *command language.*

Rather than spend a great deal of time discussing operating systems (there are excellent texts on the subject), we shall simply present the two example systems here. Much detail is left to subsequent chapters and, of course, we rely on the reader having access to the operating system manuals if they are actually to be used.

What follows, then, is largely a *functional view* of the RT-11 and UNIX systems. These systems are described from a user's view with implementation details covered later in the relevant chapters. It will be seen, however, that RT-11 is a very "transparent" system in that the user is made aware through the command language of internal details. Pedagogically this is an advantage, although RT-11 is not as convenient to use as the UNIX system. The price, however, of the UNIX system's convenience is its larger size and greater internal complexity. Together they make an excellent example of design trade-offs.

13-1 RT-11

RT-11 is primarily designed to provide a single-access local interactive facility. As such it is a small personal system which can run on the LSI-11, the smallest of the PDP-11 systems. Although there are additional capabilities, we shall focus on this basic capability of single-access, called the *single-job system*.

Since it is difficult to distinguish where the supervisor stops and the monitor begins, we shall simply adopt RT-11 terminology which lumps supervisory functions into the monitor. The clearest distinction, however, is that the primary supervisory functions are always in main memory and are concerned with handling traps and interrupts.

13-1.1 The Monitor

RT-11 comprises five components. The resident monitor RMON is always in memory and contains the functions of handling system console I/O, error traps, and the system auxiliary-memory device (containing RT-11 itself) as well as some tables describing the system configuration.

The keyboard monitor KMON contains the operator communication function. In other words, it carries out the meaning of command-language statements.

The user service routine USR contains the file management function. Every operating system is based to a large extent on its file management system and RT-11 is no exception.

Commands for file operations passed to USR are interpreted by the command string interpreter CSI. Although actually a part of USR, CSI can be accessed directly by user programs as well as by USR.

Finally, the collection of device handlers, called DH, is stored on auxiliary memory to conserve main memory. Each is simply a file and is loaded when required by USR on request from KMON.

RMON contains an absolute loader for loading the remaining monitor programs, stored on auxiliary memory as absolute load modules (Fig. 13-1). The key in operating RT-11 is to understand what programs are in memory at any particular time. Initially, when RMON is bootstrapped into memory, it loads USR and KMON into the next lower set of memory locations. In this state KMON controls communication with the console; it writes a dot (.) as a prompt character to indicate that it is waiting for a command.

A console command may result in a program being loaded from auxiliary memory. The absolute loader performs the loading into the remaining set of memory locations beginning at the low end of memory. If this amount of memory is insufficient, however, KMON and USR may be partially overwritten. Only RMON always remains in memory with a program. Further operator or

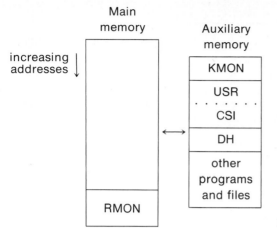

Figure 13-1 RT-11 programs.

program requests for monitor services, then, must be handled by RMON. If such requests require KMON or USR, then the program must be *swapped out* to auxiliary memory temporarily while KMON or USR are loaded to carry out the request.

Device handlers must be explicitly loaded into memory by an operator or program request. When loaded via USR, device handlers are placed in memory just below RMON with USR itself and KMON moved down if necessary (Fig. 13-2).

The monitor receives requests for service from two sources, the operator console and the loaded program. Requests from the console can come either as a *keyboard command* interpreted directly by KMON or as an I/O *command string* processed through CSI. Requests from loaded programs can also be handled directly by the monitor or be passed through CSI.

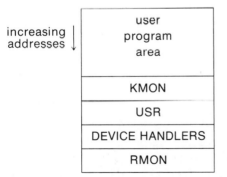

Figure 13-2 RT-11 memory allocation.

Table 13-1 Single-job commands

Command	Function
DATE	Enters or reports the current date
TIME	Enters or reports the current time
ASSIGN	Associates a logical name with a device
SET	Changes system parameters
LOAD	Loads a device handler
UNLOAD	Unloads a device handler
BASE	Sets a base address for subsequent EXAMINEs or DEPOSITs
EXAMINE	Prints the contents of specified locations
DEPOSIT	Stores into a specified location
SAVE	Writes a loaded program onto a file
CLOSE	Causes current open files to become permanent
GET	Loads a load module
START	Transfers control to a loaded program
INITIALIZE	Clears memory from previous activity
RUN	Equivalent to GET followed by START
R	Equivalent to RUN for programs on the system device
REENTER	Restarts a loaded program

Table 13-2 Special function key commands

Command	Function
CTRL/A	Displays next page of output
CTRL/C	Interrupts current program and returns control to KMON
CTRL/O	Inhibit printing on console terminal
CTRL/Q	Resume console output
CTRL/S	Suspend console output until CTRL/A or CTRL/Q
CTRL/U	Delete current input line
CTRL/X	Delete command string
CTRL/Z	End-of-file

13-1.2 Keyboard Commands

Keyboard commands from the operator console are interpreted directly by KMON. They provide the basic control over RT-11 by the operator. Table 13-1 summarizes the commands, and Table 13-2 summarizes the special function key meanings.

13-1.3 Program Requests

Requests for monitor service by a loaded program are implemented as traps to RMON, which transfers control to the appropriate monitor program. Requests can be classified as file manipulation, data transfer (I/O), and miscellaneous services. Some of the more commonly used requests are summarized in Table 13-3.

Table 13-3 Programmed requests

Request	Function
.LOOKUP	Opens an existing file via a specified channel
.CLOSE	Closes a specified channel
.DELETE	Deletes a file
.ENTER	Creates a new file for output
.READ	Initiates a file read operation
.READC	Initiates a file read operation; upon I/O completion control transfers to a specified address
.READW	Initiates and completes a file read operation; control returns only after the operation is complete
.TTY	Transfers one character from keyboard buffer to R0
.TTYOUT	Transfers one character from R0 to keyboard buffer
.WRITE	Initiates a file write
.WRITC	Similar to READC
.WRITW	Similar to READW
.EXIT	Returns control to KMON
.FETCH	Loads device handlers
.RELEAS	Removes device handlers
.WAIT	Waits for I/O completion on a specified channel
.PRINT	Prints an ASCII string

13-1.4 Command String Interpretation

A *command string* is a request to RT-11 to initialize input and output files for subsequent reading, writing, or both. A command string is normally created during a program's execution either by the operator at the console or by the program in memory. In either case, the current program can request CSI to interpret the command string and carry out the specified operations.

The general form of a command string is

DEV:OUTPUT/SWITCH=DEV:INPUT/SWITCH

which specifies from left to right an output device, output file name, output parameters, an input device, input file name, and input parameters. The actions to be carried out are all those required to locate and open the files.

A programmed request to CSI to obtain, interpret, and carry out a command string is via the macro .CSIGEN described in RT-11 manuals.

13-1.5 System Programs

In addition to the monitor, RT-11 includes a set of system programs whose function is to provide tools to develop, test, and run the user's own programs. The most commonly used of these are:

MACRO	Macro assembler	ODT	Interactive program debugger
EDIT	Text editor	PIP	File transfer and maintenance
LINK	Linker		program

and other language processors such as FORTRAN, BASIC, and Pascal.

Each of these is described in a separate manual, which must be consulted for details of operation. A typical sequence of actions, however, is to enter program text by running EDIT, assembling by running MACRO, linking by running LINK, running the load module itself, and finally debugging by linking ODT to the program and running the resulting load module.

After loading a system program via the R command, it will usually request a command string from the operator (via CSI as explained earlier). CSI writes an asterisk (*) as the prompt character to announce that a system program is waiting for input. For example, LINK expects a command string specifying input from one or more object modules and specifying the file name and device for the load-module output as well as a listing device or file.

13-2 THE UNIX SYSTEM

The UNIX operating system is primarily designed to provide a multiaccess local-remote interactive facility. It is a small- to medium-size time-sharing system requiring one of the medium-size PDP-11 family members. It is an extremely easy operating system to use and provides a rich variety of services not found in many time-sharing systems.

Since several topics involving operating system design occur in later chapters, we are not able to discuss the internal structure of the UNIX system just yet. What we can do, however, is present some of the functional characteristics as seen by each user. With some UNIX system experience behind us, later chapters should be easier to understand.

The UNIX system is written almost entirely in the systems programming language C. Source code for the system is available only under license from Western Electric.

13-2.1 The File System

The user's view of the UNIX system centers on the file system. In a sense, UNIX software provides a rich file-manipulation system. Three kinds of files exist: ordinary files, directories, and special files.

An *ordinary file* is simply a stored sequence of characters identified by a name of 14 or fewer characters. A directory, viewed by the user, is a similarly named list of file names. *Directories* are not normally accessible to a user. The names in a directory may be those of any files, ordinary, special, or directories. Thus, a directory can contain the names of subdirectories. A *special file* is similar to an ordinary file except that the physical medium manifesting the file is permanently associated with it. Thus, each peripheral and auxiliary memory device is named as a file. In addition, main memory is named as a file.

Input and output file names can be passed as parameters to functions, so a program need not be aware of the source or destination of its input and output.

This yields a great deal of flexibility in designing programs. Special files are no exception to this, although obviously one cannot write to the card reader file.

The UNIX file system maintains several directories for its own use. One of these, root, is not a subdirectory of any other directory. All other directories, however, are directly or indirectly subdirectories of root. The directory structure, then, is a "rooted tree" as each directory is constrained to appear as an entry in only one other.

Files are named within the directory structure by a *path name* of the form

/dir1/dir2/ . . . /dirn/filename

where dir1 appears in root, dir2 appears in dir1, etc., and filename appears in dirn. Normally, users do not have access to root, however, since on logging in they are assigned to a *current directory* associated with their log-in name. For example, the UNIX system writes login: to a terminal that is free. To log in, one enters an authorized name, say, joe. If the name is accepted, the terminal is then associated with the directory joe as the current directory. Path names not starting with the slash character (/) are interpreted relative to the current directory. For example, projectx/progy might refer to one of joe's programs in a subdirectory of joe called projectx.

13-2.2 The Shell and Programs

The shell is the UNIX command interpreter. Each UNIX command corresponds to a program; to invoke a UNIX function one enters the name of a program followed by arguments, thus:

command arg1 arg2 . . . argn

The shell finds a file of the same name as the command and, if found, transfers control to it. The program executes, having the argument strings passed to it by the shell, and then returns to the shell, which writes the prompt character % to the terminal, indicating completion of the command.

A command may be any path name. Common commands, however, are found in the directory /bin, and if the shell cannot find a command it looks there.

13-2.3 File Transfers

Each program, when invoked via a command, expects input from a standard input source file and writes output to a standard output destination file. The default for both of these is the user's terminal. It is easy, however, to change these standard files, and this ability is the basis of the UNIX system's file transfer capabilities.

Any argument of a command preceded by > causes the argument name to become the standard output file for the duration of the command execution.

The program never sees the argument since it is removed by the shell, which effects the file switch as well. The ls command, for example, lists the current directory. Entering

ls >filenamex

causes the listing to be written onto the file called filenamex, which may be a disk file, terminal, line printer, etc.

Prefixing an argument with < causes the argument name to become the standard input file for the duration of the command execution. For example, the command opr performs off-line printing of a file. Entering

opr

would cause all subsequent terminal input, up to an end-of-file character (which is CTRL-D) to be printed whenever the printer is free. Entering

opr <myfile

would cause the file named myfile to be printed.

Files can be passed from one program to another without the user having to explicitly name a temporary file. For example, nroff is a text formatter which could be invoked in a sequence of commands such as

nroff   <text1 >scratch
opr   <scratch

which would format and print text1. The operator would have to wait until nroff was finished to enter the second command. The same effect can be achieved by entering

nroff <text1 | opr

where the | means that the standard output file of the preceding command is passed to the succeeding command as its standard input.

Some commands accept arguments describing input and output files, and it is only when these are not given that they resort to using the standard input and output files. The commands ls, opr, and nroff are among these. So, the following commands perform the same actions as their explicitly described counterparts above.

ls filenamex
opr myfile
nroff text1 >scratch
opr scratch

Notice, however, that the output file for nroff is explicitly named, since it merely concatenates all its arguments to form its input file.

13-2.4 System Programs

The UNIX system comprises a rich variety of programs (commands), including utilities, compilers, and programming tools. A sample of some of the more commonly useful programs are described here; ls and opr have already been mentioned.

Program	Function
cat	Concatenates and writes a set of files. This is a quick way to see what is in a file or to write to a file. For example, cat x writes x to the terminal, and cat >tty2 writes subsequent terminal input to terminal tty2.
cc	Compiles C programs
chdir	Changes the current directory
cp	Copies a file
ld	Links object modules
login	Logs a user in to the UNIX system
mail	Sends a mail message to another user
mkdir	Creates a new directory
mv	Renames (moves) a file
rmdir	Deletes a directory
split	Splits a file into equal-size pieces
who	Reports who is logged in
write	Writes a message to another terminal

EXERCISES

13-1 From your perspective as a user, assess in a short report the convenience characteristics of RT-11.

13-2 Repeat Exercise 13-1 for the UNIX system.

13-3 Repeat Exercise 13-1 for your system if it is not RT-11 or the UNIX system.

13-4 From your experience as a user, assess in a short report the reliability characteristics of RT-11.

13-5 Repeat Exercise 13-4 for the UNIX system.

13-6 Repeat Exercise 13-4 for your system if it is not RT-11 or the UNIX system.

13-7 Adopt the viewpoint of a user who wishes to store private information in your computer system. Assess in a short report the security characteristics of RT-11.

13-8 Repeat Exercise 13-7 for the UNIX system. You may require some research on this.

13-9 Repeat Exercise 13-7 for your system if it is not RT-11 or the UNIX system.

REFERENCES

The prime source of material on RT-11 is the set of manuals available from Digital Equipment Corporation: "Edit-11 Text Editor," "Link-11 Linker and Libr-11 Librarian," "Macro-11 Assembler," "ODT-11R Debugging Program," and "RT-11 Monitor Handbook." The UNIX system is described in a set of documents, "Documents for Use with the UNIX Time-sharing System," available with a UNIX software license from Western Electric. Read the document entitled "UNIX for Beginners" first. In addition, a recent issue of *The Bell System Technical Journal,* published by American Telephone and Telegraph Co., contains a very comprehensive set of papers describing the design and use of the UNIX system.

FOURTEEN

AUXILIARY-MEMORY DEVICES AND PHYSICAL FILES

Long-term storage of data is one of the prime requirements of computer systems, and it is this subject to which we now turn. Long-term storage simply means that it is possible to store large amounts of data in such a way that the system can be completely shut down, and when it is again started up the data will be available. A side benefit of such a facility is the ability to transfer such stored data from one system to another.

14-1 ECONOMIC CONSIDERATIONS

Ideally, the memory for a computer should have as large a capacity as possible and be as fast as possible. Capacity is usually measured in bits and speed is usually specified in terms of *access time*, the average time required to fetch from, or to store into, a randomly chosen cell in the memory. Unfortunately, the cost per bit of storage increases as access time decreases; this is simply a characteristic of current technology and economics. The result of this cost characteristic is that designers of computers must compromise in their wish for large and fast memories, since the money available is usually limited. The compromise usually reached yields a hierarchy of memory devices: a limited amount of expensive memory, a larger amount of less expensive memory, and a very large amount of relatively cheap memory.

Figure 14-1 illustrates the capacity, cost, and access-time characteristics of memory devices available from manufacturers. As can be seen in the diagram, the devices are grouped into three classes: *Direct access* devices are character-

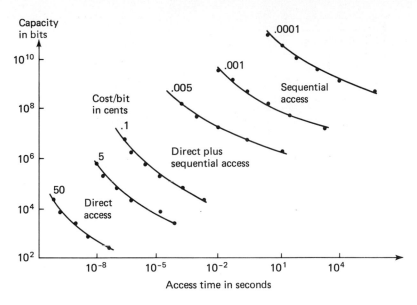

Figure 14-1 Characteristics of memory devices.

ized by an access time that is identical for all cells. *Sequential access* devices require that a cell be accessed by scanning sequentially through the cells until the one desired is found. *Direct plus sequential access* devices combine the characteristics of the two previous types.

Note how the plot of device characteristics forms a band from small, fast, and expensive devices to the larger, slower, and cheaper devices. This distribution of the characteristics of available devices results directly from the economic considerations mentioned previously. Large but fast devices are too expensive for the market. Small, slow devices are not attractive to buyers.

14-2 AUXILIARY-MEMORY DEVICES

The highest level in the hierarchy of memory devices is actually composed of the processor registers. These cells are used to hold data involved in the current state of execution of a program (Fig. 14-2).

The second level in the memory hierarchy usually consists of direct memory and is usually called *main memory*, the lower levels being called *auxiliary memory*.

The fourth level in the memory hierarchy often consists of magnetic tape drives, these being sequential access devices. (Actually, the sequential access device classification is largely a result of the existence of magnetic tapes!) Data are stored on a magnetic tape (see Fig. 14-3) by moving the tape under a write head that magnetizes small areas on the surface. Each small area is magnetized

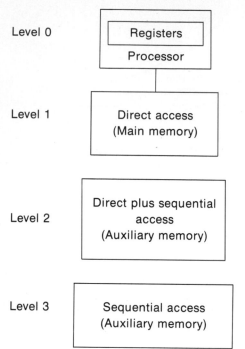

Level 0   Registers / Processor

Level 1   Direct access (Main memory)

Level 2   Direct plus sequential access (Auxiliary memory)

Level 3   Sequential access (Auxiliary memory)

Figure 14-2 The hierarchy of memory devices.

in one of two directions to encode a 0 or a 1. A tape contains a sequence of characters (usually 8-bit characters) stored in this way. Tapes are read by passing the surface under a read head that detects the stored data. Data can be written onto a tape only in a single sequence of characters, called a *block*. Once stored, data in a block can only be accessed by reading the entire block. Because of the mechanical characteristics of tape drives, blocks are separated

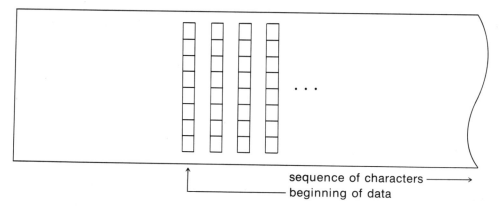

sequence of characters ⟶

beginning of data

Figure 14-3 Magnetic tape memory.

by *interrecord*[1] *gaps*. Since interrecord gaps are relatively large (about $\frac{3}{4}$ in) it is desirable to store data in large blocks so that a tape is efficiently utilized.

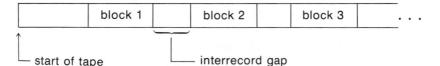

start of tape   interrecord gap

Tape drives usually offer five possible operations:

1. REWIND: Rewind the tape so that the first block is under the read-write heads.
2. READ: Read the block that is currently positioned under the heads, leaving the heads positioned over the next sequential block.
3. WRITE: Write a block at the current head position, leaving the heads ready to write the next sequential block.
4. BACKSPACE: Rewind the tape so that the heads are positioned over the preceding block.
5. END FILE: Write a special block called an END-OF-FILE mark at the current head position, leaving the heads ready to write the next sequential block.

A sequence of blocks terminated by an END-OF-FILE mark constitute a *physical file*. Because of the inexact mechanical tolerances of tape drives, it is not possible to WRITE a block onto a tape in the middle of a file and then expect to access the remainder of the file, even if the blocks are the same length. The updated block may not coincide with the old block, and erroneous data may still be stored on the tape.

Note that the source of data for a WRITE operation and the destination of the data retrieved with a READ operation have not been specified. This is discussed in the following section, but generally it will be main memory in both cases.

The block is the unit of data transfer to and from auxiliary memory devices. With tapes, the term *block* is synonymous with *physical record,* the addressable unit of data storage on auxiliary-memory devices. Another way to look at physical records is to say that they provide the storage medium on which blocks are stored. A block may occupy one or more physical records. This distinction may seem pedantic here, but it becomes important when discussing other devices and auxiliary memory in general.

The third level in the memory hierarchy is occupied largely by a class of device characterized by rotating magnetic surfaces. These devices exhibit ac-

---

[1] As will be made clear later, a *physical record* is the addressable unit of data storage, while the block is the unit of data transfer. These two terms are often confused. On tapes the terms become synonymous.

cess characteristics combining the direct and sequential modes. One of the most common of these rotating surface devices is the *movable-head disk,* shown schematically in Fig. 14-4.

A movable-head *disk module* (a disk *device* contains one or more modules) contains a set of coaxial rotating circular plates coated with a magnetic material. Data are written onto and read from the plates by a set of *read-write heads* attached to an access arm common to all heads. The arm can be moved radially to any one of a set of discrete positions. At a given arm position each head is situated so that it can read or write data from or to a ring-shaped area on the recording surface called a *track*. The set of tracks available at each arm position is called a *cylinder*. Each track contains one or more blocks. To access a block, the arm is moved to the cylinder, the head is selected, and the track is scanned until the block rotates to the head position. The block is then read or written as it passes under the head.

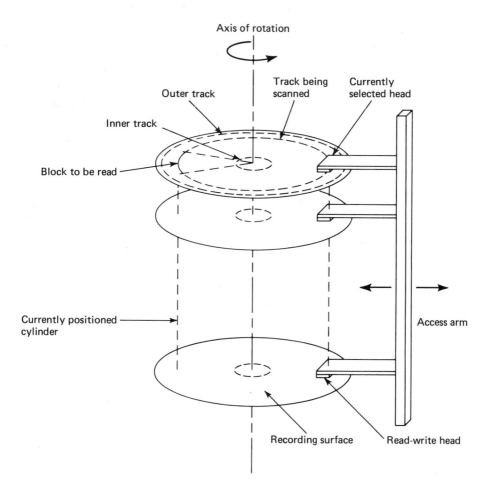

Figure 14-4 Movable-head disk module.

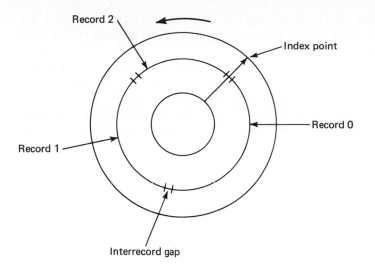

Figure 14-5 Variable-length physical records on a disk.

Some disks allow only one physical record size, while others are designed to accommodate a variable physical record size (Fig. 14-5). If a disk contains variable-size physical records, a particular record is located by first scanning the track containing the record until an *index point* appears under the heads; the record is then accessed by scanning the track and counting records until the one desired is reached. Physical records on disks are separated by interrecord gaps, as are blocks on tape. The *address* of a physical record is specified by a cylinder number, track number, and record number.

Disks with fixed-length physical records are called *sector-organized* (Fig. 14-6). The recording density varies from outer to inner tracks so that each track

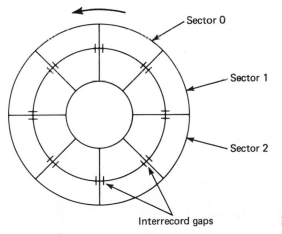

Figure 14-6 Sector-organized disk.

contains the same number of equal-capacity physical records. A physical record in a sector-organized disk is addressed by a cylinder number, track number, and sector number.

As with tapes, the unit of data that is read from, or written onto, a disk is the *block*. With disks, however, blocks and physical records need not coincide (although they often do). A block may only occupy part of a physical record, in which case the remainder of the record is unusable and thus wasted. A block may occupy several physical records; most disks allow read or write operations to transfer data from or to consecutive physical records as one continuous operation. In fact it is often possible to transfer the entire contents of a disk as one block. In such a case physical records are accessed automatically in the addressing sequence. For example, if a disk has s sectors, t tracks, and c cylinders, the sequence of disk addresses starts at cylinder 0, track 0, and sector 0 and ends at cylinder $c - 1$, track $t - 1$, and sector $s - 1$. The switching of read-write heads from one track to the next sequential track within a cylinder can be accomplished in a short enough time that each consecutive disk rotation can be used to read or write part of the block. Access arm movement is relatively slow, however, and several disk revolutions may occur before the arm can be positioned at the next consecutive cylinder.

The three basic operations of a disk are:

1. SEEK: Move the access arm to a specified cylinder and select a specified track.
2. READ: Read a block starting at a specified physical record and continuing for a specified number of characters.
3. WRITE: Write a block starting at a specified physical record and continuing for a specified number of characters.

A physical file on a disk is simply a specific collection of physical records, not necessarily contiguous.

14-2.1 RX11 Floppy Disk System

The RX11 floppy disk system, commonly found in small PDP-11s, consists of one or two disk modules. Each of these has only one recording surface (i.e., only one track per cylinder) with 77 cylinders numbered 0 to 76. Each track is divided into 26 sectors, numbered 1 to 26, which are capable of storing 128 bytes of data. Unlike most disks the RX11 is not a DMA device.

The following data describes the RX11-processor programming interface:

RX11 status register RXCS	address 177170 octal
RX11 buffer register RXDB	address 177172 octal
RX11 interrupt priority	5
RX11 interrupt vector	address 264 octal

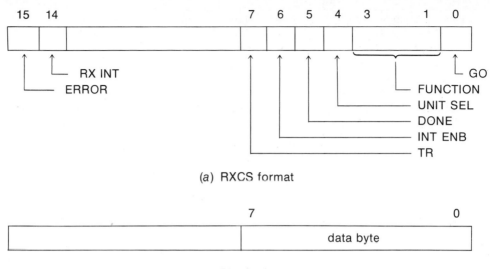

(a) RXCS format

(b) RXDB format

Figure 14-7 RX11 device registers.

The format of the RX11 registers is shown in Fig. 14-7. To write a sector, a buffer in the RX11's interface is first filled by passing data to it through the RXDB. After the buffer is filled, the actual write can be carried out. The sequence proceeds as follows. A Fill Buffer command, 000 octal, is placed in the FUNCTION field, and the GO bit is set. The program waits for TR to be set, and when this is detected a byte is moved into the RXDB, resetting TR. The wait on TR is repeated until all 128 bytes have been passed to the buffer in the RX11's interface. When the last byte is accepted, DONE will be set and an interrupt generated if INT ENB has been set.

With the buffer filled, the sector can be written as follows. A Write Sector command, 010 octal, is moved into the FUNCTION field and the GO bit set. The program waits for TR to be set, and when this is detected the sector address, as an 8-bit integer, is moved into the RXDB resetting TR. The program again waits for TR and, when it is set, moves the track address into the RXDB, resetting TR. On completion of the write, an interrupt is generated. On the average each access requires about $\frac{1}{2}$ s, so the RX11 is not a very fast device.

Reading a sector proceeds in an analogous manner to the write.

14-3 PHYSICAL FILES

Files exist in almost every computer system, and are, in some respects, the central entities about which all computing activity revolves. Computers are information processing tools, and the file is the basic unit of long-term in-

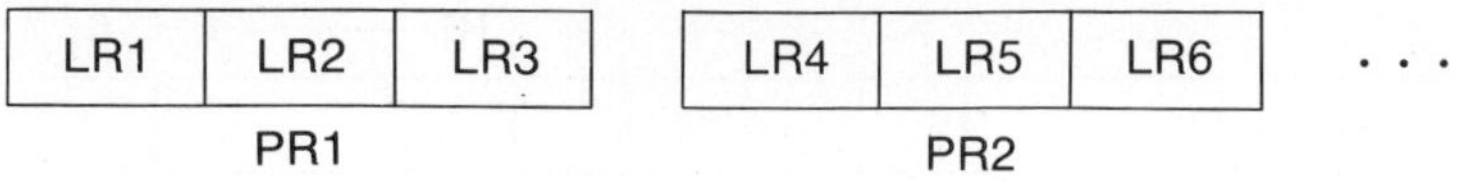

Figure 14-8 Blocked logical records.

formation storage. This section describes how a file can be stored on an auxiliary-memory device. The discussion is confined to tapes and disks.

The external view of a file is often that of a table of *logical records*. Each logical record contains related data in a set of fields. Every logical record contains the same set of fields;[1] that is, the *field format* of each logical record is identical to every other. The field chosen to identify a record is called the *key field*.

A file as just described is an example of a logical file, a file as viewed by a programmer using some particular programming language. The name *logical* file is used to indicate that the programmer sees only the logical relationships among the data in the file. That is, the programmer sees a file as simply a collection of logical records, each record having a particular field format.

The remainder of this section is concerned only with the way a file can be stored on an auxiliary-memory device. A file as stored on such a device is called a *physical file*.

The unit of storage on auxiliary-memory devices is the physical record. Consequently, physical files must be divided into physical records. Sometimes one logical record can conveniently form a physical record. For example, each logical record in a file may, coincidentally, be the same size as a physical record on a disk. In storing the file, each logical record forms a block and is stored in a single physical record. More often, however, logical record size and physical record size do not conform.

Logical records (LRs) may be smaller than physical records (PRs), in which case several logical records occupy one physical record. Packing logical records into physical records is called *blocking* (Fig. 14-8). A PR size smaller than LR size results in "spanned records," logical records divided among one or more physical records (Fig. 14-9). The choice of logical record size is determined by the application.

Physical record size may be fixed by the device manufacturer, as is the case for sector-organized disks. With tapes, physical record size is simply the same as the block size.

The choice of block size is determined by four factors:

1. *Accessing time*. The total time spent accessing a file may be decreased if blocks are made larger. This is especially true for disks, where arm-movement time and rotational time constitute significant overhead on each access.

---

[1] Logical records need not be of identical length, but the discussion can be simplified by assuming fixed-length logical records.

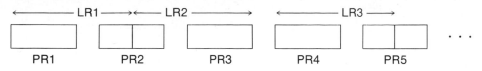

Figure 14-9 Spanned logical records.

2. *Auxiliary-memory utilization.* For devices permitting variable-length physical records, block size determines physical record size. Memory utilization, the proportion of the recording surface actually used for data storage, may be increased by making blocks larger. This results from the (often) large interrecord gaps.
3. *Main-memory utilization.* Large blocks require correspondingly large buffers in main memory into which or from which they are to be transferred. Large buffers may reduce main-memory utilization.
4. *Physical record size.* A block size less than physical record size wastes the remaining unusable portion of each physical record.

Physical files can be organized to provide access in two basic ways, *sequential* and *indexed*. In a sequentially organized file the physical records (and therefore the logical records) are accessible only by scanning sequentially through the file. A particular record is identifiable only by its relative position in the file. In an indexed file the location of a logical record is determined from its key; that is, given a key value the corresponding logical record can be found.

14-4 SEQUENTIAL FILES

Auxiliary-memory space for a file can be allocated by blocking logical records into sequential physical records taken in the normal addressing sequence. Such a file is called a *sequential file*. Tapes, of course, are almost always organized using sequential files, but disks are also used to store sequential files.

Sequential files are normally used for data processed sequentially and often sorted (Fig. 14-10). Insertions of new logical records and record deletions are awkward because the entire file following a new or deleted record must be adjusted. In addition, records on sequential tape files cannot normally be updated

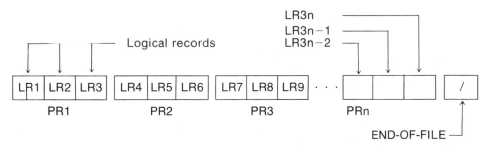

Figure 14-10 A sequential file.

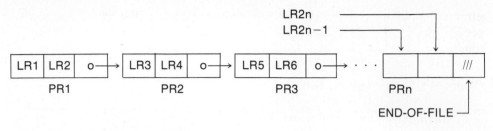

Figure 14-11 A chained sequential file.

in place, so that the entire file must be rewritten if changes are made. As shown in Fig. 14-10, a sequential file is normally terminated by a special physical record (block) called an END-OF-FILE mark.

A sequential file requires a contiguous collection of physical records. If the addition of new logical records increases the length of the file, it must be moved to a new larger location in auxiliary memory. If disks are used, however, it is not necessary to move the file; The physical records can be "chained" to-

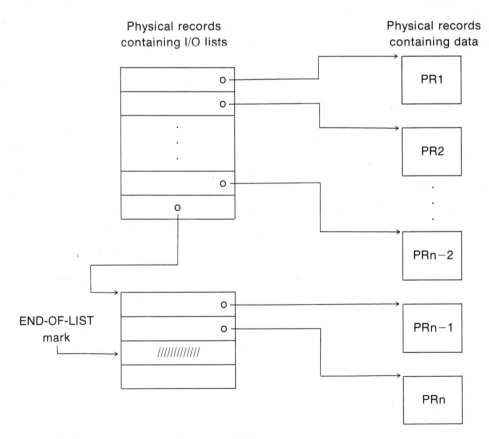

Figure 14-12 A chained sequential file using I/O lists.

gether by placing in each physical record the address of the next sequential record. Thus, space for such a *chained sequential file* can be freely allocated from any part of the disk (Fig. 14-11).

Note that the END-OF-FILE mark for a chained sequential file can be included in the last physical record in place of a chaining address.

For faster sequential searching the chaining addresses in the physical records can be removed and placed in a separate list of addresses called an *I/O list*. The I/O list for a file is itself stored in a chain of physical records. Thus space for the list and for the data records in a file can be freely allocated from the available space (Fig. 14-12).

14-5 INDEXED FILES

Each logical record in a file can be assigned to a specific physical record. If the physical record address can be determined from the logical record key, then each logical record can be accessed directly without a search. Such files can be called *directly indexed*. This technique is especially suited to disks where sectors can be directly addressed. The correspondence between keys and disk addresses can be obtained by hashing or by simply keeping in main memory a list of keys and their corresponding addresses. If logical records are blocked,

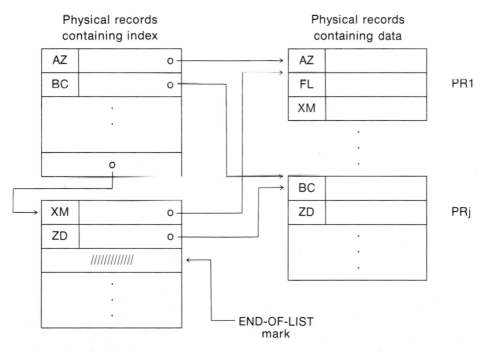

Figure 14-13 An indexed file.

then a sequential search of a physical record is necessary to locate a particular logical record.

Hashing suffers from the same problems of memory utilization discussed in a previous section. Access, however, can be fast.

Maintaining a list of keys and their corresponding addresses is expensive in terms of the space occupied by the list in main memory and, also, the time required to sort and search the list. Once an address is obtained, however, access is fast.

The list of keys and corresponding addresses just described for directly indexed files is the basic element in a file organization commonly called *indexed,* except that *the list is stored in auxiliary memory rather than main memory.* This list, containing each key value present in the file along with the address of the physical record containing the corresponding logical record, is called simply an *index.* A simple file is shown in Fig. 14-13.

Note that the index is stored in a chained list of physical records. An END-OF-LIST mark indicates the end of the index. Given a key value, the physical record address can be found by searching the index, which is normally sorted. The logical record sought is found by a sequential search of the physical record.

If the logical records are sorted within each physical record, and the index is sorted, then the index need only contain the key of the *last* logical record in each physical record (Fig. 14-14). Given a key value, say, SEARCHKEY, the index is searched until an entry is found for which SEARCHKEY $\leq$ KEY.

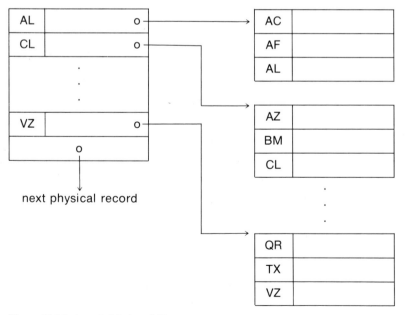

Figure 14-14 A sorted indexed file.

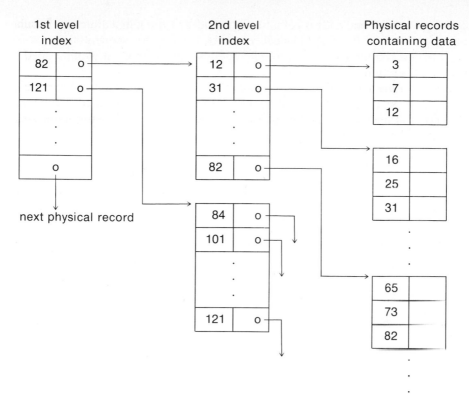

Figure 14-15 Multilevel indexing.

The logical record is then found by a sequential search of the physical record whose address is in the entry.

Note that a separate access to auxiliary memory is generally required for each physical record examined. To avoid long sequential searches of the index, several "levels" of indexing can be used. Each higher-level index contains a list of the last key values present in each physical record of the next lower-level index (Fig. 14-15).

The physical records may be stored sequentially in contiguous addresses, in which case the file may be accessed either sequentially or by indexing. Such files are fairly common and are called *indexed-sequential*.

14-6 FILE DIRECTORIES

Any large computer system contains many files of differing organizations. In order that access to files can be performed in a convenient way, each file is given a name, which can be assigned by a programmer and stored in a *file directory*. A directory is simply a file, each logical record of which contains the name, accessing method, and address of a file. The address given in a directory would normally be that of the first physical record of the file; for sequential files this record would contain data, and for indexed files, for example, it would contain the start of an index.

One file directory may contain entries for all files in the system. Such a directory is often called the *master directory*. In other systems each individual disk module, tape reel, etc., contains a *volume directory* of files stored therein.

14-7 RT-11 FILES

Physical file organization in RT-11 is quite simple; A block is synonymous with a physical record. The RX11 floppy disk, therefore, can contain a maximum of $77 \cdot 26 = 2002$ blocks of 128 bytes each.

There are three types of physical files, which are called, in PDP-11 terminology, *contiguous, linked,* and *mapped.* A *contiguous* file is what our discussion called *sequential.* That is, each block (i.e., physical record) is assigned an address immediately following its predecessor. On a direct-access device like a disk, this has the advantage that the address of any block can be determined from the address of the first, making a sequential search unnecessary.

The second type, *linked,* we have called *chained sequential.* Such files are more easily joined together or modified since there is no restriction on the addresses of the blocks. An interesting aspect of RT-11's linked files is that, when writing a file, addresses are assigned with some intervening sectors between consecutive blocks. This allows sequential processing to proceed quickly, since a block's successor should be approaching the read heads just after the block has been processed.

Finally, *mapped* files in RT-11 make use of I/O lists. Rather than placing an

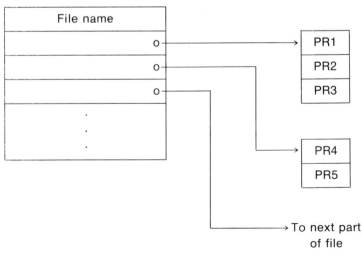

Figure 14-16 Mapped files in RT-11.

address for every block in the I/O list, however, each set of physically contiguous blocks is described in the list (Fig. 14-16).

Directories are also straightforward. Each disk module has one directory listing for each file on the module its name, address, and length. Tapes, on the other hand, have no directories. Rather, files are placed consecutively, each containing at the beginning its own descriptive information.

File names include a specification of the device containing the file. This makes life easier for the operating system, since only one device need be accessed. Also, names contain a specification of the type of the file. This information, in a one- to three-character extension, can be used to catch errors as well as identify for the user various versions of a file. For example, BAS means a BASIC source file, OBJ means a relocatable object file, and LDA is an absolute load module. The general form of file names is

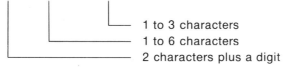

dev:filename.extension

               1 to 3 characters
               1 to 6 characters
               2 characters plus a digit

14-8 UNIX FILES

A file in the UNIX system is essentially a named character string. There is no implicit logical record organization, although one is free to insert control characters to delineate records if desired.

Each auxiliary-memory device is a self-contained file system. Physical records are each 512 bytes long, and physical record 0 is left unused. On physical record 1 is a table called the *super block* containing all the necessary descriptive information about the device. One such piece of information is the number of physical records allocated, starting at record 2, for the *inode table*.

Each file on a device has a single entry, its *inode*, in the device inode table. This inode provides the sole path to a file. Part of the C definition of an inode might appear as

```
STRUCT  inode
{ CHAR   nlink;
    INT   mode;
    INT   addr[8];
    etc.
```

For small files the array addr contains up to eight physical record addresses constituting the file. As seen in Fig. 14-17, a zero address indicates a null value.

For files that are larger than 4096 characters, called *large files*, a different scheme is used. The 15-bit field mode will contain a code indicating a large file, and the blocks pointed to by addr will each contain not data but up to 256 further physical record addresses. This is illustrated in Fig. 14-18.

As a way of increasing the maximum size of files to 2^{15} blocks (the largest

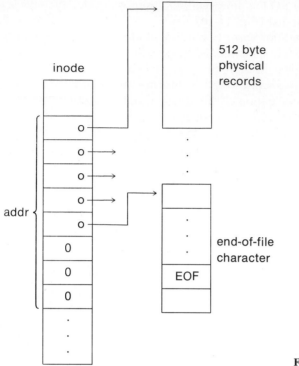

Figure 14-17 A small UNIX™ file.

positive integer range using 16-bit arithmetic!) a special meaning is given to addr[7]. If necessary, to extend the file and use addr[7], two levels of indirect addressing, rather than one, are used. The procedure that converts a block number into a physical record number simply performs one extra level of indirection if the block number is larger than $2^{11} - 2^8 - 1$.

UNIX files are, therefore, a version of the I/O list method discussed earlier. To increase the speed of access, a copy of the inode is kept in main memory for each active file, current directory, auxiliary-memory device (recall that each device is represented by a file), text file (special internal UNIX file), and the root file.

Directory files are organized in the same way as other files, the main difference being that access to them is somewhat restricted. Each block in a directory file contains up to 32 sixteen-character entries. In each such entry is a 16-bit inode pointer into the inode table and a 14-character file name. Thus, many directory entries can refer to the same file, possibly with a different name.

14-9 ACCESS METHODS AND LOGICAL FILES

Most programmers do not see the internal details of file organization as have been discussed here. Just as most programmers see the computer system via a

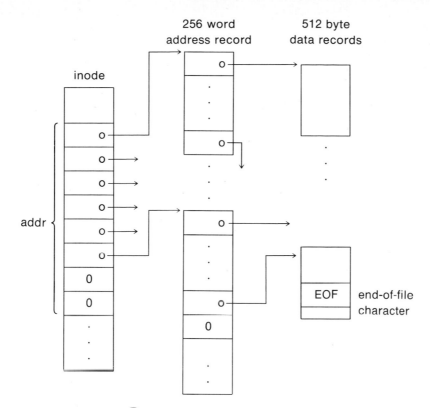

Figure 14-18 A UNIX™ large file.

high-level language, rather than assembly language, so they see the file system via a high-level file management system.

A file as seen by an applications programmer can be called a *logical file* to distinguish it from its physical file representation. Logical files are composed of logical records, and it is these records that are manipulated by applications programs. There may be a complex set of file management programs to do blocking, data transfer, buffering, allocation of auxiliary-memory space, etc., in order to present a convenient view of the files to the user. Often, different views are available. Sometimes called *access methods,* these views permit a programmer to perform access to the logical file in different ways, depending on his or her needs. For example, a file may be written as a sequential (logically sequential!) file and read as an indexed (logically indexed) file.

In principle, the physical organization is independent of the logical organization. Obviously, however, certain physical organizations are better able to support certain logical organizations. Thus many logical access methods reflect the underlying organization of the file. The main difference is likely to be the difference between logical records and physical records, as discussed earlier.

EXERCISES

14-1 A sequential file is stored on tape. Show an algorithm for searching for and updating a logical record with a given key. Assume a blocking factor of 3 (three logical records per physical record) and double buffering.

14-2 The time required to access a disk comprises three components: a fixed time incurred if the heads are moved, a head movement time proportional to the number of cylinders moved, and a rotational delay while the record moves under the heads. Suggest how each of these components might be reduced through careful allocation of disk space to files.

14-3 Assume that a 200-cylinder, eight-sector disk has a fixed-head movement time of 50 ms, a variable head movement time of 1 ms per cylinder, and a rotational speed of 1200 r/min. If files are evenly distributed on the disk and all files are equally likely to be accessed, what is the average access time for the device? [*Hint:* The mean distance between two randomly chosen points in the interval $(0,1)$ is $\frac{1}{3}$.]

14-4 Assume that a file processing program using the disk of Exercise 14-3 requires 50 ms to process one block of data. If a block comprises one sector, how many buffers would one need to eliminate delay due to file I/O?

14-5 Repeat Exercise 14-1 for the case of a chained sequential file on disk.

14-6 Repeat Exercise 14-1 for the case of a chained sequential file with I/O lists.

14-7 Repeat Exercise 14-1 for the case of an indexed file.

14-8 Consider an RT-11 contiguous file without a logical record structure. Show the algorithm for converting a character index into the file into a physical record address and character index into the physical record. Repeat this for the linked and mapped organizations.

14-9 Repeat Exercise 14-8 for each type of UNIX file, small and large.

REFERENCES

This chapter has barely scratched the surface of the subject of file systems. It has carefully avoided becoming involved in the issues regarding the facilities that a general-purpose file system should provide. This subject area considers logical views (abstractions) of files and leads into the study of *data base systems*. A more general introduction to information storage systems can be found in Freeman (1975) and in Hsiao (1975).

The UNIX file system derives largely from that of the MULTICS system developed at MIT and described in Daley (1965).

A discussion of design issues is found in Madnick (1969) and (1970). Particular techniques for organizing files are discussed in Johnson (1961), Nievergelt (1974), Schay (1962), and Sussenguth (1963).

CHAPTER FIFTEEN

MULTIPROGRAMMING

15-1 PERFORMANCE CONSIDERATIONS

In an earlier chapter, we described how the supervisor can provide an operation with which a user program can wait for some event such as an interrupt to occur. This operation might take the form of a language function call (translated by the compiler, perhaps, into a trap) such as

block (device_address)

The block will delay execution of the calling program until the next interrupt from the specified device, at which time the program can continue. As pointed out previously, a supervisor could simply implement this with a busy-wait loop.

Now suppose that the supervisor is part of a batch operating system and that user programs, once loaded, have access to one of several disk devices for file manipulation. If programs in this system tend to do little disk I/O, then they will execute quickly and be removed by the monitor, which will load the next user program. User jobs should flow through the system with a reasonably high utilization of the processor.

Suppose now that programs tend to do a great deal of disk I/O. Each time a program blocks on its disk, the entire system pauses, waiting for a disk interrupt. Since disk access times are typically 10 to 100 ms (whereas processor instruction times for even a small PDP-11 are in the range of several microseconds), processor utilization decreases and the throughput of the system can slow down dramatically.

Further suppose (1) we have a system in which each user program needs

331

only one disk drive and there are several available, and (2) a program occupies only a fraction of main memory. Then the monitor can *multiprogram* a set of user jobs by loading all of them into memory simultaneously. Only one is executing at one instant, but when the executing program enters the supervisor via a block, the supervisor can simply give processor control to one of the other programs in memory that are not also blocked on a device. Thus, the block operation not only delays program execution but also yields processor control to another program.

There are important consequences. First, the supervisor must handle and record interrupts as they occur, since, as one program executes, interrupts can occur for other blocked programs. Second, a program invoking block will regain processor control only after the interrupt occurs and another executing program yields control. Thus a program invoking block will not necessarily continue execution as soon as the supervisor has detected the interrupt. This will occur, however, in the circumstance where block is invoked and the supervisor finds all multiprogrammed programs blocked on interrupts. It then can busy-wait and, at the next interrupt, the associated waiting program will be given control immediately.

We have described how multiprogramming can increase the throughput of a batch system by sharing the processor and memory. Now consider the supervisor in an interactive operating system. In a single-access system the program interacting with the terminal will spend most of its time blocked, and the supervisor will be busy-waiting. Time-sharing is a way of utilizing this available system time by making the system multiaccess. Suppose that each of several terminals has a separate program with which it interacts. This set of programs may be multiprogrammed in exactly the same way as in the batch system. They will each be blocking on a terminal, though, instead of on a disk.

There is one important difference between the batch and interactive multiprogrammed systems. It concerns not the mechanism of multiprogramming, which is identical, but the performance. In the case of a batch program blocking on a disk, it does not matter that execution may not continue soon after the interrupt. However, with an interactive system this does matter, since the user at a terminal, unlike the disk, needs a response from the program quickly after entering a command. Therefore, the program serving a terminal needs to regain processor control soon after an interrupt.

As long as all the programs in the simple interactive system described here are I/O bound, i.e., they consume little processor time, then the response at terminals will be adequate. This will certainly be true for a small number of terminals. In this case the multiprogramming mechanism can be identical with the batch system. Later, we will consider ways of coping with a large number of terminals and compute-bound programs. Note however that it is not practical with the simple methods described here to multiprogram batch and interactive programs in the same system. This is because a compute-bound batch program could seriously affect terminal response by refusing to yield processor control.

15-2 REENTRANT PROGRAMS

In both batch and interactive systems, jobs and terminal users can share reentrant code. It is particularly common in a time-sharing system to serve a set of terminals with a single program in main memory. Each terminal has an associated data area in memory, of course. Even though there is only one program, such a system is still said to be multiprogrammed. In fact, the supervisor is not affected by code sharing; it can be exactly the same as that described in the previous section.

The concept of a process, introduced in Chap. 6, is needed to describe systems with reentrant programs. Each user terminal in a time-shared system is controlled by a process which is managed by the supervisor. Each process is represented in the system by the current state of the computation it is performing. Its state will comprise processor register contents and its private data.

15-3 THE MULTIPROGRAMMING SUPERVISOR

The multiprogramming supervisor (MS) must keep a record of the state of each process and each I/O device under its control. For devices, the important state information is whether or not an interrupt has occurred. For processes it is the processor register contents (including the PC) and the location of its private data. In the case of the PDP-11 the location of private data is simply described by R6, so we need consider only the register contents.

For simplicity we shall assume that each device is permanently associated with a process. It is necessary therefore for the supervisor to maintain this mapping information as well.

A simple supervisor's data structures, to manage np processes, can be implemented as follows:

```
CONST np = 3;
TYPE csr = 170000..177777;
     pstate = RECORD
           r : ARRAY [0..6] OF INTEGER ;
          pc : INTEGER ;
          ps : INTEGER ;
        addr : csr ;
         int : BOOLEAN
             END ;
     processtable = ARRAY [1..np] OF pstate ;
VAR pt : processtable;
    current : 1..np ;
    reg : ARRAY [0..7] OF INTEGER ;
    psw : INTEGER ;
    b, waiting: BOOLEAN;
```

The variables reg and psw are implemented in hardware, of course. Also available to the supervisor are two subprograms, push and pop, as follows:

```
PROCEDURE push (z : INTEGER);
        push z onto the system stack;
FUNCTION pop : INTEGER ;
        pop := remove top element from system stack ;
```

The processtable pt contains an entry for each process, there being np processes. Each such entry contains the register contents r and pc, the status word ps, the address of the associated device, and an interrupt flag int. Finally, to locate the currently executing process, called the *running* process, the supervisor needs the subrange variable current.

The supervisor provides two operations over these data structures, block and interrupt, shown in Fig. 15-1. Entry to block is caused by the running process. Entry to interrupt is caused by an I/O device.

```
PROCEDURE block ;
    VAR i : INTEGER ;
    BEGIN
        mask interrupts;
        FOR i := 0 TO 6 DO pt[current].r[i] := reg[i];
        pt[current].pc := pop;
        pt[current].ps := pop;
        IF NOT selectnextprocess THEN BEGIN
            waiting := TRUE;
            unmask interrupts;
            WHILE waiting DO ;
            b := selectnextprocess END;
        unmask interrupts
    END;


PROCEDURE interrupt(intaddr : csr) ;
    VAR d : 1..np;
    BEGIN
        mask interrupts;
        d := 1;
        WHILE pt[d].addr <> intaddr DO d := d + 1;
        pt[d].int := TRUE;
        IF waiting THEN waiting := FALSE
        ELSE unmask interrupts
    END
```

Figure 15-1 The block and interrupt operations.

The procedures block and interrupt will be implemented as trap and interrupt handlers respectively. Procedure return, then, will be implemented with RTT and RTI. Function selectnextprocess (Fig. 15-2) can be implemented with any reasonably efficient subroutine calling sequence. Also, since block and interrupt are not implemented as subroutines, interrupt masking and unmasking are handled by the hardware.

Notice that the supervisor executes with interrupts masked. They are masked on entry to block, and if selectnextprocess returns unsuccessfully (all processes are blocked), they are unmasked, waiting is set to TRUE, and the supervisor busy-waits.

Subsequently, interrupt is invoked with interrupts masked and the interrupt bit for the device in question is set. Procedure interrupt now examines waiting to determine the program to which it will return. If waiting is TRUE it will return to block; if waiting is FALSE it will return to some process's program. So, in the first case it simply sets waiting to FALSE and returns, *with interrupts still masked;* in the second, it unmasks interrupts before returning.

There may be a slight inefficiency in this supervisor in that the running process's registers are always stored into pt when block is called. It might be worth a check to see if the process's device has already interrupted, in which case the process can continue. This would complicate our algorithm, however, and the implementation would have to be examined to see if the change were justified.

Even if a process invokes block when its device has already interrupted, we may want other processes to have priority over the running process in gaining processor control. As explained earlier, in an interactive system response time will be affected by these considerations. Thus, having MS always rescan the process table when a process blocks gives MS a chance to employ any algorithm it wishes in selecting the next process to run. The subject of scheduling

```
FUNCTION selectnextprocess : BOOLEAN ;
     VAR i,j : 1..np; notf : BOOLEAN;
     BEGIN
        i := 1; notf := TRUE; selectnextprocess .— FALSE;
        WHILE (i <= np) AND notf DO BEGIN
           IF pt[i].int = TRUE THEN BEGIN
              pt[i].int :— FALSE;
              FOR j := 0 TO 6 DO reg[j] := pt [i].r[j];
              push (pt[i].ps);
              push (pt[i].pc);
              notf := FALSE;
              selectnextprocess := TRUE;
              current := i END
           ELSE i := i + 1
        END
     END
```

Figure 15-2 The short-term scheduler.

algorithms is an extremely large area; we shall return to this point in the following section. Our present description employs a sequential search of pt. What does this imply about the relative priorities assigned to processes with respect to scheduling?

One final point to note is that multiple interrupts from a device will be lost, since interrupt simply sets int. Our simple supervisor will work only where a device never interrupts its control process until a previous interrupt has been acknowledged via its control registers.

15-4 PROCESSOR SCHEDULING

The supervisor described in the previous section has a very simple scheduling algorithm; to select a process it scans the entire process table in sequential order. One should immediately see that with a large number of processes in an interactive system this will be quite inefficient, since most processes will be blocked, and a search of the entire table will be very time-consuming. Additionally, there still remains the problem that, with this simple supervisor, a process can seize control of the processor and keep it indefinitely.

The processor scheduling function being discussed here is called *short-term* scheduling to distinguish it from scheduling carried on by the monitor (in scheduling a batch job's entry into the system, for example) or by the operator.

15-4.1 Short-Term Scheduling

A process in a multiprogrammed system can be in one of three basic states: running, blocked, or ready. A process is said to be *running* when it has control of the processor. In terms of the algorithm shown in Fig. 15-1, it is the process to which the variable current refers. Note that a running process can be interrupted periodically, in which case its execution pauses. It still retains its running status, however, at least until it executes a block operation. A process is said to be *blocked* if it has executed a block operation on a device but an interrupt from that device has not occurred. A blocked process becomes *ready* as the result of the interrupt on which it is waiting. These states are illustrated in Fig. 15-3 along with the events and operations causing state changes. Notice that a running process that executes block after an interrupt from its device proceeds directly to the ready state.

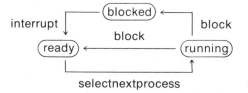

selectnextprocess

Figure 15-3 Process states.

Clearly, the short-term scheduler, selectnextprocess, needs only to examine ready processes, not the entire process table. It would help therefore to keep ready processes stored separately.

How can we solve the additional problem of processes monopolizing the system's resources in running state? One way is to require of all programs that they periodically call the supervisor via a specially supplied operation for such a voluntary preemption. This obviously will only work in carefully controlled circumstances. It is sometimes used, nevertheless, as a simple and direct solution.

A more general solution is to augment the supervisor with a third operation, called *timeout*. This requires that the hardware include a timer I/O device[1] that can be set to interrupt after a specified interval. The supervisor can then set this device like an alarm clock to regain control of the processor and invoke the scheduler. This is called *time-slicing*, and the chosen interval the *time quantum*. Let's now examine scheduling in more detail.

15-4.2 Nonpreemptive Scheduling

The scheduler of Fig. 15-2 is said to be *nonpreemptive* because it performs no time-slicing. Here, the running process is defined by the value of current, blocked processes are those for which int = 0, and ready processes are those nonrunning processes for which int = 1. Because processes are stored in a sequential table, the scheduler must search sequentially. If ready processes are stored separately, this search can be shortened. The search by interrupt can easily be eliminated by a suitable implementation since each device occupies a fixed table position. Therefore, we are concerned only about selectnextprocess.

Ready processes can be stored on a *ready list*. The organization of the list is dependent on the operations to be performed on it. Let's suppose that the scheduler is to treat the ready list as a queue (Fig. 15-4). Processes entering the ready state are appended to the list. The scheduler removes the oldest process on the list, i.e., the one at the head of the list. This scheduling algorithm, first in first out (FIFO), guarantees that a process will eventually be selected.

---

[1] The PDP-11 programmable real-time clock, KW11-P, is available for this purpose.

append $\longrightarrow$ [| | | | |] $\longrightarrow$ remove

Figure 15-4 A queue.

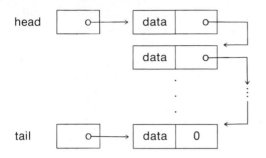

Figure 15-5 A singly linked list.

A queue can be implemented with a *singly linked* list (Fig. 15-5). As with the nodes of a singly linked tree (see Chap. 8), the physical ordering in memory of the elements on such a list is not related to their ordering on the list. This ordering is determined solely by the values in the link fields of the elements; a link field contains a reference (address or index) to another list element. Therefore, a list of arbitrary order can be created by altering the link-field values. As shown in Fig. 15-5, the first and last elements on such a list are recorded in the variables labeled *head* and *tail*.

The data structure changes that we will make to incorporate the link fields are the following:

1. Add a pointer field l to the pstate record.
2. Add ready list head and tail pointers.
3. Make current of type pointer.

The ready processes are then simply linked together as shown in Fig. 15-5. The operations append and remove, along with the required data structure changes, are shown in Fig. 15-6.

Now the ready processes are those nonrunning processes that are on the ready list. Revised programs for block, interrupt, and selectnextprocess are shown in Fig. 15-7. In interrupt, we have assumed that the implementation will make a table search unnecessary.

Notice that it has been necessary to retain int to avoid appending a process to the ready list more than once, in the event that a device can transmit an interrupt before receiving an acknowledgement.

```
CONST np = 3;

TYPE csr = 170000..177777;
     pstateptr = ↑ pstate;
     pstate = RECORD
         r : ARRAY[0..6] OF INTEGER;
         pc : INTEGER;
         ps : INTEGER;
         addr : csr;
         int : BOOLEAN;
         l : pstateptr
         END;
VAR head, tail,current : pstateptr;
     reg: ARRAY [0..7] OF INTEGER;
     psw: INTEGER;
     b,waiting: BOOLEAN;

PROCEDURE append (p : pstateptr) ;
     BEGIN
         p↑.l := nil;
         IF tail = nil THEN head .– p
         ELSE tail↑.l :– p;
         tail := p
     END;

FUNCTION remove : pstateptr;
     BEGIN
         remove := head;
         IF head <> nil THEN BEGIN
             head :– head ↑ .l;
             IF head = nil THEN tail := nil END
     END
```

Figure 15-6 Ready list implementation.

15-4.3 Preemptive Scheduling

Preemptive scheduling adds one additional state change to Fig. 15-3; the time-out operation can now be invoked independently of the running process, placing it in the ready state (Fig. 15-8). To modify the scheduler we need mainly to add the timeout operation.

Only one other modification is necessary. Since the running process may invoke block before timeout is invoked by the timer device, the timer's next interrupt must be canceled before it can occur. This can be done in the same program that starts the timer, which is most clearly accomplished by select-

```
PROCEDURE block ;
VAR i : INTEGER;
BEGIN
      mask interrupts;
      FOR i := 0 TO 6 DO current ↑ .r[i] := reg [i];
      current ↑ .pc := pop;
      current ↑ .ps := pop;
      IF NOT selectnextprocess THEN BEGIN
            waiting := TRUE;
            unmask interrupts;
            WHILE waiting DO ;
            b := selectnextprocess END;
      unmask interrupts
END;

PROCEDURE interrupt (procptr : pstateptr) ;
BEGIN
      mask interrupts;
      IF NOT procptr ↑ .int <> 1 THEN BEGIN
            procptr ↑ .int := TRUE;
            append(procptr) END;
      IF waiting THEN waiting := FALSE
      ELSE unmask interrupts
END;

FUNCTION selectnextprocess : BOOLEAN;
VAR i : pstateptr; j : 1..np;
BEGIN
      i := remove;
      selectnextprocess :=FALSE;
      IF i  <> nil THEN BEGIN
            selectnextprocess := TRUE;
            current := i;
            WITH current ↑  DO BEGIN
                  int := FALSE;
                  FOR j := 0 TO 6 DO reg[j] := r[j];
                  push(ps);
                  push(pc) END END
END
```

Figure 15-7 Nonpreemptive scheduling.

nextprocess as it loads the new current process. We then have the following sequence: The timer is started by selectnextprocess either to occur and invoke timeout or to be canceled by selectnextprocess. These modifications are all shown in Fig. 15-9. No changes in the data structures are necessary.

Notice, particularly, that timeout's call to selectnextprocess is guaranteed to return TRUE, with a process loaded into the processor, since the preempted

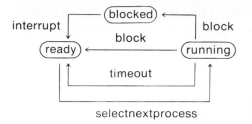

Figure 15-8 Preemptive scheduling "process states."

process is placed onto the ready list. Therefore no busy-waiting is required in timeout as it is in block.

This is a good example of a situation where software errors can be detected. If selectnextprocess returns FALSE, something is wrong! For the moment we just specify that timeout takes some "error condition" action. The subject of reliability and error conditions is treated in a later chapter.

```
PROCEDURE timeout ;
VAR i : INTEGER;
BEGIN
     mask interrupts;
     WITH current ↑ DO BEGIN
         FOR i :— 0 TO 6 DO r[i] := reg[i];
         pc := pop;
         ps := pop END;
     append(current);
     IF selectnextprocess THEN unmask interrupts
     ELSE error condition
END;


FUNCTION selectnextprocess : BOOLEAN ;
VAR i : pstateptr; j · 1  np;
BEGIN
     IF timer is on THEN stop timer;
     i := remove;
     selectnextprocess := FALSE;
     IF i <> nil THEN BEGIN
         selectnextprocess := TRUE;
         current := i;
         WITH current ↑ DO BEGIN
              int := FALSE;
              FOR j := 0 TO 6 DO reg[j] := r[j];
              push(ps);
              push(pc) END
         start timer END
END
```

Figure 15-9 Preemptive scheduling.

One final comment on program design is that it might have been clearer to have block stop the timer, because it is actually the invocation of block that necessitates this action. We have opted for placing the stopping code in the same program as the starting code to localize control of the timer device.

15-5 MEMORY MANAGEMENT

As processes execute in a multiprogramming system, such as the one described in this chapter, their memory requirements may vary. In particular, a process may periodically become inactive for a period of time because the user at its terminal has logged-off. Typically a log-off command from a user causes the terminal's process to enter a monitor program that releases any system resources (for example, memory) held by the process and then blocks the process on the terminal. Any subsequent interrupt causes the monitor to carry out the log-on conversation with the terminal. If the terminal is successful in logging-on, the monitor obtains the necessary system resources and enters the appropriate application program.

The progress of a process in the system, then, alternates between periods of activity, during which it uses resources such as memory, and periods of inactivity, during which it uses no system resources. Of course, the monitor program must remain in memory since inactive processes are blocked in this program. It will normally be reentrant and thus shared among the processes, so its memory requirements are not viewed as allocated to any particular process.

This section is concerned with managing the allocation and deallocation of memory in a multiprogrammed system. Since memory is being shared among independent processes, this task is placed in the supervisor for reliability.

To provide the memory management function we need to augment our supervisor with two operations,

FUNCTION getmem (len:1..maxlength):blockadr

to allocate memory, and

PROCEDURE relmem (adr:address; len:1..maxlength)

to release memory, where address is a subrange minadr..maxadr, maxlength has the value maxadr − minadr + 1, and blockadr is defined as the subrange minadr − 1..maxadr. The value minadr − 1 when returned by getmem indicates a null block address; in other words, no memory is available.

Since both getmem and relmem will presumably be required to examine and alter a data structure describing the state of memory, we do not want time-out to interrupt the running process in either program and cause another process to be given processor control. This second process might also enter one of the memory management programs, which would find the data structure in an inconsistent state thus causing errors.

Consequently, both getmem and relmem will execute with interrupts masked to avoid interference between processes. We shall now examine several possible methods for managing memory.

15-5.1 Fixed Allocation

The simplest way to allocate memory is to divide it into fixed-size *partitions*. The maximum number of active processes is therefore fixed (Fig. 15-10). This is called the *degree of multiprogramming,* the number of processes actively using system resources. The problem, of course, is that the process's requirement may not match the partition size. If it is less, memory is wasted; if it is more, it

```
CONST degree = degree of multiprogramming;
        minadr = smallest address;
        maxadr = largest address;
        maxlength = maxadr − minadr + 1;
        minlessone = minadr − 1;

TYPE address = minadr..maxadr;
        lengthtype = 1..maxlength;
        blockadr = minlessone..maxadr;
        partition = RECORD
              addr : address;
              length : lengthtype;
              busy : BOOLEAN END;
VAR mt : ARRAY[1..degree] OF partition;

FUNCTION getmem(len : lengthtype) : blockadr ;
      LABEL 999;
      VAR i : 1..degree;
      BEGIN
            mask interrupts;
            getmem := minadr −1;
            FOR 1 := 1 TO degree DO
                IF (0 < len) AND (len <= mt[i].length)
                      AND (mt[i].busy = FALSE) THEN BEGIN
                      getmem := mt[i].addr;
                      mt[i].busy := TRUE;
                      go to 999 END;
            999:unmask interrupts
            END;

PROCEDURE relmem(adr: address; len: lengthtype) ;
      VAR i: 1..degree;
      BEGIN
            mask interrupts;
            i := 1;
            WHILE mt[i].addr <> adr DO i := i+1;
            mt[i].busy := FALSE;
            unmask interrupts
      END
```

Figure 15-10 Fixed memory allocation.

simply cannot run (unless more than one partition is allocated—in which case we are not doing fixed allocation!).

Fixed allocation may use equal-size partitions or partitions of differing sizes. The case study described in Chap. 18 uses equal-size partitions. There, the allocated memory area is used for data only, all application programs being reentrant. Figure 15-10 shows a simple version of the memory manager for fixed allocation. Available memory is described in a table called *mt*. The variable degree, the degree of multiprogramming, is declared elsewhere.

15-5.2 First-Fit

First-fit is one of the simplest forms of variable partition allocation. Here we allocate to a process exactly the size of memory block requested. After a series of calls to getmem and relmem, memory becomes "checkerboarded" with allocated blocks alternating with available blocks. The first-fit algorithm searches memory from one end and allocates a block from the first available block of sufficient size. In Fig. 15-11, for example, a large block is split to make the allocation.

The sequential search can be organized to permit very fast releasing of blocks. To do this, the available blocks of memory are organized in a *doubly linked* list, as shown in Fig. 15-12.

Here, each contiguous available block of memory constitutes a list element. Each such block contains a pair of list link fields containing the address of the predecessor and successor list elements. Therefore, from any block it is easy to locate its predecessor and its successor.

Blocks are placed on the list in order of ascending memory address. Each block of available memory is bounded by three special words at each end. The outer words contain a marker, say the value 1, indicating a free block. The next inner pair of words contain list links; the predecessor link points to the successor link of the preceding list element and vice versa. The successor link of the last block and the predecessor link of the first block contain null pointers. Finally, the innermost pair of words[1] each contains the length in words of the block, excluding the outer pair of marker words.

---

[1] This assumes a word-organized memory rather than a byte-organized memory as in the PDP-11.

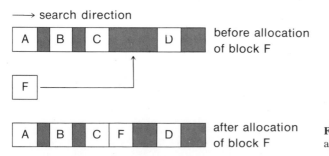

⟶ search direction

before allocation of block F

after allocation of block F

Figure 15-11 First-fit memory allocation.

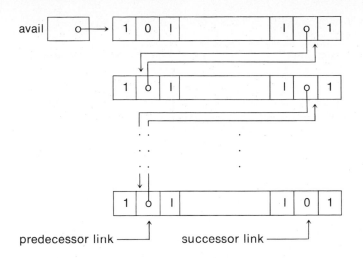

predecessor link ⎯⎯⎯⎯⎯⎯⎯⎯⎯⎯⎯⎯⎯⎯⎯⎯⎯⎯ successor link ⎯⎯⎯⎯⎯⎯⎯⎯⎯⎯⎯

Figure 15-12 Doubly linked available memory list.

Blocks of allocated memory contain one pair of marker words containing the value 0 (Fig. 15-13). The process to which the block is allocated uses only the inner part of the block and is unaware of the marker words. The initial state of allocatable memory is shown in Fig. 15-14. Notice that the available list has but one block, therefore both predecessor and successor links are zero. Also, a special pair of words containing zero bound this single block. These words simulate bounding allocated blocks; if not immediately clear, the reason for these will be evident in a moment. Now let us examine how allocation and releasing are accomplished.

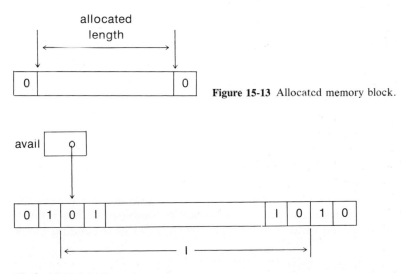

Figure 15-13 Allocated memory block.

Figure 15-14 Initial memory state.

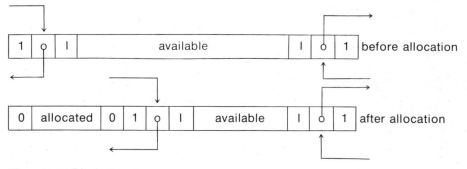

Figure 15-15 Block allocation.

Figure 15-15 shows an example of block allocation. An available block is split in two, and a new available block is placed on the list in the same position. The block being allocated is found by getmem following successor links from avail until either a block of sufficient length is found or the end of the list is encountered (Fig. 15-16).

Figures 15-17 and 15-18 show block releasing and relmem respectively. Here one can see the use of the marker words and the predecessor links. A block being released can be recombined with neighboring available blocks and the resulting larger available block placed on the list in the proper order without a search of the list. If, however, there are no neighboring available blocks, the list must be searched to find the proper position. Note that the procedures remlink and link are not shown.

15-5.3 Best-Fit

Rather than do a sequential search of memory for a sufficiently large block, the memory manager can order the available list on block size rather than memory address, thus enabling a best-fit search. As with first-fit, this method allocates a block of memory of the exact size requested. To find a memory block, the get-mem function scans the available list in order of increasing block length; the first available block equal to or larger than the requested size is used for allocation.

To allocate a block getmem performs the same actions as with first-fit except that the remaining unallocated portion of the block that is split in two is not linked back onto the list in the same position. Instead, it is removed from the list, the list is searched to find the correct position, and it is reinserted in order of ascending block length.

To release a block, relmem performs the same actions as with first-fit except that, regardless of whether the released block is combined with neighboring blocks, it is reinserted onto the available list in order of ascending block length.

```
CONST minadr = smallest address;
      maxadr = largest address;
      maxlength = maxadr − minadr + 1;
      minlessone = minadr − 1;

TYPE address = minadr..maxadr;
     lengthtype = 1..maxlength;
     blockadr = minlessone..maxadr;

VAR m : ARRAY[address] OF INTEGER;
    avail : blockadr;

FUNCTION getmem(len : lengthtype): blockadr ;
    VAR i,j : blockadr;
    BEGIN
        mask interrupts;
        getmem := minadr − 1;
        IF avail <> minadr − 1 THEN BEGIN
           i := avail;
           j := m[m[i+1]+i−1];
           WHILE((m[i+1]<len+6) AND (m[i+1] <> len) AND (j <>
                   minadr−1)) DO BEGIN
               i := j; j := m[m[i+1]+i−1] END;
           IF   m[i+1] >= len+6) OR (m[i+1] = len) THEN BEGIN
               getmem := i;
               j := m[i+1]+i−2;
           IF   m[j]−len = 0 THEN BEGIN
               m[i−1] := 0;
               m[j+2] := 0;
               remlink(m[i], m[j+1], avail)
               {This procedure removes a block from the linked list} END
           ELSE BEGIN
                   m[j] := m[j]−len  2;
                   m[len+i+3] := m[j];
                   m[len+i+2] := m[i];
           IF   i <> avail THEN m[m[i]] := len+i+2;
               ELSE avail := len+i+2;
               m[len+i+1] := 1;
               m[len+i] := 0;
               m[i−1] := 0 END END END
    END
```

Figure 15-16 First-fit getmem.

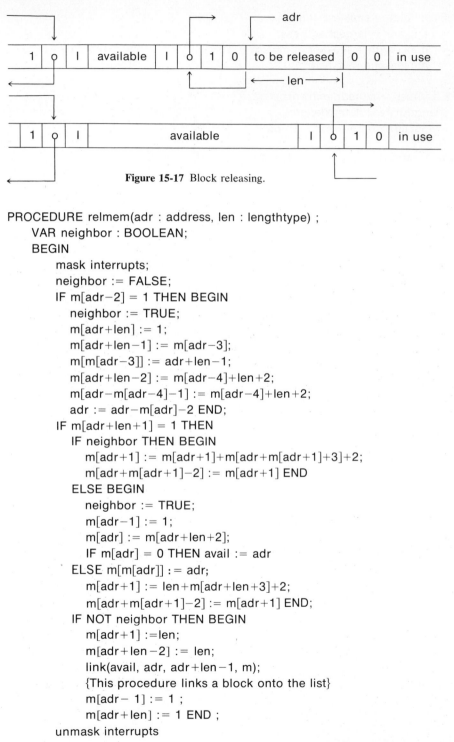

Figure 15-17 Block releasing.

```
PROCEDURE relmem(adr : address, len : lengthtype) ;
    VAR neighbor : BOOLEAN;
    BEGIN
        mask interrupts;
        neighbor := FALSE;
        IF m[adr−2] = 1 THEN BEGIN
            neighbor := TRUE;
            m[adr+len] := 1;
            m[adr+len−1] := m[adr−3];
            m[m[adr−3]] := adr+len−1;
            m[adr+len−2] := m[adr−4]+len+2;
            m[adr−m[adr−4]−1] := m[adr−4]+len+2;
            adr := adr−m[adr]−2 END;
        IF m[adr+len+1] = 1 THEN
            IF neighbor THEN BEGIN
                m[adr+1] := m[adr+1]+m[adr+m[adr+1]+3]+2;
                m[adr+m[adr+1]−2] := m[adr+1] END
            ELSE BEGIN
                neighbor := TRUE;
                m[adr−1] := 1;
                m[adr] := m[adr+len+2];
                IF m[adr] = 0 THEN avail := adr
            ELSE m[m[adr]] := adr;
                m[adr+1] := len+m[adr+len+3]+2;
                m[adr+m[adr+1]−2] := m[adr+1] END;
            IF NOT neighbor THEN BEGIN
                m[adr+1] :=len;
                m[adr+len−2] := len;
                link(avail, adr, adr+len−1, m);
                {This procedure links a block onto the list}
                m[adr− 1] := 1 ;
                m[adr+len] := 1 END ;
        unmask interrupts
    END
```

Figure 15-18 First-fit relmem.

More work is required using best-fit than with first-fit allocation because of the ordering of the available list. Whether or not this is justified depends a great deal on the characteristics of memory requests. Memory management algorithms can be compared on the basis of such performance measures as memory utilization and the proportion of refusals when the total amount of memory is actually sufficient. A decision must be based on careful analysis of the expected demands upon memory.

15-5.4 Buddy Systems

We have described two extreme cases of memory allocation. On the one hand, fixed partition allocates blocks of a permanently fixed size. It is very simple but restricts the degree of multiprogramming and is inflexible in matching the demands upon memory. On the other hand, first-fit and best-fit are perfectly flexible in matching the demands upon memory but are complex and tend to fragment memory into unusable small blocks. *Buddy systems* are a compromise between these two extremes.

The basic idea in using a buddy system is to provide a set of predetermined sizes in which memory blocks are allocated. A specific request is allocated, from this set, a block of the smallest size that is sufficiently large to meet the request.

Perhaps the simplest buddy system is the binary buddy system, in which the available sizes are

$$L_k = 2^k \qquad k = 1, 2, 3, \ldots$$

Another is the Fibonacci buddy system, with sizes that are Fibonacci numbers:

$$L_k = L_{k-1} + L_{k-2} \qquad L_1 = 1 \qquad L_2 = 1 \qquad k = 3, 4, \ldots$$

All such sequences of block sizes have the property that any block can be subdivided into two smaller blocks, both of which are also in the sequence of allowable sizes. The name *buddy system* comes from the fact that any block, when subdivided, creates a pair of buddies, blocks that will eventually be restored to a single block.

The essence of the algorithm is the following: To allocate a block find the smallest available block that is larger than the requested size. Repeatedly subdivide this block until a block is obtained that cannot be further subdivided and still meet the request. Allocate this block.

To deallocate a block, attempt to rejoin it with its (free) buddy. If successful, repeatedly rejoin resulting blocks to their buddies until a block is obtained that cannot be further rejoined to a free buddy. Place this block on the available list.

Obviously, the available list should be ordered on block size, as in best-fit. However, while best-fit places no restrictions on how memory can be partitioned, the buddy system provides a set of possible partitionings of memory. Only these are possible, since each available block, starting with all of memory, can be subdivided in only one way. Experiments have shown that under certain conditions of memory sharing the buddy systems are superior to best-fit and first-fit.

One should be careful about selecting a memory allocation algorithm, since its performance is dependent on the characteristics of memory allocation requests. As a class of algorithms, however, buddy systems represent a set of possible solutions to any particular situation.

Also note that buddy systems, as one would expect from a compromise, suffer from the disadvantages of both best-fit (or first-fit) and fixed partitioning. That is, they create some "checkerboarding" of memory and also suffer internal wastage because of the restrictions on block size.

15-5.5 Compaction

As was pointed out earlier, it is possible that a memory request can be denied although the total amount of available memory is sufficient to satisfy the request. This fragmentation is one of the fundamental problems of dynamic memory management. One alternative to simply denying the memory request is to compact memory, that is, move all of the allocated blocks to one end of memory, leaving a single block of available memory.

Compaction is time-consuming. Not only must the data structures be extensively updated (all available blocks must be collected and combined), but the program and data in allocated blocks must be moved. Experiments have shown that compaction is not normally justified because of its high cost.

A further restriction in using compaction is the requirement that all code in allocated blocks be position independent since it may be moved at any time. Hardware mechanisms that remove this restriction are described in Chap. 16.

15-6 RT-11 MULTIPROGRAMMING

As might be expected, RT-11 provides a rudimentary form of multiprogramming. Chapter 13 described memory allocations under what is called the single-job monitor. Alternatively, however, one can run RT-11 under the foreground-background monitor (FB monitor), which provides for two independent processes to share memory.

Under the FB monitor a *foreground job* can be loaded into memory along with the job that would normally run under the single-job monitor. The latter is then termed the *background job*. As shown in Fig. 15-19, the memory area allocated to the foreground job is just below the device handlers and above USR and KMON. This partition is allocated to suit the size requirements of the foreground job, and then USR and KMON are loaded below.

The background job is loaded into the lower part of memory, as indicated in Fig. 15-19. If insufficient space is available in the free area, then KMON and USR are overwritten to accommodate the background job. As a consequence these programs must be reloaded to handle background program terminations

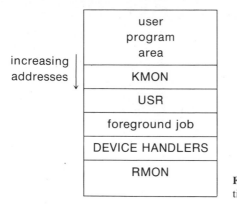

Figure 15-19 RT-11 foreground-background allocation.

and CTRL/C from the console. In both of these cases, the necessary portion of the background job is swapped out to disk and KMON and USR are swapped in. If the program is resumed then it must be reloaded, again overwriting KMON and USR.

The foreground job has priority in a preemptive processor scheduling algorithm. All interrupts from devices under the control of the foreground job cause the background job to be preempted if it is running. Thus the background job simply uses all processor time not used by the foreground job. Typically a real-time process would run in the foreground with program development (editing, compiling, etc.) running in the background.

15-7 UNIX SYSTEM MULTIPROGRAMMING

This section embarks on a risky path. Here we attempt to give a nice example of multiprogramming in the context of the previous general discussion. In taking this path, however, we bypass many of the complexities of both the UNIX system and larger PDP-11 models. Nevertheless, it should be possible to gain some feeling for the multiprogramming mechanism in the UNIX system. We take a bottom-up view, as in previous topics. With these mechanisms introduced, and after further reading from the reference list, the student should be able to acquire a more complete view of UNIX software.

Figure 15-20 shows the structure of a UNIX system process as manifested by:

1. Its control information in the UNIX supervisor (called the *kernel*)
2. Its associated program code
3. Its private data

Inside the kernel is an array of structures called *proc,* which constitutes the UNIX process table. Since an entire process description would be quite large, however, only the essential parts of a process's state are kept there. Specifi-

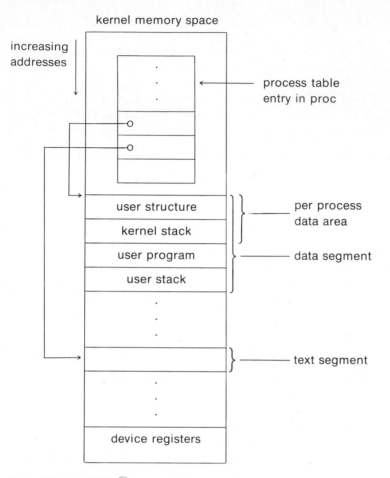

Figure 15-20 A UNIX™ process image.

cally, a process's entry in proc contains only that set of information that must be in memory at all times. One of the items in a proc entry is a reference (actually indirect through another kernel table) to a *text segment* containing shareable reentrant code.

Another item in proc is the main-memory address of the process's *data segment*.[1] Here we find the remainder of the process state information in a structure called *user*. Following the user structure is an area used by the kernel for stack space when it has been entered by the process. Next is an area for a private nonreentrant user program followed by the process stack area.

The running process is identified by the kernel maintaining a reference to that process's per process data area (see Fig. 15-20). An explanation of just how this reference is maintained must be deferred until the next chapter.

---

[1] If the process is swapped out, this item contains a disk address.

There may be many processes active in memory, each requiring space for a data segment and a text segment (which is not necessarily present if the process has not called a program). Processes share main memory and their data structures move in and out of memory under UNIX software control according to their use of the system resources. The dynamic memory management algorithm employed to allocate and deallocate space to support this sharing is first-fit. Unfortunately, licensing restrictions prevent the publishing of the two C procedures that carry out these functions, malloc and mfree. However, the programs below have been written in C to illustrate similar functions.

```
getmem(mptr,size)
STRUCT map *mptr;
{
    REGISTER INT i;
    REGISTER STRUCT map *jptr;

    i = 0;
    jptr = mptr;
    WHILE (jptr -> m_size != 0 ){
        IF (jptr->m_size >= size) {
            i - jptr -> m_addr;
            jptr -> m_addr =+ size;
            IF ((jptr -> m_size -- size) == 0){
                DO {
                    jptr -> m_addr = (jptr+1) -> m_addr;
                    jptr ++;
                }
                WHILE ((jptr-1) -> m_size = jptr -> m_size);}break;}
        ELSE
            jptr++;
    }
    RETURN(i);
}

relmem(mptr, size, addr)
STRUCT map *mptr;
{
    REGISTER STRUCT map *jptr;
    REGISTER INT i,j;

    jptr = mptr;
    WHILE ( jptr -> m_addr < addr &&
            jptr -> m_size != 0 ) jptr++;
    IF ((jptr-1) -> m_addr + (jptr-1) -> m_size == addr ){
        i = ((jptr-1) -> m_size =+ size );
```

```
        IF ((jptr−1) −> m_addr + i == jptr −> m_addr &&
            jptr −> m_size != 0){
            (jptr−1) −> m_size = jptr −> m_size + i;
            WHILE ( jptr −> m_size ) {
                jptr −> m_size = (jptr+1) −> m_size;
                jptr −> m_addr = (jptr+1) −> m_addr;
                jptr++;}
            jptr −> m_size =+ size; }}
    ELSE {
        IF (addr + size == jptr −> m_addr &&
                jptr −> m_size ){
        jptr −> m_addr = addr;
        jptr −> m_size =+ size; }
    ELSE {
        j = jptr;
        WHILE( jptr++ −> m_size);
        WHILE( jptr != j){
            jptr −> m_size = (jptr−1) −> m_size;
            jptr −> m_addr = (jptr−1) −> m_addr;
            jptr−−;}
        j −> m_size = size;
        j −> m_addr = addr;} }
}
```

The first parameter to getmem, mptr, is a pointer to the available list. The second, size, is the size of block requested. The procedure initializes the pointer jptr to point to the first element on the list and then searches the list. Figure 15-21 depicts the situation. As can be seen, the available list is a table of map structures. The last entry is denoted by a zero in the m_size component.

The WHILE statement sequences through the list via jptr++ and terminates if jptr −>m_size = 0. In the loop the address found is stored into i (to be returned) and the old block address is incremented by size. Finally, if the block has been reduced to zero size, the remainder of the list is compacted. If no block is found, then a zero is returned by the initial value of i.

The deallocation procedure relmem takes three parameters: mptr, the pointer to the list; size, the size of the returned block; and addr, the address of the returned block. This procedure finds the position in the list, which is ordered on increasing addresses, at which the block is to be inserted. It then carries out one of two possible actions. First, the preceding entry in the list may be for an adjacent block, in which case they are merged. Second, the successor entry in the list may be for an adjacent block and may be merged. If in this latter alternative no merging is carried out, then the deallocated block is inserted into the sorted list.

Process scheduling in the UNIX system is best illustrated in a procedure called *swtch,* which licensing restrictions prevent our publishing. The heart of

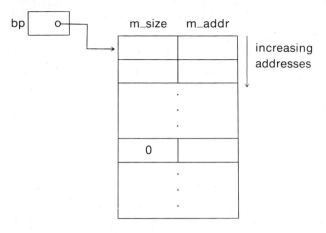

Figure 15-21 The UNIX^{TM} available list.

the UNIX scheduler is a search of the process table followed by a busy-waiting loop implemented by the procedure idle. This procedure, coded in assembler rather than C, is similar to the following:

```
IDLE:   MOV   PS,-(SP)
        BIC   #340,PS
    L:  BR    L
        MOV   (SP)+,PS
        RTS   PC
```

To understand an operating system one good place to start is its busy-waiting loop. From here, one can discover the events that take place as an interrupt arrives and causes a process to respond. At the least, we have pointed the reader to this vital spot in the UNIX operating system.

EXERCISES

15-1 Under what conditions would it be appropriate to use each of the following I/O programming techniques?
(a) Busy-waiting
(b) Interrupt-driven
(c) Multiprogramming supervisor controlled

15-2 Why is a multiprogramming supervisor not reentrant?

15-3 A small time shared system has eight terminals. Characters are received from each terminal at the rate of one per second. The average amount of processor time required to handle one character is 10 ms. If characters arrive in a random fashion, what is the proportion of unused processor time? What is the probability that an interrupt is handled without delay?
Repeat the calculation for character handling times of 50 ms and 100 ms.

15-4 What is the minimum hardware addressing capability required in order to code reentrant programs? What other features are convenient?

15-5 Modify procedure block from Fig. 15-1 to check if the process's device has already interrupted and, if so, to allow the process to continue.

15-6 Modify procedure selectnextprocess from Fig. 15-2 so that processes have equal priority. This can be done by a circular table scan starting after the last selected process.

15-7 *Medium-term scheduling* refers to the mechanism for making processes available to the short-term scheduler. Such processes are called *active* processes. Modify the data structures and programs from Fig. 15-1 and 15-2 to recognize active and inactive processes. (Interrupts to inactive processes are ignored.) Write two additional supervisor operations to make an inactive process active and vice versa. They can be called, respectively,

start(i: 1..np)
and   stop(i: 1..np)

Newly active processes should be blocked. A process may not stop itself.

15-8 Write an interrupt handler for the clock on your machine. It should transmit a short message to the console for each interrupt received. Test your program.

15-9 Is the masking of the interrupts in relmem (Fig. 15-10) necessary? Explain.

15-10 Implement and test getmem and relmem of Fig. 15-16 and 15-18.

15-11 Modify the memory management programs of Fig. 15-8 to use the best-fit algorithm.

15-12 Repeat Exercise 15-11 for the binary buddy system method.

15-13 If you were to implement the interrupt procedure of Fig. 15-1 on a small PDP-11, what stack would be used in this program in the case that no process were running? How is the interrupted PC-PS pair removed from this stack?

15-14 Write and test a small supervisor for the PDP-11. Your test program can be a reentrant program that reads and echoes characters from a terminal associated with the running process. Entry to the supervisor occurs by an EMT trap to block or by an interrupt to the interrupt procedure. Use the algorithms from Fig. 15-1 and 15-2.

15-15 Modify your supervisor of Exercise 15-14 to use a FIFO ready list scheduler.

15-16 Modify your supervisor of Exercise 15-14 to use preemptive scheduling. Test it by inserting some dummy compute-bound code into your test program.

REFERENCES

There are several excellent texts on operating systems that provide more comprehensive treatment of multiprogramming. They include Lister (1975), Madnick (1974), Shaw (1974), Watson (1970), Wilkes (1968), and Brinch-Hansen (1973). Denning (1971) contains a tutorial about the so-called "third generation" computer systems that evolved in the 1960s when multiprogramming became common. For those interested particularly in scheduling, Lampson (1968) discusses the subject in some detail.

Knuth (1968) provides a very complete discussion of memory management algorithms. For a more up-to-date discussion, particularly of the buddy system class of algorithms, see Peterson (1977).

SIXTEEN

MEMORY MAPPING AND PROTECTION

Multiprogramming creates two fundamental memory management problems. One of these, the allocation and releasing of memory blocks, has been discussed in Chap. 15. The second problem is memory protection. Even before multiprogramming was introduced, we discussed the problem of protecting the supervisor from inadvertent (or malicious) user program actions. This problem is compounded with multiprogramming, because now we must consider how to protect the user processes from each other, as well as the supervisor from the users.

This chapter discusses several hardware mechanisms that help to solve the memory allocation and protection problems. One particularly important aspect of protection is the extent to which the protection mechanism permits flexible sharing. Multiprogrammed processes often share reentrant code. Less common, but also possible is the sharing of data. There are, therefore, conflicting needs: Processes must be protected from each other in memory while being allowed shared access to common memory.

There are, then, three important needs to be kept in mind in examining the mechanisms presented in this chapter:

1. Memory allocation
2. Memory protection
3. Memory sharing

In describing each mechanism it is important to consider the extent to which each of these needs is met.

Finally, the hardware mechanisms to be described here are invoked at execution time. This is necessary since user programs may have been compiled by different compilers. In some more restricted situations where several user programs can be compiled together, it is possible to accomplish many of the objectives of memory allocation, protection, and sharing at compile time. We should keep in mind therefore that execution time memory mapping and protection are necessary because of the independent nature of the supervisor and user programs. Compile time mechanisms are best studied in the context of a course in programming languages, however, so the topic is not pursued here.

16-1 PROTECTION KEYS

Processes in a fixed-allocation memory management system can be protected with a protection key mechanism (see Fig. 16-1). Memory is partitioned into p equal-size blocks. The processor contains p *block key* registers (BK), each of length $\log_2 p$ bits, and one *process key* register (PK), of the same length. All memory references are checked by the processor, which will cause an error trap in the case that memory block i is referenced[1] and the contents of PK do not equal the contents of BK[i].

Each active process can be assigned a key in the range 0 to p − 1 so there can be up to p active processes. All blocks of memory allocated to the process with key i have their associated BK register set to contain i. The process key register PK is made part of the state of a process and is therefore loaded with the key of the running process. BK is modified only when memory allocation is altered.

[1] Some machines perform checking only on writes to memory rather than on reads and writes.

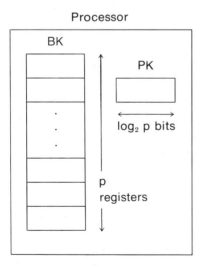
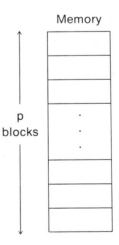

Figure 16-1 Protection keys.

The BK and PK registers must be accessible only in supervisor mode, of course, for protection to be effective. The major limitation of the protection key mechanism is that the number of blocks must be kept small to reduce cost, and since this increases the block size, the variability of partition size is restricted. Nevertheless this is an effective compromise between fixed allocation and variable-size allocation. Of course, the location of blocks is fixed, so we really have fixed allocation but with the possibility of allocating more than one contiguous partition to a process.

Interprocess protection is effective, and sharing of partitions is possible. This kind of sharing is not at a very fine level of program structure, however, since an entire partition must be shared although less might do. The problems of memory management are not significantly aided.

16-2 MEMORY MAPPING

One of the problems of memory management discussed earlier is the fact that programs, once loaded, can be moved only if all address relocation is repeated. Also, any code to be moved must not store any memory addresses in places unknown to the relocating loader. Compaction, therefore, is difficult to perform.

Rather than having the loader do the relocation, it is possible to delay it and perform it at execution time. That is, the loader places the program directly into memory, leaving all addresses relative to the beginning of the program. Addresses are then relocated at execution time by a memory mapping unit (Fig. 16-2). Without considering exactly how the memory mapping unit works, one can see that a program can be moved in memory and the only information that needs to be modified in the mapping unit is the program's actual memory location. It does not matter if the program stores memory addresses to be used later, because all addresses are relocated at the time they are used to reference memory.

Another characteristic of programs in load-module form is that they require contiguous blocks of memory. Of course, the relocating loader could break a program up and place it into whatever separate blocks might be available, but this would complicate the loader greatly and would not help protection. Alter-

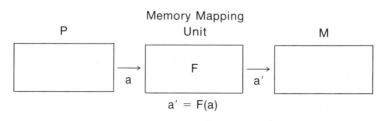

Figure 16-2 Memory mapping.

natively, the memory mapping unit can be designed so that the program can be partitioned in more than one contiguous section. The information describing the location of each section of the program is contained in the memory mapping unit, which performs the appropriate relocation as each address is used to reference memory. Figure 16-2 denotes this memory mapping function as F.

Memory mapping, then, has the potential to significantly ease memory allocation. As we shall see in the following sections, protection and sharing are also important by-products.

16-3 BASE AND BOUND REGISTERS

The simplest form of memory mapping unit contains two registers: a *base register* and a *bound register* (Fig. 16-3). These registers, accessible only in supervisor mode, provide the following mapping function:

$$a' = C(BASE) + a \qquad \text{where } 0 \leqslant a \leqslant C(BOUND)$$

An error trap occurs in the event that a does not meet the bounds condition. In other words, the running process cannot reference memory outside of its designated partition.

Using a base and bound mapping mechanism, programs can be moved about in memory, making compaction easier, but they still require a contiguous block. Protection can be applied only to the program as a whole. Sharing is only possible by appropriately overlapping the allocated memory blocks of two processes. Only one common area of memory can be shared in this way and, even then, it must be appropriately located within the *logical address space* of each process: That is, the address range 0 through $l-1$. A shared section of memory must be at the lower end of one process's address space and at the upper end of the other's space.

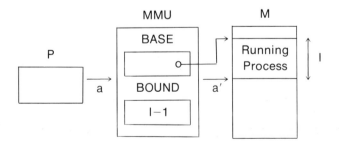

Figure 16-3 Base and bound registers.

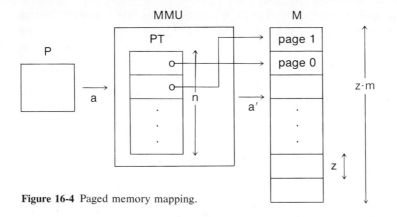

Figure 16-4 Paged memory mapping.

16-4 PAGED ALLOCATION

Paged memory mapping can be viewed as an extension to base and bound mapping. In order to relax the constraint that a process be allocated one contiguous block of memory, more than one base register is supplied.

In paging, each program is partitioned into equal-size blocks called *pages*. Correspondingly, memory is partitioned into blocks of the same size called *page frames*. Thus, one page exactly fits into a page frame.

A paging memory mapping unit (Fig. 16-4) contains a set of registers constituting a *page table* (PT). These registers, accessible only in supervisor mode, can each contain a page frame number; PT register i contains the number of the page frame currently holding page i of the running process.

Suppose the pages and page frames are of size z words. Denote with n the maximum number of pages in the logical address space of a program. Denote with m the number of page frames in memory.[1] Then, a logical address in a program can be broken down into two components, a page number, p, and a word number within the page, w.

a	
p	w

Page number   Word number

This means that z is a power of 2 (the usual situation), memory contains $z \cdot m$ words, and there are n PT registers. When a process is loaded, each of its pages is stored in any available page frame and the associated PT register updated to contain the correct page frame number. The mapping function is

$$a' = C(PT[p]) + w$$

---

[1] For the moment we assume that $n \leqslant m$.

Of course, a process may not require n pages, so each PT register must contain a *presence bit* to indicate that a page frame has been allocated. The format of a PT register then has two fields, the page frame number (PF) and the presence bit (PB):

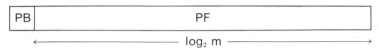

and the mapping function is

$$a' = C(PT[p].PF) + w$$

where

$$PT[p].PB = TRUE$$

An error trap occurs in the event that a process attempts to reference unallocated address space.

Paging provides a more flexible kind of partitioned allocation than base and bound registers; each process's allocation need not be contiguous and compaction is never needed, since all space is allocated in units of one page frame. The fragmentation of memory discussed earlier, which is usually called *external fragmentation,* is replaced, however, by *internal fragmentation,* since some space is usually left unused in the last page of a process's address space. There is a motivation, then (for this and other reasons), to keep page size small. Of course, page size cannot be too small, since the size of PT would increase unmanageably.

Protection and sharing are both improved with paging. Memory can now be shared on a per page basis, and any number (up to n) of pages can be shared. Not only is interprocess protection provided as with base and bound registers, but two additional benefits are obtained. Both derive from the fact that given the existence of the PT, it is relatively easy to include additional information in each PT register specifying restrictions on access to the specified page. Each page can be designated, for example, as being read-only, write, or execute-only by including two extra bits denoted below as RTS, for *rights.*

Protection bits in the PT register provide intraprocess protection as well as selective sharing between processes. Since the PT contents are part of the process state (loaded when a process becomes running), one process may have write rights to a page while another process may have read-only rights to the same page.

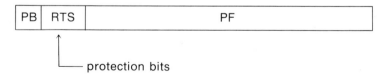

In many systems the PT is not implemented in hardware in the processor but is stored in main memory. The MMU contains only a single page table register (PTR) holding the address of the running process's PT (Fig. 16-5). This

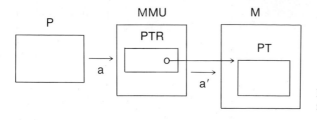

Figure 16-5 Storing the PT in memory.

reduces the size of the process state necessary to be loaded on a process switch and allows a smaller page size since a large PT size is not as serious a cost restriction as it would be if the PT is implemented in hardware. One serious complication, however, is the fact that the MMU must make a memory access to the PT in order to perform each address mapping.

16-5 SEGMENTED ALLOCATION

Protection and sharing of memory under paged allocation is seriously restricted because the unit of protection and sharing, the page, is of fixed size. A natural partitioning of a program into, for example, component procedures does not, of course, lead to fixed-size pieces but to variable-size pieces. *Segmentation* is a memory mapping mechanism in which the basic unit of memory allocation, protection, and sharing is the *segment,* which can be of varying size.

A segmented MMU is shown in Fig. 16-6. A segment table ST replaces the page table. In a segmented architecture, logical addresses, i.e., those used by the assembly-language programmer, are of the form

$$a = (s,w)$$

where s is a segment number and w is a word within the segment number. The important distinction here is that segments, unlike pages, are visible to the programmer (or to the compiler). ST registers are similar to PT registers in that

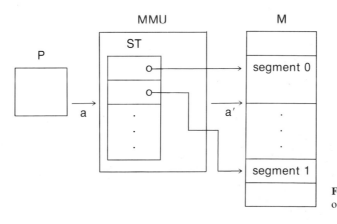

Figure 16-6 Segmented memory mapping.

ST register i contains the memory address SA of segment i. As shown below, a presence bit PB is also included along with an RTS field.

L	PB	RTS	SA

In addition to SA, PB, and RTS, the ST register contains a length specification L. This is checked by the mapping function, which is

$$a' = C(ST[s].SA) + w$$

where ST[s].PB = TRUE

$$w \leq ST[s].L - 1$$

An error trap occurs in the event that a process attempts to address beyond the end of a segment or to unallocated memory. In addition, the RTS field is checked to verify that the kind of access being performed is permitted and, if not, a trap occurs.

A clear example of the utility of segmentation is that vectors can be stored in separate segments with the MMU performing automatic subscript range checking.

With segmentation, sharing and protection can be based on the natural unit of the segment. Procedures can be stored as pure reentrant code in execute-only segments, data such as vectors can be stored in a segment of the appropriate length, and processes can share logical units of code or data rather than arbitrarily fixed size units. As with paging, no address relocation by the loader is required, and interprocess as well as intraprocess protection is provided.

As with paging, the ST is often stored in main memory with a single register, the segment table register STR, containing the main memory address of the ST for the running process.

The reader will have noticed that, while segmentation improves sharing and protection, we have reintroduced the problem of external fragmentation. Segmentation still, however, retains the property that segments can be moved about in memory without any address relocation being necessary. It is therefore feasible to perform compaction. As pointed out earlier, however, studies have shown that the overhead of compaction is not usually justified.

16-6 FURTHER STUDY IN MEMORY MAPPING

Several problems and capabilities associated with memory mapping have been purposely ignored because our scope is rather limited at this point. These should be mentioned to avoid giving a misleading impression of the subject. However, a detailed explanation of these points is not practical. The following comments, then, can be used as food for thought!

First, sharing of memory is complicated by the fact that a shared page (or segment) can be referenced in two or more logical address spaces, perhaps with different page (or segment) numbers. If such a reference exists in shared reentrant code there is a conflict; which of the page (or segment) numbers does the code contain?

Second, requiring a memory reference to perform the mapping is impractical. Usually, a special buffer memory in the MMU is used to hold recently referenced PT or ST entries. A memory reference is unnecessary if the entry sought is found in the buffer memory. If a memory reference is needed, then the entry obtained is placed in the buffer in anticipation of another reference soon after.

Third, paging and segmentation are sometimes used together to gain the advantages of both. To do this, each segment can be paged. Thus, programs are organized on the basis of a segmented memory, while physical memory management is carried out on the basis of paging.

Fourth, it is common practice to allow n to exceed m. That is, logical address space can be larger than the available memory on the machine. The presence bit PB can be used to detect a page or segment not in memory so that it can be fetched, possibly displacing another page or segment from memory. This ability is called *virtual memory*. The advantages gained are that programs need not be constrained by physical memory size and also that a running process can be allocated only sufficient memory to hold those pages (or segments) that it needs at any one time. This set of pages (or segments), called the *working set,* represents the real memory requirements of a process at any one time; thus, remaining physical memory can be allocated to other processes.

16-7 PDP-11 MEMORY MAPPING

Memory mapping in the larger PDP-11 models is a combination of paging and segmentation, although it is probably best viewed as a variant of paging called *variable-length paging.* Taking this view of paging, then, we can describe the PDP-11 mechanism with the following parameters:

$$n = 8$$

$$m = 32$$

$$z = 4K \text{ words}$$

The PT is implemented in hardware. Logical address space consists of 32K words partitioned into eight 4K-word pages. Physical memory may reach 128K words. The pages are called *segments,* so we shall keep this naming although, as indicated, they are really more like pages. Memory mapping can be disabled so that a PDP-11 with memory mapping appears like the machine described previously in the text.

There are actually three page tables, one for each processor mode: user, supervisor, and kernel. The PT registers, like device control registers, are lo-

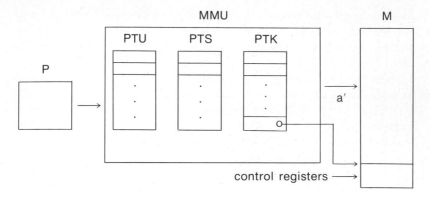

Figure 16-7 The PDP-11 memory mapping unit.

cated in the upper 4K of memory. Clearly, then, the entries in the kernel's PT should map all the PTs into the kernel's address space if the kernel is to control memory allocation. None of the PTs should map into any user's address space if proper protection is to be preserved. Figure 16-7 shows a schematic of the PDP-11 MMU, showing the three page tables as PTU, PTS, and PTK. The kernel's PT, PTK, is shown mapping the upper 4K of memory into kernel address space. Thus, the PTs and all other control registers such as device CSRs are accessible only in kernel mode. The capability exists, however, to give a user direct access to a set of device CSRs. The PDP-11 is one of only a few machines permitting such controlled access. The reason this is possible is that pages can be of variable length so that a page can contain only the words comprising the device registers.

Figure 16-8 shows the format of a PT entry, called an *active segment register* (ASR). For now, we show only the fields that are relevant. The presence bit function is incorporated into the 3-bit rights field: The value 000 binary means PB = false and any other value means PB = true.

Memory is partitioned, not into page frames, but into 4096 blocks of 32 words each. A page can be any length from 1 to 128 blocks. The block is the basic unit of memory allocation; pages in memory must start on a block boundary, and the address and length fields in the ASR are given in units of blocks.

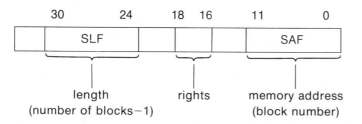

Figure 16-8 Active segment register format.

With memory mapping enabled, a 16-bit PDP-11 address is interpreted as a 3-bit page number, ASF, and a 13-bit byte number. This is further broken down into a 7-bit block number BN and a 6-bit displacement within block DIB.

15	12	6	5	0
ASF	BN		DIB	

A simplified mapping function that omits rights checking and other mechanisms not discussed is

$$a' = [C(PT[ASF].SAF) + BN] \cdot 2^6 + DIB$$

where

$$BN \leqslant C(PT[ASF].SLF)$$

In words, base address SAF is added to the block number BN and the sum concatenated with the displacement DIB. A trap occurs if the page length is exceeded or if protection rights are violated.

A rather peculiar aspect of variable-length paging is that there can be "holes" of unused locations in logical address space. Since a page can be shorter than 4096 words, the unused addresses are simply not available to the programmer although the succeeding page may be in use.

Finally, although some PDP-11 family members have three PTs as described, the larger models actually have six. There are three *data space ASRs* and three *instruction space ASRs*. All instruction references (those involving the PC) use the latter, and all other references use the former. In this way the size of logical address space is doubled to 64K words and all code is automatically protected as execute only so long as it only maps into instruction space.

16-8 UNIX SYSTEM USE OF MEMORY MAPPING

The UNIX kernel executes with the separate I and D space function disabled, so it uses one hardware page table PTK. Once initialized, all entries in PTK, except one, remain unchanged. As shown in Fig. 16-9, the first six PTK entries map to the lower six page frames in physical memory. Entry number eight maps to the last page frame containing the device registers and, among other things, the page table registers themselves. Since no process possesses a similar privilege, these registers are protected.

The seventh entry in PTK is used to identify the running process. It is set to map to the per process data area (always 1024 bytes long) of the running process. Therefore, all descriptive information about this process is directly available to the kernel. Also, this area includes a stack area for use by the kernel when entered by the running process.

The contents of all the processor registers, including those of PTU, are stored in the user structure of the per process data area when a process is blocked or otherwise ceases to be running. When a process is selected to be the

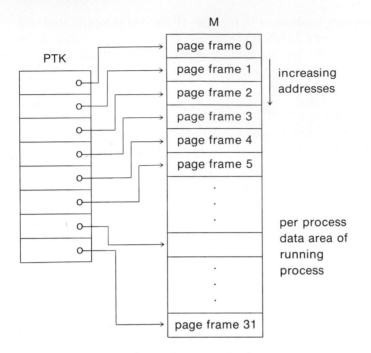

Figure 16-9 The UNIX™ kernel memory mapping.

running process, its per process data area address is placed into PTK[6]. Thereafter, the kernel can directly access the tables in the user structure describing the process's pages. The length of each page of the process can be determined from the user structure and, via malloc,[1] a suitable memory area obtained. Then the PTU is loaded for that page. The actual memory address occupied by a page need not be saved in the user structure, of course, since in general it will change each time the process runs.

EXERCISES

16-1 Some machines employ an addressing method called *base register addressing*. An operand address in an instruction is of the form (base register, displacement) where the base register is any one of a number of general registers. At run time the processor forms a logical address by adding the contents of the base register to the displacement. It is the responsibility of the programmer (or the compiler) to choose the base register and to ensure that the program initializes this register as its first action after being loaded and entered.

Base register addressing was intended as an aid to memory management.

(*a*) Explain the distinction between base addressing and memory mapping.

(*b*) What minor problem can you see as the result of the program itself, rather than the supervisor, choosing the base register?

---

[1] The memory allocation function (malloc). See Sec. 15-7.

(*c*) What more serious problem can you see occurring as one module calls another separately compiled module passing parameters by address?

16-2 Reducing page size decreases internal fragmentation while increasing page table size (table fragmentation). Assuming that page tables require two words per entry and are stored in main memory, determine the optimal page size as a function of memory size. Consider only these two factors.

16-3 How would you choose the segment table length if it were to be implemented in hardware? Comment on the practicality of using a hardware segment table.

16-4 Write the algorithm for the PDP-11 memory mapping unit.

16-5 Should the processor allow indexing across page boundaries in a paged machine? Should it be allowed in a segmented machine? Should it be allowed in a variable-length paged machine like the PDP-11? Justify your answers.

16-6 Should indexing be performed before or after memory mapping in a paged machine? In a segmented machine? In a variable length paged machine like the PDP-11? Explain.

16-7 Explain clearly with a diagram why certain logical addresses can be inaccessible in the PDP-11. Does this fact affect physical memory allocation? Explain.

16-8 Show how a process running on a PDP-11 can be given exclusive protected access to an I/O device. Is it practical to use this mechanism to give a process access to several (say, six or more) devices? Explain.

REFERENCES

Readable tutorial material on memory mapping techniques can be found in Denning (1970) and (1971). In addition, any text on operating systems or computer architecture will contain more advanced material than is found here. Some of the original research papers on the subject include Arden (1966), Dennis (1965), McGee (1965), and Randell (1965) and (1969).

SEVENTEEN

SOFTWARE DESIGN SPECIFICATION AND TESTING

Good programming is a very disciplined activity. Because of the inherent complexity in constructing large programs, it is essential to keep the programming process structured. The human mind is just not capable of comprehending all aspects of a complex program at one time. Program design, then, is based on methods of controlling this complexity. One way is to use a high-level language rather than some other form such as assembly language. We have already adopted this method in the text by using Pascal in presenting algorithms.

Even with a well-structured language such as Pascal, programming is still very complex. In this chapter, we present briefly just a few basic concepts to assist in producing good programs. Of course, these ideas are not going to solve automatically all programming problems, but adhering to some of these principles in a disciplined way will greatly help one's capabilities as a programmer.

17-1 PROGRAM QUALITY

What constitutes a good program? One might answer, "it works," but this is not sufficient. In the first place it is very hard to show whether or not a program "works." Can one prove that it works, or can one exhaustively test all possible executions of a program? Probably not, unless it is quite small. This answer recognizes only one of five important qualities of a program: *correctness, understandability, efficiency, flexibility,* and *reliability.*

The first of these, correctness, establishes that a program works; that is, it carries out a task according to a functional specification. Correctness can be established only with respect to a specification, however. This is extremely important: A program can be correct with respect to an erroneous specification. Correctness, then, is a relatively weak quality, since it assumes a correct specification and also does not consider an imperfect environment, such as bad data, malfunctioning hardware, or an inexperienced operator.

The second important quality is understandability. A program must be readable, comprehensible, and clear. The reason for this is simply that programs change, during their design and afterward. During design the programmer constantly reads the program to establish its meaning in mind. After initial design, a (possibly) different programmer is likely to need to read the program to make necessary modifications. An unclear program invites mistakes.

Third, efficiency is obviously important. The programmer should utilize the available mechanisms of language or hardware in the most appropriate way and choose algorithms that suit the situation. Efficiency should be considered *after* correctness and understandability, however. It is very much an internal property of a program, unless it relates directly to a performance specification.

Fourth, and sometimes counterbalancing efficiency, is flexibility. Since one should expect modifications or usage under differing circumstances, it is helpful if a program is designed to make changes easy. This, often, runs counter to efficiency, and circumstances will determine which is most important. But like efficiency, flexibility should be secondary to correctness and understandability.

Finally, reliability, left to the last not because of unimportance but because to a degree it encompasses all other qualities, is the basic requirement of a program. A program should perform its task when required. The last two words are critical: *when required*. A program may be required to do its job in the face of many obstacles: its own lack of correctness, errors due to poor understandability, inefficiency algorithms, inflexible design, poor hardware, operator errors, bad input data, etc.

Reliable programs are useful, even if they are not correct. A program may not conform to its specifications but because of its environment and usage may function satisfactorily. This is not to say that one should not strive for correctness, but only to point out the distinction between reliability and correctness. Many factors, then, contribute to reliability. In the remaining sections we shall attempt to further define some of them and to establish some guidelines for designing reliable programs.

17-2 ABSTRACTION

Abstraction is the process of grouping objects together on the basis of their similarities. In writing a program it is largely abstraction that one uses to control complexity. For example, the specification given to a programmer is an abstraction of many possible implementations of which it is the programmer's job to construct just one. An abstract specification, therefore, allows the program designer to concentrate on the essential features of a program and to leave all details of implementation until later.

The most familiar abstraction mechanism in programming is the procedure, which abstracts from actions. Many different procedures can perform an equivalent action. For example, a sorting procedure can use one of many possible algorithms, but the result is the same, the data involved are ordered. A programmer referencing such a procedure is not concerned about how it does a job but only that it does the job correctly. Thus, the complexity of the programmer's view of the program is reduced considerably.

A programming language can be viewed as comprising three fundamental facilities: data structures, operations on these data structures, and control flow. The primitive operations, such as addition on integers, are abstractions. The primitive data types are also abstractions. The programmer may not be concerned with how integers are implemented or how addition is implemented. Primitive control mechanisms such as the WHILE loop are also abstractions.

Given these primitive abstractions the programmer can construct programs directly. However, the programmer needs mechanisms to construct additional abstractions. Procedures provide a way of abstracting from control flow and the invocation of operations; that is, they can be used to create abstract operations. They do not, however, provide a satisfactory way of abstracting from data structures. For this, we need a different mechanism, one allowing the definition of *abstract data types*. The following sections establish some background and then describe such a mechanism.

17-3 DESIGN METHODS

Designing programs is difficult. No set of methods will solve all problems, and no method can substitute for the careful attention of the designer. Nevertheless, it is important that the novice designer be aware of some basic ideas in program design. It is especially important, in the context of a study of detailed implementation mechanisms, such as presented in this text, that the student not lose perspective on what software construction involves. First, an understanding of underlying machine and software implementation structures is essential for designing system programs. These have been discussed in detail in earlier chapters. Second, a clear understanding of more abstract design structures and of the problem structure is equally essential. These are more difficult to describe.

Abstraction is the central concept of design. In design we are creating an abstraction that will eventually be replaced by an appropriate implementation, one that matches the program's environment. It is the abstract program description that defines the set of possible implementations.

17-3.1 Top-Down Programming

Top-down programming is a systematic method for writing programs, developed largely by E. W. Dijkstra and H. D. Mills. One starts to construct a program by writing statements in an appropriate programming language (which need not have a compiler). Where complex operations are encountered, they are treated as if they exist and are simply placed in the code as appropriate invocations, such as a procedure call, perhaps. The programmer must have a clear specification of what these operations do but need not be concerned with how they do it, until he or she (or someone else) comes later to construct these operations.

For example, a large data processing program design may begin with the abstract program

```
initialize input data stream;
WHILE more data exists AND program not terminated DO
      process next transaction in data
```

Four complex operations have been included. The next design step, after verifying that the above program is correct, is to choose which of these operations is to be refined further. The process continues as each complex operation is specified and then implemented in terms of less complex operations by an abstract program. At each stage of design the key steps are the *specification* of a complex operation and then, after its implementation, the *verification* of its implementing abstract program.

Top-down programming proceeds until the complex operations can be directly implemented in some available computer system facility: a programming language or a hardware machine. Other examples of this way of designing programs have been given previously in the text. For example, the development of the assembler in Chap. 8 was given in a top-down fashion.

Problems encountered in top-down programming include the situation where the available system facilities may not match well with the operations specified in the design, and the situation where the operations were not well understood when specified. In practice, therefore, top-down programming is an iterative process, one must design top-down and then retrace one's steps "bottom-up" to a point where the design can be improved or corrected and a new design produced from that point.

17-3.2 Information-Hiding Modules

The concept of an *information-hiding module,* developed by D. L. Parnas, can be used as a complement to top-down programming. The idea here is that instead of making design decisions in the form of creating control structures and specifying imbedded operations, as in top-down programming, one *defers* design decisions in a systematic way.

One defers a design decision by specifying a module encapsulating that decision. The premise is that a good design minimizes the amount of information that each program module must know about other modules. Otherwise, this globally known information, as exists in our example in Chap. 6, becomes unmanageably complex to describe correctly. Therefore, the designer identifies design decisions that an implementation must embody and specifies the operations that will depend upon each decision. Each such set of operations then constitutes an information-hiding module.

An information-hiding module is defined only by the specifications of its component operations. No information about its internal implementation is known. The advantages of reducing the overall complexity of a large system, of assigning implementation to different programmers, and of program modification should be obvious. The large example system described in Chap. 18 is designed by defining information-hiding modules in a top-down sequence. The notion of information hiding is best understood by studying a large example such as that one.

It is very important to understand that the *design module* that we are discussing here is not the same as the *implementation module* that was discussed in Chap. 9 in the context of assemblers, linkers, etc. A design module defines a set of operations but implies nothing regarding their implementation. Thus, a design module may be directly implemented as a set of subroutines, or it may provide a set of definitions to be implemented in some other way, perhaps as macros.

In the remainder of the chapter (and in Chap. 18 as well) keep in mind this distinction between the design module and the implementation module.

17-4 SPECIFICATIONS

In Chap. 6 we introduced the concept of interface specifications as being that set of information that is globally known across a set of program modules constituting a program. These specifications included two kinds of information:

1. The syntax and parameter type rules for invoking operations of each module.
2. The description of global data structures that are accessed by more than one module. This included an informal statement of the state of such data structures before and after certain operations are performed.

In addition, the specifications included an informal statement of the semantics of the operations of each module.

This approach to specifying a program may work for small programs, but it does not provide much help when one is designing very large software systems.

The major problem is the global data. It is extremely difficult to produce reliable programs in which the implementer of each module must correctly access a large set of global data. Even more important, however, the principle of information hiding argues for the elimination of as much as possible of such global data in program design. As a result module specifications are concerned only with syntax and type rules for operations and the semantic description of each operation.

One factor that makes program design difficult is that the designer usually has an imprecise semantic specification from which to work. This results, in most cases, not only because the specification is incomplete but also because it is given in English, a very ambiguous medium of communication. As we shall see, it is very difficult to be precise in defining the semantics of programs. Consequently, until the technology of formal specification techniques improves considerably, programmers will be required to work with relatively imprecise English specifications.

Information-hiding modules and top-down designed abstract programs require somewhat different specification methods. In specifying an information-hiding module one describes the effects of invoking each of its operations. However, one should avoid referring to any internal implementation details in doing so since those, of course, are to be hidden, part of a particular implementation. The specification of an operation can be given in terms of its effects on values returned by other operations. There are two general approaches with which this can be done. First, one can *explicitly* describe the meaning of an operation by describing its effects on an abstract model of the data in the module. The abstract model is created only for describing meaning and has nothing to do with implementation (except that the meaning should be equivalent). Second, one can *implicitly* describe the meaning of an operation by describing the result of invoking certain sequences of operations. In this case, no reference to any form of internal state information is required. Examples of the implicit and the explicit approaches are given below.

A common example of an information-hiding module is a QUEUE manager. Its operations are NEW, ADD, FRONT, REMOVE and IS_EMPTY. An informal English specification of a QUEUE module that adheres to the principle of information hiding by using the implicit approach is the following:

1. NEW: returns a queue

2. ADD: maps a QUEUE and an item into a QUEUE

3. FRONT: maps a QUEUE into an item
   FRONT(NEW) is an error
   FRONT(ADD(Q,I)) returns item I if
       IS_EMPTY(Q) = TRUE and otherwise
       returns FRONT(Q)

4. REMOVE: maps a QUEUE into a QUEUE
                 REMOVE(NEW) is an error
                 REMOVE(ADD(Q,I)) returns the result of
                        NEW if IS_EMPTY(Q) = TRUE and
                        otherwise returns ADD(REMOVE(Q),I)

5. IS_EMPTY: maps a QUEUE into a BOOLEAN

The first line of each operation specification is the syntax part, expressing only the names of the operations and the types of input and output parameters. The remainder of each specification is the semantic part, expressing the effects of the operation. Notice that this is done only in terms of other operations and no details of QUEUE implementations are given. Readers should satisfy themselves that this specification conforms to their understanding of a queue.

An explicit specification of the same queue manager is shown below. Here, the specification is given in terms of two kinds of primitive objects constituting the abstract model: tuples and sequences. An abstract representation part has been added to the syntax and semantic parts to define a queue in terms of the model. To repeat, this abstract representation is given solely for descriptive purposes. In fact, when one examines the definition of sequences, it can be seen that implementation is certainly not intended!

Tuples are similar to records in Pascal except that they cannot be updated. For example,

tuple(a:integer, b:Boolean)

denotes a tuple with two components, one integer and one boolean.

{a:15, b:TRUE}

is a tuple of this type. If z denotes this tuple, then

z.a = 15 and z.b = TRUE

Sequences contain zero or more elements, all of the same type. Operations on sequences are:

<>   denotes the empty sequence

s[i]   where $1 \leq i \leq n$, denotes the i th element of s

append(s,x)   creates a new sequence with the elements of s
                   followed by x as the last element

An explicit specification of the QUEUE manager is:

QUEUE = tuple(front: integer,
                    back: integer,
                    elements: sequence(item))

1. NEW: returns a QUEUE
   NEW = {1,−1,<>}

2. ADD: maps a QUEUE and an item into a QUEUE
   ADD(q,a) = BEGIN
        q.back := q.back + 1;
        append(q,i)
       END

3. FRONT: maps a QUEUE into an item
   FRONT(q) − IF q.back ⩾ q.front THEN
        q.elements(q.back)
       ELSE error

4. REMOVE: maps a QUEUE into a QUEUE
   REMOVE(q) = IF q.back ⩾ q.front THEN
        q.front := q.front + 1
       ELSE error

5. IS_EMPTY: maps a QUEUE into a Boolean
   IS_EMPTY = IF q.back < q.front THEN
        TRUE
       ELSE FALSE

It is the programmer's job to take this explicit specification and construct an equivalent program as an implementation. Therefore, correctness verification requires showing the equivalence of two programs.

In doing top-down design one must produce a specification of an operation to be imbedded in an abstract program. The specification, then, must refer to the data structures known to the program. For example, one may design the implementation of an information-hiding module using top-down programming. Then the specification of an imbedded operation may refer to any of the data structures the module comprises.

A specification for an imbedded operation, which may be implemented by a procedure, is given as an *input-output specification*. The operation is defined as a procedural abstraction, a mapping from inputs to outputs. The syntax part describes the types of the variables in the input and output sets. The semantic part can be given in several ways. One way is to use an abstract model, as was done with information-hiding modules above. As in that former use of an abstract model, the primitive objects are chosen for clarity in producing an understandable specification. An implementation, of course, must possess all of the characteristics of a high-quality program.

An example of an abstract model input-output specification, for the greatest common divisor operation, is shown below. It is based on the primitive type INTEGER and the two primitive operations min and mod; min returns the lesser of its two arguments and mod returns the result of reducing the first argument modulo the second.

```
GCD:    maps an (INTEGER,INTEGER) into an INTEGER
        GCD(x,y) = IF x ≤ 0 OR y ≤ 0 THEN
                        error ("invalid data")
                   ELSE searchfrom(x,y,min(x,y));

where searchfrom(x,y,z) = IF mod(x,z)=0 AND mod(y,z)=0 THEN z
                          ELSE searchfrom(x,y,z−1)
```

To summarize this section, the specification of any program requires syntax and semantic parts. The latter, ideally, should not imply any internal details of implementation. An information-hiding module can be specified either implicitly, by showing the effects of each operation on the results of others, or explicitly, by basing the specification on an abstract model. An information-hiding module may be designed using top-down programming. If this is done, imbedded operations, whose implementation is deferred, must be specified before implementation can proceed. This can be done with input-output specifications based on an abstract model.

17-5 ABSTRACT DATA TYPES

Recent work in programming languages has produced a technique for constructing information-hiding modules in high-level languages. The basic notion is that the design decisions to be encapsulated in a module are all those concerned with the implementation of a specific data structure. Such a data structure is called an *abstract data type*. One can define a new abstract data type by defining the operations that are to be available for manipulating instances (variables) of that type. The language's compiler will then enforce information hiding by restricting access to the data structures so defined to those operations only.

Therefore, although it may be difficult to actually give a precise specification of an abstract data type or to prevent programmers from discovering implementation details, the compiler prevents programmers from taking advantage directly.

We now describe a notation for abstract data types based on Pascal. The fact that there may not be a compiler available to perform the checking should not deter us from using the notation.[1] It still provides a framework within which we can systematically design programs. (The project description in Chap. 18 uses this notation.)

---

[1] A compiler for this notation is currently running on a PDP-11 at Queen's University, Kingston, Canada.

The general form of an abstract data type definition, called a MODULE, is

```
MODULE <module name>;
   EXPORT <module name>,<list of operations>;
   <module name> = <data definition>;
   <definition of internal constants, types,
      variables, and procedures>;
   <definition of operations>
END
```

The module name is just the name of the type. The data definition is the internal representation of variables of the type. It is this representation that is to be "hidden," in the sense that variables of the type are to be accessed only via the operations given and not directly through knowledge of this representation. The EXPORT statement lists the operations defined on the type. These operations, given in the body of the MODULE definition, are simply function or procedure definitions. In addition, the MODULE may contain constant, type, variable, or procedure definitions used by the operations.

Variables of an abstract data type are declared outside the MODULE within a program using the MODULE definition. Such a declaration uses the normal syntax, such as

```
VAR x: <module name>
```

where module name has been defined as a MODULE. Such a declaration conceptually represents an invocation of an object creation operation that is implicitly defined with every MODULE definition.

An example is the best way to explain this notation. The following declaration defines a type queue (of integers) according to the specifications presented earlier.

```
MODULE queue ;


EXPORT queue,initq,add,front,remove,isempty;


TYPE queue = RECORD
                front : ↑ element;
                back : ↑ element
                END;


TYPE element = RECORD
                val : INTEGER;
                ptr : ↑ element
                END;
```

```
PROCEDURE initq(VAR q: queue);
    BEGIN
        q.front := NIL;
        q.back := NIL
    END;

PROCEDURE add (VAR d : INTEGER; q : queue);
    VAR el: ↑element;
    BEGIN
        new(el);
        IF q.front = NIL THEN BEGIN
            q.front := el;
            q.back := el;
            el ↑ .val := d;
            el ↑ .ptr := NIL END
        ELSE BEGIN
            q.back ↑ .ptr := el;
            el ↑ .ptr := NIL;
            q.back := d END
    END;

FUNCTION front (VAR q : queue) : INTEGER ;
    BEGIN
        IF q.front <> NIL THEN
          front := q.front ↑ .val
        ELSE front := undefined value
    END;

FUNCTION remove (VAR q : queue) : INTEGER ;
    BEGIN
        IF q.front <> NIL THEN
          front := q.front ↑ .ptr
        ELSE front := undefined value
    END;

FUNCTION isempty (VAR q : queue) : BOOLEAN ;
    BEGIN
        IF q.front <> NIL THEN
          isempty := TRUE
        ELSE isempty := FALSE
    END

END
```

A Pascal compiler with abstract data types as described here would prevent a programmer from accessing any instance of a suitably declared queue

object except through the operations given. The implementer of queues, therefore, is free to alter the representation of queues at any time without affecting other programs that use these queues.

17-6 STRUCTURAL DESIGN

The use of information-hiding modules requires that a decomposition of the program into such modules be performed. Indeed, this decomposition is one of the most important design steps; it is the structural design of the program. In creating a structural design, an activity which has been called *programming in the large,* the programmer would like to be concerned only with the relationship among modules and not with their internal design. In other words the programmer needs to be able to construct a specification, even if it be a very informal one, including syntax and semantic components.

A top-down methodology based on abstract data types can be applied to structural design. Essentially, one first produces a specification for the entire program viewed as an information-hiding module and described as a single instance of an abstract data type. One then determines a set of modules into which decisions can be encapsulated external to the former, or level 0, module. In other words, all decisions not to be encapsulated at the level 0 module are assigned to one of the set of level 1 modules. The process continues until the modules specified are small enough to be manageably implemented without further decomposition.

Consider, as an example of this top-down design process, the problem of specifying and constructing a symbol table module for the translator of a nested block structured language like Pascal. In such a language, identifiers have static scope, so that as one reads a program (or as a translator scans a program) a new set of identifiers can be declared as a block is entered. These identifiers each can supercede, for the duration of the block, an identical identifier in an enclosing block. On block exit this set of identifiers disappears. A translator, then, must have a symbol table organized so that at any point in its scan of the program, the current set of validly declared identifiers is available.

The following is an informal specification of a level 0 module providing a symbol table facility. Here, the implementation data structure is left unspecified, as is the body of each operation. The specification consists only of the syntax part, the types of functions and of parameters, and the semantic part, given as a comment in the body of each operation.

MODULE symboltable ;

EXPORT symboltable,init_symboltable,enter_block,leave_block,
       add,inblock,retrieve;

TYPE symboltable = definition of implementation deferred;

```
PROCEDURE init_symboltable(VAR s: symboltable);
    BEGIN {initializes the symboltable s}
    END;


PROCEDURE enter_block (VAR s: symboltable);
    BEGIN {causes subsequent additions of an identifier to s to
            be associated with a new block context}
    END;


PROCEDURE leave_block (VAR s: symboltable);
    BEGIN {deletes from s all identifers associated with the
            current block context and cancels the effect of the
            most recent call to enter_block}
    END;


PROCEDURE add (VAR s : symboltable;
                i : identifier;
                a : attributelist);
    BEGIN {enters into s the identifier i and its associated
            attributes a}
    END;


FUNCTION in_block (s : symboltable;
                i : identifier) : BOOLEAN;
    BEGIN {returns TRUE if i is a validly declared identifier
            in the current block context established by the most
            recent call to enter block, and FALSE otherwise}
    END;


FUNCTION retrieve (s : symboltable;
                i : identifier):attributelist;
    BEGIN {returns the attributes of the most recently added
            instance of i. An error value is returned if i has
            not been added to s.}
    END


END
```

The next step is to consider how to implement the module symboltable and to encapsulate some of these implementation considerations within one or more level 1 modules. It is at this point that the designer might start to design the algorithms for the operations of the level 0 module symboltable. Whether or not this is done at this point, the major task is to specify the data structure upon which the implementation of symboltable is to be based. With the notion of abstract data types the specification of lower-level modules is incorporated nicely within the design of the implementation data structure. Lower-level modules are just declared as abstract data types.

So one might decide to implement a symboltable with a "symstack" of arrays as follows.

```
MODULE symboltable ;
EXPORT symboltable, . . . ;
TYPE symboltable = symstack ;
.
.
.
END
```

This means that the type symboltable will be represented, within the module implementing values of this type, by the type symstack, which must now be specified. As shown below, symstack provides a stack of arrays. The operations on symstack are, then, those available to an implementation of symboltable.

```
MODULE symstack ;

EXPORT symstack,initsymstack,push,pop,top,newstack,replace;

TYPE symstack = definition of implementation deferred;

PROCEDURE initsymstack(VAR st: symstack);
    BEGIN {initializes the symstack st}
    END;

PROCEDURE push (VAR st : symstack;
                    a : array);
    BEGIN {pushes the value of a onto the stack representing st}
    END;

PROCEDURE pop (VAR st : symstack);
    BEGIN {deletes from st the most recently pushed array}
    END;

FUNCTION top (VAR st : symstack): symarray;
    BEGIN {returns the most recently pushed value or
            an error if there is no such value}
    END;

FUNCTION newstack (VAR st: symstack): BOOLEAN;
    BEGIN {returns TRUE if st was returned by initsymstack and
            FALSE otherwise}
    END;
```

```
PROCEDURE replace (VAR st : symstack;
                        a : array);
    BEGIN {replaces by a the value most recently pushed onto st}
    END


END
```

Also required for MODULE symboltable is the MODULE symarray, which constitutes the second level 1 module. Figure 17-1 shows the structure of the top-down design at this point. The diagram shows that the implementation of the MODULE symboltable is based on the use of the two MODULEs symarray and symstack.

The MODULE symarray informal specification is the following:

```
MODULE symarray ;


EXPORT symarray,initsymarray,assign,read,undefined;


TYPE symarray = definition of implementation deferred;


PROCEDURE initsymarray(VAR a : symarray);
    BEGIN {initializes the symarray a}
    END;


PROCEDURE assign (VAR a : symarray;
                        i : identifier;
                        l : attributelist);
    BEGIN {assigns the value l to the element of a indexed by i}
    END;


FUNCTION read (a : symarray,
                    i : identifier):attributelist;
    BEGIN {returns the value most recently assigned to the
            element of a indexed by i.
            An error is returned if no value has been assigned.}
    END;
```

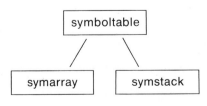

Figure 17-1 The structure of MODULE symboltable.

```
FUNCTION undefined (a : symarray;
                    i : identifier) : BOOLEAN;
    BEGIN {returns TRUE if a value has not been assigned to the
           element of a indexed by i, and FALSE otherwise}
    END

END
```

To produce a complete informal structural specification of the design of the MODULE symboltable, the process of top-down decomposition is repeated until the lowest level of types is directly available in the implementation language, i.e., is a set of primitive types. At each level one can list, within each module operation definition, the operations required for that module in lower modules. These lists then yield a complete "interface" specification which could be checked by a compiler. The complete structural specification for symboltable is shown below, followed by an actual implementation. Although the design is not carried further here (the next chapter contains a much larger complete example), the specifications for symarray and symstack can be completed in a similar way.

When, within each operation, all references to operations in other modules are listed, the references must be syntactically correct if a compiler is to check for type compatibility. This means that function calls must assign the returned value, and both functions and procedures must have valid parameters. This syntactic correctness is assured simply by using formal parameters of the operation or suitably declared local variables as actual parameters of calls and as targets of assignments. In this way the structural program description consists of dummy calls on operations whose sole purpose is to describe the relationships among the modules. Thus the structural specification is a syntactically correct program which can be checked by a compiler without altering the base language in any way.

```
MODULE symboltable ;

EXPORT  symboltable,init_symboltable,enter_block,leave_block,
        pop,top,replace;

TYPE symboltable = symstack;

PROCEDURE init_symboltable(VAR s : symboltable);
    BEGIN
        initsymstack(s)
    END;
```

```
PROCEDURE enter_block (VAR s : symboltable);
    VAR a : symarray;
    BEGIN
        initsymarray(a);
        push (s,a)
    END;

PROCEDURE leave-block (VAR s : symboltable);
    VAR b: BOOLEAN;
    BEGIN
        b := newstack(s);
        pop(s)
    END;

PROCEDURE add (VAR s : symboltable;
                    i : identifier;
                    a : attributelist);
    VAR x : symarray;
    BEGIN
        x : = top(s);
        assign (x,i,a);
        replace (s,x)
    END;

FUNCTION in_block (s : symboltable;
                    i : identifier) : BOOLEAN;
    VAR a : symarray; b: BOOLEAN;
    BEGIN
        b := newstack(s);
        a := top(s);
        b := undefined (a,i)
    END;

FUNCTION retrieve (s : symboltable;
                    i : identifier) : attributelist;
    VAR a : symarray; b: BOOLEAN;
    BEGIN
        b := newstack(s);
        a := top(s);
        pop(s);
        b := undefined (a,i);
        read (a,i)
    END

END
```

An implementation of the MODULE symboltable is

```
MODULE symboltable ;

EXPORT symboltable,init_symboltable,enter_block,leave_block,
        add,in_block,retrieve;

TYPE symboltable = symstack;

PROCEDURE init_symboltable(VAR s : symboltable);
    BEGIN
        initsymstack(s)
    END;

PROCEDURE enter_block (VAR s : symboltable);
    VAR a: symarray;
    BEGIN
      initsymarray(a);
      push (s,a)
    END;

PROCEDURE leave_block (VAR s : symboltable);
    BEGIN
        IF newstack(s) THEN return with error
        ELSE pop(s)
    END;

PROCEDURE add (VAR s : symboltable;
                    i : identifier;
                    a : attributelist);
    VAR x : symarray;
    BEGIN
        x := top(s);
        assign (x,i,a);
        replace (s,x)
    END;

FUNCTION in_block (s : symboltable;
                    i : identifier) : BOOLEAN;
    BEGIN
        in_block := TRUE;
        IF newstack(s) THEN in_block := FALSE
        ELSE IF undefined (top(s), i) THEN in_block := FALSE
    END;
```

```
FUNCTION retrieve (s : symboltable;
                   i : identifier) : attributelist;
    VAR x : BOOLEAN;
    BEGIN
        x := FALSE;
        WHILE NOT newstack(s) AND NOT x DO
            IF undefined (top(s), i) THEN pop(s)
            ELSE retrieve := read (top(s), i);
        IF NOT x THEN retrieve := error
    END

END
```

17-7 FORMAL SEMANTIC SPECIFICATIONS

Much research is being devoted to the search for a formal way to specify the meaning of programs. In the context of previous sections of this chapter, this search aims to replace the informal comment portion of a module's specification with something much less ambiguous than English prose. The previous section on specification methods gave some of the flavor of the problems of being precise in this regard. Since this research is fairly new and the methods proposed are relatively untested, some formalisms are included here mainly for completeness of our discussion. Whether these or other formalisms will become a common tool for software designers is difficult to predict. There does seem to be general agreement, however, that the abstract data type is the correct language unit upon which to base program design and specification.

Although we have used the terms *abstract data type, module,* and MODULE interchangeably, the proper perspective is that a module is an implementation of an abstract data type. Thus, while a module can be implemented in any language, an abstract data type is defined by using a particular mechanism, such as the MODULE, in a high-level language. Most of the time we use the term *module* to describe this basic unit of specification and design.

17-7.1 Axiomatic Specifications

Axiomatic specifications are an example of the implicit variety of specifications; they define the operations of a module by relating, via a set of axioms, these operations. In defining the queue of Sec. 17-4, for example, the operations NEW, ADD, FRONT, REMOVE, and IS_EMPTY were defined by relating them to each other to preserve the principle of information hiding. The only difference in using axiomatic specifications is that formal axioms, rather than informal English, are used to do this. The advantages of formal axioms is that they are well defined mathematically without the ambiguities of English.

A formal specification corresponding to the informal specification presented in Sec. 17-4 is shown below. The notation, adapted from J. V. Guttag's thesis, is the same, except that English statements are replaced by axioms and expressions.

TYPE QUEUE

1. NEW : -> QUEUE

2. ADD : QUEUE × item -> QUEUE

3. FRONT : QUEUE -> item

    AXIOM 1) FRONT (NEW) = error
    AXIOM 2) FRONT (ADD(Q,I)) = IF IS_EMPTY (Q) THEN I
                                 ELSE FRONT (Q)

4. REMOVE : QUEUE -> QUEUE

    AXIOM 3) REMOVE (NEW) = error
    AXIOM 4) REMOVE (ADD(Q,I)) = IF IS _EMPTY(Q) THEN NEW
                                   ELSE ADD (REMOVE (Q), I)

5. IS_EMPTY : QUEUE -> BOOLEAN

    AXIOM 5) IS_EMPTY (NEW) = TRUE
    AXIOM 6) IS_EMPTY (ADD(Q,I)) = FALSE

Nine axioms are required to specify the operations of the module symboltable presented in the previous section. These are, as presented by Guttag:

TYPE SYMBOLTABLE

1. NEW_SYMBOLTABLE : -> SYMBOLTABLE

2. ENTER_BLOCK : SYMBOLTABLE -> SYMBOLTABLE

3. LEAVE_BLOCK : SYMBOLTABLE -> SYMBOLTABLE

    AXIOM 1) LEAVE_BLOCK(NEW_SYMBOLTABLE) = error
    AXIOM 2) LEAVE_BLOCK(ENTER_BLOCK(symtab)) = symtab
    AXIOM 3) LEAVE_BLOCK(ADD(symtab,id,attrs)) = LEAVE_BLOCK(symtab)

4. ADD : SYMBOLTABLE × IDENTIFIER × ATTRIBUTELIST -> SYMBOLTABLE

5. IN_BLOCK : SYMBOLTABLE × IDENTIFIER −> BOOLEAN

> AXIOM 4) IN_BLOCK(NEW_SYMBOLTABLE,id)   = FALSE
> AXIOM 5) IN_BLOCK(ENTER_BLOCK(symtab),id) = FALSE
> AXIOM 6) IN_BLOCK(ADD(symtab,id,attrs),id1) =
>   IF EQUAL(id,id1) THEN TRUE ELSE IN BLOCK(symtab,id1)

6. RETRIEVE : SYMBOLTABLE × IDENTIFIER −> ATTRIBUTELIST

> AXIOM 7) RETRIEVE(NEW_SYMBOLTABLE,id) = error
> AXIOM 8) RETRIEVE(ENTER_BLOCK(symtab),id) = RETRIEVE(symtab,id)
> AXIOM 9) RETRIEVE(ADD(symtab,id,attrs),id1) =
>   IF EQUAL(id,id1) THEN attrs ELSE RETRIEVE(symtab,id1)

The operation EQUAL is assumed to be specified as part of the primitive type IDENTIFIER.

These axioms, which are not unique, represent one way of saying what the operations of SYMBOLTABLE do in a very concise way. Axiom 1 says that LEAVE_BLOCK cannot be applied to an empty SYMBOLTABLE. Axiom 2 says that applying LEAVE_BLOCK to a SYMBOLTABLE produced by applying ENTER_BLOCK yields the SYMBOLTABLE to which ENTER_ BLOCK was applied. In other words, the effect of the previous ENTER_ BLOCK is canceled. Notice how our English explanation of this axiom becomes verbose! Axiom 3 says that ADD has no effect on the result of LEAVE_ BLOCK. This axiom should be read in a recursive way; considering a sequence of SYMBOLTABLE values produced by a sequence of ADDs, the axiom is repeatedly applied until axiom 2 or axiom 1 can be applied, thus yielding a value, either an error or a SYMBOLTABLE.

A careful reading of axioms 4 to 9 is left to the reader.

Axiomatic specifications yield all the advantages of formal specifications. They provide a basis upon which statements about the correctness of a program can be made. They form an important part of system documentation, telling a programmer what a program is to do and providing a precise means for communicating among programmers.

The major disadvantages of axiomatic specifications is that they seem unfamiliar and difficult to read. Whether this will be mitigated by increased usage remains to be seen. In any case, the technique requires much development before it can be practically applied.

17-7.2 Abstract Model Specifications

Another approach to formal specification which does not suffer so much from the problems of unfamiliarity and poor readability is the abstract model specification. We have already seen specifications of this flavor in the previous section on specifications. Here, the definition of operations is based on predefined objects of some primitive type. These primitive objects must be defined elsewhere, of course, perhaps axiomatically. They are normally chosen to be of well-known types so that no extra confusion is introduced.

The advantage of using an abstract model, besides the fact that familiar primitives can be chosen, is that each operation can be specified *operationally*, that is, by explaining its effects on the primitive objects implementing the abstract data type. These specifications, therefore, read more like programs and are often more intelligible to a trained programmer.

The disadvantage is that the specification can be viewed as implying some particular implementation because of the way that the primitive objects are treated. Although free to construct his or her own implementation, the programmer may be led to follow the specifications. This, of course, may not yield the most efficient or flexible result.

An abstract model specification for a SYMARRAY can be based on the primitive object types TUPLE, LISTIDENTIFIER, and ATTRIBUTELIST. Assuming that these have all been specified, and using mnemonics for the primitive operations that for our purposes convey meaning, we can specify SYMARRAY as follows:

TYPE SYMARRAY

```
SYMARRAY − TUPLE[low : IDENTIFIER,
                high : IDENTIFIER,
                elements : LIST [TUPLE[index:IDENTIFIER,
                                       value:ATTRIBUTELIST]]]
```

1. NEW_SYMARRAY : −> SYMARRAY

```
    NEW_SYMARRAY = {low : NULL,
                    high : NULL,
                    elements : NULL}
```

2. ASSIGN : SYMARRAY × IDENTIFIER × ATTRIBUTELIST −> SYMARRAY

```
    ASSIGN(s,i,a) = IF INRANGE(s.low,i,s.high) THEN
                    {low : s.low,
                     high : s.high,
                     elements:APPEND(s.elements,i,a)}
                    ELSE IF LESS(i,s.low) THEN
                    {low : i,
                     high : s.high,
                     elements : APPEND(s.elements,i,a)}
                    ELSE
                    {low : s.low,
                     high : i,
                     elements : APPEND(s.elements,i,a)}
```

3. READ : SYMARRAY × IDENTIFIER −> ATTRIBUTELIST

   READ(s,i) = IF INRANGE(s.low,i,s.high) THEN
             GETVAL(s.elements,i)
        ELSE error

   Note here that GETVAL can return an error if no value
   is found on the list.

4. UNDEFINED : SYMARRAY × IDENTIFIER −> BOOLEAN

   UNDEFINED(s,i) = IF GETVAL(s.elements,i) = error THEN
             TRUE
           ELSE FALSE

Notice that the representation of a SYMARRAY as a TUPLE is given as part of the specification. The operations are then defined with respect to their effects on parameters so represented. This is not intended to imply that an implementation must adhere to the same representation. Whatever representation is used, however, must be shown to be consistent with the specification.

An abstract model specification for a SYMBOLTABLE is as follows. Again, it is assumed that the types SYMARRAY and SYMSTACK are independently specified.

TYPE SYMBOLTABLE

SYMBOLTABLE = SYMSTACK

1. NEW_SYMBOLTABLE : −> SYMBOLTABLE

   NEW_SYMBOLTABLE = PUSH(NEW_SYMSTACK,NEW_SYMARRAY)

2. ENTER_BLOCK : SYMBOLTABLE −> SYMBOLTABLE

   ENTER_BLOCK(S) = PUSH(S,NEW_SYMARRAY)

3. LEAVE_BLOCK : SYMBOLTABLE −> SYMBCLTABLE

   LEAVE_BLOCK(S) = IF NEW_STACK(S) THEN error
             ELSE POP(S)

4. ADD : SYMBOLTABLE × IDENTIFIER × ATTRIBUTELIST −> SYMBOLTABLE

   ADD(s,i,a) = REPLACE(s,ASSIGN(TOP(S),i,a))

5. IN_BLOCK : SYMBOLTABLE × IDENTIFIER −> BOOLEAN

    IN_BLOCK(s,i) = IF NEW_STACK(S) THEN FALSE
                   ELSE IF UNDEFINED (TOP(S),i) THEN
                        FALSE
                   ELSE TRUE

6. RETRIEVE : SYMBOLTABLE × IDENTIFIER −> ATTRIBUTELIST

    RETRIEVE(s,i) × IF NEW_STACK(S) THEN error
                  ELSE IF UNDEFINED (TOP(S),i) THEN
                       RETRIEVE (POP(S),i)
                  ELSE READ (TOP(S),i)

Notice how similar this operational abstract model specification appears to the implementation of the module symboltable shown in the previous section.

17-8 ERROR HANDLING

The intelligent handling of errors is a critical part of any reliable software system. Its importance should not be thought lessened because the subject has been left to this late chapter. In fact, it is most properly discussed in the context of module design, the topic of this chapter.

An *error* is an event that occurs as the result of a flaw in the design of software, or as the result of an unexpected condition in the environment of the software. The latter conditions include human errors, hardware faults (including faults that alter the software), and external equipment faults. The two important aspects of error handling are the detection of errors and the recovery from errors.

Errors can be detected either by the hardware or by the software. In the former case either a trap occurs which transfers control to a place specified by the software, or an error code is deposited somewhere for software inspection. More difficult to detect are those errors that do not result in error traps or hardware signals. In fact, some errors can go undetected for long periods. For example, a bad datum can contaminate a file and if the value is plausible it may never be detected.

The detection of errors by software is largely a matter of (1) checking for out-of-range data, or (2) recognizing redundancies in data and checking these for consistency. The discovery of out-of-range or inconsistent data then constitutes the detection of an error. Note that, according to our definition, the error may have occurred long before it was detected. Where sufficient redundancy does not occur naturally, it must be added. The parity bit in the 8-bit ASCII code is an example.

Assuming that an error has been detected, either by hardware assistance or by detecting incorrect data, what should happen? It is here that the effects of good design are felt very directly on the reliability of a program. Certain designs preclude intelligent action on detecting errors, leaving the programmer no choice but to specify that the program abort its execution. A good design gives the programmer alternatives that can be followed after detecting an error. Such alternatives constitute the error-recovery procedures. It is this subject of error recovery to which we shall direct our attention.

First, consider the simple method of giving total responsibility for error recovery to the caller of a module operation. This is accomplished by not specifying trap routines for hardware error traps, thus causing these traps to transfer to whatever routine was specified in the caller. Of course the caller might have similarly yielded trap-handling control. In addition, the detection of errors by software can be handled by invoking a software-generated trap, thus causing control to transfer to the caller's (or to its caller's) trap-handling routine.

Responsibility for error recovery is thus totally a function of the caller of a module operation. As indicated, this responsibility can be abdicated, in which case it falls to the previous caller in the sequence, until ultimately some program must assume the responsibility. Typically, this ultimate responsibility is taken by the operating system, which normally aborts the offending program.

Even if traps are handled by a calling module in an application program, however, there are fundamental problems. In order for such a calling module to take intelligent corrective action, it must have some knowledge of the internal structure of the module that generated the trap. This, of course, violates the principle of information hiding. Therefore, it is difficult for the trap handler in the calling module to perhaps make a change to the offending module and execute a trap return to permit it to continue. Furthermore, if it is impossible to allow the trapped module to continue, the caller is in an awkward position to continue itself because it is in a trap handler with an outstanding call to the trapped module. The only alternative is to generate a trap itself, since it probably does not have the capability to take system action to abort this outstanding call, something that only the operating system normally can do.

A second possible error-handling method is to require that every call to a module include a parameter specifying an error-recovery procedure. A module can then field its own error traps and on detecting an error invoke this error-recovery procedure. Aside from the extra overhead involved with the extra parameter (which can be reduced by suitable hardware mechanism), there are two serious problems. The error-recovery procedure still has no access to the internal structure of the erroneous module. Furthermore, should the error-recovery procedure not want to continue the erroneous module by executing a return to it, then it must invoke some system action to abort the two calls, the one resulting in the error detection and the subsequent one to the error-recovery procedure. Such an action is likely a trap to the operating system, which probably aborts the entire program.

Third, one could provide, with each subsystem collection of modules, an error-recovery module that specializes in recovery. This solution suffers the same problems as the second alternative, although the idea of centralizing the function of error recovery has some attraction.

Finally, one could require all modules to field their own error traps and on detecting an error to take any corrective action themselves, based on the available information. In the event that continuation is impossible, the module can return to its caller, passing a suitable error code as an output parameter. This has the distinct advantage that all error-recovery decisions are made in the context of the error condition. Only in the case of failure to recover does the module yield control. Such a yielding of control, of course, creates a different error condition to be handled in the context of the calling program. As with the second proposed method, the extra parameter overhead can be reduced by suitable hardware assistance.

The example system described in Chap. 18 assumes that all module operations include an error code output parameter. For reasons of clarity, however, this parameter is not shown in the programs. A particular implementation would, of course, need to provide the mechanism. Furthermore, for the same reasons of clarity, the programs in most cases do not check the return code of called operations. For our purposes, this makes the programs easier to read and understand. Deferring error-recovery details is of more general utility, however. A good design principle to follow is to decide on an error-recovery method and ensure that the program structure supports it adequately. The program can then be written in a careful structured way with concentration on the correctness of the code. Afterward, in a way similar to applying optimizations after structured coding, the error-recovery modifications to the code can be added where they have been omitted. Thus the programmer has the option of doing error recovery where he or she sees fit, but it need not interfere with the process of obtaining correct code.

17-9 TESTING

The best way to ensure correct programs is by careful design. Some suggestions for how to approach this problem have already been given at some length. We have also alluded to the process of verifying by formal proof, during or after design, that a program satisfies its specifications. However for most programs, especially those that are not small, formal verification by proof is impractical. Either the specifications are unsuitable or the program is unsuitable because of its size or structure.

Almost all programs, then, need to be tested in order to gain evidence that they are ready for operational use. In fact, program testing and related tasks often consume most of the total program production process. Despite the significance of testing, however, methods employed are largely nonsystematic. Only recently has work been devoted to developing systematic test methods.

Our goal in this section is simply to emphasize the significance of testing and to make the reader aware of the fact that, despite the lack of systematic methods, as much care is required in testing programs as is required in designing them.

17-9.1 Objectives of Testing

As stated above, the primary reason for testing is to gain evidence that a program is ready for operational use. One assumes, then, that the program in question behaves in a satisfactory manner and it is necessary to verify this. Not included in this primary reason are several other reasons often associated with testing. First, the phase of software construction commonly known as *debugging,* looking for a known flaw, is different from testing. Second, *performance evaluation,* which is concerned with determining where certain optimizations may be applied in a program's construction, also is a different task requiring different techniques.

What, then, are the objectives of testing? To answer this, recall the list of important program qualities. Of these, understandability, efficiency, and flexibility are largely untestable in the sense we are discussing, although performance evaluation can be applied to measure efficiency. What we are testing, then, is a program's correctness and reliability. It is a process of increasing one's confidence that a program is consistent with its specifications and that it yields desirable behavior when operated in an environment different from that assumed by its specifications.

17-9.2 Test Data Selection

A test consists of executing a program with a chosen set of input data and observing the results. If the chosen test data are within the domain of input assumed in the specifications, then for the test to be successful the results must be consistent with those given by the specifications. Or, if the chosen test data are not within the assumed domain (i.e., invalid input formats) then a more subjective judgment must be made as to the test's success. For example, an error message is normally expected if input data are not as required by the specifications.

A test is wholly determined by the choice of test data. Governing this choice is the *test data criterion.* This criterion constitutes a test method. What one needs for testing a program, then, is a systematic criterion for choosing one's test data.

J. B. Goodenough introduces two important qualities of a test data criterion: validity and reliability (not to be confused with program reliability). Essentially, a *valid* criterion is one that does not systematically exclude test data cases that could potentially cause an unsuccessful test, i.e., expose an error. A program designed to handle real-time input but tested on simulated input is in danger of invalid testing. *Reliability* of a criterion requires that a given application of the criterion to choosing a test data case must *always* yield either a successful or an unsuccessful test. In other words, if one test case chosen according to a criterion yields a successful test, all others chosen in the same way must also be successful.

While validity is relatively easy to discover by examining a test data selection criterion, reliability is difficult because it is dependent on the program under test. For example, suppose a program expects an input variable t in the range $0 < t < n$ and one of these values $, 0 < x < n$, causes an overflow. Then if the test data criterion for the input variable t is chosen to be [$t = 0$ or $t = n$ or $0 < t < n$], it is unreliable.

In choosing test data criteria one common guideline is that every code sequence in a program must be exercised by a test plan. That this is necessary is obvious, since one has little confidence in code that has never executed satisfactorily in a controlled test. *Path testing,* as this is called, is a relatively weak method, however, since many types of errors will not be exposed even if all sequences of code (or path segments, as they are called) are exercised. Rather, path testing should be regarded as the minimum effort to be invested in any thorough test.

17-9.3 Test Management

Just as it is important to carefully modularize the design of a program, so it is equally important to modularize the test plan of the program. Naturally, the management of testing can follow the design methodology employed, since this is likely to be the most appropriate approach. For example, *top-down* testing is most naturally applied to a program developed in this way. Here, submodules are replaced by dummy modules, sometimes called *stubs,* in order to test an upper-level module. On the other hand, *bottom-up* testing is more appropriate for a program developed in this way. In this case, driving programs need to be written to exercise the lower-level modules.

We find that top-down testing is more natural, since the stubs can evolve into the actual modules required. Also, the driving program for the module at level 0 is the only one required for a complete sequence of top-down tests, although it may need to be enlarged or modified as the sequence proceeds. On the other hand, a sequence of bottom-up tests requires that a new driving program be written at each level. Of course, either technique can borrow from the other where necessary: A bottom-up test can insert stubs in place of lower-level modules, and a top-down test can bypass the upper levels and directly test lower levels.

Very large programs must be tested in a carefully controlled sequence. The basic unit of testing is, quite naturally, the information-hiding module, in whatever form it appears. The first step, *unit testing,* is to test each such module. When each appears to meet its specifications (i.e., be correct) and to function reliably, then *integration testing* proceeds. Here, whether it be top-down, bottom-up, or another structure, it is the module interactions that must be tested.

Once a complete set of programs, intended to work together, has been integrated, it is tested as a whole. This step, *subsystem testing,* is really just the final step of integration testing. Finally, the programs are given to their intended operators for *field testing.* It is here that the programs finally operate in the intended environment and reveal whether all the care in design and testing was well spent.

There are two notable pitfalls in testing that can be avoided with some extra work. The first is *black box testing,* in which the test data selection is made independent of the internal structure of the program. This is inherently unreliable and, in any case, the structural information is available, so why not use it? The one place where black box testing is useful, however, is in field testing where, of course, the users cannot be expected to do anything other than provide a real environment independent of the internal program structure.

The second pitfall is that once an incorrect or undesirable test result is found and its source identified and corrected, the testing sequence should not simply be resumed at that point. Experience has shown that the correction of errors, or any modification of a program, often introduces other errors. Thus a program may regress in its correctness when modified. *Regression testing* is simply the process of backing up in the test plan sequence to gain assurance that this has not happened. Of course, one must decide how much retesting is required. A minimum guideline is to retest every interaction that a modified module has with other modules. A clean module interconnection structure with a high degree of information hiding helps immensely, of course. Retesting of the modified module itself must depend on the internal structure of the module.

EXERCISES

17-1 Redesign the desk calculator example of Chap. 6, using the principle of information hiding. One possible design consists of a main program plus two information-hiding modules. The first module could be an I/O module with operations to read and write "elements"; that is, numbers and special characters. The second could be the calculator module containing all stored data. Your design should consist of an algorithm for the main program plus informal specifications for each operation of the two modules.

17-2 Redesign the example assembler of Chap. 8, using the principle of information-hiding modules.

17-3 Write a set of formal specifications for an abstract data type "array of integers" having the properties that you would expect of a type with this name, (a) using an explicit method, and (b) using an implicit method.

17-4 Implement the program designed in Exercise 17-1. Write and carry out a systematic test plan for this program. Carefully explain your reasoning in designing this test plan.

17-5 Modify the program from Exercise 17-4 to include complete error-handling capabilities using the return code method. Discuss how you might approach the problem of testing this modified program.

REFERENCES

This chapter has attempted a great deal in a few pages. Consequently, the ideas have not been explained to the depth required for more than a very introductory treatment. Fortunately, a wealth of further reading exists. Kerighan (1974) contains many hints and principles for improving coding practice. Myers (1976) discusses a variety of aspects of reliability from a very practical viewpoint. The excellent four-volume series "Current Trends in Programming Methodology," edited by Yeh (1977 and 1978), comprises a collection of tutorial papers covering the current state of technology in software development. This series is an important source of material for the student serious about further study in software engineering.

Much of the impetus for the systematic top-down development of software derives from Dijkstra (1972) and Mills (1971). These should be read by any serious student. Another important source document is Parnas (December, 1972) which discusses some principles to be applied in decomposing a large program into modules.

Guttag (1978) provides a more detailed explanation of abstract data types. Much of the material in this chapter derives from that paper and others by J. V. Guttag. Goodenough (1977) provides a very readable tutorial on testing theory and principles.

CHAPTER EIGHTEEN

THE MITE SYSTEM

This chapter contains the detailed design of a program that is small enough to be comprehended and yet large enough to exhibit sufficient complexity for careful design methods to be necessary. The program, a multiprogramming interactive text editor called MITE, provides a rudimentary text editing capability for several alphanumeric screen terminals with the capability for long-term storage of text. MITE is intended to provide three things for the student: (1) a demonstration of a well-structured design, (2) an example of some of the mechanisms presented earlier, principally multiprogramming, and (3) an exercise in programming and testing a large system. As such, much value may be gained by studying the project even if an implementation is not attempted. However, implementation would undoubtedly clarify much for the student.

A structural design for MITE is described in this chapter. An example implementation is available from the author.

18-1 MITE FUNCTIONAL SPECIFICATIONS

The following specifications for MITE are admittedly ambiguous and incomplete. Current specification methods are not yet sufficiently well developed to allow us to attempt a formal specification. However, the detail in additional informal specifications would probably obscure the overall structure. Therefore, for our purpose here of showing a systematic design process we shall simply fill in the specification details as we proceed.

MITE is an in-memory text editor that manipulates text of up to 128 lines of 72 characters each. Only 20 lines may be displayed at any one time on the screen of an alphanumeric display. A user of MITE can sign on, initialize the text by asking MITE to read input from a specified place, enter text directly from the terminal, edit the text, store or print the text by asking MITE to write output to a specified place, and finally sign off.

As shown in Fig. 18-1, each line of text is displayed with an eight-character line number on the right, making a total display size of 20 by 80 characters. Lines are numbered 1 to 128, and line numbers are displayed with leading blanks.

Signing on is accomplished by turning on the terminal and typing CON-TROL L. The system responds with the prompt word MITE at the bottom of the screen and expects the user to answer with a two-digit user code. If the code is invalid, MITE responds with the message INVALID and waits for another sign on attempt. If the code is valid, MITE responds with the message START and displays lines 1 to 20, which are initially blank.

Along with the normal typewriter characters, MITE responds to characters which cause the cursor to move one position either up, down, left, or right. MITE automatically scrolls the display up or down when necessary.

When text is entered, characters are stored at a position determined by the current cursor position within the displayed 20 lines. The user types in the normal way to enter text and the cursor is automatically advanced when a

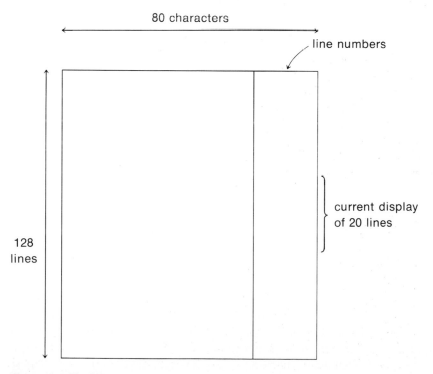

Figure 18-1 The MITE text structure.

character is entered. The cursor may be moved anywhere on the screen to specify the entry point of the text. Typing on top of an existing character causes it to be replaced. Typing a RETURN causes the cursor to be positioned at the first character of the following line with the screen scrolled up if necessary.

Alternatively, characters at the present cursor position may be deleted, or characters may be inserted before the character at the present cursor position. A character is deleted by typing a CONTROL D character, which causes the rest of the line to be shifted left and a blank inserted at the end of the line. The cursor remains stationary. To insert characters a user must first enter "insert mode" by typing CONTROL I. While in insert mode, any character typed is inserted before the character at the present cursor position; the rest of the line is shifted to the right, and the last character is lost. To leave insert mode, the user must again type CONTROL I.

Typing CONTROL N deletes the line containing the cursor. Typing CONTROL S inserts a blank line before the line containing the cursor. In both cases, the physical cursor position remains constant.

MITE also allows the user to execute the following commands by typing a CONTROL character followed by the command's parameter which is typed, followed by a RETURN, on the bottom line of the screen following a prompt word:

1. DISPLAY TO(CONTROL T) displays the text. The first line to appear on the screen is specified by the line number parameter; if a line number is omitted, the default is one.
2. FIND(CONTROL F) finds the first occurrence of the string given as a parameter at or after the current cursor position. The cursor is positioned at the first character of the string if it exists or else at the last character of the text.
3. READ(CONTROL R) reads a new text file from a specified file given as parameter. The first twenty lines are automatically displayed.
4. WRITE(CONTROL W) writes the text file to a specified file given as parameter.

QUIT(CONTROL U) terminates a session.

18-2 MITE STRUCTURAL DESIGN USING ABSTRACT DATA TYPES

The structural description of a system is produced to allow the designer to concretely exhibit the module relationships and to perform some consistency checks on the design before any extensive internal module design begins. The consistency checking of the module interfaces could be performed automatically by a compiler for the language in use here. However, as noted in the last chapter, we shall use a language which, although close to Pascal, does not have a generally available compiler. If used, a compiler could check a structural description to ensure that all operations expected by a module, and used to implement its own operations, are provided by lower-level modules. It could also ensure that the upper-level module uses the operations correctly (the types of the formal and actual parameters are identical).

The structural design does not describe the algorithms used to implement the operations. It only indicates the representation of each type in terms of its component abstract types and primitive types of the base language (in our case Pascal) and describes the operations of a type solely in terms of calls to operations of its component types. The operations of the lowest-level modules (types with no component types) are left with a null procedure body.

An operation's description consists of a procedure heading, specifying the operation's name and all names and types of its formal parameters, and a procedure body made up of calls to other operations if any are required. We have given the description in a top-down manner, starting with the complete main program of MITE, which contains calls on operations of the most abstract type (a text editor), and proceeding through the more "concrete" types. If we were to actually feed this description through a compiler, the order would have to be reversed to satisfy Pascal scope and identification rules.

The system data type "text_ed," of which MITE is a particular instance, is decomposed into the three component types "user_id_table," "text," and "device_set" (see Fig. 18-2).

The type "user_id_table" provides a table of all valid user codes for the system. It is used during the log-on to a terminal. "User_id_table" is implemented in terms of the abstract type "list" and the primitive type "user_id."

The type "text" provides the text storage area for the system and has operations to enter, insert, and delete characters, insert and delete lines, and so on. It is implemented in terms of the type "text_store," which in turn uses the type "list." There is one instance of "text_store" for each terminal in the system.

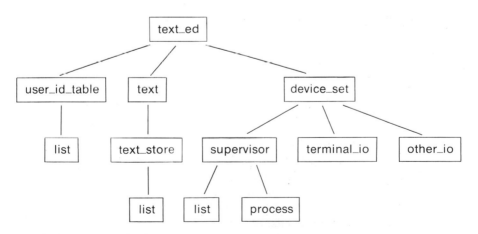

Figure 18-2 MITE structural decomposition.

The type "device_set" provides all the peripherals, such as terminals, disks, tapes, and line printer for the system. All system peripherals are grouped in the single component type "device_set" to allow the scheduling and synchronizing of the processes associated with these peripherals to be completely hidden; "device_set" is decomposed into the component types "supervisor," "terminal_io," and "other_io." The terminals of the system are implemented by "terminal_io," and all other peripherals are implemented by the type "other_io." The type "supervisor" provides all scheduling and synchronization of the peripherals. It is implemented by using the type "process" and by a set of queues implemented by the type "list." The queues are used to provide exclusive control for the disks, tapes, line printer, and so on. There is a queue to hold the waiting processes for each of these peripherals.

The main program of MITE is shown below. It is the starting point of the design and shows how the operations of the major data type, text_ed, are employed to implement MITE.

Before we plunge into the details of this design, several comments are needed to put it in a proper context. First, the list module provides more facilities than are required by the other modules in MITE. This is to be expected in a design of this sort since, in creating a generally useful module, one may choose to put more function in it than the immediate application dictates. The catch, however, is that the resultant "overkill" may affect the efficiency of the job at hand. Second, this design is a pure top-down system. As a result, in several places there occur several levels of indirect procedure calls from higher levels to lower levels. These have been left in MITE for clarity, but in an actual implementation either they should be eliminated in an optimization phase following the design phase, or some alternative to procedure calls should be used for implementation. Finally, we have taken some liberties with Pascal syntax in the interest of simplicity and clarity. These mostly take the form of comments where certain syntactic forms are required. The result is that certain details have been omitted; these must be completed with regard to the particular programming environment in use.

```
PROGRAM mite_text_editor;

    CONSTANT max = 128; { size of text area }
             n = 3; { number of interactive terminals }
             m = 3; { number of other I/O devices }

    MODULE text_ed;

    EXPORT text_ed,new_text_ed,create_processes,
           get_next_char,logon,cursor_up,cursor_down,
           cursor_right,cursor_left,return,enter_char,
           change_mode,delete_char,delete_line,insert_line,
           display_to,find,read,write,quit;
```

```
TYPE text_ed = definition deferred;

PROCEDURE new_text_ed(VAR mite: text_ed;
                      t1, . . . ,tn: terminal_add;
                      d1, . . . ,dm: device_add);
   { initializes a new system mite supporting
     terminals t1 through tn and file devices d1
     through dm };

PROCEDURE create_processes( VAR mite: text_ed;
                            VAR t: terminal_add;
                            s: stack_size );
   { creates n−1 identical copies of the calling process.
     t is an output parameter containing a unique terminal
     address };

FUNCTION get_next_char( VAR mite: text_ed;
                        t: terminal_add): CHAR ,
   { reads a character from terminal t.
     Any character, other than a CTRL L, is ignored
     unless a logon has been carried out };

PROCEDURE logon( VAR mite: text_ed;
                 t: terminal_add);
   { carries out the logon sequence with the user };

PROCEDURE cursor right(VAR mite: text_ed;
                       t: terminal_add) ;
   { moves the cursor of terminal t up one
     position from its current position. If
     necessary the display is scrolled down one line };

PROCEDURE cursor_down( VAR mite: text_ed;
                       t: terminal_add);
   { moves the cursor of terminal t down one
     position from its current position. If
     necessary the display is scrolled up one line };

PROCEDURE cursor_right(VAR mite: text_ed;
                       t: terminal_add);
   { moves the cursor of terminal t right one
     position from its current position and to
     the beginning of the next line down if necessary.
     The display is scrolled up one line if required };
```

```
PROCEDURE cursor_left( VAR mite: text_ed;
                       t: terminal_add);
  { moves the cursor of terminal t left one
    position from its current position and to
    the end of the next line up if necessary.
    The display is scrolled down one line if required };


PROCEDURE return( VAR mite: text_ed;
                  t: terminal_add );
  { moves the cursor of terminal t to the beginning
    of the text line following the current line. This procedure
    is similar to cursor_down };


PROCEDURE enter_char( VAR mite: text_ed;
                      t: terminal_add;
                      a: CHAR);
  { enters the character a into the text at the position
    of the cursor of terminal t. If the terminal is in
    insert mode the character is inserted with the
    rightmost character of the line being lost. The
    screen is scrolled if necessary. };


PROCEDURE change_mode( VAR mite: text_ed;
                       t: terminal add);
  { changes from normal to insert mode or vice versa };


PROCEDURE delete_char( VAR mite: text_ed;
                       t: terminal_add);
  { deletes the character at the position of the cursor
    of terminal t. The line is shifted left with a blank
    inserted at the right. The display is updated. };


PROCEDURE delete_line( VAR mite: text_ed;
                       t: terminal_add );
  { deletes the line containing the cursor of
    terminal t and updates the screen };


PROCEDURE insert_line( VAR mite: text_ed;
                       t: terminal_add );
  { inserts a blank line before the line containing
    the cursor of terminal t and updates the screen };
```

PROCEDURE display_to(VAR mite: text_ed;
                    t: terminal_add);
    { reads a line number i from terminal t and
      rewrites the screen so that line number i
      appears as the top line };

PROCEDURE find(VAR mite: text_ed;
                    t: terminal_add);
    { reads a string a from terminal t.
      The cursor of terminal t is advanced to the first
      character of the first occurrence of string a at or
      after the current cursor position. If no such string
      exists the cursor is positioned at the last character
      in the text };

PROCEDURE read(VAR mite: text_ed;
                    t: terminal_add);
    { reads into the text area for terminal t a text
      copy that was previously stored in file fn by a MITE
      write command. fn is read as a command parameter };

PROCEDURE write(VAR mite: text_ed;
                    t: terminal_add);
    { writes a copy of the text for terminal t into the
      file fn. The previous contents of fn are lost.
      fn is read as a command parameter. };

PROCEDURE quit(VAR mite: text_ed;
                    t: terminal_add);
    { terminates a session so that all further input
      is ignored until a log-on is carried out }

END; {text_ed}

VAR te: text_ed;
VAR ch: character;
    t,t1, . . . ,tn: terminal_add;
    d1, . . . ,dm: device_add;

BEGIN

    assign values to t1, . . . ,tn,d1, . . . ,dm;
    new_text_ed(te,t1, . . . ,tn,d1, . . . ,dm);
    {determine size ssize of process stack

```
        at this point so that the process can
        be copied correctly};
        create_processes(te,t,ssize);

    REPEAT

        ch := get_next_char(te,t);

        CASE ch OF

            CTRL L:  logon (te,t);
                 ↑ : cursor_up(te,t);
                 ↓ : cursor_down(te,t);
                 →:  cursor_right(te,t);
                 ←:  cursor_left(te,t);
            CTRL I:   change_mode(te,t);
            CTRL D:  delete_char(te,t);
            CTRL N:  delete_line(te,t);
            CTRL S:  insert_line(te,t);
            CTRL T:  display_to(te,t);
            CTRL F:  find(le,t);
            CTRL R:  read(te,t);
            CTRL W:  write(te,t);
            CTRL Q:  quit(te,t);
            printable character: enter_char(te,t,ch);
            carriage return: return(te,t)


    UNTIL FALSE

END.
```

At this point we have a specification of the type text_ed in the form of informal semantic and precise syntax specifications. Our task now is to make decisions as to the representation of an instance of text_ed. To make this task more manageable, these decisions are in the form of the definition of other abstract data types upon which the representation of text_ed can be based. These component types encapsulate design decisions that we wish to defer as we design text_ed. With some thought one might identify the three types already discussed: user_id_table, text, and device_set. There are certainly other reasonable designs as well. Definition of the data structure of text_ed proceeds as follows:

```
TYPE text_ed = RECORD
            u : user_id_table;
            tx : text;
            d : device_set
            END;
```

Semantic and syntactic specifications for these three types are now defined and, to complete the structural specification, representative calls on these operations are shown within the operations of text_ed. In each of these calls representative parameters are shown merely to make a syntactically correct program that could be checked by a compiler. The relationships between the operations of text_ed and its component types are, therefore, explicitly shown. The design process continues until the types defined are either directly available in the base language or are trivial to implement. The resulting structural design is shown below.

{ The primitive data types used in the design }

```
TYPE device_add = nullterm . . devm;
        { device_add consists of the sequence of values
          nullterm,term1, . . . ,termn,nulldev,dev1, . . . ,devm.
          The mapping from these addresses to physical
          machine addresses is implementation dependent.}
        terminal_add = nullterm . . termn;
        user_id = 0 . . 99;
        charno = 1 . . 80;
        lineno = 0 . . max;
        line_buffer = ARRAY[1 . . 72] OF CHAR;
        dev_use = (in, out, aux);
        filename = ARRAY[0 . . 5] OF CHAR;
        condition = (blocked,ready,running);
        string = RECORD
                l : 0 . .72;
                s: ARRAY[0 . . 72] OF CHAR
                END;

MODULE text_ed;

    EXPORT text_ed,new_text_ed,create_processes,
            get_next_char,logon,cursor_up,cursor_down,
            cursor_right,cursor_left,return,enter_char,
            change_mode,delete_char,delete_line,insert_line,
            display_to,find,read,write,quit;

    TYPE text_ed = RECORD
                u : user_id_table;
                tx : text;
                d : device_set
                END;

    PROCEDURE new_text_ed ( VAR mite: text_ed;
                            t1, . . . , tn: terminal_add;
                            d1, . . . , dm: device_add );
```

```
      { initializes a new text editor mite}
      VAR t: terminal_add;
           c: CHAR;
           i : INTEGER;
      BEGIN
        new_device_set( mite.d, t1, . . . , tn, d1, . . . ,dm );
        new_text( mite.tx, t1, . . . , tn );
        new_user_id_table( mite.u );
        move_cursor( mite.d, t, i, i );
        i := adv_cursor( mite.d, t );
        i := screensz( mite.d, t );
        i := linesz( mite.d, t );
        put_char( mite.d, t, c )
      END;


  PROCEDURE create_processes ( VAR mite: text_ed;
                               VAR t: terminal_add;
                               s: stack_size );
      { creates n−1 identical copies of the calling process.
        t is an output parameter containing a unique
        terminal address }
      BEGIN
          start_processes( mite.d, t, s)
      END;


  FUNCTION get_next_char(VAR mite: text_ed;
                         t: terminal_add): CHAR ;
      { reads a character from terminal t. Any character
        other than a CTRL L is ignored unless a logon has
        been carried out. }
      BEGIN
        get_next_char := get_char( mite.d, t)
      END;


  PROCEDURE logon ( VAR mite : text_ed;
                    t : terminal_add );
      { provides the log on for the system }
      VAR a : user_id;
          i: INTEGER;
          c: CHAR;
          b: BOOLEAN;
      BEGIN
          i := screensz( mite.d, t);
          put_char( mite.d, t, c);
```

```
            i := adv_cursor( mite.d, t);
            c := get_char(mite.d, t);
            b := search( mite.u, a);
            activate_process( mite.d, t, a);
            move_cursor( mite.d, t, i, i)
      END;

   PROCEDURE cursor_up ( VAR mite : text_ed;
                         t : terminal_add );
      { This procedure moves the cursor of terminal t
        up one position from its current position. If
        necessary the display is scrolled down a line. }
      VAR i: INTEGER;
          c: CHAR;
          ln: lineno;
          cn: charno;
      BEGIN
            move_cursor ( mite.d, t, i, i );
            i := adv_cursor ( mite.d, t );
            i := crow ( mite.d, t );
            i := ccolm ( mite.d, t );
            stored (mite.d, t, ln );
            i := getdsp ( mite.d, t );
            put_char ( mite.d, t, c );
            c := get_text char ( mite.tx, t, ln, cn )
      END;

   PROCEDURE cursor_down( VAR mite : text_ed;
                          t : terminal_add );
      { moves the cursor of terminal t down one
        position. This procedure is similar to
        cursor_up. };

   PROCEDURE cursor_right( VAR mite : text_ed;
                           t : terminal_add );
      { moves the cursor of terminal t right one position
        and moves to the start of the next line down if
        necessary. This procedure is similar to cursor_up. };

   PROCEDURE cursor_left( VAR mite : text_ed;
                          t : terminal_add );
      { moves the cursor of terminal t left one position
        and moves to the end of the next line up if
        necessary. This procedure is similar to
        cursor_up. };
```

```
PROCEDURE enter_char ( VAR mite : text_ed;
                            t: terminal_add;
                            a : CHAR );
    { enters the character a into the text at a
      position corresponding to the position of the
      cursor of terminal t, moves the cursor one
      to the right and alters the screen. The
      character is written or inserted according to
      the current mode of t. }
    VAR i: INTEGER;
        c: CHAR;
        ln: lineno;
        cn: charno;
    BEGIN
        storec( mite.tx, t, ln, cn, c);
        i := crow( mite.d, t);
        i := ccolm( mite.d, t);
        normal_mode(mite.tx, t);
        put_char( mite.d, t, c);
        i := adv_cursor( mite.d, t);
        move_cursor( mite.d, t, i, i );
        stored( mite.tx, t, ln );
        ln := getdsp( mite.tx, t);
        c :=get_text_char( mite.tx, t, ln, cn)
    END;


PROCEDURE change_mode( VAR mite: text_ed,
                            t: terminal_add);
    { changes from insert to normal mode or vice versa }
    BEGIN
        switch_mode( mite.tx, t)
    END;


PROCEDURE delete_char( VAR mite: text_ed;
                            t: terminal_add );
    { deletes the character at the position determined by
      the cursor position of terminal t. The rest of the
      line is shifted left and a blank added on the end.}
    VAR i: INTEGER;
        c: CHAR;
        ln: lineno;
        cn: charno;
    BEGIN
        i := crow( mite.d, t );
        i := ccolm( mite.d, t );
```

```
        ln := getdsp( mite.tx, t);
        deletc( mite.tx, t, ln, cn );
        ln := adv_cursor( mite.d, t);
        put_char( mite.d, t, c );
        c := get_text_char( mite.tx, t, ln, cn );
        move_cursor( mite.d, t, i, i )
    END;


PROCEDURE delete_line( VAR mite: text_ed;
                            t: terminal_add );
    { deletes the line corresponding to the line
      containing the cursor of terminal t and updates
      the screen }
    VAR i: INTEGER;
        c: CHAR;
        ln: lineno;
    BEGIN
        i := crow( mite.d, t);
        i := ccolm( mite.d, t);
        ln := getdsp( mite.tx, t);
        deletl( mite.tx, t, ln);
        move_cursor( mite.d, l, i, i);
        i := adv_cursor( mitc.d, t);
        put_char( mite.d, t, c);
        c := get_text_char( mite.tx, t, ln, cn)
    END;


PROCEDURE Insert_line( VAR mite: text_ed;
                            t: terminal_add ),
    { inserts a blank line before the line in the
      text corresponding to the line containing the
      cursor of terminal t and updates the screen.
      This procedure is similar to delete_line.};


PROCEDURE display_to ( VAR mite: text_ed );
                            t: terminal_add );
    { rewrites the screen starting from line ln
      where ln is read from the terminal }
    VAR i: INTEGER;
        c: CHAR;
        ln: lineno;
        cn: charno;
    BEGIN
        i := screensz( mite.d, t);
        c := get_char( mite.d, t);
```

```
            stored( mite.tx, t, ln );
            move_cursor( mite.d, t, i, i );
            i := adv_cursor( mite.d, t );
            put_char( mite.d, t, c );
            c := get_text_char( mite.tx, t, ln, cn )
        END;

    PROCEDURE find ( VAR mite: text_ed;
                         t: terminal_add );
        VAR i: INTEGER;
            c: CHAR;
            a: string;
            b: BOOLEAN;
            ln: lineno;
            cn: charno;
        BEGIN
            c := get_char( mite.d, t);
            i := screensz( mite.d, t);
            b := scan( mite.tx, t, a, ln, cn, ln, cn);
            move_cursor( mite.d, t, i, i);
            i := adv_cursor( mite.d, t);
            put_char( mite.d, t, c);
            i := crow( mite.d, t);
            i := ccolm( mite.d, t);
            i := txtmax( mite.tx);
            stored( mite.tx, t, i);
            c := get_text_char( mite.tx, t, i, i);
            i := getdsp( mite.tx, i)
        END;

    PROCEDURE read( VAR mite: text_ed;
                        t: terminal_add);
        { implements the read command }
        VAR buf: ARRAY[0 . . 71] OF CHAR;
            i: INTEGER;
            c: CHAR;
            fn: ARRAY[0 . . 5] OF CHAR;
            ln: lineno;
            cn: charno;
        BEGIN
            open_file_input( mite.d, t, fn);
            close_file( mite.d, t, fn);
            read_file( mite.d, t, fn, buf);
            storel( mite.tx, t, ln, buf);
            stored( mite.tx, t, ln);
```

```
        move_cursor( mite.d, t, i, i);
        i := screensz( mite.d, t);
        put_char( mite.d, t, c);
        i := adv_cursor( mite.d, t);
        c := get_text_char( mite.tx, t, ln, cn);
        c := get_char( mite.d, t)
    END;


PROCEDURE write( VAR mite: text_ed;
                     t: terminal_add);
    { implements the write command }
    VAR buf: ARRAY[0 . . 71] OF CHAR;
        i: INTEGER;
        c: CHAR;
        fn: ARRAY[0 . . 5] OF CHAR;
        ln: lineno;
        cn: charno;
    BEGIN
        ln := txtmax( mite.tx, t);
        open_file_output( mite.d, t, fn);
        olooc file( mite.d, t, fn),
        write_file( mite.d, t, fn, buf);
        getline( mite.tx, t, ln, buf);
        move_cursor( mite.d, t, i, i);
        i := screensz( mite.d, t);
        put_char( mite.d, t, c);
        i := adv_cursor( mite.d, t);
        storec( mite.tx, t, ln, cn);
        c := get_char( mite.d, t)
    END;


PROCEDURE quit( VAR mite: text_ed;
                     t: terminal_add );
    { implements the quit command }
    VAR i: INTEGER;
        c: CHAR;
        ln: lineno;
        cn: charno;
    BEGIN
        deactivate_process( mite.d, t );
        clear_text( mite.tx, t);
        c := get_text_char( mite.tx, t, ln, cn);
        move_cursor( mite.d, t, i, i);
        i := adv_cursor( mite.d, t);
```

```
            i := screensz( mite.d, t);
            put_char( mite.d, t, c)
        END;

    PROCEDURE return( VAR mite: text_ed;
                         t: terminal_add );
            { moves the cursor to the beginning of the line
              following the current line. This procedure is
              similar to cursor-down. }
END; {text_ed}
```

{ The type "user_id_table" represents a table of valid user codes that can only be altered at program creation time }

```
MODULE user_id_table;

        EXPORT user_id_table,new_user_id_table,search;

        TYPE user_id_table = list ;

        PROCEDURE new_user_id_table( VAR u: user_id_table) ;
            { creates a list of programmer determined codes }
            VAR i: user_id;
            CONST c = programmer determined;
            BEGIN
                new_list( u, c);
                append( u, i)
            END;

        FUNCTION search( VAR u: user_id_table;
                            a: user_id ): BOOLEAN ;
            { returns TRUE if the id is valid }
            VAR i: INTEGER;
            BEGIN
                i := select( u, a)
            END

    END; { user_id_table}
```

{ The type "text" represents the text storage area for all the terminals. The operations allow the user to enter, insert, and delete characters, get a character from the text, insert and delete lines, and so on. }

```
    MODULE text;
```

```
EXPORT text,new_text,get_text_char,switch_mode,clear_text,
        storec,deletc,insrtc,insrtl, deletl,stored,getdsp,
        getline,storel,txtmax,scan;


TYPE text = ARRAY[term1 . . termn] OF text_store;


PROCEDURE new_text( VAR y: text; t1, . . . , tn: terminal_add);
        { associates a text storage area with each terminal
          in the system identified by t1, . . . , tn }
        VAR i: terminal_add;
        BEGIN
            new_text_store(y[i], max)
        END;


FUNCTION get_text_char( VAR y: text
                        t: terminal_add;
                        l: lineno;
                        c: charno) : CHAR ;
        { reads a character from a text area. Line numbers
          are generated for character positions 73 to 80. }
        VAR ch: CHAR,
        BEGIN
            ch := char_value( y[t], l, c)
        END;


PROCEDURE switch_mode( VAR y: text;
                        t: terminal_add );
        { changes a terminal from normal to insert mode
          or vice versa }
        BEGIN
            change_mode(y[t])
        END;


PROCEDURE clear_text( VAR y: text;
                        t: terminal_add );
        { sets a text area to blanks }
        VAR l: lineno; c: charno,
        BEGIN
            set_char_value( y[t], l, c, ' ')
        END;


PROCEDURE storec( VAR y: text;
                        t: terminal_add;
                        l: lineno;
```

```
                    c: charno;
                    a: CHAR );
    { stores the character a in the text for
      terminal t at the position determined by l
      and c }
    BEGIN
        set_char_value( y[t], l, c, a )
    END;


PROCEDURE deletc( VAR y: text;
                    t: terminal_add;
                    l: lineno;
                    c: charno );
    { deletes the character at the position determined
      by l and c in terminal t's text }
    VAR ch: CHAR;
    BEGIN
        ch := char_value( y [t], l, c );
        set_char_value( y[t], l, c, ch )
    END;


PROCEDURE insrtc( VAR y: text;
                    t: terminal_add;
                    l: lineno;
                    c: charno;
                    a: CHAR );
    { inserts character a at position determined by l
      and c into t's text }
    VAR ch: CHAR;
    BEGIN
        ch := char_value( y[t], l, c );
        set_char_value( y[t], l, c, ch )
    END;


PROCEDURE deletl( VAR y: text;
                    t: terminal_add;
                    l : lineno );
    { deletes line l from t's text. }
BEGIN
    delete_line2(y[t], l)
END;


PROCEDURE insrtl( VAR y: text;
                    t: terminal_add;
                    l : lineno );
    { inserts a blank line in t's text before line l. }
```

```
BEGIN
    insert_line( y[t], I )
END;


PROCEDURE stored ( VAR y: text;
                        t: terminal_add;
                        I : lineno );
    { sets the top line number displayed on screen
      to I }
    BEGIN
        set_display( y[t], I)
    END;


FUNCTION getdsp ( VAR y: text;
                        t: terminal_add ):lineno;
    { function returning the line number of the top
      line currently displayed }
    BEGIN
        getdsp := display ( y[t] )
    END;


PROCEDURE getline( VAR y: text;
                        t: terminal_add;
                        l: lineno;
                        VAR buf: line_buffer );
    { function returning line l of t's text in buf }
    VAR c: charno;
        ch: CHAR;
    BEGIN
        ch := char_value( y[t], l, c )
    END;


PROCEDURE storel ( VAR y: text;
                        t: terminal_add;
                        l: lineno;
                        buf: line_buffer );
    { writes the line buf into line l of t's text }
    VAR c: charno;
        ch: CHAR;
    BEGIN
        set_char_value( y[t], l, c, ch )
    END;


FUNCTION txtmax ( VAR y : text;
                        t: terminal_add ): lineno ;
```

```
                { function returning the length of the
                   user's non-blank text area in lines }
                BEGIN
                     txtmax := length( y[t])
                END;

        FUNCTION scan( VAR y : text;
                            t: terminal_add;
                            a : string;
                            l: lineno;
                            c : charno;
                            VAR lf: lineno;
                            VAR cf: charno ): BOOLEAN ;
             { function returning in lf and cf the position of the first
               occurrence of a starting at the position determined
               by l and c in t's text. A FALSE result indicates
               an unsuccessful search. }
        VAR c: CHAR;
        BEGIN
             c := char_value( y[t], l, c )
        END;

END; {text}

{ The type "text_store" represents the storage for a
  terminal. There is one instance of "text_store" for
  each terminal in the system. The operations return the
  line number of the current top line of the display,
  change this number, access data in the store, and maintain
  the terminal mode. }

MODULE text_store;

        EXPORT  text_store,new_text_store,delete_line2,change_mode,
                insert_line,display,set_display,clear_value,
                set_char_value,clear_store,char_value,length;

        TYPE text_store = RECORD
                            mode: BOOLEAN;
                            dsp: 1 . . max−19;
                            data: ARRAY[1 . . max] OF
                                    ARRAY[1 . . 72] OF CHAR;
                            lines: list;
                            length: lineno
                          END;
```

```
PROCEDURE new_text_store( VAR t: text_store;
                              m: lineno);
    { initializes a new blank text area of m lines. }
    VAR i: INTEGER;
    BEGIN
        new_list( t.lines, m);
        append( t.lines, i)
    END;


PROCEDURE delete_line( VAR t: text_store;
                          l:lineno );
    { deletes line l from text store t and adds a
      new blank line to the end of the store }
    VAR i: INTEGER;
    BEGIN
        value( t.lines, l, i);
        delete( t.lines, l);
        append( t.lines, i)
    END;


PROCEDURE change_mode( VAR t: text_store);
        { changes the mode of terminal t from normal
          to insert or vice versa };


PROCEDURE insert_line( VAR t: text_store;
                          l: lineno );
    VAR i: INTEGER;
    BEGIN
        value( t.lines, max, i);
        delete( t.lines, max);
        insert( t.lines, l, i)
    END;


FUNCTION display( VAR t: text_store): lineno;
    { function returning the line number of the top line
      of displayed text };


PROCEDURE set_display( VAR t: text_store;
                          l: lineno );
    { sets the display pointer to l };


FUNCTION char_value( VAR t: text_store;
                        l: lineno;
                        c: charno): CHAR;
```

```
                   { returns the value of character stores at position
                     determined by I and c };

        PROCEDURE set_char_value( VAR t: text_store;
                                       I: lineno;
                                       c: charno;
                                       a: CHAR );
                   { sets the character at position determined by I
                     and c to a };

        PROCEDURE clear_store( VAR t: text_store );
                   { sets the storage t to all blanks }

END; {text_store}
```

{ The type representing the set of all peripheral devices
 in the system—terminals, disks, tapes, line printer.
 These are grouped together to allow the synchronizing
 and scheduling of the processes associated with these
 devices to be hidden from the user. }

```
MODULE device_set;

        EXPORT device_set,new_device_set,put_char,get_char,
               activate_process,deactivate_process,crow,
               ccolm,move_cursor,read_file,write_file,
               open_file_input,open_file_output,close_file,
               start_processes,adv_cursor,linesz,screensz;

        TYPE device_set = RECORD
                             sup: supervisor;
                             tml: ARRAY[term1 . . termn] OF terminal_io;
                             o: ARRAY[dev1 . . devm] OF other_io;
                             use: ARRAY[dev1 . . devm] OF dev_use;
                             sz: ARRAY[term1 . . termn] OF INTEGER;
                             id: ARRAY[term1 . . termn] OF user_id
                          END;

        PROCEDURE new_device_set( VAR z: device_set;
                                       t1, . . . ,tn: terminal_add;
                                       d1, . . . ,dm: device_add );
                   { returns an initialized device_set. Each terminal writer
                     is initialized to be ready. }
                   VAR t: terminal_add;
```

```
BEGIN
    new_supervisor( z.sup,t1, . . . ,tn,d1, . . . ,dm);
    new_terminal_io( z.tml[t],t1 );
    new_other_io( z.o[d1], d1 )
    fill_output_buffer( z.tml[t],' ')
END;

PROCEDURE put_char( VAR z: device_set;
                    t: terminal_add;
                    a: CHAR );
    { places character a on t's screen at present
      cursor position }
    BEGIN
        block( z.sup, t, t );
        fill_output_buffer( z.tml[t], a )
    END;

FUNCTION get_char( VAR z: device_set;
                   t: terminal_add ): CHAR;
    { function returning the next character from
      terminal t }
    BEGIN
        get_char := take_input_buffer( z.tml[t]);
        block( z.sup, t, t )
    END;

PROCEDURE activate_process( VAR z: device_set;
                            t: terminal_add;
                            a: user_id );
    { assigns terminal t to user a } ;

PROCEDURE deactivate_process ( VAR z: device_set;
                               t: terminal_add );
    { removes terminal t from last user };

FUNCTION crow( VAR z: device_set;
               t: terminal_add ): INTEGER ;
    { function returning value of line containing
      cursor }
    BEGIN
        crow :=  cursor_row( z.tml[t]
    END;

FUNCTION ccolm( VAR z: device_set;
                t: terminal_add ): INTEGER;
```

```
    { function returning the column number containing
      cursor }
    BEGIN
        ccolm :=  cursor_colm( z.tml[t] )
    END;


FUNCTION adv_cursor( VAR z: device_set;
                            t: terminal_add): INTEGER;
    { advances the cursor one position to the right or,
    if required, to the beginning of the next line.
    A value of -1 is returned if scrolling is required.
    A value of 0 indicates no scrolling. }
    VAR a: CHAR;
        l,c: INTEGER;
    BEGIN
        block( z.sup, t, t);
        fill_output_buffer( z.tml[t], a);
        set_cursor_row( z.tml[t], l);
        set_cursor_colm( z.tml[t], c)
    END;


PROCEDURE move_cursor( VAR z: device_set;
                           t: terminal_add;
                           !: INTEGER;
                           c: INTEGER ) ;
    { changes the position of the cursor to the
      position (l,c) }
    VAR a: CHAR;
    BEGIN
        block( z.sup, t, t);
        fill_output_buffer( z.tml[t], a);
        set_cursor_row( z.tml[t], l);
        set_cursor_colm( z.tml[t], c)
    END;


FUNCTION readfile ( VAR z: device_set;
                        t: terminal_add;
                        fn: filename;
                        buf: line_buffer ): BOOLEAN ;
    { function returning a line of text from a
      peripheral device }
    VAR d: device_add;
        b: BOOLEAN;
```

```
      BEGIN
          line_from_dev( z.o[d], buf, b);
          block( z.sup, t, d )
      END;


PROCEDURE writefile( VAR z: device_set;
                          t: terminal_add;
                          fn: filename;
                          buf: line_buffer );
      { writes the value of buf into the next line of
        file fn };
      VAR d: device_add;
      BEGIN
          line_to_dev( z.o[d], buf);
          block( z.sup, t, d)
      END;


PROCEDURE open_file_input( VAR z: device_set;
                                t: terminal_add;
                                fn: filename );
      { opens file fn for input }
      VAR d: device_add;
      BEGIN
          request( z.sup, t, d);
          openinput( z.o[d], fn,d)
      END;


PROCEDURE open_file_output( VAR z: device_set;
                                 t: terminal_add;
                                 fn: filename );
      { opens file fn for output }
      VAR d: device_add;
      BEGIN
          request( z.sup, t, d);
          openoutput( z.o[d], fn,d)
      END;


PROCEDURE close_file ( VAR z: device_set;
                            t: terminal_add;
                            fn: filename );
      { closes file fn }
      VAR d: device_add;
```

```
            BEGIN
                release(z.sup, d);
                close( z.o[d], fn,d)
            END;

        PROCEDURE start_processes( VAR z: device_set;
                                   VAR t: terminal_add;
                                   s: INTEGER );
            { creates n copies of the calling process and
              returns with a unique terminal address in
              parameter t }
            BEGIN
                initialize_processes( z.sup, t, s)
            END;

        FUNCTION screensz(z: device_set;
                          t: terminal_add): INTEGER;
            {returns the number of screen lines};
        FUNCTION linesz(z: device_set;
                        t: terminal_add): INTEGER;
            {returns the number of characters per line}
END; {device_set}

{ The type representing the scheduler of all processes
  in the system. }
    MODULE supervisor;

    EXPORT supervisor,new_supervisor,request,release,
           block,interrupt,initialize_processes;

    TYPE supervisor = RECORD
                        procmap: ARRAY[term1 . . termn] OF process;
                        processtab: list;
                        device_qs: ARRAY[dev1 . . devm] OF list;
                        waiting: BOOLEAN;
                        ints: ARRAY[dev1 . . devm] OF BOOLEAN;
                        busy: ARRAY[dev1 . . devm] OF BOOLEAN;
                        stacks: ARRAY[term1 . . termn] OF
                                ARRAY[0 . . stackmax] OF INTEGER
                      END;

    PROCEDURE new_supervisor( VAR m: supervisor;
                              t1, . . . ,tn: terminal_add;
                              d1, . . . ,dm: device_add );
```

```
    { initializes a new supervisor. No processes are
      made ready in this function, however. }
    VAR t: terminal_add;
    BEGIN
        new_list( m.processtab, n);
        new_process( m.procmap[t]);
        append( m.processtab, t)
    END;


PROCEDURE request( VAR m: supervisor;
                        t: terminal_add;
                        d: device_add );
    { obtains exclusive control of the peripheral d.
      If d is busy, the running process is put on a
      waiting queue for d and a new process is set
      running.}
    VAR term: terminal_add;
        i: INTEGER;
        c: condition;
    BEGIN
        append( m.device_qs[d], t);
        append( m.processtab, term);
        c := status( m.procmap[term]);
        set_status( m.procmap[term], running);
        load_regs( m.procmap[term]);
        remove( m.processtab, term);
        i := select( m.processtab, t);
        delete( m.processtab, i);
        unload_regs( m.procmap[t])
    END;


PROCEDURE release( VAR m: supervisor;
                        d: device_add );
    { releases control of the peripheral d }
    VAR t: terminal_add;
    BEGIN
        remove( m.device_qs[d], t);
        append( m.processtab, t);
        set_status( m.procmap[t], ready )
    END;


PROCEDURE block( VAR m: supervisor;
                        t: terminal_add;
                        d: device_add );
```

```
        { blocks a process until an interrupt occurs. A new
         process is set running if possible.}
        VAR c: condition;
            term: terminal_add;
        BEGIN
            set_status( m.procmap[t], c);
            c := status( m.procmap[term]);
            unload_regs( m.procmap[t]);
            remove( m.processtab, term);
            append( m.processtab, term);
            load-regs( m.procmap[term]);
            reset_int_bit( m.procmap[t]);
            set_mask( m.procmap[t], d)
        END;


    PROCEDURE interrupt( VAR m: supervisor;
                              d: device_add );
        { signals that an interrupt from device d has
          occurred by setting an interrupt bit in the
          process table. If waiting, the process is
          made ready and the bit reset.}
        VAR t: terminal_add;
            c: condition;
            dev: device_add;
        BEGIN
            remove( m.processtab, t);
            append( m.processtab, t);
            dev := mask( m.procmap[t]);
            set_mask( m.procmap[t], dev);
            set_int_bit( m.procmap[t]);
            set_status( m.procmap[t], ready);
            c := status( procmap[t])
        END;


    PROCEDURE initialize_processes( VAR m: supervisor;
                                    VAR t: terminal_add;
                                        s: INTEGER );
        { creates n identical copies of the calling process
          and inserts a unique return value in parameter t
          for each of these. All copies are initialized to
          the ready state except for one which is running
          and which returns immediately from the call.}
        VAR tm: terminal_add;
        VAR c: condition;
```

```
    BEGIN
        copy_process( m.procmap[tm], m.stacks[tm], t, tm, s, c)
    END

END; {supervisor}

{The type implementing a process. There is one instance for each terminal.}
MODULE process;

    EXPORT process,new_process,status,set_status,int_bit,
            set_int_bit,reset_int_bit,load_regs,unload_regs,
            mask,set_mask,copy_process;

    TYPE process = RECORD
                        msk : device_add;
                        regs : ARRAY[0 . . 9] OF INTEGER;
                        stat : condition;
                        ints : BOOLEAN
                    END;
            stackarr = ARRAY[0 . . stackmax] OF INTEGER;

    PROCEDURE new_process( VAR p: process),
            { initializes a new process data structure without
                making it ready };

    FUNCTION status( VAR p: process ): condition;
            {function returning the status of process p };

    PROCEDURE set_status( VAR p: process;
                                c: condition );
            { sets the status of process p to c };

    FUNCTION int_bit( VAR p: process ): BOOLEAN;
            { function returning the value of the interrupt
                bit for process p };

    PROCEDURE set_int_bit( VAR p: process );
            { sets the interrupt bit for process p to TRUE };

    PROCEDURE reset_int_bit( VAR p: process );
            { resets the interrupt bit for process p to FALSE };

    PROCEDURE load_regs( VAR p: process );
            { loads the processor registers with values
                from process p, which becomes the
                running process. };
```

```
PROCEDURE unload_regs( VAR p: process );
    { saves the current register contents in process p };

FUNCTION mask( VAR p: process ): device_add;
    { function returning the value of the mask—
      an indication of what peripheral process p
      is blocked on };

PROCEDURE set_mask( VAR p: process;
                         d: device_add );
    { sets the mask of process p to d };

PROCEDURE copy_process( VAR p: process;
                        VAR stk: stackarr;
                        VAR t: terminal_add;
                        tm: terminal_add;
                        s: INTEGER;
                        c: condition );
    { This is a key procedure in initializing the text editor.
      A copy of the calling process is created in p. A stack
      of depth s is allocated in stk, and a copy of the caller's
      stack made therein. The status of p is set to c. The
      return value for parameter t of p is set to tm.}

END; {process}

{ the type representing a terminal to the system.
  There is one instance for each terminal. }
MODULE terminal_io;

    EXPORT terminal_io,new_terminal_io,fill_output_buffer,
           take_input_buffer,cursor_row,set_cursor_row,
           cursor_colm,set_cursor_colm;

    TYPE terminal_io = RECORD
                        row: INTEGER;
                        col: INTEGER;
                        input_buffer: CHAR;
                        output_buffer: CHAR
                       END;

    PROCEDURE new_terminal_io ( VAR t: terminal_io;
                                term: terminal_add );
        { initializes a new terminal_io data structure for
          terminal term };
```

```
PROCEDURE fill_output_buffer( VAR t: terminal_io;
                              a: CHAR );
    { transmits character a to terminal t };

FUNCTION take_input_buffer( VAR t: terminal_io ): CHAR;
    { returns the next character from terminal t };

FUNCTION cursor_row( VAR t: terminal_io ): INTEGER;
    { returns the row of the cursor of terminal t };

PROCEDURE set_cursor_row( VAR t: terminal_io;
                          r: INTEGER );
    { records the row position of the cursor of terminal
      t as r };

FUNCTION cursor_colm( VAR t: terminal_io ): INTEGER;
    { returns the column of the cursor of terminal t };

PROCEDURE set cursor colm( VAR t: terminal_io;
                           c: INTEGER );
    { records the column position of the cursor of terminal
      t as c }

END; {terminal_io}

{ the type representing peripherals other than
  terminals. There is one instance for each disk,
  tape, line printer, etc.}
MODULE other_io;

    EXPORT other_io,new other io,line_to_dev,line_from_dev,
           openinput,openoutput,close;

    TYPE other_io = device dependent code;

    PROCEDURE new_other_io ( VAR o: other_io;
                             d: device_add );
        { initializes a new other_io data structure for device d };

    PROCEDURE line_to_dev( VAR o: other_io;
                           buf: line_buffer );
        { writes buf to device o };

    PROCEDURE line_from_dev( VAR o: other_io;
                             VAR buf: line_buffer;
                             VAR eof: BOOLEAN );
```

```
                { returns a block from device o in buf.
                  eof is set to TRUE if end-of-file occurs.};

          PROCEDURE openinput( VAR o: other_io;
                               fn: filename;
                               d: device_add );
             { opens file fn for input };

          PROCEDURE openoutput( VAR o: other_i;
                                fn: filename;
                                d: device_add );
             { opens file fn for output };

          PROCEDURE close( VAR o: other_io;
                           fn: filename;
                           d: device_add );
             { closes file fn }

     END; {other_io}

  { the type implementing an unordered list of any type.
    The element type is specified manually by the TYPE kind.}

  MODULE list;

        EXPORT list,new_list,first,append,delete,insert,select,
               remove, value, list_bounds;

        CONSTANT list_pool_size = implementation dependent;
                 max_list_length = implementation dependent;

        TYPE listref = 0 . . list_pool_size;
             list_bounds = 1 . . max_list_length;
             list = RECORD
                       max_list_size: list_bounds;
                       no_of_elements: INTEGER;
                       head,tail: listref
                    END;
             kind = INTEGER;

        VAR free:listref;
            ptrs: ARRAY[listref] OF listref;
            values: ARRAY[listref] OF kind;
            { Some implementation-dependent initialization
              of these data is required.}
```

```
PROCEDURE new_list ( VAR l: list;
                          maxlength : INTEGER);
    { creates a new list of length maxlength };

PROCEDURE first ( VAR l : list;
                      VAR v : kind );
{ function returning the value, in v, of the first
  element of list l. Returns an error if the
  list is empty.};

PROCEDURE append ( VAR l : list;
                       VAR v : kind );
    { appends the element v to the end of list l };

PROCEDURE remove ( VAR l : list;
                       VAR v : kind );
    { returns the value, in v, of the first element
      on the list l and deletes it from the list.
      Returns an error if the list is empty.};

PROCEDURE delete ( VAR l : list;
                       i : list bounds );
    { removes the element at position i from list l.
      Returns an error if the list length is less than i.};

PROCEDURE insert ( VAR l : list;
                       i : list_bounds );
                       v : kind );
    { inserts the value v at position i on list l.
      Returns an error if the list length is less than i−1.};

FUNCTION select ( VAR l : list;
                      VAR v : kind ): list_bounds;
    { function returning the position of the first
      element with value v found on the list.
      Returns an error if an element is not found. };

PROCEDURE value ( VAR l: list;
                      i : list_bounds;
                      VAR v: kind );

    { returns in v the value of the list element at
      position i. Returns an error if the list length
      is less than i.}

END; {list}
```

18-3 IMPLEMENTATION NOTES

In implementing MODULEs in assembly language, the semantics of language statements must, of course, be carried out manually. To assist in this process, so that the discipline of designing in a high-level language is not negated by detailed programming errors, the MACRO facility can be used. Obviously, however, implementation in a high-level compiled language is preferable.

We can define types in a top-down fashion with MACROs in the following way. (Unfortunately, names must be compressed to six characters or less reducing the readability considerably.) A type definition can appear as

```
.MACRO TEXTED
USRTAB
TEXT
DEVSET
.ENDM
```

where USRTAB, TEXT, and DEVSET are also defined as macros in their respective modules as follows:

```
.MACRO   USRTAB
LIST
.ENDM

.MACRO   TEXT
.REPT    n
TXTSTR
.ENDR
.ENDM

.MACRO   DEVSET
SUP
.REPT    n
TML
.ENDR
.REPT    m
AUXIO
.ENDR
.REPT    m
USE
```

```
.ENDR
.REPT     n
SZ
.ENDR
.REPT     n
ID
.ENDR
.ENDM
```

Lower-level modules define nested-type structures until the entire data structure is defined. We shall refer to these definitions as *type definition* MACROs. A program using these definitions can then implement the statements

```
VAR tx: text_ed;
    term: terminal_add;
```

with the assembly-language statements

```
TX:    TEXTED
TERM:  .WORD TTYNUM  ; TTYNUM IS DEFINED
                     ; ELSEWHERE AS A TERMINAL
                     ; ADDRESS
```

and operations can be invoked (using log-on as an example) with the statement

```
CALL LOGON <#TX,TERM>
```

The foregoing is very straightforward. The problem comes within a MODULE as the programmer that defined an abstract type with abstract components references one of these components. For example, the programmer of the MODULE for type TEXTED needs to be able to reference its components, namely, USRTAB, TEXT, and DEVSET, in any particular variable of the type. The first component, USRTAB, can be referenced, because it is located at the same address as the variable itself. However, the implementer of TEXTED does not know how much memory is allocated to USRTAB or TEXT, so the other components are not so easily located. Any solution must be based on obtaining this information (the size of memory allocated to an abstract type) from the definition of the type.

One possible solution is to require the implementer of a type to define another MACRO to be associated with the type definition MACRO. The purpose of this associated MACRO is to inform users of the type as to how much memory is allocated to any representation of the type. Suppose that we write all of these MACROs, which can be called *type structure* MACROs, in the general form TYPxxx. The type structure MACRO for TEXTED can then be written

```
.MACRO TYPTE
TYPTE1=TYPCNT
TYPUT
TYPTE1=TYPCNT-TYPTE1
TYPTE2=TYPCNT
TYPTX
TYPTE2=TYPCNT-TYPTE2
.ENDM
```

where TYPCNT is initialized to zero at the beginning of an assembly. It is used to count memory locations allocated in any MACRO named TYPxxx. Each such type structure MACRO will increment TYPCNT if memory is defined in the type definition. Where a component is an abstract type, such a MACRO definition contains a call to the type structure MACRO for that type.

For example, to determine the memory allocated to a representation of the type TEXTED, the implementer of TEXTED writes

```
TYPTE
```

to initialize the following variables at assembly time:

```
U:  .WORD  0
T:  .WORD  TYPTE1
D:  .WORD  TYPTE1+TYPTE2
```

Within a procedure of the MODULE TEXTED, then, a component of a variable TX of type TEXTED can be referenced as shown in the following example:

```
C:  .BYTE 0

    . . .

    MOV   #TX,TEMP
    ADD    D,TEMP
    CALL  PUTCHAR <TEMP,TERM,C>
```

In this way an abstract data type can be defined by one type definition MACRO and associated operations. These are all that the user of the type needs to define and manipulate variables of the type. If, however, the user of a type z is the implementer of a higher-level type including z as a component, then the type structure MACRO for z is required in addition to the type definition MACRO and the operations.

The above definition method using MACROs has two serious deficiencies. First, it is not very readable and somewhat clumsy to write. Second, it leaves responsibility for correct access to the representation of abstract types to the user of these types. This is directly contrary to the fundamental property that the representation of abstract types should not be accessible to users. The

method does, however, allow a program designed with the dis
level notation to be implemented in a systematic manual fashi
direct ad hoc methods. It is with this approach in mind tha
sented here.

If tighter control over access to representations is desired, then mem
can be allocated internally to the defining MODULE as with the list module in
MITE. Then the representation made available to the user is simply a reference
to the representation maintained by the MODULE. If memory is to be allocated at run time, then, of course, this approach must be used.

EXERCISES

18-1 Implement and test the MODULE list.

18-2 Implement and test the MODULE user_id.

18-3 Implement the MODULE text_ed and partially test the log-on and log-off functions. Why can
you not test them completely?

18-4 Implement device_set. Complete the test of log-on and log-off.

18-5 Implement terminal_io.

18-6 Test (partially) device_set and terminal_io by providing dummy text and supervisor MOD-
ULEs.

18-7 Implement text and text_store.

18-8 Test all functions of MITE that exercise the text MODULE.

18-9 Implement the MODULEs supervisor and process.

18-10 Test MITE for more than one simultaneous user.

18-11 Implement and test other_io.

18-12 List is the only module in MITE, other than the supervisor, with local variable data. Explain
why processes do not interfere with each other in manipulating this data in list. Why is it necessary
to prevent interference in accessing the local data of the supervisor?

18-13 Optimize your complete program by eliminating indirect calls. Are there other optimizations
that you can suggest?

REFERENCES

Texts with large examples and case studies that can be used as projects are fairly rare. Donovan
(1977) and Halstead (1974) are two of which the author is aware, although there may be others that
are not as available.

FLOATING-POINT NUMBERS

Numbers with an integer part and a fractional part can be represented in n bits by simply assuming the existence of a binary point within the n-bit number.

<— i bits —> <——— f bits ———>

```
┌──────────────┬─────────────────────┐
│              │                     │
└──────────────┴─────────────────────┘
```
—binary point

<——————— n bits ———————>

All arithmetic algorithms remain the same as for pure integers. The programmer must, however, keep track of the location of the binary point and interpret the stored value accordingly.

Choosing the location of the binary point creates a conflict. Making the fractional part (f bits) large yields better accuracy but a smaller possible range of values. Making the integer part (i bits) large yields a larger possible range of values but poorer accuracy in the fractional part. The solution lies in making the fractional part as large as practical and not storing the complete integer part. Rather, the number is expressed in exponential or *floating-point* form, in which only the fraction part and exponent parts are stored.

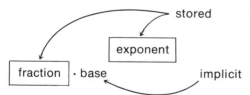

The base is implicitly assumed to be some fixed value.

For example, using decimal notation, 523.64 can be written as

$$0.52364 \cdot 10^3$$

Only the fraction 0.52364 and the exponent 3 need be stored to record the value of the number. It can be assumed that the base is always 10.

Floating-point number systems thus permit the representation of numbers that are large in magnitude as well as the representation of numbers accurate to a reasonably large number of digits.

There are many possible forms for floating-point numbers. One simple format is shown below.

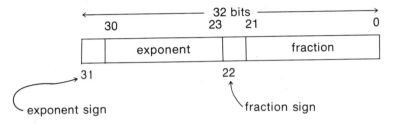

Bits 0 to 21: Fraction magnitude
Bit 22: Fraction sign; 0 denotes positive, 1 denotes negative
Bits 23 to 30: Exponent magnitude
Bit 31: Exponent sign; 0 denotes positive, 1 denotes negative

The value of numbers represented in the format shown above is

$$\text{fraction} \cdot 2^{\text{exponent}}$$

For example, -3.5_{10} is represented as

| 000000010111100000000000000000000 |

since

$$-3.5_{10} = -11.1_2 = -.111_2 \cdot 10_2{}^{10_2}$$

12.75 is represented as

| 000000100011001100000000000000000 |

since

$$12.75 = 1100.11_2 = .110011_2 \cdot 10_2{}^{100_2}$$

In order to gain the most accuracy possible, one should almost always normalize floating-point numbers after every arithmetic operation. Normalization involves shifting the fraction part left and subtracting 1 from the exponent for every digit position shifted, until leading zeros are eliminated. Thus, the leading fractional digit is always nonzero.

The representation just described uses signed-magnitude representation for the exponent and fraction parts. It is possible, of course, to use other representations, such as 2's complement.

Before describing some existing floating-point number representations, the term *fraction* will be dropped and the "fraction" part will be called *mantissa*. As will be seen in a moment, the former term is misleading in some cases.

The floating-point representations of three machines will be described. All of these machines, the Burroughs B6500, the IBM System/370 and the PDP-11, have floating-point instructions (optional on the PDP-11) that take floating-point numbers as operands.

IBM System/370 floating-point numbers can occupy one 32-bit word,

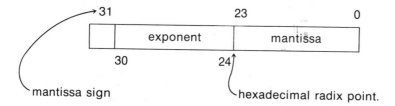

Bits 0 to 23: Mantissa as six binary-coded hexadecimal digits
Bits 24 to 30: Exponent in binary excess − 64 representation
Bit 31: Mantissa sign

Example: IBM System/370 format

The mantissa is stored as six binary-coded hexadecimal digits with the radix point at the left. The assumed base is, therefore, 16. The exponent is a 7-bit integer in excess − 64 representation; the value of the exponent part is the magnitude of this 7-bit integer minus 64. For example,

Exponent value	Stored as
−64	0000000
−63	0000001
.	.
.	.
.	.
−1	0111111
0	1000000
1	1000001
.	.
.	.
63	1111111

Using an "excess" representation eliminates the double zero of normal signed-magnitude representation. The following are examples of IBM System/370 floating-point numbers:

Value	Representation
-3.5_{10}	`1100000100111000000000000000000000`
12.75_{10}	`0100000111001100000000000000000000`
0.03125_{10}	`0011111110000000000000000000000000`

Burroughs B6500 floating-point numbers can occupy one 47-bit word.

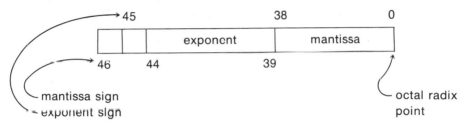

Bits 0 to 38: Mantissa as 13 binary-coded octal digits
Bits 39 to 44: Exponent magnitude
Bit 45: Exponent sign
Bit 46: Mantissa sign

Example: Burroughs B6500 format

The mantissa is stored as 13 binary-coded octal digits with radix point at the right. The assumed base is, therefore, 8. The exponent is stored as a 7-bit signed magnitude integer.

Placing the radix point at the right yields a number representation in which integers are not distinguished from other floating-point numbers. An integer is simply a floating-point number with a zero exponent. The following are examples of Burroughs B6500 floating-point numbers:

Value	Representation
-3.5_{10}	`11000001000000000000000000011100`
12.75_{10}	`01000001000000000000001100110`
-5_{10}	`1000000000000000000000000000101`

PDP-11 floating-point numbers occupy 32-bits in 4 consecutive bytes.

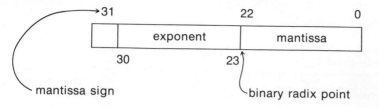

Bits 0 to 22: Mantissa magnitude in binary with leftmost bit not stored
Bits 23 to 30: Exponent in excess 128 notation
Bit 32: Mantissa sign

The mantissa is stored in binary signed magnitude. Although there are 24 bits of accuracy in the mantissa, only the least significant 23 are stored. This is possible since the mantissa is always normalized (as is usual in floating-point representations) so that the significant bit is always 1. Therefore, it need not be explicitly stored. The exponent is stored in excess 128 notation, giving an exponent range of -128 to 127.

The following are examples of PDP-11 floating-point numbers:

Value	Representation
-3.5_{10}	11000001011000000000000000000000
12.75_{10}	01000010010011000000000000000000
0.03125_{10}	00111111000000000000000000000000

SUMMARY OF PDP-11/03 INSTRUCTIONS

Notation	Meaning
$-$	Not affected
?	Conditionally set
,	Concatenated
$dst_{i,j}$ or $src_{i,j}$	Bits i to j inclusive
dst_i or src_i	Bit i
reg	Register operand
$\otimes$	Exclusive or (XOR)
ψ	Optional instruction

Single address

Mnemonic	Name	Operation	N	Z	V	C
CLR(B)	Clear	$0 \rightarrow dst$	0	1	0	0
COM(B)	Complement(1's)	$\sim C(dst) \rightarrow dst$	?	?	0	1
INC(B)	Increment	$C(dst)+1 \rightarrow dst$	?	?	?	$-$
DEC(B)	Decrement	$C(dst)-1 \rightarrow dst$	?	?	?	$-$
NEG(B)	Negate	$-C(dst) \rightarrow dst$	?	?	?	?
TST(B)	Test	examine $C(dst)$	?	?	0	0
ROR(B)	Rotate right	$C,C(dst_{n-1,1}) \rightarrow dst$ $C(dst_0) \rightarrow C$	?	?	?	?
ROL(B)	Rotate left	$C(dst_{n-2,0}),C \rightarrow dst$ $C \rightarrow dst_0$	?	?	?	?
ASR(B)	Arithmetic shift right	$C(dst)/2 \rightarrow dst$	?	?	?	?
ASL(B)	Arithmetic shift left	$C(dst)\cdot2 \rightarrow dst$	?	?	?	?
SWAB	Swap bytes	$C(dst_{7,0}) \rightarrow dst_{15,8}$ $C(dst_{15,8}) \rightarrow dst_{7,0}$	?	?	0	0
ADC(B)	Add carry	$C(dst)+C \rightarrow dst$	?	?	?	?
SBC(B)	Subtract carry	$C(dst)-C \rightarrow dst$	?	?	?	?
SXT	Sign extend	IF n=1 THEN $0 \rightarrow dst$ ELSE $-1 \rightarrow dst$	$-$	?	0	$-$
MFPS	Move byte from PS	$C(PS) \rightarrow dst$	?	?	0	$-$
MTPS	Move byte to PS	$C(src) \rightarrow PS$	?	?	?	?

Double address

Mnemonic	Name	Operation	N	Z	V	C
MOV(B)	Move	C(src) −> dst	?	?	0	−
CMP(B)	Compare	Examine C(src)−C(dst)	?	?	?	?
ADD	Add	C(src)+C(dst) −> dst	?	?	?	?
SUB	Subtract	C(dst)−C(src) −> dst	?	?	?	?
BIT(B)	Bit test	Examine C(src)∧C(dst)	?	?	0	−
BIC(B)	Bit clear	~C(src)∧(C(dst) −> dst	?	?	0	−
BIS(B)	Bit set	C(src)∨C(dst) −> dst	?	?	0	−
XOR	Exclusive or	C(reg)⊗C(dst) −> dst	?	?	0	−
MUL*	Multiply	C(reg)·C(src) −> reg	?	?	0	?
DIV*	Divide	C(reg)/C(src) −> reg	?	?	?	?
ASH*	Arithmetic shift	C(reg) shifted arithmetically number of bits given in $src_{5,0}$	?	?	?	?
ASHC*	Arithmetic shift combined	Same as for ASH on double register	?	?	?	?
FADD*	Floating add	See manual				
FSUB*	Floating subtract	See manual				
FMUL*	Floating multiply	See manual				
FDIV*	Floating divide	See manual				

Branches

Mnemonic	Name	Branch condition
BR	Branch	Always
BNE	Branch if not equal to zero	Z = 0
BEQ	Branch if equal to zero	Z = 1
BPL	Branch if plus	N = 0
BMI	Branch if minus	N = 1
BVC	Branch if overflow clear	V = 0
BVS	Branch if overflow set	V = 1
BCC	Branch if carry clear	C = 0
BCS	Branch if carry set	C = 1
BGE	Branch if greater than or equal to zero	N⊗V = 0
BLT	Branch if less than zero	N⊗V = 1
BGT	Branch if greater than zero	Z ∨ (N ⊗ V) = 0
BLE	Branch if less than or equal to zero	Z ∨ (N ⊗ V) = 1
BHI	Branch if higher	C ∨ Z = 0
BLOS	Branch on lower if same	C ∨ Z = 1
BHIS	Branch on higher if same	C = 0
BLO	Branch if lower	C = 1

Control flow

Mnemonic	Name	Operation
JMP	Jump	C(dst) $->$ PC
JSR	Jump to subroutine	dst $->$ temp
		C(reg) $->$ $\downarrow$(SP)
		C(PC) $->$ reg
		temp $->$ PC
RTS	Return from subroutine	C(reg) $->$ PC
		$\uparrow$(SP) $->$ reg
MARK	See manual	
SOB	Subtract one and branch	C(reg)-1 $->$ reg
		branch if C(reg)
		not equal to zero

Trap and Interrupt

Mnemonic	Name	Operation
EMT	Emulator trap	C(PS) $->$ $\downarrow$(SP)
		C(PC) $->$ $\downarrow$(SP)
		C(30) $->$ PS
		C(32) $->$ PC
TRAP	Trap	Trap with vector at 34
BPT	Breakpoint trap	Trap with vector at 14
IOT	Input-output trap	Trap with vector at 20
RTI	Return from interrupt	$\uparrow$(SP) $->$ PC
		$\uparrow$(SP) $->$ PS
RTT	Return from trap	Same as RTI with T bit
		trap inhibited

General

Mnemonic	Name	Operation
HALT	Halt	Stops processor from any execution
WAIT	Wait for interrupt	Stops processor instruction fetching until next interrupt
RESET	Reset bus	Initializes processor-device communication
NOP	No operation	
CLN	Clear N	
CLV	Clear V	
CLZ	Clear Z	
CLC	Clear C	
CCC	Clear all codes	
SEN	Set N	
SEV	Set V	
SEZ	Set Z	
SEC	Set C	
SCC	Set all codes	

PASCAL SYNTAX

identifier

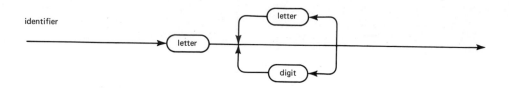

unsigned integer

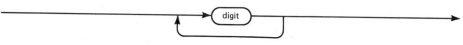

unsigned number

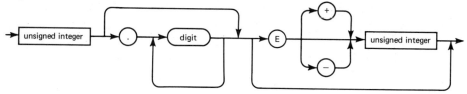

unsigned constant

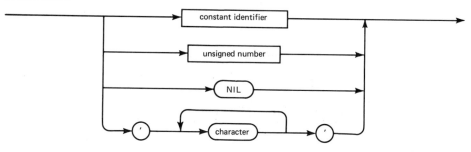

constant

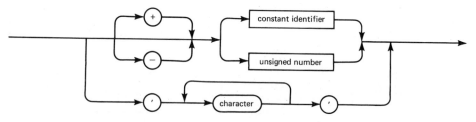

simple type

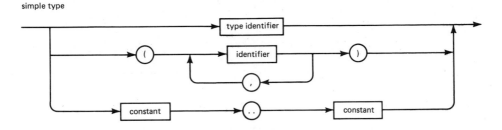

type

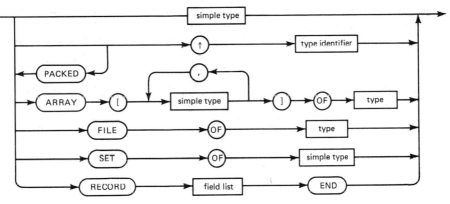

field list

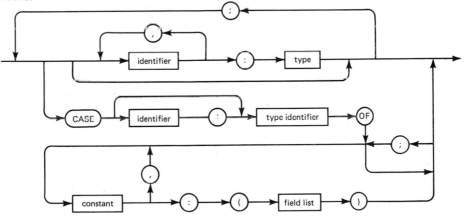

variable

field identifier

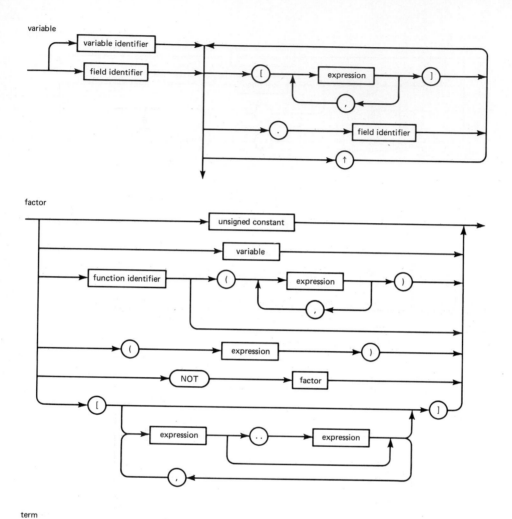

factor

term

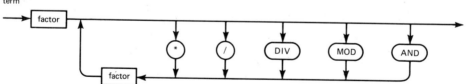

simple expression

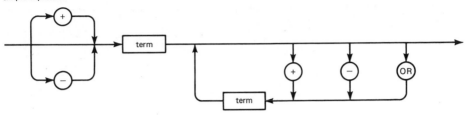

expression

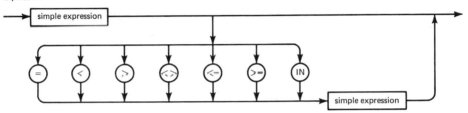

parameter list

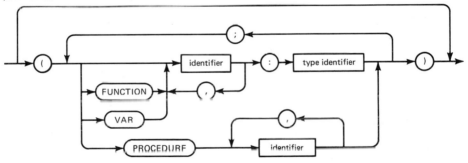

statement

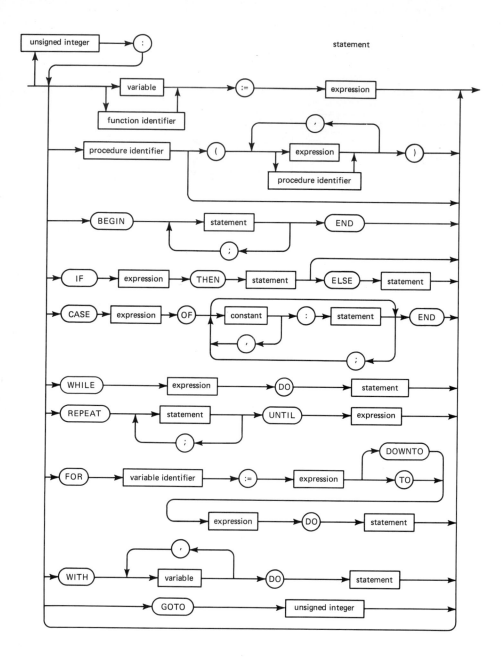

block

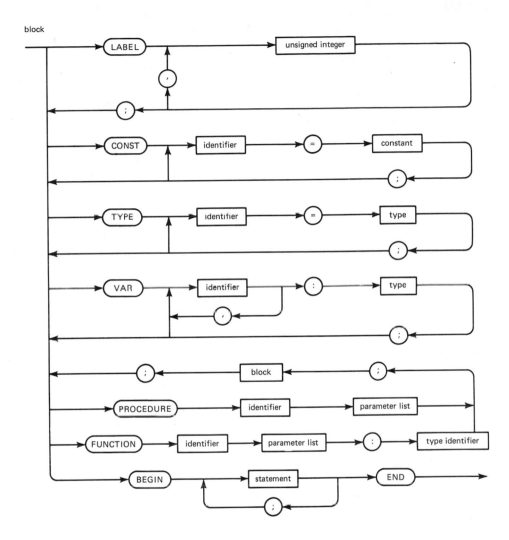

program

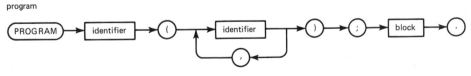

BIBLIOGRAPHY

American Telephone and Telegraph Co.: *The Bell System Technical Journal*, vol. 57, no. 6, part 2, 1978.

Arden, B. W., B. A. Galler, T. C. O'Brien, and F. H. Westervelt: Programming and Addressing Structure in a Time-Sharing Environment, *JACM*, vol. 13, no. 1, pp. 1–16, January, 1966.

Arora, S. R., and W. T. Dent: Randomized Binary Search Technique, *CACM*, vol. 12, no. 2, pp. 77–80, February, 1969.

Barron, D. W.: "Assemblers and Loaders," American Elsevier, New York, 1969.

Batson, A.: The Organization of Symbol Tables, *CACM*, vol. 8, no. 2, pp. 111–112, February, 1965.

Bell, G., et al.: A New Architecture for Mini-Computers—The DEC PDP-11, *Proc. AFIPS, SJCC*, vol. 36, pp. 657–675, 1970.

Berztiss, A. T.: "Data Structures—Theory and Practice," Academic, New York, 1971.

Bowles, K. L.: "Microcomputer Problem Solving Using Pascal," Springer-Verlag, New York, 1978.

Brinch-Hansen, P.: "The Architecture of Concurrent Programs," Prentice-Hall, Englewood Cliffs, N.J., 1977.

————: "Operating Systems Principles," Prentice-Hall, Englewood Cliffs, N.J., 1973.

Brown, P. J.: "Macroprocessors," Wiley, New York, 1974.

Clampett, H. A. Jr.: Randomized Binary Searching With Tree Structures, *CACM*, vol. 7, no. 3, pp. 163–165, March, 1964.

Colin, A. J. T.: "Introduction To Operating Systems," American Elsevier, New York, 1971.

Conway, M.: Design of a Separable Transition Compiler, *CACM*, vol. 6, no. 7, pp. 396–408, July, 1963.

Corbato, F. J.: PL/I As a Tool for Systems Programming, *Datamation*, vol. 15, no. 5, pp. 68–76, May, 1969.

Daley, R. C., and P. G. Neumann: A General-Purpose File System for Secondary Storage, *Proc. FJCC*, pt. 1, pp. 213–229, 1965.

Denning, P. J.: Third Generation Computer Systems, *Computing Surveys*, vol. 3, no. 4, 1971.

————: Virtual Memory, *Computing Surveys*, vol. 2, no. 4, pp. 153–187, September, 1970.

Dennis, J. B.: Segmentation and the Design of Multiprogrammed Computer Systems, *JACM*, vol. 12, no. 4, pp. 589–602, October, 1965.

Digital Equipment Corp.: "Edit-11 Text Editor," Maynard, Mass.

————: "Link-11 Linker and Libr-11 Librarian," Maynard, Mass.

————: "Macro-11 Assembler," Maynard, Mass.

————: "Microcomputer Handbook," Maynard, Mass., 1976.

————: "ODT-11R Debugging Program," Maynard, Mass.

————: "RT-11 Monitor Handbook," Maynard, Mass.

Dijkstra, E. W.: Notes on Structured Programming, in "Structured Programming," Academic, New York, 1972.

Donovan, J. J.: "Systems Programming," McGraw-Hill, New York, 1972.

Eckhouse, R. H. Jr.: "Minicomputer Systems: Organization and Programming," Prentice-Hall, Englewood Cliffs, N.J., 1975.

Elson, M.: "Data Structures," Science Research, Chicago, 1975.

Floyd, R. W.: Algorithm 245, Treesort 3, *CACM,* vol. 7, no. 12, p. 701, December, 1964.

Freeman, P.: "Software System Principles," Science Research, Chicago, 1975.

Gear, C. W.: "Computer Organization and Programming," 2d ed., McGraw-Hill, New York, 1974.

Genuys, F. (ed.): "Programming Languages," Academic, New York, 1968.

Goldstine, H. H.: "The Computer From Pascal to von Neumann," Princeton, 1972.

Goodenough, J. B., and S. L. Gerhart: Toward a Theory of Testing: Data Selection Criteria, in R. T. Yeh (ed.), "Current Trends in Programming Methodology," vol. 2, pp. 44–79, Prentice-Hall, Englewood Cliffs, N.J., 1977.

Graham, R. M.: "Principles of System Programming," Wiley, New York, 1975.

Greenwald, I. D.: A Technique for Handling Macro Instructions, *CACM,* vol. 2, no. 11, pp. 21–22, December, 1959.

Guttag, J. V.: The Specification and Application to Programming of Abstract Data Types, Computer Systems Research Group Tech. Rep. CSRG-59, University of Toronto, 1975.

————, E. Horowitz, and D. R. Musser: Abstract Data Types and Software Validation, *CACM,* vol. 21, no. 12, pp. 1048–1064, December, 1978.

Harrison, M. C.: "Data Structures and Programming," Scott, Foresman, Glenview, Ill., 1973.

Heising, W. P.: Note on Random Addressing Techniques, *IBM Systems Journal,* vol. 2, pp. 112–116, June, 1963.

Hellerman, H.: "Digital Computer Systems Principles," McGraw-Hill, New York, 1967.

Holt, R. C., et al.: "Structured Concurrent Programming with Operating System Examples," Addison-Wesley, Reading, Mass., 1978.

Hsiao, D. K.: "System Programming," Addison-Wesley, Reading, Mass., 1975.

Jensen, K., and N. Wirth: "Pascal User Manual and Report," 2d ed., Springer-Verlag, New York, 1974.

Johnson, L. R.: An Indirect Chaining Method for Addressing on Secondary Storage Keys, *CACM,* vol. 4, no. 5, pp. 218–222, May, 1961.

Joy, W. N., S. L. Graham, and C. B. Haley: UNIX Pascal User's Manual, Dept. Electrical Engineering and Computer Science, U. California, Berkeley, 1977.

Katzan, H.: "Computer Organization and the System/370," Van Nostrand Reinhold, New York, 1971.

————: "Computer Systems Organization and Programming," Science Research, Chicago, 1976.

Keiburtz, R.: "Structured Programming and Problem Solving with Pascal," Prentice-Hall, Englewood Cliffs, N.J., 1978.

Kent, W.: Assembler-Language Macroprogramming, *Computing Surveys,* vol. 1, no. 4, pp. 183–196, 1969.

Kernighan, B. W.: "Programming in C: A Tutorial," Bell Labs, Murray Hill, N.J.

———— and P. J. Plauger: "The Elements of Programming Style," McGraw-Hill, New York, 1974.

———— and P. J. Plauger: "Software Tools," Addison-Wesley, Reading, Mass., 1976.

———— and D. Ritchie: "The C Programming Language," Prentice-Hall, Englewood Cliffs, N.J., 1978.

Knuth, D. E.: "The Art of Computer Programming: Fundamental Algorithms," Addison-Wesley, Reading, Mass., 1968.

————: "The Art of Computer Programming: Seminumerical Algorithms," Addison-Wesley, Reading, Mass., 1969.

————: "The Art of Computer Programming: Sorting and Searching," Addison-Wesley, Reading, Mass., 1973.

Lampson, B. W.: A Scheduling Philosophy for Multiprocessing Systems, *CACM,* vol. 11, no. 5, pp. 347–360, May, 1968.

Lions, J.: A Commentary on the UNIX Operating System, Dept. Computer Science, U. New South Wales, Australia, 1977.

———: UNIX Operating System Source Code, Level Six, Dept. Computer Science, U. New South Wales, Australia, 1977.

Lister, A. M.: "Fundamentals of Operating Systems," Macmillan, New York, 1975.

Madnick, S. E.: Design Strategies for File Systems, MIT Project MAC Rep. TR78, October, 1970.

——— and J. W. Alsop: A Modular Approach to File System Design, *Proc. SJCC,* vol. 34, pp. 1–14, 1969.

——— and J. J. Donovan: "Operating Systems," McGraw-Hill, New York, 1974.

Mano, M. M.: "Computer Systems Architecture," Prentice-Hall, Englewood Cliffs, N.J., 1976.

Maurer, W. D.: An Improved Hash Code for Scatter Storage, *CACM,* vol. 11, no. 1, pp. 35–38, January, 1968.

——— and T. G. Lewis: Hash Table Methods, *Computing Surveys,* vol. 7, no. 1, pp. 5–19, March, 1975.

McCarthy, J., F. J. Corbato, and M. M. Daggett: The Linking Segment Subprogram Language and Linking Loader, *CACM,* vol. 6, no. 7, pp. 391–395, June, 1963.

McGee, W. C.: On Dynamic Program Relocation, *IBM Systems Journal,* vol. 4, no. 3, pp. 184–199, 1965.

McIlroy, M. D.: Macro Instruction Extensions of Compiler Language, *CACM,* vol. 3, no. 4, pp. 214–220, April, 1960.

Mills, H. D.: Top-Down Programming in Large Systems, in Rustin (ed.), "Debugging Techniques in Large Systems," pp. 41–55, Prentice-Hall, Englewood Cliffs, N.J., 1971.

Mooers, C. N.: TRAC, A Procedure Describing Language for the Reactive Typewriter, *CACM,* vol. 9, no. 3, pp. 215–219, March, 1966.

Myers, G. J.: "Software Reliability: Principles and Practices," Wiley, New York, 1976.

Nievergelt, J.: Binary Search Trees and File Organization, *Computing Surveys,* vol. 6, no. 3, pp. 195–207, September, 1974.

Organick, E.: "Computer System Organization: The B5700/B6700," Academic, New York, 1973.

Parnas, D. L.: On the Criteria To Be Used In Decomposing Systems Into Modules, *CACM,* vol. 15, no. 12, pp. 1053–1058, December, 1972.

———: A Technique for the Specification of Software Modules with Examples, *CACM,* vol. 15, no. 5, pp. 330–336, May, 1972.

Patt, Y. N.: Variable Length Tree Structures Having Minimum Average Search Time, *CACM,* vol. 12, no. 2, pp. 72–76, February, 1969.

Peterson, J. J., and T. A. Norman: Buddy Systems, *CACM,* vol. 20, no. 6, pp. 421–430, June, 1977.

Presser, L., and J. R. White: Linkers and Loaders, *Computing Surveys,* vol. 4, no. 3, pp. 149–167, 1972.

Proceedings of the Sixth Symposium on Operating System Principles, *Operating Systems Review,* vol. 11, no. 5, 1977.

Randell, B.: A Note on Storage Fragmentation and Program Segmentation, *CACM,* vol. 12, no. 7, pp. 365–369, 372, July, 1969.

——— and C. J. Kuehner: Dynamic Storage Allocation Systems, *CACM,* vol. 8, no. 5, pp. 297–306, May, 1965.

Ritchie, D. M.: "C Reference Manual," Bell Labs, Murray Hill, N. J.

Rosen, S.: Electronic Computers: A Historical Survey, *Computing Surveys,* vol. 1, no. 1, pp. 7–36, March, 1969.

———: "Programming Systems and Languages," McGraw-Hill, New York, 1967.

Schay, G. Jr., and W. G. Spruth: Analysis of a File Addressing Method, *CACM,* vol. 5, no. 8, pp. 459–462, August, 1962.

Shaw, A. C.: "The Logical Design of Operating Systems," Prentice-Hall, Englewood Cliffs, N.J., 1974.

Shell, D. L.: A High Speed Sorting Procedure, *CACM,* vol. 2, no. 1, pp. 30–32, January, 1959.

Stone, H. S., and D. P. Siewiorek: "Introduction to Computer Organization and Data Structures," McGraw-Hill, New York, 1975.

Strachey, C.: A General Purpose Macrogenerator, *Computer Journal,* vol. 8, no. 3, pp. 225–241, 1965.

Sussenguth, E. H. Jr.: Use of Tree Structures for Processing Files, *CACM,* vol. 6, no. 5, pp. 272–279, May, 1963.

Tremblay, J. P., and P. G. Sorenson: "An Introduction to Data Structures with Applications," McGraw-Hill, New York, 1976.

Watson, R. W.: "Timesharing System Design Concepts," McGraw-Hill, New York, 1970.

Webster, C. A. G.: "Introduction to Pascal," Heyden and Son, Philadelphia, 1976.

Western Electric Co.: "Documents for Use with the UNIX Time-Sharing System," 6th ed., 1974.

Wilkes, M. V.: "Time-Sharing Computer Systems," American Elsevier, New York, 1968.

Wirth, N.: "Algorithms + Data Structures = Programs," Prentice-Hall, Englewood Cliffs, N.J., 1976.

————: On Multiprogramming, Machine Coding, and Computer Organization, *CACM,* vol. 12, no. 9, pp. 489–498, September, 1969.

————: "Systematic Programming: An Introduction," Prentice-Hall, Englewood Cliffs, N.J., 1973.

Yeh, R. T. (ed.): "Current Trends in Programming Methodology," vol. 1: "Software Specification and Design," Prentice-Hall, Englewood Cliffs, N.J., 1977; vol. 2: "Program Validation," 1977; vol. 3: "Software Modeling," 1978, vol. 4. "Data Structuring," 1978.

INDEX